User's Guide

Version 4 for Macintosh

New version created by
Joseph Jacobs
Bob Schulman
Karen Weiss
Glenn R. Wichman

Manuals and Help

Cynthia Gingerich   Denise Lau   Suzanne Schrader

Development Team

Kate Atwood	Patrick Kennedy	Fred Rusko
Jill Baird	Tom Klemzak	Joseph A. Schrader
Brian Davis	Christopher Lee	Terry Tierney
David Epstein	Jimmy Lee	Eric Tilenius
Greg Harlow	Mick McCaffrey	Maggie Ward
Bruce Hertzfeld	Marcos Montenegro	William Weisman
Judee Humberg	Richard Petit	
Linda Itskovitz	John Rathbone	

Special thanks

Bob Carr	Roger Hain	Chuck O'Brien
Richard Gray	Laurie Lasslo	Stan Shoemaker
Paul Grand	David Lippman	Steve Weiss

QuickStart Card

User's Guide

Getting started

Setting up your finances

Entering your data

Completing your financial picture

Analyzing your finances

Quicken provides insight into your finances

Quicken is very easy to use; it's even easier when you're aware of all the ways Quicken can help you.

This chapter covers the basics of what Quicken does and explains how Quicken can help you organize your personal and business finances.

Welcome to Quicken for Macintosh

Welcome to the large family of Quicken users. Thank you for selecting Quicken for Macintosh; we hope our product and service will earn your trust.

Quicken is flexible, easy to use, and powerful. Use it to keep track of all your financial transactions, no matter how simple or complex, for personal or business use, or both.

If you're new to Quicken, you'll find it provides an easy, useful way to keep track of your finances without learning accounting jargon or techniques. With Quicken you can easily handle all the tasks you once had to do manually:

- Writing checks
- Updating your check register
- Balancing (reconciling) your account
- Setting up and adjusting a budget for your income and expenses
- Reminding yourself of upcoming bills you have to pay
- Keeping track of your current net worth, including investments, assets such as your home, liabilities such as credit card debt, and of course all your bank accounts
- Much, much more

This chapter quickly highlights what Quicken can do for you. After you start the program, special hints called *Qcards* pop up in Quicken to help you set up your first account.

As you use Quicken more, you'll discover that it can also handle:

- **Financial planning.** You can try out "what-if" scenarios for loan planning, loan refinancing, savings planning, college planning, and retirement planning.
- **Income tax planning.** Quicken gathers information from your tax-related transactions to make it easier for you to fill out federal and state tax forms such as Form 1040, Schedule A, and Schedule C.
- **Business bookkeeping.** You can use Quicken to manage accounts receivable, payroll, accounts payable, and cash flow forecasting for a small business.

Quicken manages your check register

You enter most transactions for a Quicken bank account in the register, which looks just like a paper check register. The register for a bank account is where Quicken stores all transactions that affect your account balance; for example, payments, deposits, ATM (automated teller machine) transactions, and electronic fund transfers.

The sample register below contains some of the transactions for a Quicken bank account called "Checking."

Quicken displays the name of the account ("Checking") in the window title.

Quicken's register

Notice that the check numbers are from two different series. Check number 5003 was written by hand from a paper checkbook at the grocery store, and check number 124 was an Intuit check printed directly from Quicken. Quicken has no problem if you use more than one series of check numbers at a time.

Choose Register (⌘ R) from the View menu to display the register for an account.

DATE	NUMBER	DESCRIPTION		PAYMENT		✓	DEPOSIT		BALANCE	
		CATEGORY/CLASS	MEMO							
1/11 1994	ATM	ATM Withdrawal [Cash]		200	00	✓			5,902	96
1/11 1994	5003	Central Market Groceries		102	92	✓			5,800	04
1/13 1994	124	Macy's Clothing	New Jacket	129	87	✓			5,670	17
1/13 1994	125	TGRK Charity		150	00	✓			5,520	17
1/15 1994	EFT	Interest Earned Interest Inco...				✓	0	42	5,520	59
1/15 1994	DEP	Sally's Paycheck *split*				✓	2,162	97	7,683	56
1/15 1994	PRINT	American Lending Corp. *split*	Account #93-	1,533	91	✓			6,149	65

Checking: Register

Record	Restore	SPLITS	Current Balance	$3,230.00
			Ending Balance:	$8,283.70

Quicken computes the account balance automatically when you record a transaction.

The register contains all bank account transactions, including checks that you plan to print with Quicken. You'll enter checks that you plan to print in the Write Checks window. When you record a check in the Write Checks window, Quicken adds the check to the register automatically. For complete information about writing checks to print with Quicken, see Chapter 8, *Writing checks,* beginning on page 103.

Because you can print the register for a Quicken account at any time, you will now need a paper check register only to record handwritten checks. If you enter transactions into Quicken often enough, you may stop using your paper check register altogether. In any case, you will never again have to do arithmetic by hand in a paper register.

Categories keep track of your income and expenses

Income and expense *categories* are what make Quicken so informative: they help you understand and organize your finances. If you had to track your expenses by hand, you might put all your grocery receipts in an envelope labeled "Groceries" and all your charge slips for gasoline in an envelope labeled "Gas." Then, at the end of the month, you'd have to tally up the contents of each envelope to find out how much you spent on each category.

In contrast to the laborious task of tallying expenses by hand, the simple act of assigning a transaction to a category in Quicken gives you the power to easily create reports, graphs, and budgets that offer true insight into your finances.

For example, if you buy groceries at several different stores, Quicken uses the same "Groceries" category each time you record a payment to one of those stores in the check register. At the end of the month, you can press a few keys to create a report or a graph that shows how much you spent on groceries that month.

Entering categories is easy. As soon as you type the letters "gr," Quicken completes the category name "Groceries" in the Category field of the transaction you are recording.

		Checking: Register				
DATE	NUMBER	DESCRIPTION		PAYMENT	✓	DEPOSIT
		CATEGORY/CLASS	MEMO			
2/8 1994	132	Central Market groceries		89 90	✓	

When you set up your first file as described in "Setting up your first bank account" on page 33, we recommend that you use one of Quicken's preset lists of standard categories, which have been carefully designed to work for most homes and businesses. You can add, change, and delete categories all at once or "on the fly" while using Quicken. See Chapter 5, *Setting up categories and classes*, beginning on page 43, for more information.

Quicken's category list

Subcategories, indented under the category they belong to, help you track your income and expenses in more detail.

Choose Categories & Transfers (⌘L) from the View menu to display the category list.

"Bank Charges" is a category for tracking bank service charges such as the cost of checks and overdrafts. This category is listed in Quicken's standard home category list.

"Books, Music" is not listed in Quicken's standard home category list, so this family added it to their list to meet their needs.

Use Quicken categories to get the information you need to prepare income tax returns. See Chapter 22, *Preparing your income taxes*, beginning on page 361, for detailed information.

Reports and graphs highlight information

In a category report, Quicken totals income and spending for all your accounts and displays the report on the screen. Print the report if you like.

Quicken's flexible reporting allows you to include information from any or all of your Quicken accounts. Create a preset report, or customize a report by choosing the accounts and categories, the layout, and the level of detail in the report.

Note the subcategories for the expense categories "Auto" and "Utilities." Subcategories add detail to help you analyze your spending or income patterns.

Quicken can create many different kinds of personal and business reports and graphs to give you insight into your finances. Suppose that you want to look at your income and expenses for the month of January. You can see the information you want in a category report or on an income and expense graph.

```
┌─────────────── Category Report ───────────────┐
  Thursday, January 14, 1993

                 Category Report
               1/1/93 Through 3/31/93
                                      1/1/93-
              Category                 3/31/93

  Inflows
    Salary                           36,250.02

  Total Inflows                      36,250.02
  Outflows
    Auto:
      Fuel                              191.00
      Loan Int                          580.49
      Repairs                           165.98

    Total Auto                          937.47
    Charity                             350.00
    Clothing                          1,842.54
    Dining                              988.61
    Entertain                         1,214.63
    Gifts                               240.40
    Groceries                         1,092.44
    Household                           795.64
    Insurance                           454.56
    Marmona Fund                        969.58
    Mortgage Int                      3,242.30
    Taxes:
      Federal                         8,612.52
      FICA                            1,812.48
      State                           2,899.98

    Total Taxes                      13,324.98
    Telephone                           277.07
    Utilities:
      Garbage                           130.00
      Gas & Electric                    187.14

    Total Utilities                     317.14
    Outflows - Other                    200.00

  Total Outflows                    26,247.36

  Overall Total                     10,002.66

  Full Columns
└────────────────────────────────────────────────┘
```

If you want to view the transactions that make up a value in a report, double-click the value to get a *detail* report (a list of transactions). To change one of the transactions in that list, double-click it to go to the register with that transaction selected.

Quicken graphs make the significance of your financial records jump right out at you.

For example, income and expense graphs show how much you are spending in individual categories in relation to your total spending and to other major categories. You can create these graphs anytime to spot spending patterns, show your top ten expenses, alert yourself to overspending, and compare historical data. In graphs, the values of subcategories are rolled into the value of the main categories.

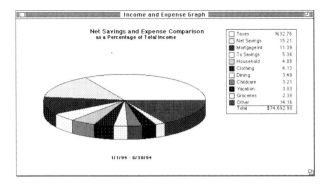

If you want to see more detail about a value in a graph (for example, a particular bar, pie slice, or point on a line), double-click the value to get a *QuickZoom* graph.

Quicken shortcuts save you time

Quicken has many features that work together to save you time. For example, paying your bills typically requires writing many checks that are exactly the same each month, or are the same except for the dollar amount. Because many of the checks you write recur regularly, Quicken has a shortcut called *QuickFill* that *memorizes* each transaction the first time you enter it.

Suppose you write a check to pay this month's gas and electric bill. Next month, when you start to enter a payment to the same utility company in the register or in the Write Checks window, QuickFill automatically completes the payee name. Here's how QuickFill helps you complete the check with a minimum of effort.

Quicken displays the name of the account ("Checking") in the window title.

Quicken's Write Checks window

When you type "val" QuickFill automatically completes the name of the utility company name (Valley Gas & Electric). When you press Tab after QuickFill completes the payee name, QuickFill enters the rest of the transaction, including the address and the category for utilities. All you have to do is change the amount.

This automatic entry of a memorized transaction is part of the QuickFill feature.

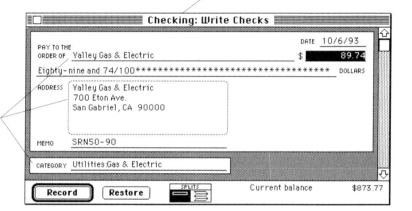

After you record the check in the Write Checks window, Quicken automatically enters the transaction in the check register and can print the check any time you're ready. (If you are writing checks by hand, you would enter the transaction directly into the Register window.)

You can set up a reminder to yourself to recall the same transaction at regular intervals. (See "Using Billminder" on page 169.)

You might have several transactions that you want to enter on the same date (for example, a group of bills that you pay at the same time each month). To save even more time, you can memorize these transactions with the special ⌘ M shortcut, put them in a transaction group, and recall them all at once. Quicken can notify you when this group of bills is due, and it can even enter the transactions for you. (See "Using transaction groups" on page 165.)

Quicken has special account types for tracking different kinds of transactions

After you work with a Quicken checking account for a month or two, you may want to set up additional accounts for savings, credit cards, investments, loans, or other items. Quicken has 7 different account types specifically adapted to handle these items and others. A single Quicken data file can hold all the accounts you need.

For example, you might have three checking accounts, two credit card accounts, and a money market account. Quicken can combine the data from all these accounts into any reports and graphs that you request. (Or you can limit any report or graph to selected accounts.)

Quicken displays the name of the Quicken data file ("My accounts") in the window title.

Quicken's account list

My accounts

Account Name	Account Type	Balance
AMX	Credit	235.00
Auto Loan	Liab	17,396.23
Cash	Cash	39.00
Chandler Inc.	Invest	16,602.38
Checking	Bank	2,204.40
House	Asset	152,879.50
IRA-Sally	Invest	168.20
IRA-Steve	Invest	2,210.56
Margin Loan	Liab	14,935.61
Marmona Fund	Fund	1,212.95
Mortgage	Liab	132,664.41
Quicken Visa	Credit	48.56
Sally's 401k	Asset	5,431.11
Savings	Bank	8,500.00

Open   New   Edit   Delete

Choose Accounts (⌘ A) from the View menu to display the account list.

Next to the account list is the icon for the Quicken data file named "My accounts." This data file contains all the accounts you see in the list.

You can add a new account to your Quicken data file at any time.

Set up all your accounts in one Quicken data file

When you first use Quicken, limit yourself to one or two bank accounts for the first month or two. A simple approach with fewer Quicken accounts will work best when you're getting started.

Later, you can add more accounts to your file, up to a total of 255. (Most people never have more than 10 accounts.)

Bank Accounts	Cash Accounts	Credit Card Accounts
Asset Accounts	**Liability Accounts**	**Investment Accounts**

To set up a new account, choose New Account from the File menu. For more information about setting up new accounts, see Chapter 4, *Setting up additional accounts*, beginning on page 35.

Quicken transfers money between accounts automatically

After you've set up more than one account, you may want to transfer money from one to another. Here's an example. Suppose you want to transfer $200 from your checking account to your savings account. You can choose Transfer Money from the Activities menu and select the source and destination accounts from two popup menus.

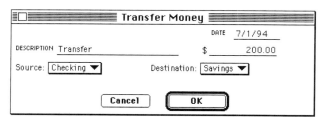

When you click OK, Quicken automatically records a withdrawal of $200 from the checking account and a deposit of $200 in the savings account.

This is the withdrawal of $200 from the checking account. Note the brackets around the transfer account name [Savings] in the Category field.

DATE	NUMBER	DESCRIPTION	PAYMENT	✓	DEPOSIT	BALANCE	⇧
		CATEGORY/CLASS MEMO					
7/1 1994		Transfer [Savings]	200 00			8,083 70	

Checking: Register

Here's the other side of the transfer above: $200 deposited into the savings account. Note the brackets around the transfer account name [Checking]. You can press ⌘ [to move from one side of the transfer to the other.

DATE	NUMBER	DESCRIPTION	PAYMENT	✓	DEPOSIT	BALANCE	⇧
		CATEGORY/CLASS MEMO					
7/1 1994		Transfer [Checking]			200 00	9,014 86	

Savings: Register

To create a transfer transaction, you can also enter a transaction in the source account with the name of the destination account in the Category field. When you record the *source* transaction, Quicken automatically creates a matching entry in the *destination* account.

Quicken displays account names in brackets at the end of the category list to distinguish them from categories.

When you double-click the name of the transfer account, Quicken inserts the account name [Savings] in the Category field of the selected transaction.

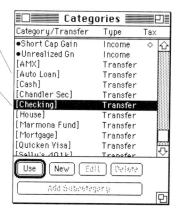

No income or expense is created by a transfer, so you can't categorize a transfer. You're just moving money from one account to another. Categories allow you to track income and expenses, and a transfer is simply a way to record the movement of funds.

You'll love balancing your bank statement (really!)

Quicken can automatically reconcile your bank, credit card, portfolio, and mutual fund accounts with your bank, credit card, brokerage, and mutual fund statements. The following example balances, or *reconciles*, the June bank statement for a sample checking account.

Sample Bank Statement for a Checking Account

Last statement date:		05/19/93	Beginning balance:	1454.31
This statement date:		06/19/93	Ending balance:	102.12
			Interest earned:	4.04
Payments:		5	Deposits:	1
477	6/1	59.97	6/4	2,425.00
478	6/15	1,158.39		
479	6/15	241.89	Withdrawals:	2
480	6/16	35.00	6/5	2,000.00
3031	6/2	185.98	6/9	100.00

Some bank statements call the beginning balance the "opening balance" or "starting balance."

Some bank statements call the ending balance the "closing balance" or "new balance."

Reconciling with Quicken requires only two steps:

Step 1. Copy information from your bank account statement.

Check the Previous Balance and New Balance amounts and any service charges or interest from your statement. If necessary, correct this information to match your bank statement.

"Interest Earned" is a category for interest that you earn. Be sure to assign income categories to all amounts you earn or receive.

Step 2. Mark off transactions from the bank statement in the list that Quicken displays in the Reconcile window.

Don't mark transactions that do not appear on the bank statement. These transactions have not cleared the bank yet.

The Reconcile window displays one line for each transaction in your Quicken check register.

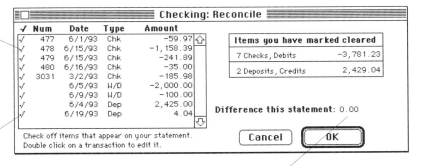

As you mark items as cleared, the Difference This Statement amount changes. When the amount in the Difference field reaches zero, you have successfully balanced your account! (If the account doesn't balance, Quicken will offer to make an adjusting entry for you. If you accept the adjusting entry, your Quicken bank account balance will be correctly synchronized with the bank's records.)

Using Qcards and Help

Using Qcards

Quicken displays Qcards automatically for five major activities where you may need some help. Qcards tell you what type of information to enter in a field or what other type of action is appropriate.

The Qcard instructions change each time you press Tab to move to another field in the window or click in another field.

Quicken displays onscreen messages called Qcards to help you enter the correct information.

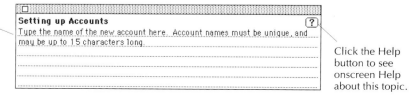

Setting up Accounts

Type the name of the new account here. Account names must be unique, and may be up to 15 characters long.

Click the Help button to see onscreen Help about this topic.

You can turn off all the Qcards for an activity by clicking the close box in the Qcard window. If you close a Qcard, however, you turn off all Qcards for that activity.

System 7 Help menu icon

You can turn any set of Qcards on or off at any time. If you are using System 7, you can turn on Qcards for an activity by choosing Show Qcard from the Help menu in the right corner of the Quicken menu bar.

Another way to turn Qcards on and off is to choose Qcards from the Settings menu. Then select the Qcard area that you want to turn on or off and click OK.

Qcards for entering transactions in the register of any account.

Qcards for setting up accounts.

Qcards for reconciling bank, credit card, portfolio, and mutual fund accounts.

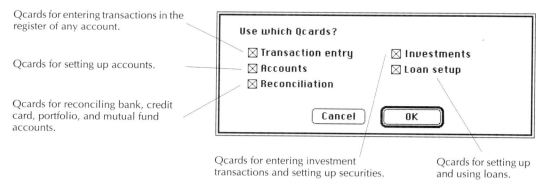

Use which Qcards?

☒ Transaction entry   ☒ Investments
☒ Accounts   ☒ Loan setup
☒ Reconciliation

[Cancel]   [OK]

Qcards for entering investment transactions and setting up securities.

Qcards for setting up and using loans.

Using System 7 Balloon Help

To turn on System 7 Balloon Help, choose Show Balloons from the Help menu in the right corner of the Quicken menu bar. Then point to items on the screen to see help balloons about them.

Point to any item on the screen to learn more about it. For example, you can see help balloons for buttons, text fields, options, and more.

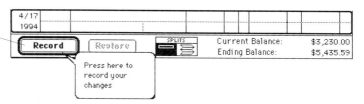

Using the ⌘ ? Quicken Help system

When you are working in Quicken, specific help about a task is always available. For example, if you are working in Write Checks and need information about filling out a check, you can press ⌘ ? (or the Help key on an extended keyboard) to get specific details about writing checks. You can also press ⌘ ? (or the Help key) and click Topics to browse through the topics list for areas of Quicken you'd like to know more about.

If Quicken can't open the Quicken Help file, copy the Quicken Help file from the folder where you installed Quicken to the folder where you are running Quicken.

If you see an item in **bold** when you are reading a Help topic, you can click on the item to learn more about it. All words in bold are links to related topics in the Help system.

You can also look up a topic in the Help system. For example, the following technical topics appear in the Help system only (we don't repeat them in this *User's Guide*). To print any Help topic, choose Print Help Text from the File menu.

Topic	Location in Help
Information about QIF files	Choose "Transferring data" from the Topics list, and then click "Information about QIF files" in the Sub-topics list.
Memory management tips	Choose "Memory" from the Topics list, and then click "Memory management tips."
Quicken files on your disk	Choose "Technical information" from the Topics list, and then click "Quicken files on your hard disk" in the Subtopics list.

1 **Press ⌘ ? to choose Quicken Help from the Help menu.**

You can also press the Help key on an extended keyboard or choose Quicken Help from the System 7 Help menu in the right corner of the Quicken menu bar.

2 **If necessary, click the Topics button at the bottom of the Help window.**

3 **Scroll in the list of topics on the left side of the Help window and select the topic you want.**

You can scroll to select a topic, or press the first letter of the topic name. For example, you can press the letters **cat** to select "Categories."

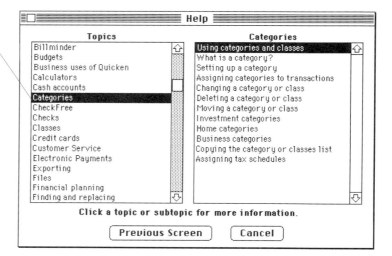

4 **On the right side of the Help window, click the subtopic you want.**

Quicken displays the Help screen for the subtopic.

5 **(Optional) To print a Help screen, choose Print Help Text from the File menu.**

6 **When you have finished with the Help window, click Cancel or click the close box.**

For people who have used other Quicken versions

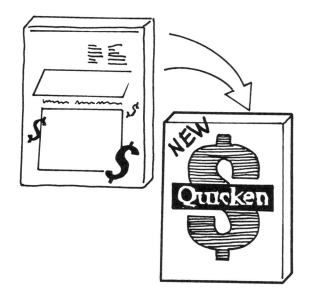

If you are new to Quicken, you can skip this chapter.

If you have used an earlier version of Quicken for Macintosh, the chapter will help you update your data files. It also describes how to transfer data from Quicken for Windows or DOS Quicken to your Macintosh.

If you already use Quicken, you don't need to read the *User's Guide* over again. "What's New in Quicken" on page 19 highlights the areas of Quicken that contain new features, and tells you which sections in this manual describe these new features.

Updating from Quicken 3 to Quicken 4

If you haven't already installed the new version of Quicken, do so now using the QuickStart Card.

Before you start Quicken 4, we recommend that you move any data files out of the Quicken 3 folder. Drag the data files to the folder where you installed Quicken 4 (the Quicken 4 Folder).

The Installer may already have moved any data files that were loose in the same folder as the Quicken 3 application file (not in a subfolder).

This is a Quicken 3 data file.

Your financial data is stored in one or more files like these, not in the Quicken 3 application file.

My accounts

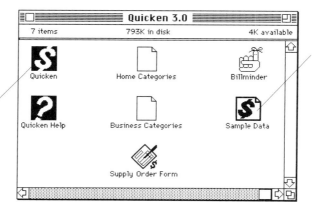

This is the Quicken 3 application file. The Quicken 3.0 folder shown here contains the program files that came on your original Quicken 3 Master Disk. (You may have given your Quicken 3 folder a different name.)

This is the Quicken 3 Sample Data file. Do not move this file unless you are sure that you have added your own financial data to the file.

This is the Quicken 4 Folder that the Installer put on your hard disk.

This is the Quicken 4 application file.

We recommend that you move all Quicken data files to the new Quicken 4 Folder where you installed Quicken.

Check carefully to make sure the old Quicken 3 folder contains no data files or folders that contain data files. (You can move your data files to any folder, but we recommend that you move them to the new Quicken 4 Folder.) Now, if you still have your Quicken 3 Master Disk, you can delete the entire Quicken 3 folder. If you don't still have your Quicken 3 Master Disk, back up the Quicken 3 folder to a floppy disk and then delete the entire Quicken 3 folder.

1　After you have removed all your Quicken data files and deleted the old Quicken 3 folder, you can upgrade your Quicken data files three different ways:

- Open the Quicken 4 Folder and double-click the Quicken 4 application file. Quicken will prompt you to open your Quicken data file.

- Double-click your Quicken data file.

- If you have System 7, you can drag your Quicken data file to the Quicken 4 application file.

  When you do any of these, Quicken asks you to personalize your copy of Quicken.

2　Type your name and click OK.

If you double-clicked the Quicken 4 application to start with, Quicken displays a standard Open File dialog box. Continue to step 3.

If you double-clicked your data file or dragged the file to the Quicken 4 application, Quicken 4 updates your data at once and you are ready to work. If you need to update any other Quicken data files, continue to step 3.

3　Select your Quicken 3 file and click Open.

Quicken 4 reads your data directly and you're ready to work. When Quicken updates your data file to work with Quicken 4, it also creates a backup file in the original Quicken 3 format. The name of the Quicken 3 backup file will be the name of your original file plus "(Q3)"—for example, "My accounts (Q3)."

A Quicken 4 data file icon.

My accounts

After you update your file to the Quicken 4 format, you CANNOT go back and use the same file with an earlier version of Quicken. If you ever need to go back and use your old data with Quicken 3, open the file with "(Q3)" at the end of the file name.

Updating Quicken 1 or 1.5 data files to Quicken 4

If you haven't already installed the new version of Quicken, do so now using the QuickStart Card.

When you start using Quicken 1 or 1.5 data in Quicken 4, Quicken will help you create a new Quicken 4 data file to hold your accounts. A single Quicken 4 data file can hold 255 accounts.

Locating and updating Quicken 1 or 1.5 data files

Follow the steps below to start Quicken, create a file for your accounts, and copy your existing accounts into it. When you finish, you will have a new Quicken 4 data file that contains all your existing accounts.

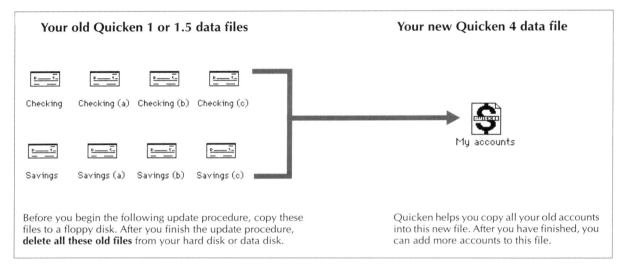

Your old Quicken 1 or 1.5 data files

Checking   Checking (a)   Checking (b)   Checking (c)

Savings   Savings (a)   Savings (b)   Savings (c)

Before you begin the following update procedure, copy these files to a floppy disk. After you finish the update procedure, **delete all these old files** from your hard disk or data disk.

Your new Quicken 4 data file

My accounts

Quicken helps you copy all your old accounts into this new file. After you have finished, you can add more accounts to this file.

1   **Back up your Quicken 1 or 1.5 data files to a floppy disk.**

The Quicken 4 application icon.

Quicken 4

2   **Double-click the Quicken 4 application icon.**

Quicken asks you to personalize your copy of Quicken.

3   **Type your name and click OK.**

Quicken displays a window where you can choose the categories that you want to use with Quicken.

4   **Select the categories you want to use and click OK.**

Important! If you already have a Quicken 1 or 1.5 category list set up the way you want it, do not select any categories here.

The data file Quicken creates for you.

Quicken uses the name you typed in step 2 to name the new Quicken 4 data file (it adds the word "Finances" to your name. For example, Quicken creates a file called "Murphy's Finances" if you typed the name "Murphy."

Quicken opens the Set Up Account window.

Instead of setting up a new account, you need to add your existing Quicken 1 or 1.5 accounts to this file.

5 **Click Cancel in the Set Up Account window.**

6 **Choose Open File from the File menu.**

Quicken displays a standard Open File dialog box.

7 **In the Open File dialog box, go to the folder that contains your Quicken 1 or 1.5 accounts. Select one of your accounts and click Open.**

Quicken displays a window which explains that a Quicken 4 data file can contain several different accounts.

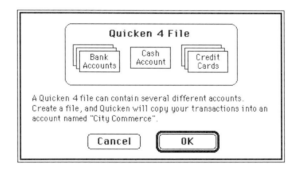

We recommend that you put all your accounts in one file. Most people use just one Quicken data file. If you find that you need to create another file after working with Quicken for a while (to separate business data from personal data, for example), read "Setting up additional files" on page 61.

8 **Click OK.**

Quicken copies the data from your existing account (including categories and recurring transactions) into the new Quicken 4 file. When Quicken finishes copying the data, you will be in the Register window for your updated account.

Your original data file is not affected. Note that you cannot go back to a previous version of Quicken and use the version of your data that has been copied into a Quicken 4 data file.

9 **If you have another account that you want to add to the same Quicken 4 data file, repeat steps 6, 7, and 8.**

Repeat until you have copied all your accounts into the Quicken 4 data file.

10 **Delete your old data files and the earlier version of Quicken (Quicken 1 or 1.5) from your hard disk.**

> If you have removed the earlier version of Quicken from your hard disk and Quicken 4 still doesn't start when you double-click a data file, try rebuilding your desktop. To rebuild your desktop, restart your computer and hold down the Option and ⌘ (command) keys as your computer starts up until you see a message that the desktop is being rebuilt.

How Quicken converts zero-amount transactions

In Quicken 1 or 1.5, some people set up categories for assets, liabilities, or credit cards, and they used zero-amount transactions to track those items in a Quicken bank account without affecting the balance of that account.

When Quicken 4 converts zero-amount transactions that were created in Quicken 1 or 1.5, it treats them all as deposits. The result may be reversed signs for amounts from zero-amount transactions.

If you used zero-amount transactions to track assets, liabilities, or credit cards in a Quicken 1 or 1.5 bank account, you might have to change the signs in those zero-amount transactions to make the category totals correct in Quicken 4 reports and graphs.

What's New in Quicken

This section is for people upgrading from Quicken 3 for the Macintosh. Each new area in Quicken 4 is packed with new features, so this section tells you how to find each new area in the Quicken software, and it includes page references to other sections in this manual that describe all the new features available in those areas.

IntelliCharge

Eliminate the "grunt work" of tracking your credit card purchases. IntelliCharge, when used with a special Quicken credit card, automatically records your credit card transactions, complete with categories, in seconds.

Simply use your Quicken credit card for purchases anywhere. Each month, you'll get your own electronic credit card statement delivered through your modem or on a diskette. IntelliCharge reads the electronic statement and displays it on screen. For each transaction, it proposes a category based on how you've categorized such transactions in the past. (You can easily change the categories however you like.) Then click one button and IntelliCharge adds the transactions to your register.

To apply for a Quicken credit card, see the application included in your Quicken package.

For more information, see "Using IntelliCharge" on page 201.

Investments

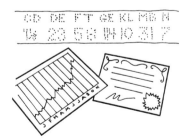

Let Quicken analyze the performance of your investments, saving you time and expense. Now Quicken has the power to track investments in stocks, bonds, mutual funds, and other investments that fluctuate in price. New investment reports and graphs can show you capital gains, rate of return, the market value of any or all of the investments in your portfolio and much more.

You can even import security prices downloaded from an online service such as Prodigy's QuoteTrack into your Quicken portfolio.

Choose New Account from the File menu to set up a portfolio account or a mutual fund account.

For more information, see "Tracking investments" on page 231.

Loans

Why wait for your lender's statement to find out what your outstanding loan balance is or how much interest you've paid this year? Let Quicken track your loan amortization and you'll have the status of your loans any time you want it.

In addition to conventional loans, Quicken can handle a variety of loan features, including variable interest rates, balloon payments, and negative amortization. And if the lender is *you*, Quicken can even track payments you receive for loans you've made.

Choose Loans from the View menu.

For more information, see "Tracking loans" on page 279.

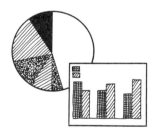

Graphs

Get the picture fast! Graphs transform rows and columns of data in registers and reports into financial information you can understand immediately.

Create graphs to help analyze your income and expenses, track your budget activity, determine your net worth, and evaluate the performance of your investment portfolio.

If you need more information about an item you see in a pie chart or bar graph, you can get it quickly using *QuickZoom* to move to another, more detailed graph or report.

Choose Graphs from the Reports menu.

For more information, see "Creating graphs" on page 341.

Financial planning calculators

Now Quicken can help you plan for the future as ably as it keeps you informed today. Five financial planning calculators provide the information you need to make smart financial decisions. You can perform "what if" calculations by playing around with the numbers and choosing different values to calculate.

Use the financial planning calculators to evaluate options for loans, mortgage refinancing, investment and savings growth, retirement income, and college financing.

Choose a financial planning calculator from the Planning menu.

For more information, see "Using financial planning calculators" on page 379.

QuickFill

QuickFill saves you time and keystrokes by automatically filling in transaction fields when you type a few characters.

You can use QuickFill to recall entire transactions that you've either memorized or already recorded in the register. Or use it to quickly enter categories, classes, and investment securities and actions.

QuickFill is preset to start recalling your memorized transactions right away. As you add more transactions in the Quicken 4 register, QuickFill remembers those, too. If QuickFill isn't active, choose General from the Settings menu, and then select the setting to use QuickFill.

For more information, see "Using QuickFill to complete transactions" on page 158.

```
Outflows
   Auto:
      Fuel            191.00
      Loan Int        580.49
      Repairs          1⊙⊙8

   Total Auto         937.47
```

QuickZoom

In previous versions of Quicken, if you wanted to look at detail for an item in a report, you had to search for the transaction or transactions that made up that amount yourself.

Now, if you need more information about an item you see in a report, you can get it quickly using *QuickZoom* to move to another, more detailed report or to the actual transaction in an account register.

To see the detail for an amount in any Quicken report, select that amount and double-click.

For more information, see "Investigating items in reports using QuickZoom" on page 337.

Transaction group automatic entry

Transaction groups make it easy for you to enter recurring transactions on a regular basis. And with automatic entry, it's even easier because Quicken does the work for you.

Normally, Quicken simply reminds you when it's time to recall a transaction group. But when you turn on automatic entry for a specific group, Quicken recalls the group for you on the scheduled date, and records the group's transactions in the destination account.

To turn on the automatic entry feature for a transaction group, choose Transaction Groups from the View menu.

For more information, see "Setting up a transaction group" on page 165.

Qcards and Balloon Help

Instant help is always on hand when you need it most. If you use System 7, you can point at any item in Quicken to see a help balloon that tells you about it.

In addition to Balloon Help, Quicken has special tip windows called Qcards that pop up when you might need help. These Qcards contain hints and guidelines for data entry.

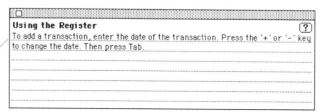

This Qcard pops up when you're in typing a date in the check register.

Each time you Tab to a different place in a window, Quicken displays a new Qcard.

To turn on System 7 Balloon Help, choose Show Balloons from the System 7 Help menu in the right corner of the menu bar. To turn off Balloon Help, choose Hide Balloons from the Help menu.

To turn Qcards on or off for any of seven different areas in Quicken, choose Qcards from the Settings menu and select the Qcard area you want to use.

For more information, see "Using Qcards and Help" on page 10.

More new features

Publishing Quicken reports. If you want to use data from a Quicken report in documents created in other applications, and you use System 7, you can now publish all or part of a Quicken report.

To share data from a Quicken report with a document in a different application, you select part or all of a Quicken report and then create a *publisher* for the selected report data.

The publisher creates an *edition*, which is a file that contains the selected report data and is still linked to Quicken. You control which documents subscribe to this edition of Quicken data, and when and if the edition is updated.

For more information, see "Publishing Quicken report data for use in other applications" on page 399.

Line Items

```
EE US svgs bonds proceeds
Nontaxable ed. benefits
Post:89 EE US savings b...
Qual. higher ed. expenses
Schedule A
  Cash charity contributi...
  Gambling losses
  Home mortgage interest
  Investment man. fees
```

Tax schedule reports and tax line item assignments. Quicken simplifies the dreaded chore of tax preparation if you set up categories and classes with tax time in mind. Now you can assign line items from tax forms and schedules to your Quicken categories. Then whenever you assign a category to a transaction throughout the year, tax information is also attached to the transaction.

The new tax schedule report and capital gains report group and subtotal your tax-related transactions. You can use the information in these reports whether you prepare your taxes yourself or provide information to a tax preparer. You can also transfer data directly from these reports to tax preparation software.

For more information, see "Preparing your income taxes" on page 361.

```
Year-to-date
Current Month
Current Quarter
Current Year
Last Month
Last Quarter
Last Year
All Transactions

Custom...
```

Reports and preset text dates. We've added preset text dates for your convenience when setting up reports. Now you can use text date templates such as "End of last quarter" or "Yesterday" instead of typing dates.

For more information, see "Creating reports" on page 320.

Transaction Report
1/1/93 Through 3/31/93

Description	Memo	Category
Opening Balance		[AMX]
Sam's Restaurant	Steve Lunch	Dining
Park Restaurant		Dining

Drag under the column heading to widen or narrow the column.

Resizable report columns. Now the width of columns in Quicken reports is completely under your control. You can widen them or narrow them as you prefer. Whether you want to resize column widths in an onscreen report for your viewing comfort, or because you want all the columns to fit on a single sheet of paper when you print the report, it's easy to widen or narrow the columns as you see fit.

For more information, see page 321 and "Previewing page breaks in a report" on page 326.

QuickBudget. Create budgets automatically using last year's Quicken data as a starting point. When you click the QuickBudget button, actual amounts from your existing Quicken data move into the budget. You can keep those amounts or edit them. When you know what you spent on items last year, it's easier to set realistic goals for this year.

Display or enter budget amounts by month, quarter, or year.

For more information, see "Budgeting your income and expenses" on page 351.

Other improvements

Here are enhancements we've made to existing features in this version of Quicken for Macintosh. Many are the result of requests from our users.

- Quicken menus are organized better than ever. See Appendix B, *Menus and command keys,* beginning on page 391, for a complete overview of the new menus.

- You'll notice that, if you type the amount of a transaction in the account register and press Tab, you now reach the Category/Class field immediately. Most Quicken users enter Category/Class information for every transaction, so we made Tabbing to that field more convenient.

- All Quicken list windows now have convenient buttons that let you add, edit, change, or delete list items without leaving the list window.

- By popular demand, you can now print the account list!

Press ⌘ G

- We added a new Find Again command on the Edit menu, so it's easier to continue a search.

- Our new Transfer Money command on the Activities menu automates Quicken's important transfer feature.

Press ⌘ M

- The Memorize command on the Edit menu works both to memorize a transaction *and* to memorize a custom report setup for later use.

Transferring files from IBM Quicken (DOS or Windows)

More information about QIF files is in Help. (Press ⌘ ? and then click Topics. Click "Technical Information" on the Topics list, and then click "Information about QIF files" in the Subtopics list on the right.)

You might want to transfer data from DOS Quicken or Quicken for Windows to Quicken for the Macintosh. To do this, you must export the data from each of your IBM Quicken accounts to a QIF file. A QIF file is a text file in a special format called Quicken Interchange Format. Then, you must import each of these QIF files into Quicken for the Macintosh.

◆ **Export your accounts from your DOS Quicken or Quicken for Windows to QIF files.**
See "Exporting your accounts from DOS Quicken" on page 27 or "Exporting your accounts from Quicken for Windows" on page 28.

◆ **Move the files to your Macintosh.**
See "Moving the QIF files to your Macintosh" on page 29.

◆ **Import the files into Quicken for Macintosh.**
See "Importing the files into Quicken for Macintosh" on page 30.

After you have finished transferring transactions from a DOS Quicken or Quicken for Windows investment account to a Quicken for Macintosh portfolio or mutual fund account, the price history of the securities in the Quicken for Macintosh account may not be complete.

To enter the prices:

• If you exported accounts from DOS Quicken, you can export security prices from the Update Prices and Market Values window in a DOS file, and then import the prices into the Portfolio window of your Quicken for Macintosh portfolio or mutual fund account as described in "Importing prices" on page 272.

• If you exported accounts from Quicken for Windows, you can print your security prices in the Update Prices and Market Values window and enter the prices manually as described in "Updating the prices of your securities" on page 267.

Exporting your accounts from DOS Quicken

1   **Open the account you want to export data from.**

2   **Choose Export from the Print/Acct menu.**

Use the drive letter for the floppy drive that contains a 3.5-inch floppy disk.

If you accept the dates Quicken fills in, the export file will contain all the current year's transactions.

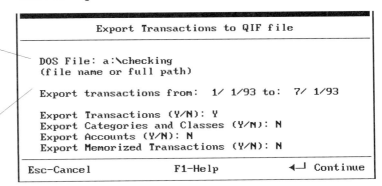

```
      Export Transactions to QIF file

  DOS File: a:\checking
  (file name or full path)

  Export transactions from:  1/ 1/93 to:  7/ 1/93

  Export Transactions (Y/N): Y
  Export Categories and Classes (Y/N): N
  Export Accounts (Y/N): N
  Export Memorized Transactions (Y/N): N

 Esc-Cancel            F1-Help          ◄┘ Continue
```

3   **Enter the name of a new QIF file to receive the exported data. For example, enter** a:\checking **to export the transactions from an account called Checking to a 3.5-inch floppy disk in drive A.**

4   **Enter the date of the first and last transactions to be included in the exported text file.**

5   **Set Export Transactions to Y. All other export options should be set to N.**

6   **Press Enter to begin exporting the transactions.**

Quicken exports the transactions to a temporary QIF file.

7   **Repeat steps 1 to 6 for each account in the DOS Quicken file, and then continue to "Moving the QIF files to your Macintosh" on page 29.**

Exporting your accounts from Quicken for Windows

1 **Open the account you want to export data from.**

2 **Choose Export from the File menu.**

Enter the name of a file to receive the exported data. You can keep the .QIF extension to remind you what the file is for.

Quicken will create the QIF file on this drive and in this directory. If you want the file to be created elsewhere...

...double-click the directory you want in this list (you can double-click c:\ to see other directories on the C: drive)...

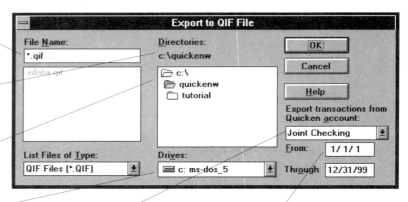

...or select the drive you want from this drop-down list.

This is the account you are exporting transactions from.

Enter the starting and ending dates of the transactions to be imported in these boxes.

3 **In the File Name box, enter the name of a file to receive the exported data.**

You don't have to give the file any particular extension. But if you keep the .QIF extension that is already in the box, it will remind you what the file is for.

4 **Enter the date of the first and last transactions to be included in the exported text file.**

5 **Click OK to begin exporting the transactions.**

Quicken exports the transactions to a temporary QIF file.

6 **Repeat steps 1 to 5 for each account in the Windows Quicken file, and then continue to "Moving the QIF files to your Macintosh" on page 29.**

Moving the QIF files to your Macintosh

If you have a network, you can probably move the QIF files from the IBM computer to your Macintosh over the network.

If you don't have a network that connects the IBM computer to your Macintosh, you can use the Apple File Exchange utility program that came with your Macintosh System Software to translate the QIF files for use on your Macintosh. You must have the following things:

- A Macintosh with a SuperDrive.
- A DOS machine with a 3.5-inch floppy drive.
- Apple File Exchange. (See your Macintosh System Software reference manuals to find Apple File Exchange.)
- A 3.5-inch floppy disk formatted for DOS.

1   **Start Apple File Exchange on your Macintosh.**

2   **Insert the 3.5-inch DOS floppy disk that contains the exported QIF files in the floppy drive.**

3   **Choose Text Translation from the MS-DOS to Mac menu.**

4   **Select the files you exported from DOS Quicken and click Translate.**

In this example, Apple File Exchange will place the translated files in a folder called "DOS Quicken Files" on the Macintosh.

It doesn't matter which side the DOS files appear on (left or right).

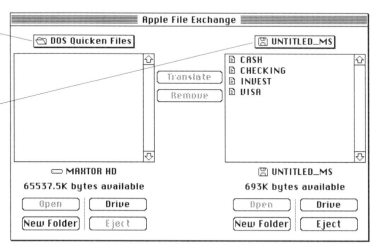

Apple File Exchange translates the QIF files to Macintosh format and moves them from the floppy disk to your Macintosh.

Or press ⌘ Q

5   **After translating the files, choose Quit from the File menu to leave Apple File Exchange.**

Importing the files into Quicken for Macintosh

1   **In Quicken for the Macintosh, create a new file. (Choose New File from the File menu.)**

    See page 61 for complete information about creating a file.

2   **Set up a new account in the Quicken for Macintosh file for EVERY account that you exported. (Choose New Account from the File menu.)**

    Each account should have an opening balance of $0.00 with a transaction date prior to any actual IBM Quicken transaction.

    See page 36 for complete information about setting up an account.

    When you have set up all the accounts in Quicken for the Macintosh, you can start importing the QIF files.

3   **Choose Open Account from the File menu and open the account register of the first account that you want to transfer from IBM Quicken.**

4   **Choose Import from the File menu.**

5   **Import the file that matches the account register you have open.**

    The Import procedure is described in detail in "Importing the transactions from the QIF file into an account" on page 70.

6   **Open the next account you want to transfer data into.**

7   **Repeat the Import procedure for each account.**

    Congratulations! You have completed the IBM to Macintosh transfer.

    If you ever want to transfer transactions from Macintosh to IBM, the process is similar: export each account from Quicken for the Macintosh to a QIF file and then import each QIF file to an IBM Quicken account.

Setting up your first bank account

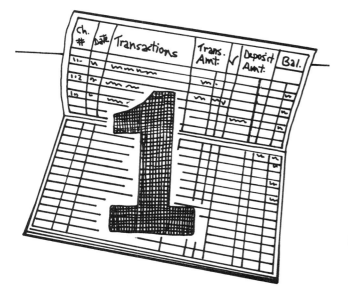

T his chapter helps you set up your first Quicken file and bank account.

If you have used a previous version of Quicken for Macintosh or IBM Quicken (DOS or Windows), see Chapter 2, *For people who have used other Quicken versions,* beginning on page 13.

Starting Quicken for the first time

If this is the first time you've ever used Quicken, follow the instructions on the QuickStart Card to install Quicken. If you are upgrading from another version of Quicken for Macintosh, skip now to the instructions in "For people who have used other Quicken versions" on page 13 for starting Quicken.

If you want to learn more about how Quicken works before opening Quicken and setting up your first bank account, read Chapter 1, *Quicken provides insight into your finances,* beginning on page 1.

1   Open the folder where you installed Quicken 4.

The Quicken 4 application icon.

Quicken 4

2   Double-click the Quicken 4 application icon.

Quicken asks you to personalize your copy of Quicken. If Quicken does not ask you to personalize your copy of Quicken, choose New File from the File menu and skip to step 4 below.

3   Type your name and click OK.

Quicken uses your name to set up a new Quicken data file named *"Your Name*'s Finances." Quicken also displays a window where you can select the categories that you want to use with this file.

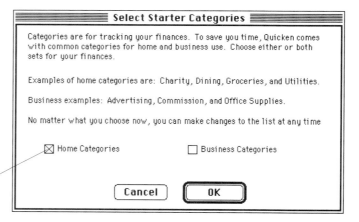

Select the categories you want to use. Quicken's preset list of Home categories is illustrated on page 46.

4   Select the categories you want to use.

To learn more about categories, see "Categories keep track of your income and expenses" on page 4.

5   Click OK.

The data file Quicken set up for you (if you typed in "Murphy" as your name).

Murphy's Finances

Quicken stores your data in the data file it just created. You'll need to back up this data file regularly after you start using Quicken. Continue to "Setting up your first bank account" on page 33.

Setting up your first bank account

Leave Bank Account selected if you plan to set up a checking, savings, or money market account as your first Quicken account.

After you select categories and click OK as described on page 32, Quicken displays the Set Up Account window. Before setting up your bank account, find your last bank statement.

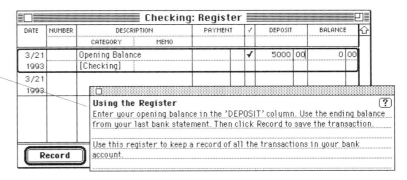

Click here to add optional notes about the account. Quicken opens a text window where you can enter five lines of notes. (Press Return to start a new line.)

1 **Enter a name and description for your bank account.**

When you're ready to add another bank account or a different type of account, see Chapter 4, *Setting up additional accounts*, beginning on page 35.

2 **Click Create.**

Quicken creates a new bank account and opens the Register window for the new account so you can begin entering transactions.

Follow the instructions in the Qcard to enter an opening balance in the Deposit column.

Quicken displays a new Qcard each time you press Tab.

See page 10 for information about turning Qcards on and off.

3 **Enter the opening balance for the account in the Deposit field of the Opening Balance transaction.**

The date and amount of the Opening Balance transaction should be the same as the ending balance amount and the closing date from your most recent bank statement.

4   **Click Record to save the Opening Balance transaction.**

Your first account is set up. Now you can add transactions to the register. See "Bringing your account up to date" on page 34.

Bringing your account up to date

After Quicken sets up your bank account and displays the new account register, you can start entering transactions.

Enter these transactions first:

- All transactions that have occurred between the ending balance on your last bank statement and today. These transactions may be checks that you have written and recorded in your paper check register, electronic funds transfers to or from your account, or ATM deposits to or withdrawals from the account you just set up.

- All transactions dated before the statement ending balance date that have not yet appeared on any bank statement.

From now on, you can enter transactions into Quicken on a regular basis as they occur or whenever it's convenient for you. Entering data in a Quicken register is described in Chapter 7, *Using the register,* beginning on page 79.

When your next bank statement arrives, use it to balance your bank account with the transactions you've recorded in the Quicken account. See Chapter 10, *Balancing your checkbook,* beginning on page 141.

If you would like to enter transactions from a period earlier than the date of your opening balance transaction, (for example, from the beginning of this year), you can do so. Wait until after your next bank statement arrives and you've balanced your account for the first time. Then see "Adding earlier transactions to Quicken" on page 155.

When you first start using Quicken, limit yourself to one or two bank accounts for the first month or so. You can even track your credit card and cash spending in your single Quicken bank account. (See "Tracking credit card transactions in Quicken bank accounts" on page 195 and "Entering cash transactions in bank accounts" on page 218.) When you decide to set up additional accounts, read Chapter 4, *Setting up additional accounts,* beginning on page 35.

Setting up additional accounts

You can add more accounts to your Quicken file to track your finances in greater detail.

Quicken has seven account types with features tailored to different tracking needs:
bank
cash
credit card
asset
liability
portfolio
mutual fund

Follow the same basic steps to create and use any account type.

Setting up additional Quicken accounts

With Quicken, you can create up to 255 related accounts in a single Quicken file. The steps to set up additional accounts are basically the same as those you followed to set up your first Quicken account.

If you have not already set up your first Quicken account, see "Setting up your first bank account" on page 33. If you want to set up an account to track an amortized loan, see Chapter 17, *Tracking loans*, beginning on page 279.

1 If you have more than one file, be sure to open the one you want before setting up the new account.

In most cases, you'll want to set up all your accounts in the same file so you can create reports based on data from all of them. However, in some cases you might want separate Quicken files (for example, one file for home accounts, another file for business accounts). When you set up a new account, Quicken adds it to the current Quicken file. For information about when and how to create more than one Quicken file, see "Setting up additional files" on page 61.

2 Choose New Account from the File menu.

Use the descriptions to help you decide which type to create. Then click the button of the account type you want.

If you decide later that you selected the wrong type, you can edit the account information to change the type in most cases. See page 40.

Enter a unique name for the account, up to 15 characters long. Use your own name, your bank name, or a descriptive name such as Checking, Visa, or Mortgage. The name can include letters, numbers, spaces, and any characters except these:
/ : [ ] ^ ! < > ( ) "

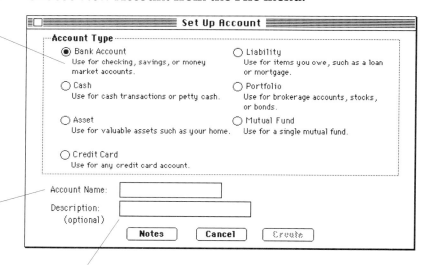

You can enter an account description up to 30 characters long.

3 Click a button to select the type of account to create.

4 Enter a name for the account.

5   **(Optional) Enter an account description.**

6   **(Optional) To add any notes about the account, click Notes.**

Quicken opens a window where you can enter five lines of notes, such as the account number, branch address, or telephone number. (Press Return to start a new line.) When you've finished, click OK in the Notes window. Then when you want to read or change the notes, edit the account. See "Editing account information" on page 40.

7   **(Credit card accounts only) Enter the credit limit.**

8   **Click Create.**

Quicken creates the new account, adds its name to the account list, and opens the register for it.

Quicken places the cursor in the column where you'll enter the opening balance. The name of this column varies depending on the type of account you're creating.

If you need to change the opening balance for an account after the account is set up, come back to this transaction. Enter the revised opening balance (replacing what you had originally entered in the column), and change the date if necessary. See page 41 for more information about changing the opening balance.

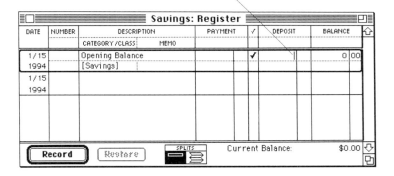

9   **Enter the opening balance.**

Use the table on page 38 to determine the amount to enter as the opening balance.

10   **Change the date if necessary.**

Use the table on page 38 to determine the date to enter for the Opening Balance transaction.

Account type	Balance	Date
Bank	Ending balance shown on your last bank statement (also called "current" or "new" balance)	Date of your last bank statement
Cash	Amount of cash you have on hand	Today's date
Credit card	Balance due shown on your last credit card statement (also called "new" balance)	Date of your last credit statement
Asset	Current value of the asset	Today's date
Liability	Current amount owed on the liability	Today's date
Portfolio	See "Choosing an option for first-time setup" on page 236.	
Mutual fund	See "Choosing an option for first-time setup" on page 236.	

11   **Click Record.**

- To enable electronic payments for a bank account, see Chapter 12, *Paying bills electronically,* beginning on page 171.

- To enable IntelliCharge for a credit card account, see "Setting up a credit card account to use IntelliCharge" on page 201.

Selecting an account to use

You can work with many accounts at one time by opening multiple account windows on your desktop. You can tell which account you are working in because the account name is part of the Write Checks and Register window titles.

The account list shows you the accounts you've set up in the current file. To open the account list, choose Accounts from the View menu.

Or press ⌘ A

The account list shows the name, type, and balance of every account in the current file.

To print the account list, open it and choose Print Accounts from the File menu.

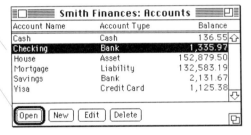

There are three ways to switch to a different account in the current file:

- Open an account from the account list.

Double-click the account you want to use.

OR

Select the account and then click Open.

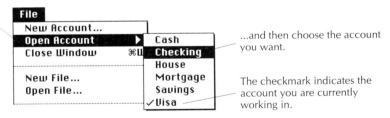

- Choose Open Account from the File menu, and then choose the account you want.

Choose this command....

...and then choose the account you want.

The checkmark indicates the account you are currently working in.

- Click in any window that belongs to the account.

Editing account information

You can rename a Quicken account, change the account description, and read any notes you may have added about the account. You can also change the credit limit for a credit card account.

You can change the account type in most cases. However, you cannot change the type if the account is a:

- Portfolio account
- Mutual fund account
- Bank account with untransmitted CheckFree payments
- Liability account or asset account used with Quicken's loan feature
- Non-investment account that you want to change to a portfolio account or mutual fund account

Or press ⌘ A

1 **Choose Accounts from the View menu.**

2 **Select the account you want to edit.**

This is an account list for a sample file called "Smith Finances."

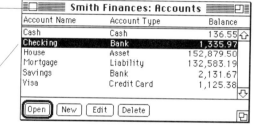

To select an account, click it.

Or press ⌘ E

3 **Click Edit.**

You see the same Set Up Account window that you used to create a new account.

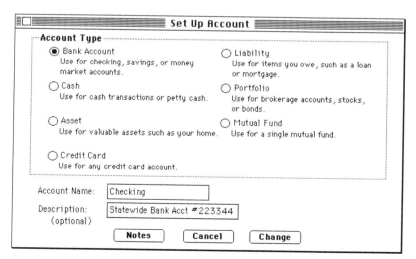

4 **You can change the account name, type, description, notes, and credit limit (for credit card accounts).**

If you change the name of an account, Quicken automatically updates any transactions linked to this account through transfers to show the new name. (For more information about account transfers, see "Transferring money between accounts" on page 86.)

5 **Click Change.**

Quicken makes any changes to the account information and updates the account list and the category and transfer list. Quicken also updates the account name in the Category field of any transfer transactions.

If you need to change the opening balance for an account after the account is set up, you can go directly to the Opening Balance transaction in the register and change the date or amount of the transaction. (See the illustration of the register on page 37 for details.) The next time you reconcile this account, Quicken displays an opening balance difference. See "Letting Quicken adjust for differences" on page 151.

Deleting an account

Deleting a Quicken account permanently removes all of that account's records from your file. Once you delete an account, there is no way to recover it. Be certain you want to delete an account before doing so.

When Quicken deletes the account, it also deletes the account name from the Category field of any transfer transactions.

Or press ⌘ A

1   **Choose Accounts from the View menu.**

2   **Select the account you want to delete in the account list.**

Or press ⌘ D

3   **Click Delete.**

Quicken warns that you are about to permanently remove this account from your file.

If the account contains transactions that are protected with a modify transaction password, Quicken will ask you to enter the password before it deletes the account.

4   **Click Yes if you are certain you want to delete the account.**

Quicken permanently removes the account from your file. The account name is also removed from the category and transfer list and from the Category field of any transfer transactions.

If you delete a liability account or asset account that you use with Quicken's loan feature, Quicken deletes the loan from the loan list as well.

Setting up categories and classes

Categories and classes are labels that you can apply to transactions to track how much you are spending on particular items.

When you "categorize" and "classify" transactions, Quicken can provide you with insight into your finances through reports, graphs, and budgets.

This chapter explains how to set up and change categories and classes. Chapter 7, *Using the register,* beginning on page 79, explains how to assign categories and classes to transactions.

About categories

Quicken categories are flexible and easy to use. You can name your categories using words, numbers, or characters in any combination. You can set up categories before you categorize transactions, or set them up "on the fly" as you enter transactions. You can enter categories for some or all of your transactions.

Think about what questions you would like Quicken reports, graphs, and budgets to answer. If you are tracking your home finances, you probably want reports and graphs to tell you:

- How much you spend each month on groceries, mortgage interest, utilities, auto maintenance, medical fees, entertainment, or charity. These items are your *expense categories*.

- How much you receive each month in salary, bonuses, dividends, interest income, or rent from investment properties. These items are your *income categories*.

You can also categorize different parts of the same transaction with multiple category names. Categorizing one transaction with multiple categories or classes is called "splitting" a transaction. For example, if you spend $120 at a department store, you may not spend the entire amount on one item. A split transaction allows you to track more specifically where the money went: $17 on books, $39 on clothing, and $64 on housewares.

Assign categories to all your transactions when you enter them in Quicken so that you can:

- Generate Quicken's income- and expense-based reports and graphs. (See "Category" on page 300 for a sample category report and "Analyzing income and expenses" on page 345 for a sample category graph.)

- Set up budget amounts for each category in the budget spreadsheet. Then you can quickly compare your actual expenses with your budget amounts by creating a budget report or a budget variance graph. (See Chapter 21, *Budgeting your income and expenses,* beginning on page 351.)

- Prepare for your tax returns by printing a report that lists all tax-related income and expenses. (See "Creating tax reports" on page 374.)

- Export your transaction data to tax software. (See "Transferring Quicken data to tax preparation software" on page 377.)

Using Quicken's preset category lists

Whether you want to modify Quicken's preset lists of home or business categories or start from scratch, the way you organize your category list affects how Quicken organizes all your income and expense-based reports and graphs, and your budget.

If you're the type of person who likes to get started quickly and learn by trial and error, you probably want to start using Quicken's preset category list and add new categories as you need them. Review Quicken's preset list of categories illustrated below and see if it's similar to the way you mentally organize your finances.

If you prefer to spend some time thinking about how you want Quicken to organize your finances, review the preset category list illustrated below, and then take a look at the modified category lists on page 47.

When you started Quicken for the first time, you had an opportunity to choose Quicken's home or business categories. (See "Starting Quicken for the first time" on page 32.) If you selected the Home checkbox, Quicken displays these categories when you choose Categories & Transfers from the View menu.

Here is the list of Quicken's preset categories for personal finances. Quicken also has a preset list of categories for small business (not illustrated here). The complete lists of Quicken's standard home and business categories are in Help. (Press ⌘ ? and then click Contents. Click "Setting up categories and classes," and then click "Quicken's home categories" or "Quicken's business categories.")

The preset list of categories contains some subcategories. Subcategories are indented under the main category. In this example, "Insurance" is the main category and "Auto" and "Home" are the subcategories.

Quicken organizes categories alphabetically in the category list. If you would like to change the order of some categories, you can add spaces or numbers in front of category names to change the order of the list. See "Setting up categories" on page 47 for more information about how to add categories to this preset list.

If you are using Quicken in the U.S., you may want to delete these Canadian categories from the list: CPP, RRSP, and UIC. If you are using Quicken in Canada, you may want to rename the subcategories under "Taxes."

```
≣▢▭≣ Categories ≣≣◲▯
Category/Transfer     Type      Tax
Auto                 Expense          ⇧
  Fuel
  Service
Bank Charges         Expense
Bonus                Income      ◇
Charity              Expense     ◇
Child Care           Expense     ◇
Clothing             Expense
CPP                  Income      ◇
Dining               Expense
Education            Expense
Entertainment        Expense
Gift Received        Income      ◇
Gifts                Expense
Groceries            Expense
Home Repair          Expense
Household            Expense
Insurance            Expense
  Auto
  Home
Interest Earned      Income      ◇
Interest Paid        Expense     ◇
Investment Exp       Expense     ◇
Medical              Expense     ◇
Miscellaneous        Expense
Mortgage Int         Expense     ◇
Old Age Pension      Income      ◇
Recreation           Expense
RRSP                 Expense
Salary               Income      ◇
Subscriptions        Expense
Taxes                Expense     ◇
  Federal                        ◇
  Medicare                       ◇
  Other                          ◇
  Property                       ◇
  Soc Sec                        ◇
  State                          ◇
Telephone            Expense
Travel               Expense
UIC                  Expense     ◇
Utilities            Expense
  Gas & Electric
  Water                          ⇩
```

Each category's type (income or expense) is listed next to the category name. Generally, you assign income categories to transactions that increase the balance of your account and you assign expense categories to transactions that decreases the balance of the account. However, sometimes you should use an expense category for a transaction that increases the balance of your account.

For example, if you assign the *expense* category "Clothing" to a transaction, you would assign the same *expense* category "Clothing" to a transaction for the return of the clothing. The net result of a credit for returned merchandise is a decrease in your clothing expenses in a report or graph.

In Quicken, you may set up many accounts, but you have only one category list. Whether you enter a transaction into one Quicken account or another, the category you apply to the transaction is the same.

For example, if you write a check for some food you bought at the market, you would enter a transaction into your Quicken checking account and assign the category "Groceries" to the transaction. If you pay for the food by credit card instead of check, you would enter a transaction into your Quicken credit card account instead of your checking account, but you'd still assign the category "Groceries" to the transaction.

You can assign tax information to tax-related categories. Chapter 22, *Preparing your income taxes,* beginning on page 361.

Here are two sample category lists:

- The list on the right is used by a family that wants to track their income and expenses in more detail than provided by Quicken's preset list. You may want to add more levels of detail to Quicken's preset list of categories.

- The list below is shorter than Quicken's preset category list. It contains main categories only. You may want to delete some of the categories in Quicken's preset list if you know you'll never use them.

Modifying Quicken's preset category lists

There are many ways to organize your categories. You can modify Quicken's preset category list by reducing or adding to the number of categories, by editing the names of the categories, and by reducing or adding to the number of levels of categories.

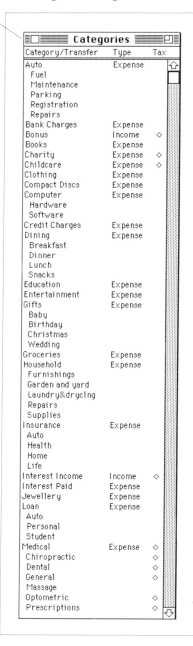

The organization of your categories affects the organization of your budget and all income and expense-based reports and graphs. If you have a long, detailed category list similar to the one illustrated on the right, your budget and reports will also be long, but more detailed. If you have many subcategories, they will appear in budget and reports, but subcategories are rolled up into the main categories in graphs. To see how Quicken uses categories in reports, graphs, and budgets, review the sample category report on page 300, the income and expense graph on page 345, and the budget on page 353.

Setting up categories and subcategories

Quicken maintains a list that includes the names of all the categories and accounts in the current Quicken file. Whenever you set up a new category or account, Quicken adds it to the category and transfer list.

You can set up all your categories on one level or in a hierarchy with main categories and subcategories. Subcategories offer an additional level of detail. It's up to you if you want to use one category called "Utilities" for all your utility transactions, or if you want to have subcategories under "Utilities" called "Cable," "Gas and Electricity," "Trash," "Water," and so on.

You can set up your category names before you enter transactions, or you can set them up as you enter transactions. Whenever you type a new category name in a transaction, Quicken offers to set up the new category.

After you are finished setting up your categories and subcategories, you are ready to assign them to transactions in the register. See Chapter 7, *Using the register,* beginning on page 79.

Setting up categories

Or press ⌘ L

1   Choose Categories & Transfers from the View menu.

Quicken lists income and expense categories alphabetically at the top of the category and transfer list followed by investment categories and transfers.

These are typical expense categories in a category and transfer list. Subcategories are indented under the main categories.

Account names (enclosed in square brackets) are included in this list because you can double-click an account name to create an automatic transfer between accounts. See "Transferring money between accounts" on page 86 for complete information about transfers between accounts.

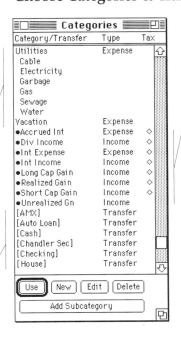

The first time you set up a Quicken portfolio or mutual fund account, Quicken automatically adds these investment categories to your category and transfer list.

You can add more investment categories to your category and transfer list if necessary. See the first table footnote on page 251.

You can print the category and transfer list. Open the list and then choose Print Categories from the File menu.

Or press ⌘ N

2   Click New.

Quicken displays the Set Up Categories dialog box.

3 Enter information for the category in the Set Up Categories dialog box.

Click a category type:

- Click Income if this is a category such as salary, bonuses, dividends, interest income, or rent from an investment property.

- Click Expense if this is a category such as groceries, mortgage interest, utilities, auto maintenance, medical fees, entertainment, or charity.

To assign a tax schedule to this category, see "Assigning line items from tax forms and schedules to categories" on page 364.

Enter a name for the new category or subcategory. You can use up to 15 characters.

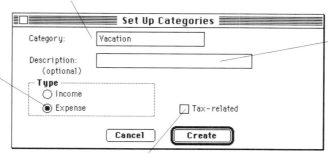

(Optional) Enter a description of the category or subcategory in the Description box. You can use up to 30 characters.

(Optional) Click the Tax-related checkbox if you want to use this category to track a particular type of tax information.

4 Click Create to add the category name to the list.

Setting up subcategories

Or press ⌘ L

1 Choose Categories & Transfers from the View menu.

2 Select the category you want to create a subcategory for.

Or press ⌘ N

3 Click the Add Subcategory button.

4 Enter information for the subcategory the same way you'd enter information for a category.

5 Click Create to add the subcategory name to the list.

Quicken displays the new subcategory alphabetically below the main category in the categories and transfers list.

To add a subcategory called "Insurance" under the main category "Auto," select the main category and click Add Subcategory.

Type "Insurance" in the Category field, and click Create.

In this example, Quicken would display the subcategory "Insurance" between "Fuel" and "Maintenance."

Quicken doesn't display an income or expense type here; subcategories are always the same expense type as the main category.

Changing and deleting categories and subcategories

When you change a category name, Quicken automatically changes all transactions categorized with the old name.

When you delete a category or subcategory, Quicken erases the name from the category and transfer list and the Category field of any transactions currently assigned to it. Don't delete a category or subcategory name as a step in changing it. See "Moving categories and subcategories" on page 51 instead.

Delete a category only if you don't expect ever to use it.

You cannot edit or delete transfers. Quicken uses the accounts you've set up and displays them at the bottom of the category and transfer list. You use the accounts to show transfers of funds from one Quicken account to another. If you no longer use one of your Quicken accounts and you'd like to delete the account, see "Deleting an account" on page 42.

You cannot edit or delete investment categories. Quicken adds predefined investment categories to your category and transfer list the first time you create an investment account (portfolio or mutual fund account).

Changing categories and subcategories

Or press ⌘ L

1   Choose Categories & Transfers from the View menu.

2   Select the category or subcategory you want to change.

Or press ⌘ E

3   Click Edit.
Quicken displays the Edit Categories dialog box.

4   Make any changes you want to the information displayed.

5   Click Change to record the changed category or subcategory information.

Deleting categories and subcategories

Or press ⌘ L

1 Choose Categories & Transfers from the View menu.

2 Select the category or subcategory you want to delete.

If you delete a category that has subcategories under it, Quicken will delete the main category *and* all the subcategories that belong to it. If you want to keep some or all of the subcategories, change them into categories before deleting the main category. See "Changing (promoting) a subcategory into a category" on page 52.

Or press ⌘ D

3 Click Delete.

Quicken asks you to confirm that you want to delete the category or subcategory.

4 Click Yes.

Quicken deletes the category or subcategory name from the category and transfer list and erases it from the Category field of any transactions to which it has been assigned, including memorized transactions.

Moving categories and subcategories

After working with Quicken for a while, you'll understand better how Quicken uses categories in reports, graphs, and budgets. You may want to move categories within the category and transfer list. You can easily change a category into a subcategory, change a subcategory into a category, or move a subcategory from one category to another.

When you change the name or level of a category, Quicken automatically changes the name in each of the transactions that you've previously categorized with the old name.

Changing (demoting) a category into a subcategory

Or press ⌘ L

1   Choose Categories & Transfers from the View menu.

2   Select the category you want to demote.

3   Drag the category up or down.

When you drag the category vertically, the mouse pointer changes to a double-pointed arrow and a horizontal line shows you when you've reached the destination category name.

You may decide to change the category "Telephone" into a subcategory of "Utilities."

Select "Telephone" and drag it down to just below "Utilities." This line and a double-pointed arrow appear.

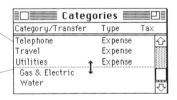

4   Release the mouse button when the horizontal line is just underneath the destination category.

After you move the category, Quicken changes it into a subcategory of the destination category and updates the alphabetic order of the list. Any subcategories that belonged to the demoted category stay with it (creating three or more levels).

When you release the mouse button, Quicken realphabetizes the subcategory list. Now "Telephone" is a subcategory of "Utilities."

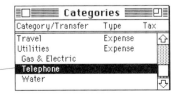

Changing (promoting) a subcategory into a category

Or press ⌘ L

1 Choose Categories & Transfers from the View menu.

2 Select the subcategory you want to promote.

3 Drag the subcategory to the left to promote it by one or more category levels.

When you drag the category to the left, the mouse pointer changes to a left-pointed arrow and a vertical line shows you to align it with any category level you choose.

You may decide to change the subcategory "Bonus" into a category.

Select "Bonus" and drag it left to the same place where main categories begin in the list. This line and left-pointed arrow appear.

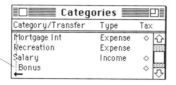

4 Release the mouse button when the vertical line is aligned with the correct level of category.

Quicken promotes the category you moved to the category level you indicated and updates the alphabetic order of the list. Any subsubcategories that belonged to the promoted category stay with it.

When you release the mouse button, Quicken updates the list. Now "Bonus" is a main category.

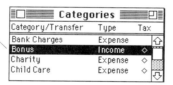

Moving a subcategory from one category to another

Or press ⌘ L

1 Choose Categories & Transfers from the View menu.

2 Select the subcategory you want to move and drag it up or down the list.

3 Release the mouse button when the horizontal line is just below the destination category name.

Quicken changes the subcategory you moved into a subcategory of the destination category you indicated and updates the alphabetic order of the list. Any subcategories that belonged to the subcategory stay with it.

Copying categories from one file to another

All the accounts in one Quicken file share the same categories. You can copy the categories (including budget amounts you may have already entered for each category) from one Quicken data file to another in two steps. First, export the categories from one Quicken data file to a separate text file, and then import the separate text file with the categories into the second Quicken data file.

See Chapter 6, *Setting up and using Quicken data files*, beginning on page 59 for more information about Quicken files.

To copy all the categories from the Quicken data file "Smith Finances" into the Quicken data file "Smith Consulting," you first export the categories from "Smith Finances" into a text file called "ExportedCats".

Smith Finances   ExportedCats   Smith Consulting

Exporting categories from one Quicken data file to an export file

1   **Choose Open File from the File menu, and then select the Quicken data file that contains the categories you want to copy and click Open.**

Or press ⌘ L

2   **Choose Categories & Transfers from the View menu.**

3   **Choose Export Categories from the File menu.**

4   **In the Export Category List To field, specify the name of the export file (such as ExportedCats) that will contain the category information.**

5   **Click Save.**

Quicken copies the categories and budget amounts into the text file.

Now you can copy the categories from the text file into a different Quicken data file. See "Importing the exported categories into another Quicken file" on page 54.

Importing the exported categories into another Quicken file

1 **Choose Open File from the File menu, and then select the Quicken data file that you want to copy the categories into (the "destination" data file) and click Open.**

   This destination Quicken data file needs to exist before you can import anything into it. If you have not set up the destination Quicken data file yet, see "Setting up additional files" on page 61.

2 **Choose Import from the File menu.**

3 **Select the export file that you just created.**

4 **Click Open to import the text file that contains the category information.**

   Quicken adds the imported categories and budget amounts to your destination Quicken data file.

About classes

You can use classes to specify where, to what, or to whom your transactions apply. Classes do not replace categories. Rather, classes complement categories by adding a second dimension to reports, graphs, and budgets. You should assign categories to transactions, but you don't have to assign classes to transactions.

Your use of classes can be as simple or as intricate as your finances require. You might use just one class, for example, to distinguish business transactions in a file that contains both personal and business expenses. Or you might use a number of classes; for example, if you work with a number of clients, you could set up a class for each client.

It's helpful to use Quicken for a while before you start using classes. Because people use classes in so many different ways, Quicken does not provide a preset list of classes. To use classes efficiently, think about what kind of reports, graphs, and budgets you might need. (See "Job/project" on page 314 for a sample report that uses classes to separate the income and expenses for multiple projects.)

There may be times when you want reports based on categories, other times when you want reports based on classes, and other times when you want a report that includes both category and class information.

You might want to use classes in situations like these:

- If you work with multiple clients, you can identify transactions by client name. Then you can report separately on the income and expenses related to each client.

- If you manage properties, you can identify transactions by property name or address. That way, six different utility bills could be marked clearly as utility expenses applying to six different properties.

- If you use your personal checking account for business as well as personal expenses, you can identify business transactions with the class name Business.

Examples of classes and their uses are illustrated in the table on page 56.

Use classes to specify	Reason for using classes	Examples of classes
Who the transaction is for		
• Your clients	Track income and expense by client	SellCo, Whitman, Taylor, Hill
• Your salespeople	Track commissions	Bob, Karen, Glenn, Kate, Eric, Jill
• You or your spouse	Track income and expense by individual	Steve, Sally
Where the transaction applies		
• Sales regions	Track performance by division	Midwest, West, East, North, South
• Property names	Track income and expense by property	Harlow St, Ward Way, Rusko Avenue
What the transaction is for		
• Job or project names	Perform job costing	Tierney, Epstein, McCaffrey, Petit
• Equipment or vehicle	Track expenses by item	Macintosh, truck, phone, FAX, copier
• Business use	Separate business income and expense from personal income and expense in the same Quicken data file.	Business (Leave all your personal transactions unclassified, but assign the class called "Business" to all your business expenses.)

Setting up classes and subclasses

You can set up classes before you categorize transactions, or set them up "on the fly" as you enter transactions. You can enter classes in some or all of your transactions.

Quicken displays class names in the class list, which is shared by all the accounts in the file.

You cannot change a class into a category, or vice versa.

After you are finished setting up any classes you want to use, you are ready to assign them to the transactions you enter in the register. See Chapter 7, *Using the register,* beginning on page 79.

Setting up classes

Or press ⌘ K

1 Choose Classes from the View menu.

Each item in the list is a class. The property classes in this list make it possible for Quicken to track rental income and expense by property.

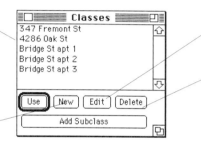

To view or change the information for an existing class, select it in the list and click Edit.

To delete a class, select it in the list and click Delete.

You can print your class list. Open the list and choose Print Classes from the File menu.

If this is the first time you're setting up a class, this list is empty. Click New to set up a new class.

Or press ⌘ N

2 Click New.

You can use up to 15 characters to enter a class name.

You can use up to 30 characters to enter a description.

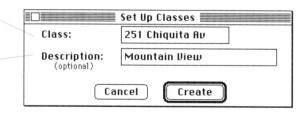

3 Enter a name in the Class field.

4 (Optional) Enter a description of the class in the Description field.

A typical class list for personal finances might contain several classes for tracking the income or expenses related to these items:
• vehicles
• individuals
• properties

5 **Click Create to add the class name to the class list.**

If you use the same Quicken data file to track your personal finances and a personal business such as consulting, you might use only one class called "Business." Assign this class to transactions that are related to the income or expenses of your business.

See "Assigning classes consistently" on page 91 for more information about using a class for business transactions.

Setting up subclasses

Using subclasses lets you further refine your reports. The steps to add a subclass to a class are the same as those to add a subcategory to a category, except that you start by choosing Classes from the View menu. Then click Add Subclass instead of Add Subcategory. See "Setting up subcategories" on page 48.

Changing and deleting classes and subclasses

The steps to change or delete a class are the same as those to change or delete a category, except that you start by choosing Classes from the View menu. See "Changing and deleting categories and subcategories" on page 49.

Moving classes and subclasses

The steps to move existing classes and subclasses in the class list are the same as those to rearrange categories in the category and transfer list, except that you start by choosing Classes from the View menu. See "Moving categories and subcategories" on page 51.

Copying classes from one file to another

All the accounts in one Quicken file share the same class list. You can copy classes from one Quicken file to another by exporting the classes to a separate file, and then importing the separate file with the classes into the second Quicken file. The steps to copy classes from one Quicken file to another are the same as those to copy categories from one Quicken file to another, except that you start by choosing Classes from the View menu. Then choose Export Classes from the File menu. See "Copying categories from one file to another" on page 53.

6

Setting up and using Quicken data files

This chapter describes what a Quicken data file is and how to set up and use additional Quicken data files.

You'll also learn how to back up your work, copy data between files and accounts, set up passwords to protect your data from unauthorized access, and create a new file for a new year.

About Quicken data files

Your Quicken accounts are grouped in one or more Quicken data files. Each separate file is unrelated to any other Quicken data file, which means that reports and graphs show data from only one file at a time. **Most people need only one Quicken file.**

> A Quicken account is not the same as a Quicken file. You need to set up a new Quicken account for each real-life account that you have (for example, your checking account, savings account, VISA account, MasterCard account, mortgages, car loans, and investment accounts). You can set up as many accounts as you need in one file (up to 255).

All the accounts in one file are related to each other—they share the same categories, classes, memorized transactions, and other information.

Your Quicken data file might contain a checking account, a savings account, two credit card accounts, a portfolio account, and a mutual fund account. (If you have a file for business use, your file might contain a business checking account, an A/R account, an A/P account, and a capital equipment account.) You can transfer amounts from one account to another within the same file.

When you run a Quicken report or graph, you see data from all the accounts in the current Quicken data file. For example, a net worth report calculates your net worth based on the balances of all the accounts in your file, and the summary report shows income and expense totals from all the accounts in your file.

The accounts in a Quicken data file are like the folders in a file drawer. For example, you might label these folders "Checking Account," "Savings Account," "Individual Retirement Accounts," "VISA Account," and so on.

A Quicken data file is like a drawer in a filing cabinet (it holds many accounts). For example, you might label this drawer "Our Finances."

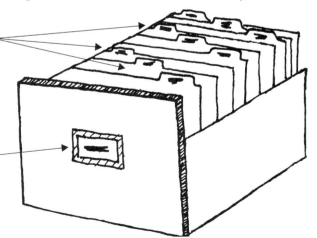

If you want to find out more about Quicken accounts, see "Quicken has special account types for tracking different kinds of transactions" on page 7.

Setting up additional files

If you use Quicken for personal finances, you probably need only one file. When you store all your accounts in just one file, Quicken gives you important benefits that it cannot provide for separate files. With all your accounts in one file, Quicken can:

- Keep one list of income and expense categories for all your accounts

- Combine data from all accounts in a single report or graph to track your income and expenses, net worth, and other important information

- Transfer money from one account to another in the same file

With separate files, there is no connection between the accounts in one file and the accounts in another. Of course there are some good reasons to have more than one file:

- To keep information separate for business purposes, if your personal and business finances are entirely separate and have different checking accounts.

- To keep a separate file for each year's accounts. See "Creating a new file for a new fiscal or calendar year" on page 76.

1   Choose New File from the File menu.

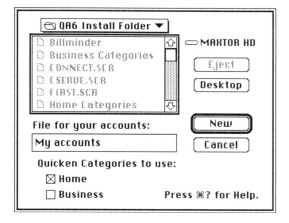

2   Specify a location and name for your new Quicken file.

3   (Optional) Select home or business categories.

Quicken provides preset home and business categories so you can identify transactions by income or expense type (for example, salary income or mortgage expense). Categories also let you produce meaningful reports using your Quicken data.

Selecting predefined categories now does not limit you in any way, as you can always add, edit, or delete categories later. However, if you do not want to use predefined categories with your file, clear the checkbox for either or both category types.

4   Click New.

Quicken creates a new file with the location and name you specified and opens the Set Up Account window.

Set up accounts within this file as described in "Setting up additional Quicken accounts" on page 36.

To copy categories from an existing Quicken file to a new Quicken file, see "Copying categories from one file to another" on page 53.

Opening a file

When you start Quicken, it opens the last file you used in the previous session. To work in another file, open it.

Or press ⌘ O

1   Choose Open File from the File menu.

2   Select the file you want to open.

3   Click Open.

4   Type a password if Quicken asks you for one. Then click OK.

Quicken closes all the open account windows before it opens the new file. The next time you open the file, Quicken reopens all the account windows you used in the last session and positions them in the same places on the desktop.

Assigning a password to your file.
You can assign a file password to your Quicken file to prevent unauthorized access. See "Requiring a password to open a file" on page 72.

Renaming or deleting a file

See page 4 of your QuickStart Card for tips about working with Quicken data files in the Finder. You rename or delete a Quicken data file the same way you rename or delete any file in the Finder. For a quick tutorial about the Finder and other Macintosh basics, find the "Macintosh Basics" disk that came with your computer and run the Macintosh Basics tutorial.

Backing up your Quicken data file

It's a good idea to back up your Quicken data file every time you use Quicken. You might also want to create a special backup at the end of a fiscal or calendar year.

Creating a regular backup

Or press ⌘ Q

1   **If Quicken is running, choose Quit from the File menu.**

2   **Insert your backup disk.**

A Quicken data file icon

Murphy's Finances

3   **Open the folder that contains your Quicken data file.**

4   **Drag the icon for the Quicken data file to the backup disk.**

5   **When the backup disk icon is selected (black), release the mouse button.**

The System software copies the file to the backup disk. If a file with the same name already exists on the disk, the System software asks you to confirm that you want the file replaced before it copies the file.

6   **Eject the backup disk and store it in a safe place.**

You can use the same backup disk the next time you back up your work.

Drag your Quicken data file to the backup disk. The Quicken data file in this example is "Murphy's Finances."

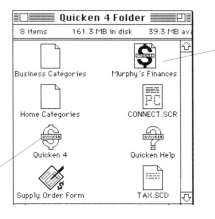

This is the Quicken application file. It does not contain your data.

If you ever need to restore this file from the backup disk to your hard disk, insert your backup disk. Then drag the backup copy from the backup disk into the folder on your hard disk where you keep your Quicken data files.

Creating a year-end backup

This method allows you to back up the previous year's transactions and continue to use the current Quicken data file. We recommend this method unless your Quicken data file gets very large and you run out of space on your hard disk or backup disk.

If you want to start a new file for the new year that contains only transactions for the new year, see "Creating a new file for a new fiscal or calendar year" on page 76.

Or press ⌘ Q

1   Choose Quit from the File menu to leave Quicken.

2   Insert your backup disk.

A Quicken data file icon

Murphy's Finances

3   Open the folder that contains your Quicken data file.

4   Click on the icon for the Quicken data file to select it.

Or press ⌘ D

5   Choose Duplicate from the File menu.

The System software creates a copy of your file. For example, if your file name is "Murphy's Finances," the System creates a file called "Murphy's Finances copy."

6   Rename the copy by typing a new name immediately.

Click on an item to select (highlight) it.

For example, if you are creating a backup copy of all your transactions for 1993, rename the copy "Murphy's Finances 1993." "Murphy's Finances" is your archive file for 1993.

7   Copy the archive file to a floppy disk, store it in a safe place, and delete it from your hard disk.

8   Continue to work with your original Quicken data file.

In this example, your original Quicken data file is "Murphy's Finances."

9   (Optional) To prevent access to the previous year's transactions in the current file, you can set up a transaction password.

See "Requiring a password to change earlier transactions" on page 74.

10   (Optional) If you want the archive file to contain only transactions from the previous year, use the Save a Copy command to purge all transactions from the current year.

For example, if you want "Murphy's Finances 1993" to include only transactions for 1993, you can use the Save a Copy command to purge all 1994 transactions from the file. See "Purging any later transactions in the archive file" on page 78.

Copying part of a file

You can copy part of a file to create a new file. You specify a date range, and then Quicken transfers all the transactions that fall within that date range to a new file. Quicken does not change the original file in any way. The new file will have all the same lists as the original file: accounts, categories, classes, and so on.

> Save a Copy will copy transactions from all the accounts in your file. If you want to copy transactions from one account to another account, see "Copying transactions from one account to another" on page 68.

You might want to copy part of a Quicken file for one of these reasons:

- Your Quicken data file is too large to fit on your backup floppy disk. You want to remove some of your older data from your working file.

- You want to copy your memorized transactions, transaction groups, categories, classes, and merchants to a new file without copying any transactions.

> You might want to copy transactions within a certain date range to start a new file for a new fiscal year. If so, see "Creating a new file for a new fiscal or calendar year" on page 76.

1   Open the file you want to copy.

2   Choose Save a Copy from the File menu.

See "How Save a Copy treats prior uncleared transactions" on page 66 before selecting or clearing this checkbox.

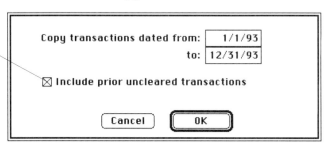

```
Copy transactions dated from:    1/1/93
                          to:   12/31/93

☒ Include prior uncleared transactions

              Cancel          OK
```

3   Enter the date range of transactions to be included in the new file.

By default, Quicken uses the dates of the oldest and newest transactions in the current file as the date range of transactions to be included in the new file.

If you want to create a new file that contains only your memorized transactions, transaction groups, and categories (but no transactions), enter dates that are later than the last transaction in the existing file. You must also perform steps 6 and 7 below.

4   **Decide what you want Quicken to do with prior uncleared transactions.**

For most people, selecting the Include Prior Uncleared Transactions checkbox is the right choice. When the checkbox is selected, Quicken transfers all uncleared transactions to the new file. See "How Save a Copy treats prior uncleared transactions" on this page for details.

5   **Click OK.**

Quicken displays a dialog box where you can name the copy.

6   **Specify a name and location for the new Quicken file.**

7   **Click Save.**

Quicken begins copying the data from all the accounts in the file. The original file is still the current file, and it is unaffected.

8   **If you wish to work in the new file, choose Open File from the File menu and select that file.**

How Save a Copy treats prior uncleared transactions

Prior uncleared transactions are transactions that occurred before the date range but haven't yet been cleared (marked with a √) or reconciled (marked with a ✓) in the √ (cleared) column.

If you include prior uncleared transactions when you copy a file, Quicken transfers the information to the new file as follows:

- For each account in the original file, Quicken summarizes (that is, sums the amounts of) all prior cleared transactions. Quicken then uses this total amount as the opening balance of the corresponding account in the new file.

- Quicken copies all prior uncleared transactions from each account in the original file to the corresponding account in the new file.

When should you include prior uncleared transactions?

Include prior uncleared transactions to the new file if you use Quicken to do any of these tasks:

- Reconcile bank or credit card accounts
- Track assets
- Track business payables and receivables

For such tasks, it's important to include uncleared transactions in the new copy of the file, even when those transactions occur before the beginning of the current period. To include these transactions, select the Include Prior Uncleared Transactions checkbox.

If your cash, asset, or liability account contains prior cleared transactions, Quicken does not copy these transactions to the account in the new file. Instead, Quicken summarizes the transactions and uses this sum as the opening balance of the account in the new file.

Remember that transfer transactions are special because they might include cases where one side of a transfer has cleared, but not the other. For example, a check to VISA might have appeared on a bank statement, but not on a VISA statement. In this example, if you include prior uncleared transactions when you copy and the check date is prior to the beginning date you specify, Quicken summarizes the bank account side of the transfer and copies the credit card account side. This partial summary is not harmful, but it does cause Quicken to display the message, "Transfer not present" if you use the Go to Transfer (⌘ [) command in the VISA account transaction. Also, the TOTAL TRANSFERS line item in a summary report might not be zero.

When should you exclude prior uncleared transactions?

You should exclude prior uncleared transactions from the new file only if you perform none of the tasks listed in the previous section using Quicken. You want the new file to include only transactions in the date range for the current period, regardless of their cleared status. To exclude prior uncleared transactions, clear the Include Prior Uncleared Transactions checkbox.

Copying transactions from one account to another

Although you cannot move or copy transactions directly from one Quicken account to another, you can do so indirectly by exporting and importing transactions.

If you want to add transactions from other programs or from IBM Quicken (DOS or Windows) to your Quicken file, see "Transferring files from IBM Quicken (DOS or Windows)" on page 26.

You might want to import and export transactions for any of the following reasons:

● To consolidate transactions from the same Quicken account in two different locations. To consolidate transactions from an account in one location with the same account in another location, export the transactions from the account in the first location to a QIF file, and then import the transactions to the account in the other location.

A QIF file is a text file in a special format called "Quicken interchange format."

More information about QIF files is in Help. (Press ⌘ ? and then click Topics. Click "Technical Information" in the Topics list, and then click "Information about QIF files" in the Subtopics list on the right.)

● To move transactions from one account to another in the same Quicken data file. For example, suppose you entered some transactions in the wrong account. You can export the transactions from the incorrect account to a QIF file, and then import them into the correct account. (Be sure to delete the transactions from the first account when you have finished.)

● To merge two different Quicken data files. If you want to combine accounts from two Quicken data files into one Quicken data file, export the transactions from the first Quicken data file to separate QIF files (one QIF file per account). Then, in the second Quicken data file, set up the accounts and import the transactions.

Copying transactions from one account to another takes two steps:

◆ **Export the transactions from the source account to a QIF file. You can export transactions within a date range only; you cannot specify individual transactions.**
See "Exporting transactions from an account to a QIF file" on page 69.

◆ **Import the QIF file into the destination account in the same Quicken data file or in a different Quicken data file.**
See "Importing the transactions from the QIF file into an account" on page 70.

Exporting transactions from an account to a QIF file

1   **Open the account you want to export data from.**

2   **Choose Export Transactions from the File menu.**

Enter the starting and ending dates of the transactions to be exported.

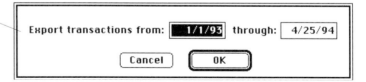

Export transactions from: 1/1/93   through: 4/25/94

Cancel   OK

3   **Enter the dates of the first and last transactions to be included in the exported text file.**

You can specify only a date range, not specific transactions.

4   **Click OK.**

Quicken displays a dialog box where you can name the export file.

5   **In the Export Current Account To field, enter the name of a temporary file to receive the exported transactions.**

> **Important!** Do not use the name of any Quicken data file! Make up a new name that you will recognize. This temporary file is just a "transition" container for the exported transactions. For example, if you are exporting transactions from a bank account called "Savings," name the temporary file "Temp Savings."

6   **Click Save to export the transactions to a text file.**

Now you are ready to import the QIF file you just created into the destination account.

Importing the transactions from the QIF file into an account

1 **If the account you want to import data into does not yet exist, set up the account.**

See "Setting up additional Quicken accounts" on page 36.

2 **Open the register for the account that you want to import data into.**

3 **Choose Import from the File menu.**

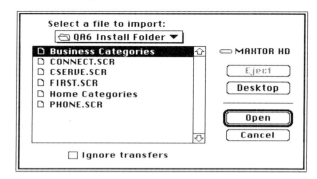

4 **Choose the QIF file that contains the exported data.**

5 **Click Open.**

Quicken imports the transactions from the text file into the current account register, adding new categories and classes as it imports the transactions that contain them.

If the imported file contains transfers to accounts that don't exist in the current Quicken file, Quicken replaces the bracketed account name in the Category field of the transfers with one asterisk and the account name like this: *Checking.

An example of the latter result: if the imported file contains transfers to an account called Savings that doesn't exist in the current file, Quicken replaces the [Savings] account name in the Category field of the transfers with the name *Savings.

Later, if you wish, you can set up the missing account and restore the transfer information to these transactions with multiple Replace commands. Or change the *Savings category name into something else.

Combining two Quicken accounts

1 Export the transactions from one account to a text file.

2 (Optional) If you want a record of the account from which you exported the transactions, choose Print Transactions from the File menu to print the account register.

Or press ⌘ D

3 Select the account from which you exported the transactions in the account list and choose Delete from the Edit menu to delete it.

4 Open the second account and import the text file.

Merging two Quicken files

1 Export the transactions from each account in the first Quicken file to a separate text file.

2 Open the second Quicken file.

3 Set up new accounts or open existing accounts and import the data from each of the text files, one account at a time.

Setting up passwords

You might want to protect all or some of the transactions in a Quicken file from unauthorized changes. You can set up two different types of password in Quicken:

- You can discourage unauthorized access to your Quicken data by requiring a file password before your file can be opened.

- You can also set up a separate transaction password that protects all transactions before a certain date.

Requiring a password to open a file

Use a file password to protect an entire file. After you set up a file password, you cannot open your Quicken file unless you enter the password correctly. However, a file password cannot protect your file from being copied, deleted, or renamed. If your file is renamed or copied to a different place, the password is still in effect.

When you set up a password, it protects only the current file. Make sure that the current file is the one you want to assign a password to.

Important! Write down the password and keep the written password in a safe place. If you forget your password, the only way to remove it from your Quicken data file is to send your file to Intuit's Password Removal Team. The service fee for password removal is $5.00. Please allow 10 business days for password removal.

---

1   **Open the file you want to protect with a password.**

2   **From the Settings menu, choose Passwords and then choose Open File.**

As you enter your password, Quicken displays a bullet (•) in place of the character you typed to ensure privacy.

3   **Enter a private password that is easy for you to remember and click OK.**

You can enter up to 16 characters, including spaces. It doesn't matter whether you type upper- or lowercase characters when you set up or later enter a password.

4   **Enter the password again to confirm it and click OK.**

From now on, Quicken prompts you for the password before allowing you to open this Quicken file.

Changing or removing the file password

You can change or remove a password from a file if you want to allow access to it by other individuals.

Important! Write down the password and keep the written password in a safe place. If you forget your password, the only way to remove it from your Quicken data file is to send your file to Intuit's Password Removal Team. The service fee for password removal is $5.00. Please allow 10 business days for password removal.

---

1   **Open the file whose password you want to change or remove.**

2   **From the Settings menu, choose Passwords and then choose File.**

3   **Enter the current password and click OK.**

Quicken displays the Open File Password dialog box.

4   **Enter a new password or leave the field blank to remove the password for the file.**

5   **Click OK and enter the new password again to confirm it.**

6   **Click OK.**

Quicken activates the new password or removes the current password immediately.

Requiring a password to change earlier transactions

Use a transaction password to protect transactions within a date range from inadvertent change. After you set up a transaction password, you cannot make changes to transactions prior to a given date unless you enter the password correctly. For example, you might want to *close* an accounting period so that no changes can be made inadvertently to transactions in it.

When you create a transaction password, you specify the password you want to use and a date. The date you specify is the date of the last transaction you want this password to protect.

Important! Write down the password and keep the written password in a safe place. If you forget your password, the only way to remove it from your Quicken data file is to send your file to Intuit's Password Removal Team. The service fee for password removal is $5.00. Please allow 10 business days for password removal.

1 **From the Settings menu, choose Passwords and then choose Transaction.**

As you enter your password, Quicken displays a bullet (•) in place of the character you typed to ensure privacy.

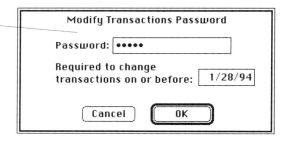

2 **Enter a private password that is easy for you to remember.**

You can enter up to 16 characters, including spaces. It doesn't matter whether you use lowercase or uppercase letters.

3 **(Optional) Enter the date of the last transaction you want the password to protect.**

Quicken presets the date to today's date.

4 **Click OK.**

5 **Enter the password again to confirm and click OK.**

From now on, Quicken prompts you for the password before it allows you to record changes to any of the transactions dated on or before the date you specified.

Changing or removing the transaction password

You can change or delete a password from a range of transactions if you want to allow access to it by other individuals. You can also change the date of the last transaction protected by the password.

Important! Write down the password and keep the written password in a safe place. If you forget your password, the only way to remove it from your Quicken data file is to send your file to Intuit's Password Removal Team. The service fee for password removal is $5.00. Please allow 10 business days for password removal.

---

1   **From the File menu, choose Passwords and then choose Transaction.**

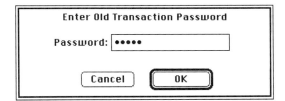

2   **Enter the current password and click OK.**

Quicken displays the Modify Transactions Password dialog box.

3   **Make your changes:**

• To change the transaction password, enter a new password.

• To remove the transaction password, leave the password field blank.

• To change the date of the last transaction you want the password to protect, change the date in the date field.

4   **Click OK.**

If you changed the password, Quicken asks to re-type the new password.

5   **Click OK again.**

Quicken activates the new password, removes the current password, or changes the protected date range immediately.

Creating a new file for a new fiscal or calendar year

Many people think that they should "close out" their accounts at the end of a fiscal or calendar year. To "close out" accounts means to *archive* (or store) the previous year's data and create a new file for the current year.

Some accounting programs require you to close out your accounts at the end of a year, but Quicken does not. In fact, one of the great advantages of Quicken is the ability to create reports and graphs that include several years' worth of information. If you close out a Quicken data file at the end of a year, you sacrifice the ability to create reports and graphs that include information from previous years. For maximum flexibility, we recommend that you make a simple year-end backup of your file as described in "Creating a year-end backup" on page 63 instead of closing out your accounts.

In many cases, the reason people want to close out a previous year is to protect historical data from changes. If you're worried about protecting historical data, you can always set up a password. See "Requiring a password to change earlier transactions" on page 74.

Creating a new file for the new year

If your accountant insists that you create a new Quicken data file for a new fiscal or calendar year, or if your working Quicken data file has become too large and unwieldy, you can use the Save a Copy command to start a new file. The new Quicken data file will contain:

- The ending balance from each account in the previous year (plus all transactions from the previous year that have not been reconciled, if that is what you want)
- Categories and classes
- Memorized transactions
- CheckFree merchants and account information
- All your custom settings

Before the Save a Copy procedure, your working file contains all transactions to date.

After the Save a Copy procedure, your new file will contain only transactions for the new year.

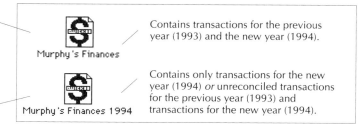

Murphy's Finances — Contains transactions for the previous year (1993) and the new year (1994).

Murphy's Finances 1994 — Contains only transactions for the new year (1994) *or* unreconciled transactions for the previous year (1993) and transactions for the new year (1994).

1 Open the working copy of your Quicken data file.

This file contains all your transactions to date. In this example, the working file is "Murphy's Finances."

2 Choose Save a Copy from the File menu.

Enter the beginning and ending dates for the NEW year, not the previous year.

For example, if you want to start a new file for 1994, enter 1/1/94 and 12/31/94.

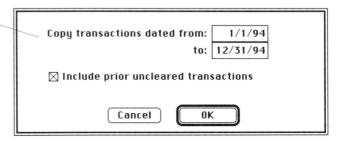

Copy transactions dated from: `1/1/94`
to: `12/31/94`

☒ Include prior uncleared transactions

Cancel   OK

3 Enter the date range of the new year.

In this example, the new year is 1994, so you would enter 1/1/94 to 12/31/94.

4 Decide how you want Quicken to handle uncleared transactions from the previous year:

An uncleared transaction is a transaction that contains nothing in the √ (cleared) field—no thin checkmark or bold checkmark.

- If you have been reconciling all your Quicken accounts since you set them up, select the Include Prior Uncleared Transactions checkbox. Quicken will bring forward all uncleared transactions from the working file to the new file for the new year.

- If you do not reconcile all your Quicken accounts, clear the Include Prior Uncleared Transactions checkbox.

For more information about Include Prior Cleared Transactions, see "How Save a Copy treats prior uncleared transactions" on page 66.

5 Click OK.

Quicken starts out by naming the new file "Copy of *filename*." We suggest that you rename the file to distinguish it as the new year's data.

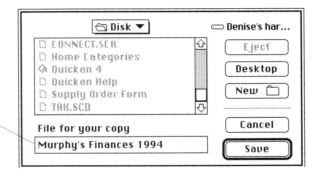

🖿 Disk ▼   ⬭ Denise's har...

☐ CONNECT.SCR   Eject
☐ Home Categories
◈ Quicken 4   Desktop
☐ Quicken Help
☐ Supply Order Form   New 🗀
☐ TRK.SCD

File for your copy   Cancel

Murphy's Finances 1994   Save

6   **Enter a new name for your new Quicken data file.**

For example, if the working copy of your file is named "Murphy's Finances," we suggest naming the new file "Murphy's Finances 1994."

7   **Click Save.**

Quicken creates a copy of your file that includes only transactions for the new year (1994 in this example).

The file may also include prior uncleared transactions if you requested them.

8   **Choose Open File from the File menu. Open the new file and use it to continue your work in the new year.**

In this example, the new file is called "Murphy's Finances 1994."

Archiving the old file

You now have two different Quicken data files:

- The old file ("Murphy's Finances") contains all your transactions to date. This is your archive file.
- The new file ("Murphy's Finances 1994") contains only transactions for the new year. From now on, you will do all your work in this file.

Rename the old file "Murphy's Finances 1993," copy it to a floppy disk, label the disk, and store it in a safe place. If you don't need frequent access to data from the previous year, you can delete the old file from your hard disk.

Purging any later transactions in the archive file

If you want the archive file to contain only transactions from the previous period, instead of all the transactions in the original file, open the archive file and use Save a Copy to purge transactions that occurred after the end of the period. For example, if you want your archive file to contain transactions from 1993 only, enter 1/1/93 to 12/31/93 as the Save a Copy date range.

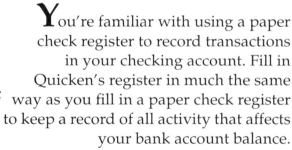

Using the register

Y ou're familiar with using a paper check register to record transactions in your checking account. Fill in Quicken's register in much the same way as you fill in a paper check register to keep a record of all activity that affects your bank account balance.

Each Quicken account has a register associated with it. This chapter describes using the check register for bank accounts. The basic steps for working in all Quicken account registers are the same. Once you learn to work with one check register, you know most of what you need to know about any Quicken register.

Adding transactions to the register

When you set up a Quicken bank account for the first time, you find yourself in the Register window. Use the register to record all transactions, except checks you plan to print. (If you plan to print checks with Quicken, enter them at the Write Checks window, not the Register window. When you create a check in the Write Checks window, Quicken automatically adds that transaction to your register.)

Transactions are items that affect the balance in your account. Common transactions include:

- Checks written by hand
- ATM (automatic teller machine) transactions
- Deposits
- Electronic funds transfers (deposits or withdrawals)
- Checking account fees and interest
- Bank service charges

1 If you don't already have the account open that you want to use, choose Open Account from the File menu, and then choose the account you want to use.

Or press ⌘ A

Or choose Accounts from the View menu, select the account you want to work with, and click Open.

Or press ⌘ R

2 If you're not already in the Register window, choose Register from the View menu.

Quicken opens the register for the account and selects the transaction you entered last.

Or press ⌘ N

3 If the transaction that Quicken selects is not a blank transaction, choose New Transaction from the Edit menu.

Quicken places the insertion point into a blank transaction and enters today's date in the Date field.

4 Enter information about the new transaction into each field.

"Enter" means type the information in a field and then press Tab. When you press Tab, the insertion point moves forward to the next field. If you prefer to press Return instead of Tab to move from field to field, you can change Quicken's settings. See "Changing register settings" on page 102.

See the illustration on page 81 for more information about each field.

5 When you have finished entering the transaction, click Record to record it as a permanent part of your records.

Each time you record a transaction, Quicken sorts it in the register first by date and then by check number and recalculates all subsequent balances. Quicken's automatic sorting keeps your records in order no matter when you enter transactions. For example, suppose the date at the end of the check register is 2/27/93 and you want to enter an ATM withdrawal made on 2/10/93. When you enter the transaction at the end of the check register and click Record, Quicken automatically moves the transaction to where it belongs chronologically.

Each time you record a new transaction, Quicken remembers it. This feature can save you time for transactions that recur month after month, like depositing your salary. See Chapter 11, *Saving time with memorized transactions,* beginning on page 157, for more information about using memorized transactions.

You can enter dates quickly in the date field. Place the cursor in the Date field you want to change, then press these keys:

- **+** next day
- **—** previous day
- **t** Today
- **m** beginning of the **M**onth
- **h** end of the mont**H**
- **y** beginning of the **Y**ear
- **r** end of the yea**R**

The active, selected transaction has a bold box around it.

In the Category field, enter categories to track your income and expenses. See "Assigning categories to transactions" on page 82.

(Optional) In the Memo field, enter a memo if you want to record more information about this transaction.

Click Record when you have finished entering a transaction.

Click Restore if you make a mistake while entering or editing a transaction. The transaction reverts to the way it was before you started to change it.

In the Number field, enter the number of a printed check, handwritten check, or the type of transaction. Press + to enter the next check number quickly.

In the Payment field, enter the amount of each check or payment.

A checkmark in the √ (cleared) field indicates the cleared status of each transaction. See page 148.

In the Deposit field, enter the amount of each deposit.

Checking: Register

DATE	NUMBER	DESCRIPTION / CATEGORY/CLASS　MEMO	PAYMENT	√	DEPOSIT	BALANCE
6/4 1994	DEP	Sally's Paycheck *split*			2,162 97	5,930 68
6/8 1994	172	Atwood's Athletic Attic Clothing　Avia shoes	42 38			5,888 30
6/8 1994	174	Central Market Groceries	22 18			5,866 12
6/8 1994	PRINT	City of Valley Utilities:Garbage　May	65 00			5,801 12
6/8 1994	ATM	Cook's Esso Auto:Fuel	15 28			5,785 84
6/8 1994	175	Garden Grill Dining　lunch w...	37 00			5,748 84
6/8 1994	PRINT	Humberg's Landscaping Household:Gard...　Spring 94	650 00			5,098 84
6/8 1994	177	Holt Renfrew Clothing　New Jac...	129 87			4,968 97

Record　　Restore　　SPLITS　　Current Balance　$3,230.00　　Ending Balance:　$6,435.59

Click the right side of the Splits button to assign more than one category to a transaction. See "Sample split transactions" on page 94.

You cannot edit values in the Balance column. Quicken automatically calculates your new balance each time you record a transaction.

The Current Balance is the balance of all transactions entered through today. If you postdate transactions, Quicken also displays an Ending Balance, which is the balance of all transactions entered.

Assigning categories to transactions

Use categories to identify exactly where your income comes from and where your expenses go. When you enter a category name in the Category field of a transaction, you *categorize* the transaction with that income or expense category. It's important to categorize your transactions because Quicken uses the category information you assign to transactions to create reports, graphs, and budgets about your income and expenses.

Quicken provides standard home and business categories for you to use, but you can modify them or create your own. To create your own set of categories or to customize the standard home or business categories before you start assigning them to transactions, see "Setting up categories and subcategories" on page 47.

You can enter these items in the Category field

Categories	Categories let you identify transactions by type. This section briefly describes what categories are for and how to assign them to transactions. You can categorize a transaction with multiple categories by "splitting" the transaction. See page 92.
Transfers	You can choose the name of another Quicken account from the category and transfer list to transfer money to that account. For example, you can withdraw money from your savings account and have Quicken automatically transfer the amount as a deposit to your checking account. Transfers are explained on page 86. You can categorize a transaction with multiple transfers by "splitting" the transaction. See page 92.
Classes	Classes let you define a transaction even more specifically than with a category alone. Some Quicken users benefit from using classes; others find that categories are all they need to track their finances. To decide whether classes can help you, see page 55.You can categorize a transaction with multiple classes by "splitting" the transaction. See page 92.

Entering categories

You can enter an existing category name in the Category field by:

- Typing it in the Category field
- Choosing it from the category and transfer list

Typing the category name in the Category field

1   Click in the Category field of the transaction you want to categorize.

2   Begin typing the category name in the Category field.

Continue typing until Quicken fills in the correct category.

Begin typing the category until QuickFill completes the name. In this example, we typed "ch" and QuickFill added "arity."

| 4/12 | 5080 | World's Children | | | 300 | 00 | | | | |
| 1994 | | charity | | | | | | | | |

If the first few characters you type match the beginning of more than one category name, QuickFill enters the first category that begins with the letters you typed. Keep typing until QuickFill enters the correct category. If you have turned the QuickFill setting off, press Tab. Quicken fills in the correct category.

If you enter a category name that isn't already in the category list, Quicken lets you decide whether to set up a new category or select an existing one instead.

If Quicken displays this message:

- Click Cancel if you made a typing error and want to return to the register to enter the correct category.
- Click Set Up to create a new category.
- Click Select to choose an existing category from the list.

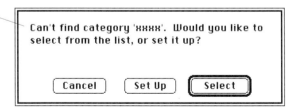

Can't find category 'xxxx'. Would you like to select from the list, or set it up?

[Cancel]   [Set Up]   [Select]

3   If you are entering a subcategory, type a colon (:) after the category to separate the main category from the subcategory: Auto:Fuel

Choosing categories from the category and transfer list

1 **Click in the Category field of the transaction you want to categorize.**

Or press ⌘ L

2 **Choose Categories & Transfers from the View menu.**

3 **Double-click the category name in the list to paste it in the Category field of the Register window.**

You can also select the category name you want and click Use or select the category name you want and press Return to paste it in the Category field.

There are three ways to enter a category from the category and transfer list:

- Double-click the category.
- Select the category and press Return.
- Select the category and click Use.

Assigning categories consistently

Quicken uses the category information you assign to each transaction to create income and expense-based reports and graphs and to format your budget.

Assign at least one category to each transaction you enter. If you don't assign a category, Quicken uses the label "Other" to refer to uncategorized amounts in reports and the label "Uncategorized" to refer to uncategorized amounts in graphs.

Whenever you find an uncategorized transaction in a report or graph, double-click the transaction until you reach the transaction in the register. Then assign a category to the transaction. See "Investigating items in reports using QuickZoom" on page 337 or "Investigating items in graphs using QuickZoom" on page 344.

If you want Quicken to help remind you to enter a category for every transaction as you are entering transactions in the register, you can turn on a setting so that Quicken displays a message whenever you don't assign a category to a transaction. See "Changing register settings" on page 102.

Assign categories and subcategories consistently. For example, if you sometimes assign the category Auto to transactions for gasoline that you purchase and other times you assign the category *and subcategory* Auto:Fuel, Quicken displays two amounts in a report. One amount represents all transactions that have Auto assigned to them, and another amount represents all transactions that have Auto:Fuel assigned to them.

Transferring money between accounts

You can use account transfers for many types of transactions. When you set up a new account, Quicken adds the new account name to the account lists and to the category and transfer list so you can select the account for transfers.

Transfers can record these and other common transactions:

- Movement of funds from a checking account to a savings account

- Cash advances from your credit card account to your checking account

- Loan payments from a checking account into a liability account that tracks the balance of your loan principal

When you record a transfer transaction in the source account, Quicken automatically creates a parallel transaction in the destination account. If the source transaction is a payment or decrease, the destination transaction is a deposit or increase.

For example: If you record a transaction with $2,000.00 in the Payment field in your checking account and the name of your savings account in the Category field, Quicken automatically records a corresponding transaction of $2,000.00 in the Deposit field of your savings account.

Here's the original transaction that you record in "Checking" (the source account).

Note the square brackets around the transfer account name in the Category field.

Here's the corresponding transaction that Quicken automatically records in "Savings" (the destination account) as a result of the transfer.

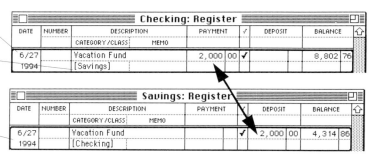

You cannot include a transfer and a category in the same Category field. A transfer is simply a movement of funds between one account and another. For example, every month you and your spouse both transfer $1000 from your individual checking accounts to your joint checking account to cover household expenses. In the register of your personal checking account, you would enter the name of your joint account in the Category field: [Joint Checking]

You can enter a transfer for part of the total amount of a transaction by using splits. For example, see the paycheck deposit illustrated on page 94 to see how funds are transferred from a checking account into an account for a retirement plan.

Likewise, in a mortgage payment, the principal amount of the mortgage transaction is transferred to a liability account, and the interest part of the mortgage transaction is assigned to an expense category. See Chapter 17, *Tracking loans*, beginning on page 279 to set up and enter mortgage payments.

You can include class information with transfer information in the Category field. For example, if you pay for an antique table from a checking account and you want to record the purchase in an asset account called "Personal Assets," you would enter [Personal Assets]/Antiques in the Category field.

Entering transfers

You can enter a transfer transaction between accounts by:

- Choosing Transfer Money from the Activities menu

  This method is fast when you want to transfer money from one Quicken account to another and neither account is open.

- Choosing the destination from the category and transfer list

  If you want to transfer money from one Quicken account to another and the register for the source account is already open, it's easiest to enter the information into the Category field.

Using the Transfer Money command

1   Choose Transfer Money from the Activities menu.

2   Enter information in the Transfer Money dialog box.

(Optional) Enter the description or payee right over "Transfer" if you want your Quicken records to be more descriptive about this transaction.

Enter the amount of money you want to transfer in the $ (amount) field.

Click the arrow to display the list of your accounts. Select the source account you are transferring money *from*.

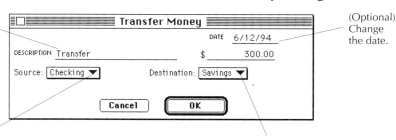

(Optional) Change the date.

Click the arrow to display the list of your accounts. Select the destination account you are transferring money *to*.

3   Click OK.

Quicken records the transfer transaction in the source and destination accounts you selected and adjusts the balances of each account. The amount you specified ($2,000.00 in the example above) is withdrawn from the source account and deposited in the destination account.

Typing transfers in the Category field

Or press ⌘ N

1 Start a new transaction in the Register or Write Checks window of the source account.

(Or select an existing transaction to change it into a transfer.)

2 Enter all the information for the transaction as usual, except not in the Category field.

3 Enter the name of the destination account in the Category field:

• If you know the name of the account you want to transfer the money to, type [and then start typing the name of the account in the Category field. QuickFill enters the name of the account and adds the end bracket to show it's a transfer.

Or press ⌘ L

• If you're not sure of the name of the account you want to transfer to, place the insertion point in the Category field and choose Categories & Transfers from the View menu. When Quicken displays the category and transfer list, double-click the account name to enter it into the Category field.

There are three ways to enter a transfer from the category and transfer list:

• Double-click the transfer.

• Select the transfer and press Return.

• Select the transfer and click Use.

You can quickly spot account names in the list: they appear at the bottom in square brackets (after all your categories), and Transfer is listed in the Type column.

4 Click Record to record the transfer transaction.

Quicken records the check in the register *and* creates a parallel transaction in the other account register for that amount.

Changing a transaction that includes a transfer

When you change a transaction that includes a transfer to or from another account, the transaction created by the transfer also changes in some cases:

- If you delete the transaction, Quicken deletes it from both the source and destination accounts.

- If you change the date or amount of the transaction, the information changes in both source and destination accounts. But, if you change the transaction description, check number, memo, or cleared status, the information changes only in the account in which you made the change.

- If you rename an account, Quicken updates every occurrence of the name in all transactions, including transfers.

- If a transfer was made in a split transaction, you can change it only from the original transaction in the source account. You cannot change it in the destination account that received the transfer.

Going to a transfer transaction

You can go directly from a transaction that includes a transfer to the parallel transaction in another account. The Go to Transfer command is useful when you want to see the transaction created by a transfer or when you want to make a change to a transfer that originated in a split transaction (you can change such transfers only in the split line item of the original transaction in the source account).

1   **In the Register window, select the transaction that includes the transfer information.**

    (Or in the Write Checks window, display the check containing the transfer information.)

Or press ⌘ E   2   **If the transaction is split, click Splits to open it and click anywhere on the split line containing the name of the transfer account.**

Or press ⌘ [3   **Choose Go to Transfer from the Activities menu.**

    Quicken displays the register for the transfer account and selects the parallel transfer transaction in that account.

Assigning classes to transactions

You can enter an existing class name in the Category field by choosing it from the class list or by typing it after a category in the Category field. (You can also assign a class to a transaction without assigning a category to the transaction.)

Classes let you define a transaction even more specifically than with a category alone. Some Quicken users benefit from using classes; others find that categories are all they need to track their finances. To decide whether classes can help you, see page 55.

Entering classes

You can enter an existing class name in the Category field by:

- Typing the class name in the Category field
- Choosing it from the class list

Typing a class in the Category field

1 Click immediately after the category in the Category field of the transaction you want to classify.

2 Type a forward slash (/).

The forward slash separates the category from the class.

3 Begin typing the class name in the Category field and continue until QuickFill enters the correct class.

As soon as you type a forward slash, Quicken recognizes that you are entering a class.

In this example, the category is "Repairs" and the class is "Oak Street."

		Checking: Register						
DATE	NUMBER	DESCRIPTION		PAYMENT	√	DEPOSIT	BALANCE	
		CATEGORY/CLASS	MEMO					
5/23 1994	478	SDP's Carpentry Repairs/Oak St		1,250 00			3,930 04	

If the first few characters you type match the beginning of more than one class name, QuickFill enters the first class that begins with the letters you typed. Keep typing until QuickFill enters the correct class. If you have turned the QuickFill setting off, press Tab. If you enter a class name that you haven't already set up, Quicken lets you decide whether to set up a new class or select an existing one instead.

4 If you are entering a subclass, type a colon (:) after the class to separate the main class from the subclass: Repairs/OakStreet:Apt1

Choosing a class from the class list

1   Click after the category in the Category field of the transaction you want to classify.

Or press ⌘ K

2   Choose Classes from the View menu.

3   Double-click the class name in the list to paste it after a category.

You can also select the class name you want and click Use or select the class name you want and press Enter to paste it in the Category field.

There are three ways to enter a class from the class list:

- Double-click the class.
- Select the class and press Return.
- Select the class and click Use.

Assigning classes consistently

Quicken uses the class information you assign to transactions to create class-based reports. Although you should assign at least one category to each transaction you enter, you should assign classes only to those transactions that require classes.

If this business is your main source of income, you'll probably want to track your expenses in a separate Quicken data file. See "Setting up additional files" on page 61.

For example, if you run a small home business, you might have a separate business checking account or use your personal checking account for business expenses. In either case, you'll want to report separately on your business transactions for tax purposes.

Set up a class named "Business." (See "Setting up categories and subcategories" on page 47.) Categorize all business-related transactions (payments, deposits, cash purchases, and credit card transactions) as usual, and always classify them with the class name "Business." For example, you might categorize a transaction for business travel: Travel/Business

By using the class "Business" for all business expenses, you can exclude business data from personal reports and exclude personal data from business reports.

Splitting transactions

Sometimes you may want to assign more than one category, transfer, or class to a single transaction. For example, a check you write to a department store might cover clothing, office supplies, and home furnishings. You can split transactions that are withdrawals from or deposits to an account.

"Entering a split transaction" below describes how to split a transaction by assigning several categories to a single transaction. You can split a transaction to assign multiple transfers or multiple classes in the same way.

"Sample split transactions" on page 94 illustrates other common split transactions, such as entering your paycheck deposit into a Quicken account.

Entering a split transaction

When you create a split transaction, you enter category names and amounts to identify each line of the split. You can enter this information when you first record a transaction, or you can add it later.

1   Select the transaction you want to split.

Or begin with a new transaction and enter information into the Date, Number, and Description fields.

2   If the Amount field of the transaction is blank, enter the total amount of the transaction.

Or press ⌘ E

The Splits button is at the bottom of the register. Click the left side of the Splits button to close an open split.

3   Click Splits to open the split transaction.

 Click the right side of the Splits button to display the lines of a split transaction.

Quicken displays the lines of the split transaction and copies any information you may have already entered in the Category, Payment, or Deposit field of the transaction to the first split line.

4   If the first Category field of the split is blank, enter a category and press Tab.

If a category name is in the field, press Tab to move to the next field.

5   (Optional) If the first memo field of the split is blank, enter a memo.

If a memo is already in the field, press Tab to move to the next field.

6   In the first Amount field, enter the amount you want to assign to the first category.

The amount for the entire transaction is already selected. Type the amount of the first category right on top of the amount of the entire transaction.

7   Press Tab to move to the next Category field in the split transaction.

Quicken subtracts the amount you typed in the Amount field of the first split line ($31.00) from the total amount you entered for the transaction ($124.57) and displays the remainder ($93.57) in the next Amount field.

4/30 1994	Emporium		124	57			4,118	92
CATEGORY/CLASS		MEMO				AMOUNT		
Clothing		shoes for Karen				31	00	
						93	57	

8   Continue to add categories, memos, and amounts until you have added one split line for each part of the transaction.

Categorize each line of the split with any category you choose.

There are four lines in this example of a split transaction, but you can enter as many lines as you need in a split transaction.

4/30 1994	Emporium		124	57			4,118	92
CATEGORY/CLASS		MEMO				AMOUNT		
Clothing		shoes for Karen				31	00	
Household		mini vac				60	00	
Gifts		book for Glenn				21	57	
Entertainment		video				12	00	

If you have an uncategorized remainder on the last line of the split and you want to recalculate the transaction total, select the remainder, delete it, and press Tab to move to the next field. Quicken recalculates the amount in the split transaction according to the total amount you entered in the Payment or Charge field

Or press ⌘ E

9   Click Splits to close the split transaction.

10   Click Record to record the split transaction.

If you see the message "This split transaction contains one or more uncategorized items. Save changes?" you have not entered a category for at least one of the amounts in the transaction. Click Cancel to go back to the split transaction and enter the categories, click Discard to delete the transaction, or click OK to leave the transaction uncategorized.

Sample split transactions

You can enter negative amounts in split transactions.

The split transaction in this example is a paycheck deposit.

Enter your *net* pay as the total amount for the transaction.

Enter your *gross* pay in the Amount field of the first split line.

Enter all deductions from your gross pay on the next lines as negative amounts.

		Checking: Register					
DATE	NUMBER	DESCRIPTION	PAYMENT	√	DEPOSIT	BALANCE	
		MEMO					
3/15 1994	DEP	Steve's Paycheck			2,467 97	7,164 38	

CATEGORY/CLASS	MEMO	AMOUNT
Salary		3,941 67
Taxes:FWH		-885 42
Taxes:FICA		-283 33
Taxes:SWH		-177 08
Taxes:SDI		-32 87

If you have more than four deductions, use the scroll box in the split transaction to scroll down and enter information on the split lines below.

You can assign transfers to amounts in split transactions. See "Transferring money between accounts" on page 86 for more information about entering transfer transactions.

The split transaction in this example is also a paycheck deposit.

You can enter a transfer of money from this account ("Checking") to another account, such as the Quicken account that tracks your retirement plan ("Sally's 401k").

		Checking: Register					
DATE	NUMBER	DESCRIPTION	PAYMENT	√	DEPOSIT	BALANCE	
		MEMO					
4/23 1994	DEP	Sally's Paycheck			2,162 97	13,019 49	

CATEGORY/CLASS	MEMO	AMOUNT
Salary		3,541 67
Taxes:FWH		-785 42
Taxes:SWH		-283 33
Taxes:FICA		-177 08
[Sally's 401k]		-32 87

You can assign classes to amounts in split transactions. See "About classes" on page 55 and "Assigning classes to transactions" on page 90 for more information about using classes.

If you use a class called "Business" to separate your small business finances from your personal finances in the same Quicken data file, you can enter the class on one line of the split transaction without applying the class to the other lines of the split transaction.

	AMX: Register					
DATE	DESCRIPTION	CHARGE	√	PAYMENT	BALANCE	
	MEMO		?			
5/13 1994	Montenegro Travel Agency	601 76			4,766 07	

CATEGORY/CLASS	MEMO	AMOUNT
Vacation	train tickets to San Diego	183 95
Travel/Business	plane ticket for Anders account	417 81

Reviewing and changing split transactions

Edit split transactions much as you edit other transactions. A few additional keys work in a split transaction.

1   Double-click the word "split" in an existing split transaction.

Or press ⌘ E

Double-click the word "split" to open an existing split transaction.

Or select the transaction and click Splits.

| 4/15 | 5074 | American Lending Corp. | | 1,533 | 91 | ✓ | | | 10,908 | 41 |
| 1994 | | *split* | Account # | | | | | | | |

2   Make the changes you want in the split transaction.

If you want to	Do this
Delete an entire line in a split transaction	Move the insertion point to the line. Choose Delete Split Line from the Edit menu.
Enter a new split line in a split transaction	Move the insertion point to the line below where you want to insert a new line. Choose New Split Line from the Edit menu.

Or press ⌘ D

Or press ⌘ N

Or press ⌘ E

3   Click Splits to close the Split Transaction window.

4   Click Record to record the transaction.

Reviewing the register

You can review a register to find specific transactions at any time by scrolling through it, using keyboard shortcuts, or by using the Find command. And you can change the size of the Category and Memo fields if you prefer to view more of the categories than the memos.

Scrolling through the register

Use the scroll bar to move through the Register window and locate specific transactions quickly. When you drag the scroll box in the scroll bar, you'll see a date appear and change as you scroll. This date represents the date of the transaction that is at the bottom of the Register window when you release the scroll box.

Drag the scroll box in the scroll bar...

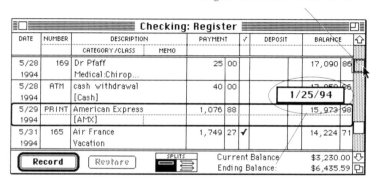

... and the *QuickScroll* box appears to displays dates of specific transactions.

Using keyboard shortcuts

You can also use keyboard shortcuts to move through the register transaction by transaction, or page by page, or to jump directly to the first or last transaction.

The Home, End, Page Up, and Page Down keys are available only on the Macintosh extended keyboard.

Keystroke	Result
Page Up or ⌘ ↑	Scrolls up one screen at a time.
Page Down or ⌘ ↓	Scrolls down one screen at a time.
Tab	Goes to the next field.
Shift+Tab	Goes to the previous field.
Home	Goes to the first transaction in the register.
End	Goes to the last transaction in the register.

Finding a specific transaction

Quicken's Find command locates specific transactions in the Register or Write Checks window. You can find a transaction even if you don't know all the information contained in the transaction. You might want to find a check with a specific number or payee. In an investment account, you can search for securities and actions.

1   Choose Find from the Edit menu.

Or press ⌘ F

Type some or all of the text or the exact amount to find here. (The text can be uppercase or lowercase and contain characters and numbers.)

The field names in the Search popup menu depend on the type of account you have open.

More information about choices in the Match If popup menu is in Help. (Press ⌘ ? and then click Topics. Click "Register," and then click Finding transactions."

This menu item is available only when the credit card account is set up to use IntelliCharge. See page 212.

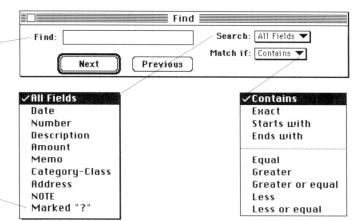

2   Type the word, phrase, or amount you want to find in the Find field.

You can also use match characters with the word, phrase, or amount. See "Using wildcard characters to restrict reports" on page 336.

3   (Optional) Choose a field name from the Search popup menu.

Find searches all fields for the text or amount you want to find. If you know which field contains the text or amount, you can speed up the search by looking only in that field.

4   (Optional) Choose a search criterion from the Match If popup menu.

5   Start to search:

- Click Previous to search backward for the transaction (toward the beginning of your register).

- Click Next to search forward for the transaction (toward the end of your register).

Quicken selects the first match it finds or tells you that it cannot find a match.

Or press ⌘ G

6 **(Optional) To continue finding items, click Previous or Next or choose Find Again from the Edit menu.**

Quicken stops searching when it reaches the last transaction in the register (or the first transaction for backward searches). If you want Quicken to continue searching, you can change this setting. See "Changing register settings" on page 102.

7 **When you are done with the search, close the Find window.**

Changing the size of the Category and Memo fields

The Category and Memo fields share the second line of a transaction. To increase the width of one of the fields, drag the border between the fields to the left or right.

Drag the border between the fields to the left or right. The mouse pointer changes to a double-pointed arrow.

		Checking: Register					
DATE	NUMBER	DESCRIPTION	PAYMENT	√	DEPOSIT	BALANCE	⇧
		CATEGORY/CLASS ↔ MEMO					
5/11	5078	Valley Gas & Electric	64 97	√		3,480 82	
1994		Utilities:Electric April					
5/11	5079	Western Bell	87 52	√		3,393 30	
1994		Telephone March/A...					

Revising transactions

This section explains how to correct mistakes and void and delete transactions. You can edit any transaction in the register. When you finish recording changes to transactions, Quicken recalculates all subsequent balances if necessary.

Correcting mistakes

Or press ⌘ Z

To correct a single mistake you make while you are editing a field, choose Undo from the Edit menu.

To restore an entire transaction to the way it was before you started to change it, click the Restore button at the bottom of the window.

The only item in the register you cannot change by normal editing is the Balance column. If you need to change the balance during reconciliation, you must do so by adding a payment or deposit as an adjustment in the register or by having Quicken adjust the difference for you. (See "Letting Quicken adjust for differences" on page 151.)

Changing or deleting a reconciled transaction affects future reconciliations. Quicken lets you know if you are about to change a reconciled transaction and asks you to confirm the change.

Your ability to change transactions after they are entered or even reconciled gives you complete control of your finances. However, if you think you need to protect your data from accidental or unauthorized changes, Quicken has two kinds of passwords:

- A File password requires users to enter a password before opening a file. (See "Requiring a password to open a file" on page 72.)
- A Transaction password protects transactions prior to a specified date. (See "Requiring a password to change earlier transactions" on page 74.)

Voiding a transaction

Rubber checks?

If you're using Quicken to manage your finances and balance your checkbook, you don't need to worry about bouncing checks. If you do bounce a check that you've entered into your Quicken checking register:

- Void the original transaction.
- Enter a new transaction for the bank's NSF (non sufficient funds) charge.
- Enter a new transaction for the merchant's service charge.
- Write and print a new check.

From time to time you might need to void a transaction. By marking a printed or handwritten check as void instead of just deleting it, you'll have an accurate record of each numbered check.

When Quicken voids a transaction, it:

- Inserts the word *void* before the payee name
- Marks the transaction as reconciled with a ✓ (bold checkmark), so it doesn't interfere with reconciling
- Removes the dollar amount from the transaction and splits
- Removes information from the Category field

If you void a transfer transaction, Quicken changes the transaction in the source account and deletes the amount in the corresponding transaction in the destination account.

1 **Select the check or other transaction you want to void.**

   If the check was one you wrote by hand and have not yet entered in the check register, enter the date and check number in a new transaction in the register now.

2 **Choose Void Transaction from the Edit menu.**

3 **Click Record to record the transaction as void.**

Deleting a transaction

Once you delete a transaction and confirm the deletion, Quicken can't recover it. Be sure you really want to delete a transaction before doing so.

To protect previous transactions from accidental change or deletion, you can assign a transaction password to them. See "Setting up passwords" on page 72.

1   Select the transaction you want to delete.

Or press ⌘ D

2   Choose Delete Transaction from the Edit menu.

Quicken asks "Are you sure you want to delete?"

3   Click Delete to delete the transaction.

Quicken removes the transaction from the register and recalculates all subsequent balances.

If you've deleted a transfer transaction, Quicken removes the transaction from the register of both the source account and the destination account and recalculates the balances in both accounts.

Printing the register

You can print all or some of the transactions in a register. You can specify a time period of a day, a week, a month, a year, or more so you will have a printed record of the period of time covered.

1   Open the register you want to print.

2   Choose Print Register from the File menu.

3   (Optional) Change the range of dates to print.

The preset range is for the year to date. You can use the + or – key to increase or decrease the date in any Quicken Date field.

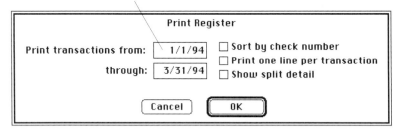

```
                              Print Register

    Print transactions from:    1/1/94     □ Sort by check number
                                           □ Print one line per transaction
                 through:       3/31/94    □ Show split detail

                              Cancel        OK
```

4   (Optional) Select any printing options you want to use:

•   Quicken ordinarily sorts the register first by date and then by check number. If you select the Sort By Check Number checkbox, Quicken does not generate or display a running balance. The Balance column on your printout will be blank.

•   Select the Print One Line Per Transaction checkbox to abbreviate each transaction to fit on one line.

•   Quicken normally prints three lines per transaction. Select the Show Split Detail checkbox to display all the lines in a split transaction.

5   Click OK.

The printer dialog box appears.

6   Set the print options you need.

7   Click Print to print the register.

Changing register settings

This illustration shows the settings that are selected when Quicken is installed.

If a checkbox is selected, the setting is turned on.

If a checkbox is cleared, the setting is turned off.

Click in a checkbox to select or clear it.

You can change many of Quicken's settings with commands on the Settings menu.

1   **Choose General from the Settings menu.**

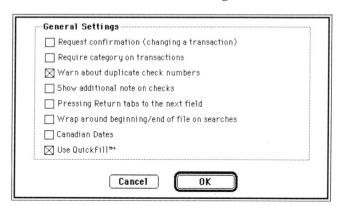

2   **Select or clear the settings you want to change, then click OK.**

General settings	Quicken does this when the setting is selected
Request confirmation (changing a transaction)	Requires you to confirm any changes made to a transaction before going to a new transaction or a new window.
Require category on transactions	Prompts you to identify a category in a transaction that you are recording if you have not already entered one. This helps you remember to categorize all your transactions for accurate reports, graphs, and budgets.
Warn about duplicate check numbers	Displays a warning message if you enter a check number that is already entered in the register.
Show additional note on checks	Adds an extra Note field to the checks displayed onscreen. See "Adding a note to checks" on page 108.
Pressing Return tabs to the next field	Uses the Return key as well as the Tab key to move between fields in any account register and the Write Checks window. You'll probably want to turn this option on if you are accustomed to using DOS Quicken or other DOS applications.
Wrap around beginning/end of file on searches	When you are using the Find command, Quicken stops searching when it reaches the last transaction in the register (or the first transaction for backward searches). Select this setting if you want Quicken to continue searching.
Canadian dates	Displays the date format DD/MM/YY instead of the format MM/DD/YY in the register and Write Checks window.
Use QuickFill	Fills names in transaction fields automatically when you type the first few characters of the name. QuickFill "guesses" the rest of the name you began typing from an appropriate list based on previous transactions you've entered. See "Using QuickFill to complete transactions" on page 158.

8

Writing checks

Having Quicken prepare your checks is a great convenience. If you print checks, you avoid the duplicate work of writing checks and then recording them in Quicken. You will save hours of valuable time, avoid clerical errors, and prevent unnecessary financial hassle every month.

For information about how to order different kinds of Intuit checks, consult the check catalog in your Quicken package or see Appendix A, *Ordering supplies and other Intuit products*, beginning on page 387.

Filling out a check

Use the Write Checks window to enter checks that you plan to print with Quicken. Enter other transactions, such as checks that you've written by hand, deposits, or bank fees in the check register. When you record a check in the Write Checks window, Quicken adds it automatically to the check register.

You can write checks in any Quicken bank account: checking, money market, or savings. You can write checks as bills arrive or at regular intervals: weekly, biweekly, or monthly.

You can order printable check forms from Intuit. Intuit checks are accepted everywhere. See Appendix A, *Ordering supplies and other Intuit products,* beginning on page 387. Or, see the catalog included with your Quicken package.

1   Open the bank account that you want to write checks from.

Or press ⌘ J

2   Choose Write Checks from the Activities menu.

Quicken displays the Write Checks window.

If you plan to mail the check in an Intuit window envelope, enter the payee name and mailing address. Include the payee name, address, city, state, and zip code. You can use up to five lines (press Enter to start a new line). Press the Quote key (' or ") to copy the payee name here.

Enter the payee name here (the person or organization to whom you are writing the check). When you view this check later in the check register, the payee information appears in the Description field.

When you enter the dollar amount in the $ (amount) field, Quicken automatically spells out the amount on the next line.

The date appears on the check when you print it. To change the date to today's date, enter the date you want to be printed on the check.

If you want to send a message to the payee or if you want to provide additional information on the check for your own records, enter it as a memo on the check, up to 31 characters long. The contents of the Memo field may be visible when you mail the check in an Intuit window envelope. If you need to ensure that the information is not visible through the envelope window, you can display a Note field and enter information here instead of the Memo line. (See "Adding a note to checks" on page 108 if you can't see the Note field.)

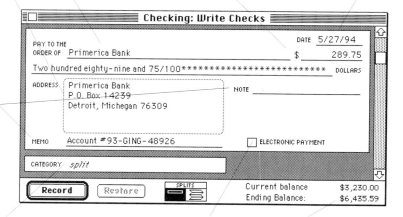

Enter the category, class, or transfer information in the Category field. Click Splits to split a check just as you split transactions in the register. (See page 92.)

Quicken displays this option if you have set up this checking account for sending electronic payments. See "Setting up an account for electronic payments" on page 177.

The Ending Balance is the balance in the account based on all entered transactions, including any postdated transactions.

3   (Optional) Change the selected date and press Tab.

4   **Enter the payee name as you want it to appear on the check and press Tab.**

5   **Enter the amount of the check in the $ (amount) field.**

Quicken automatically spells out the amount of the check in words on the next line.

6   **If you plan to mail the check in an Intuit window envelope, enter the payee name and mailing address in the Address field.**

Press the Quote key (') to copy the payee name in the first line of the address. Press Return to move to each new line in the Address field. Press Tab to move to the Memo field.

7   **(Optional) Enter a note in the Memo field or the Note field.**

If the field is not already displayed in the Write Checks window, see "Adding a note to checks" on page 108 to display the Note field.

8   **Enter a category in the Category field.**

Enter categories, splits, or transfers the same way that you split a transaction in the check register. If you use Intuit voucher checks, Quicken prints up to nine lines of split information on the perforated voucher attachment. If you write a single check that covers twenty invoices, Quicken prints the first nine invoice numbers and the amount to be applied to each invoice on the voucher attachment.

9   **If you plan to pay the check electronically with CheckFree, select the Electronic Payment checkbox.**

If the Electronic Payment checkbox is not displayed, this account is not set up to use CheckFree. See "Entering electronic payments" on page 179.

10   **When you have finished writing the check, click Record to save it as a permanent part of your records.**

Quicken enters the information on the check into your register and memorizes the transaction. Until you print the checks, Quicken displays "Print" in the Number field of each printable transaction in the register. Quicken inserts the correct check number in the check register after it has finished printing the check. The Write Checks window does not display a check number. Intuit checks are prenumbered because most banks require prenumbered checks for stop payment purposes.

Reviewing checks you've written

Once you've written and recorded your checks, you can review them before printing either by scrolling through the Write Checks window or by reviewing them in the register. After you've already printed a check, you cannot review it in the Write Checks window. You can review printed checks only in the register.

You can add to, change, delete, or void any check in the Write Checks window exactly the same way you edit transactions in the register. When you finish changing a transaction, Quicken recalculates all subsequent balances if necessary.

Or press ⌘ R

1   Choose Register from the View menu.

The Register window displays checks and other transactions by date, and it also shows the information written on the checks (except for the Address and Note fields). Unprinted checks appear in the register with "Print" in the Number field. After you print the check, Quicken replaces "Print" with the actual check number.

After you print a check, Quicken inserts the check number in the Number field.

To view or edit splits (if any), select a split transaction and click the Splits button at the bottom of the register.

Unprinted checks have **Print** in the Number field.

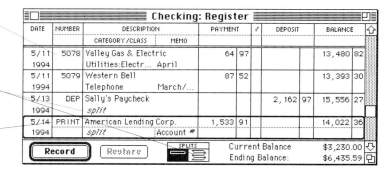

2   Scroll through the register.

You can also drag the scroll box to search by date, or use the Find command to locate the transaction you want. (See "Finding a specific transaction" on page 97.)

3   As you review checks in the check register, you can delete or change them any way you like.

Changes you make to an unprinted check in the register will appear on the printed check. For more information about changing transactions in the register, see "Revising transactions" on page 98.

Or press ⌘ J

4   Click in the Write Checks window to return to it.

Writing postdated checks

By postdating, you can schedule checks for future payment. You can also forecast how much money you need in the coming weeks. Later, when you print checks, you can have Quicken print checks dated through a specific date. Except for changing the date, writing postdated checks is the same as writing regular checks with Quicken.

Caution:

This postdating technique serves scheduling and forecasting purposes in Quicken. We are not suggesting that you mail postdated checks.

---

1   **In the Write Checks window, change the current date to the date in the future when you want to print the check.**

2   **Complete the check as described on page 104.**

3   **Click Record to record the check.**

When you have postdated checks in your account, Quicken calculates a Current Balance and Ending Balance and displays them both at the bottom of the Write Checks window.

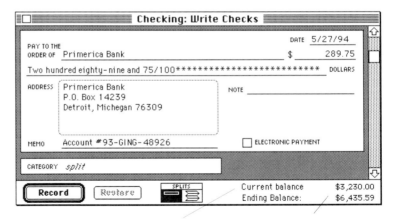

The Current Balance amount shows the balance in your account before any postdated transactions.	The Ending Balance amount shows the balance after all postdated transactions.

Quicken's Billminder can remind you to print postdated checks and other scheduled transactions up to 30 days before their scheduled dates. Billminder helps you pay bills on time even though you don't use Quicken every day. See "Using Billminder" on page 169.

Adding a note to checks

The contents of the Memo field may be visible when you mail a printed check in an Intuit window envelope. If you need to ensure that confidential information (such as an account number you want to print on the check) is not visible from the envelope, you can display a Note field in the Write Checks window and enter information there instead of the Memo field.

1   Choose General from the Settings menu.

2   Select the Show Additional Note On Checks checkbox.

Select this checkbox to display the Note field onscreen in the Write Checks window.

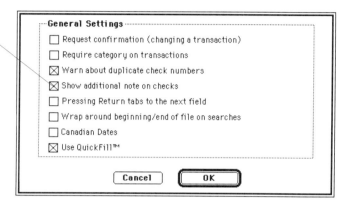

```
General Settings
 ☐ Request confirmation (changing a transaction)
 ☐ Require category on transactions
 ☒ Warn about duplicate check numbers
 ☒ Show additional note on checks
 ☐ Pressing Return tabs to the next field
 ☐ Wrap around beginning/end of file on searches
 ☐ Canadian Dates
 ☒ Use QuickFill™

                    [ Cancel ]   [ OK ]
```

3   Click OK.

Quicken displays a Note field onscreen in the Write Checks window to the right of the Address field. Enter up to 19 characters in the Note field.

```
                                    DATE 6/17/93
PAY TO THE
ORDER OF _____   $ _____
_____ DOLLARS

ADDRESS  ┌─────────────────┐  NOTE _____
         │                 │
         │                 │
         └─────────────────┘
MEMO _____      ☐ ELECTRONIC PAYMENT
```

To turn off the display of the Note field, clear the Show Additional Note On Checks checkbox. If you turn off the display of the Note field, Quicken saves any information that you may have entered into this box previously in the Write Checks window. Turn on the display of the message box to display the text again.

Printing checks

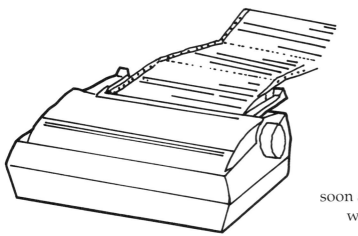

When you print checks with Quicken, you use special personalized checks from Intuit, designed to work with Quicken.

Intuit makes checks for page-oriented printers and continuous-feed printers.

You can print a batch of checks as soon as you've written them, or you can wait and print them at another time.

About printing checks

You can print checks as soon as you've written them, or you can wait and print them at another time. For example, you can enter checks in the Write Checks window at various times throughout the month, but wait and print them only once or twice each month.

When you order personalized Intuit checks, Intuit prints your name, address, account number, bank name, check numbers, and all the information required by financial institutions on your checks. Intuit guarantees their acceptance everywhere your checks are accepted now.

Intuit checks are economical and come in a variety of styles for Macintosh-compatible printers. All Intuit checks fit one of the two sizes of Intuit double-window envelopes. Both your address and the payee address appear in the windows, eliminating the need to address envelopes. See Appendix A, *Ordering supplies and other Intuit products,* beginning on page 387.

Before you begin to print your checks, make sure that your printer is using the correct printer driver. See "About printer drivers" on page 111.

Then, if you plan to print checks using a laser, inkjet, postscript, or other sheet-fed, *page-oriented* printer (including a dot matrix printer that has a paper tray), see "Printing checks on page-oriented printers" on page 112.

Or, if you plan to print checks using a *continuous-feed* (also known as tractor-feed, pin-feed, or dot matrix) printer, see "Printing checks on continuous-feed printers" on page 122.

To reprint checks that you have already printed, see "Reprinting checks" on page 131.

About printer drivers

You need a Macintosh-compatible printer and the correct version of printer driver for the printer that you plan to use to print Quicken checks.

If you don't know the version of the printer driver your Macintosh is using, open any Macintosh application and choose Page Setup from the File menu. The version of your printer driver is displayed in the Page Setup dialog box, just left of the Print button. Click Cancel to close the Page Setup dialog box.

The version of your printer driver is displayed to the left of the Print button.

```
┌──────────────────────────────────────────────────────────────┐
│ LaserWriter Page Setup                          7.0    ┌──OK──┐│
│ Paper: ◉ US Letter  ○ A4 Letter                        └──────┘│
│        ○ US Legal   ○ B5 Letter  ○ │ Tabloid    ▼│  [ Cancel ] │
└──────────────────────────────────────────────────────────────┘
```

Use the table below to make sure your printer driver is compatible with Quicken. If you don't have a recent version of the printer driver, contact your Apple dealer.

Installing a printer driver

To install the required version of an Apple printer driver, or to reinstall the existing printer driver, see the Macintosh User's Guide.

If your printer is not an Apple printer, review the instructions that came with the printer for information about installing or reinstalling its printer driver.

After installing a new printer driver or reinstalling the existing printer driver:

- Restart your Macintosh.
- Open Quicken.
- Choose Chooser from the Apple menu.
- In the left box, click the icon that represents the printer you want to use.
- In the right box, if your printer is not on a network, click the icon for the modem port or the icon for the printer port that represents the port you used to connect the printer. If your printer is on a network, click the name of the printer.
- Close the Chooser.

You're ready to print checks now.

Printer	Required printer driver version
GCC Personal Laser Printer	4.0 or later
GCC Personal Laser Printer II	4.0 or later
HP DeskWriter	2.0 or later
HP Desk Writer C	2.0 or later
ImageWriter	2.6 or later
ImageWriter II	2.6 or later
ImageWriter LQ	2.0 or later
LaserWriter	5.0 or later
LaserWriter II	5.0 or later
LaserWriter II NT	5.0 or later
LaserWriter II NTX	5.0 or later
Personal LaserWriter	1.0 or later
Personal LaserWriter LS	1.0 or later
Personal LaserWriter NT	1.0 or later
Personal LaserWriter SC	1.0 or later
StyleWriter	1.0 or later
StyleWriter II	1.0 or later

Printing checks on page-oriented printers

This section explains how to print checks on a laser, inkjet, postscript, or other page-oriented printer (including a dot matrix printer that has a paper tray). If you have an ImageWriter or other continuous-feed (also known as tractor-feed, pin-feed, or dot-matrix) printer, skip to page 122.

◆ **Set up your check printer.**
   See "Setting up page-oriented printers" on page 113.

◆ **Load the checks in your printer.**
   See "Positioning checks in page-oriented printers" on page 114.

◆ **Print your checks.**
   See "Printing checks from your account" on page 116.

◆ **Make sure the checks all printed correctly.**
   See "Examining printed checks" on page 118.

Using continuous-feed checks in page-oriented printers

If you used to print your checks on a continuous-feed printer, but now you want to print checks on your new page-oriented printer, you may still have some continuous-feed checks left over. You can keeping using your old checks, but you need to turn the continuous-feed checks into page-oriented checks first and then change a setting in the Check Printing Settings dialog box before you print the checks.

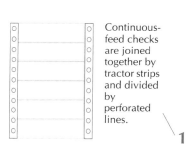

Continuous-feed checks are joined together by tractor strips and divided by perforated lines.

1 Get the continuous-feed checks that you want to print in a page-oriented printer.

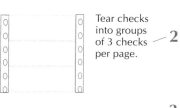

Tear checks into groups of 3 checks per page.

2 Tear the checks into groups of three.

Do not tear apart checks at each perforated line to create individual checks.

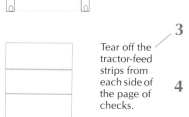

Tear off the tractor-feed strips from each side of the page of checks.

3 Tear off the tractor-feed strips along the sides of the checks.

Each page you create should have three checks on it.

4 Change a setting in Check Printing Settings dialog box before you print checks.

See "Using trailer strip options" on page 121.

Setting up page-oriented printers

Before you print any checks from a Quicken account, you need to select the page-oriented printer you're going to use to print checks. Once you set up your printer, you don't have to change the check printing settings unless you change Intuit check styles, change printers, or decide to place a custom logo on your checks.

1   Select the printer you plan to use in the Chooser.

- Choose the Chooser from the Apple menu.

- In the left box, click the icon that represents the printer you want to use.

- In the right box, if your printer is not on a network, click the icon for the modem port or the icon for the printer port that represents the port you used to connect the printer. If your printer is on a network, click the name of the printer.

- Close the Chooser.

2   Choose Check Printing from the Settings menu.

There are three types of Intuit checks:

- Standard checks are 3.5 inches high.
- Voucher checks are 3.5 inches high, with a 3.5-inch tear-off voucher attachment below each check. Quicken prints the check date, payee, and amount on the perforated voucher attachment.
- Wallet checks are about 2.8 inches high, with a removable stub on the left.

Times is the default font for page-oriented printers. The Sample box shows the currently selected font and size.
Make sure the Sheet Feeder checkbox is selected as illustrated.

Choose one of these icons when you want to print starting with a partial page of checks.

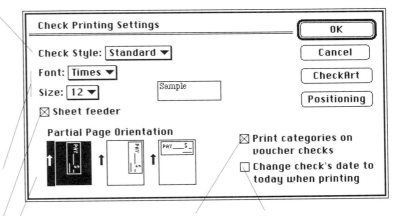

Select the Print Categories on Voucher Checks checkbox if you want to print category information from a split check on the perforated attachment to voucher checks. See "Splitting transactions" on page 92 for more information.

Select the Change Check's Date to Today When Printing checkbox if you want Quicken to change the dates on the checks to the current date when you print the checks.

3   Choose the Intuit check style you plan to print from the Check Style popup menu.

This arrow tells you that there is a popup list here that contains more than one item. Click the arrow and drag down the mouse button to select a different item.

4 **(Optional) Choose a different font name and size for the text that prints on checks from the Font and Size popup menus.**

The Sample box shows the currently selected font and size.

5 **Make sure that the Sheet Feeder checkbox is selected.**

6 **Leave the Partial Page Orientation icons as they are until you need to print a partial first page of checks.**

7 **(Optional) To print category information from a split check on the perforated attachment to voucher checks, select the Print Categories on Voucher Checks checkbox.**

See "Splitting transactions" on page 92 for more information.

8 **(Optional) To have Quicken change check dates to the current date at print time, select the Change Check's Date to Today When Printing checkbox.**

9 **Click OK to save your check printing setup.**

Positioning checks in page-oriented printers

When you order checks for your page-oriented printer, order the laser/inkjet checks. These checks work for all single-sheet-fed, page-oriented printers, not just laser or inkjet printers.

Standard or wallet laser/inkjet checks come grouped three to a page, ready to be inserted in your page-oriented printer paper tray. There is one voucher check on each page.

The table on page 115 describes how to position a full page of checks in your printer. If you are planning to start printing less than a full page of three standard or wallet checks, see "Printing a partial first page of checks" on page 119.

Position the checks according to your printer type. If your printer is not listed in the table below, assume that you should insert checks in the envelope feeder, with the checks facing up, and the top of the page of checks facing toward the printer as you insert the paper tray into the printer.

You do not need to print a sample check to test alignment, but you might want to test one check before you print a large batch. After positioning the checks in your printer, continue to "Printing checks from your account" on page 116.

Printer type	Checks in the paper tray or envelope feeder?	Checks face up or face down?	Top of the page of checks points to the printer?
GCC Personal Laser Printer GCC Personal Laser Printer II	Paper tray	Load checks face up	Point the top of the page toward the printer
HP DeskWriter HP DeskWriter C	Paper tray	Load checks face down✻	Point the top of the page toward the printer
HP LaserJet	Paper tray	Load checks face down✻	Point the top of the page toward the printer
HP LaserJet II HP LaserJet III HP LaserJet IV	Paper tray	Load checks face up	Point the top of the page toward the printer
LaserWriter LaserWriter II LaserWriter II NT LaserWriter II NTX	Envelope feeder or paper tray	Load checks face up	Point the top of the page toward the printer
StyleWriter StyleWriter II	Paper tray	Load checks face up	Point the top of the page toward the printer
Personal LaserWriter Personal LaserWriter LS Personal LaserWriter NT Personal LaserWriter SC	Paper tray	Load checks face down✻	Point the top of the page toward the printer

✻ When you load checks face down, you must reverse the order of the sheets so that the first sheet of checks is on top when you're looking at the stack of checks turned facedown. (This method ensures that printed check numbers match the numbers in the Quicken check register.)

Printing checks from your account

1 **If you haven't already inserted the checks in the printer, insert them now.**

See "Positioning checks in page-oriented printers" on page 114.

2 **Make sure your printer is turned on and online.**

If you're using a LaserWriter, the green light should be lit.

3 **Open the account you want to print checks from.**

Or press ⌘ P

4 **Choose Print Checks from the File menu.**

Quicken displays the Print Checks dialog box.

If you receive a message that you don't have any checks selected to print, you need to enter the checks you want to print in the Write Checks window (see "Filling out a check" on page 104). If you have already entered the checks into the register instead of the Write Checks window, you need to show Quicken which checks in the register you want to print (see "Reprinting checks" on page 131).

Enter the number shown on the first check positioned in the printer here.

Choose an option for printing:

- Click Checks Dated Through and then change the date range of the checks to be printed; by default, the date is the current date.

- Click Selected Checks to print only specified checks.

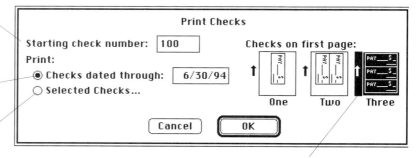

Select the icon for three checks. If you need to print less than a full page of three checks, see "Printing a partial first page of checks" on page 119.

5 **If the number in the Starting Check Number field is not the same as the number of the first check in your printer, enter the number of the first check in your printer.**

6 **Select an option for the checks you want to print.**

7 **(Optional) Change the date range of the checks you want to be printed.**

8   **If you chose Selected Checks, mark each check you want to print, and then click OK.**

Quicken lists in chronological order all the checks you've written and not yet printed.

```
                  Select Checks to Print

 Print   Date      Payee                          Amount
   √    5/15/94  American Lending Corp.           1,533.91 ⬆
   √    5/16/94  Dr. Chris Lee                       70.00
   √    5/20/94  Davis, Baird and Hertseld          215.00
   √    5/27/94  Primerica Bank                     289.75
        5/29/94  American Express                 1,076.88
         6/8/94  City of Valley                      65.00      ┌─────────┐
   √     6/8/94  Valley Gas & Electric               64.97      │   All   │
   √     6/8/94  Atwood Leisure                     106.83      └─────────┘
   √    6/12/94  Montenegro Consulting              125.00      ┌─────────┐
        6/15/94  GMAC Financing                     587.55      │  None   │
        6/15/94  American Lending Corp.           1,533.91      └─────────┘
   √    6/27/94  Primerica Bank                     289.75
        6/28/94  Western Bell                        87.52 ⬇

  ┌──────────┐   ┌──────────┐   Selected Checks:      $2,695.21
  │  Cancel  │   │    OK    │   Current Balance:      $3,230.00
  └──────────┘   └──────────┘   Ending Balance:       $7,766.87
```

To mark a check to be printed, click the check. Quicken displays a checkmark in the Print column when you've selected a check to be printed. If you accidentally mark a check that you do not want to print, click the transaction again to deselect it.

9   **Make sure that the icon for three checks is selected.**

If you are planning to start printing less than a full page of three standard or wallet checks, see "Printing a partial first page of checks" on page 119.

10   **Click OK in the Print Checks window to open the printer dialog box.**

The settings in the printer dialog box vary for various printer types.

```
 LaserWriter                                    7.0     ┌─────────┐
                                                        │  Print  │
 Copies: 1           Pages: ⦿ All ○ From:    To:       └─────────┘
                                                        ┌─────────┐
 Cover Page:    ⦿ No ○ First Page ○ Last Page          │ Cancel  │
 Paper Source: ⦿ Paper Cassette ○ Manual Feed          └─────────┘
 Print:        ⦿ Black & White   ○ Color/Grayscale
 Destination:  ⦿ Printer         ○ PostScript® File
```

11   **Click Print in the printer dialog box to start printing your checks.**

Stopping a print job

Press ⌘ .

If you notice a problem while your checks are being printed, stop the printing process by pressing the command key and the period key together. If your printer continues to print, turn its power switch off.

Examining printed checks

After the checks have finished printing, Quicken needs to know if your checks printed correctly.

If all the checks printed correctly, click Yes. Until you click Yes, unprinted checks in the register that you've selected to print have Print in the Number field. After you click Yes, Quicken inserts check numbers in the Number field.

If any of the checks did not print correctly, click No.

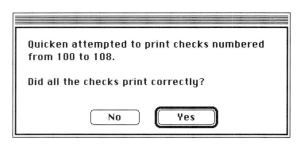

Using a LaserWriter?

Sometimes Quicken displays this message before the printer is finished printing your checks.

Wait a few moments before you examine the checks and click Yes or No.

1 Examine the printed checks.

2 If the checks printed correctly, click Yes.

Quicken inserts check numbers in the Number field of the printed checks in the register. You are finished printing.

3 If any of the checks did not print correctly:

- Quicken asks you to type the number of the first unprinted or incorrectly printed check. Type the number of the first check that printed incorrectly (or did not print) and click OK.

- Examine your printer to see if the checks jammed or the printer ran out of checks. If the text on the checks in your printer is not aligned correctly, you may need to adjust the check printing settings. See "Adjusting check alignment" on page 138.

4 Start printing again after you've fixed the problem:

Or press ⌘ P

- Choose Print Checks from the File menu.

- Select an option to specify the checks you want to print.

- Click Print in the printer dialog box.

Saving sample check stock

If you have trouble getting your checks to print at first, don't continue to use the sample checks that came with Quicken. Instead, print sample checks on blank paper. After printing a sample check, place the paper on top of the sample check page and hold them both up to the light to see if the text printed correctly.

Printing a partial first page of checks

If you use standard or wallet checks in your page-oriented printer, you'll sometimes find that a *partial page* of one or two blank checks remains after you have finished printing. You can start printing onto that partial page the next time you begin to print checks.

You can print partial pages of standard or wallet checks, but not voucher checks, since they come one per page only.

1   Before you start printing, turn on your printer, but don't load your checks yet.

2   Choose Check Printing from the Settings menu.

3   Select one of the Partial Page Orientation icons to show Quicken how you insert envelopes into your printer and click OK.

You feed checks into your printer the same way you feed envelopes. Before you insert your checks into the envelope feeder you need to know:

- The type of envelope feeder your printer has

- If you should insert the check face up or face down

- If you should insert the left edge, right edge, top, or bottom of the check into the printer first.

You feed checks into your printer the same way you feed envelopes. Consult your printer manual to find out which of these three basic positions the printer manufacturer recommends for loading envelopes in the envelope feeder or cassette.

If your checks print upside down or on the wrong side, reverse the way you load the checks into the envelope feeder.

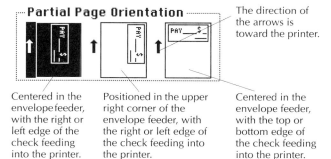

Partial Page Orientation

The direction of the arrows is toward the printer.

Centered in the envelope feeder, with the right or left edge of the check feeding into the printer.

Positioned in the upper right corner of the envelope feeder, with the right or left edge of the check feeding into the printer.

Centered in the envelope feeder, with the top or bottom edge of the check feeding into the printer.

Or press ⌘ P

4   Choose Print Checks from the File menu.

5   Be sure the number in the Starting Check Number field is the same as the number of the first check on your partial page of checks.

6 **Select the checks you want to print in the Print Checks dialog box.**

7 **Choose a Checks on First Page icon:**
- Click One if your first page has one check on it.
- Click Two if your first page has two checks on it.

Choose the icon that represents the number of checks you will be printing. Depending on the printer you use to print checks, the orientation of the check icons on the buttons may be horizontal instead of vertical as shown here in the first two icons.

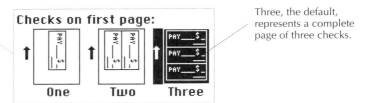

Three, the default, represents a complete page of three checks.

8 **Load the one or two checks into your envelope feeder or cassette as pictured in the partial-sheet icon you selected.**

If your printer requires that you load letterhead face down (as the Apple Personal LaserWriter does), load your checks that way. Look in your printer manual if you aren't sure.

Preventing wasted checks with forms leaders
You may need to use Intuit forms leaders to prevent wasted checks if your page-oriented printer does not have an envelope feeder, *and* you are using standard three-to-a-page checks, *and* you want to print checks on partial pages. See "Forms leaders" on page 390.

---

9 **Click Print to start printing the checks.**

After the partial page of checks is printed, begin printing checks to a full page of checks by choosing Print Checks from the File menu.

Using trailer strip options

In some situations you may need to display and use a special option for handling existing trailer strips or missing trailer strips on your checks.

Use the trailer strip option	Check printing situation
Clear the checkbox.	Intuit laser/inkjet checks have an extra 1/2" trailer strip at the bottom of each sheet. (When you order checks for your page-oriented printer, you order laser/inkjet checks. These checks work for all single-sheet fed, page-oriented printers.) If you are printing a partial page of page-oriented checks, Quicken may display a message telling you that the page is shorter than the size selected in the Page Setup dialog box. Check to see if the trailer strip is missing from the bottom of the page of checks.
Clear the checkbox.	You have turned continuous-feed checks into pages with three checks per page to be able to print checks on a page-oriented printer. (See "Using continuous-feed checks in page-oriented printers" on page 112.)
Select the checkbox.	You use a LaserWriter SC to print a partial page of checks with one check on it.
Clear the checkbox.	You use a LaserWriter SC to print a partial page of checks with two checks on it.

To clear or select the Use Trailer Strip checkbox:

1   **Choose Check Printing from the Settings menu.**

2   **Press Option-T.**

Quicken displays a Use Trailer Strip checkbox in the Check Printing Settings dialog box just below the Sample box.

3   **Select or clear the Use Trailer Strip checkbox according to your situation described in the table above.**

4   **Click OK to save the check printing settings.**

Although Quicken hides the Use Trailer Strip checkbox after you close the Check Printing Settings dialog box, Quicken does save the setting. You can display the checkbox again by pressing Option-T.

Printing checks on continuous-feed printers

This section explains how to print checks on ImageWriter or other continuous-feed (also known as tractor-feed, pin-feed, or dot-matrix) printers. If you have a laser, inkjet, postscript, or other sheet-fed, page-oriented printer (including a dot-matrix printer that has a paper tray), turn to page 112.

◆ **Set up your check printer.**
See "Setting up continuous-feed printers" on this page.

◆ **Load the checks in your printer.**
See "Positioning checks in continuous-feed printers" on page 124.

◆ **If this is the first time you've printed an Intuit check, print a sample check to make sure the alignment is correct.**
See "Printing a sample check on continuous-feed printers" on page 125.

◆ **Print your checks.**
See "Printing checks from your account" on page 116.

◆ **Make sure the checks all printed correctly.**
See "Examining printed checks" on page 118.

Setting up continuous-feed printers

Before you print any checks from a Quicken account, you need to select the continuous-feed printer you're going to use to print checks. Once you set up your printer, you don't have to change the check printing settings unless you change Intuit check styles, change printers, or decide to place a custom logo on your checks.

1 **Select the printer you plan to use in the Chooser.**

● Choose the Chooser from the Apple menu.

● In the left box, click the icon that represents the printer you want to use.

● In the right box, if your printer is not on a network, click the icon for the modem port or the icon for the printer port that represents the port you used to connect the printer. If your printer is on a network, click the name of the printer.

● Close the Chooser.

2   Choose Check Printing from the Settings menu.

There are three types of Intuit checks:

- Standard checks are 3.5 inches high.
- Voucher checks are 3.5 inches high, with a 3.5-inch tear-off voucher attachment below each check. Quicken prints the check date, payee, and amount on the perforated voucher attachment.
- Wallet checks are about 2.8 inches high, with a removable stub on the left.

Geneva is the default font for continuous-feed printers. The Sample box shows the currently selected font and size.

If the Sheet Feeder checkbox is selected, clear the checkbox as illustrated.

Using a continuous-feed printer, you don't need to select any partial page orientation options.

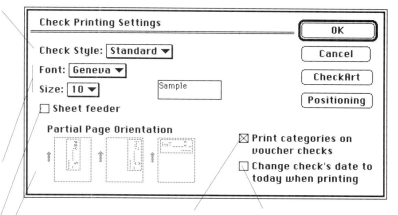

Select the Print Categories on Voucher Checks checkbox if you want to print category information from a split check on the perforated attachment to voucher checks. See "Splitting transactions" on page 92 for more information.

Select the Change Check's Date to Today When Printing checkbox if you want Quicken to change the dates on the checks to the current date when you print the checks.

3   Choose the Intuit check style you plan to print from the Check Style popup menu.

This arrow tells you that there is a popup list here that contains more than one item. Click the arrow and drag down the mouse button to select a different item.

4   (Optional) Choose a different font name and size for the text that prints on checks from the Font and Size popup menus.

The Sample box shows the currently selected font and size.

5   Make sure that the Sheet Feeder checkbox is cleared.

6   (Optional) To print category information from a split check on the perforated attachment to voucher checks, select the Print Categories on Voucher Checks checkbox.

See "Splitting transactions" on page 92 for more information.

7   (Optional) To have Quicken change check dates to the current date at print time, select the Change Check's Date to Today When Printing checkbox.

8   Click OK to save your check printing setup.

Positioning checks in continuous-feed printers

Intuit's patented automatic alignment helps you line up the checks correctly in your printer. Insert the checks in your printer as you would in any continuous-feed printer paper.

Position the checks horizontally in the same position you normally use for printing on 8.5-by-11-inch paper. You probably won't need to change the position of the paper clamps.

Position the checks according to your printer type.

Printer type	How to position the checks
ImageWriter I	Align the line for position number five on the check with the top of the type head. Snap the roller into place against the checks to hold the checks firmly in place.
	If the checks still print too high: • Choose Check Printing from the Settings menu. • Click Positioning. • Enter −30 in the Fine Tuning field.
ImageWriter II	Align the top of the first check with the top of the plastic guard in front of the print head.
ImageWriter LQ	Align the top of the first check with the top of the print head.

Preventing wasted checks with forms leaders
You may need to use Intuit forms leaders to prevent wasted checks if your continuous-feed printer has a tractor head above the print head and you cannot print on the first check. See "Forms leaders" on page 390.

Printing a sample check on continuous-feed printers

Quicken lets you print a sample check to make sure the checks are properly aligned in the printer before you print the rest of the checks. Your Quicken package includes sample checks for continuous-feed printers.

1 **If you haven't already inserted the checks in the printer, insert them now.**

See "Positioning checks in continuous-feed printers" on page 124.

2 **Make sure your printer is turned on and online.**

If you're using an ImageWriter, the green "Select" light should be lit.

3 **Choose Page Setup from the File menu and make sure that the Paper option selected is US Letter.**

4 **Open the account you want to print checks from.**

Or press ⌘ P

5 **Choose Print Checks from the File menu.**

When you test the check alignment, Quicken prints a sample check with a pointer line printed on it. Use the pointer line on the sample check to find and note the physical spot on your printer you will use to line up checks in the future.

```
          Print Checks

Starting check number:  [100]
Print:
  ○ Checks dated through:  [5/23/94]
  ○ Selected Checks...
  ⦿ Check Alignment Test

        [ Cancel ]  [[  OK  ]]
```

6 **Click Check Alignment Test.**

Quicken displays the printer dialog box.

7 **Click Print.**

Quicken prints a sample check.

8 **Without moving the check in the printer, look at the sample check.**

Check the horizontal alignment. Does the text appear too far to the left or right? Check the vertical alignment. If the check is aligned correctly, the type rests just above the lines on the check.

- If the sample check printed correctly, click Cancel in the Check Alignment window and see "Printing checks from your account" on page 116.

  OR

- If the sample check *did not* print correctly, see "Correcting continuous-feed check alignment" next.

Correcting continuous-feed check alignment

1 **Look at the pointer line that printed in the middle of the check and note the position number that the arrows point to.**

Quicken prints a pointer line on the sample check. The arrows at each end of the pointer line point to position numbers printed along the edges of the check.

In this example, the pointer line points to position number 26.

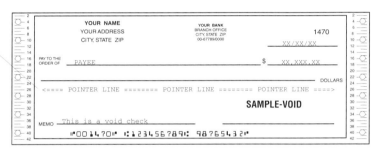

2 **In the Check Alignment dialog box, click the position number pointed to by the pointer line arrows on the printed check.**

Indicate the number the pointer line is pointing to on the check you just printed here. (The number 26 is just an example.)

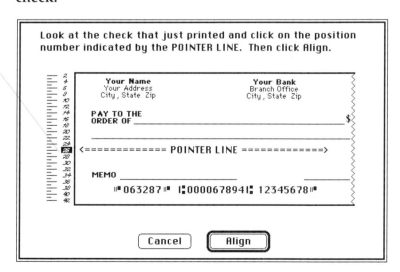

3 **Make any side-to-side, horizontal positioning adjustments by hand now, moving the paper clamps on the printer as necessary.**

4 **Click OK.**

Quicken aligns the check vertically in the printer, advances the checks, and prints another sample.

5 **Without moving the check in the printer, look at the second sample check.**

The vertical positioning of the second check should be almost perfect. If it's off by a noticeable amount, repeat the above steps until a sample check prints correctly.

OR

If a half-line adjustment is needed, use the Line Feed button on the top of your printer or the knob on the side of your printer to move the check up or down half a line.

6 **Note the correct position of the check for future positioning.**

Visually line up part of your printer, such as the sprocket cover or print head, with one of the position numbers at the edge of the check. Make a note of this spot on the printer. From now on, use this spot on the printer as an alignment cue to position your checks visually each time you insert them in your printer, so you won't have to test your check alignment again by printing more sample checks.

You are now ready to print your checks.

Printing checks from your account

1 **If you haven't already inserted the checks in the printer, insert them now.**

See "Positioning checks in continuous-feed printers" on page 124.

2 **Make sure your printer is turned on and online.**

If you're using an ImageWriter, the green "Select" light should be lit.

3 **Open the account you want to print checks from.**

Or press ⌘ P 4 **Choose Print Checks from the File menu.**

Quicken displays the Print Checks dialog box.

If you receive a message that you don't have any checks selected to print, you need to enter the checks you want to print in the Write Checks window (see "Filling out a check" on page 104). If you have already entered the checks into the register instead of the Write Checks window, you need to show Quicken which checks in the register you want to print (see "Reprinting checks" on page 131).

Enter the number shown on the first check positioned in the printer here.

Choose an option for printing:

- Click Checks Dated Through and then change the date range of the checks to be printed; by default, the date is the current date.
- Click Selected Checks to print only specified checks.

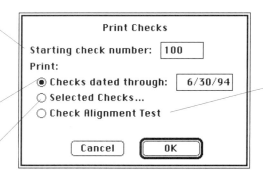

If you click Check Alignment Test, Quicken prints a check with a pointer line printed on it. You print a sample check the first time you print checks with Quicken to find and note the physical spot on your printer you will use to line up checks in the future. See "Printing a sample check on continuous-feed printers" on page 125.

5 **If the number in the Starting Check Number field is not the same as the number of the first check in your printer, enter the number of the first check in your printer.**

6 **Select an option for the checks you want to print.**

7 **(Optional) Change the date range of the checks to be printed.**

8 **If you chose Selected Checks, mark each check you want to print, and then click OK.**

Quicken lists in chronological order all the checks you've written and not yet printed.

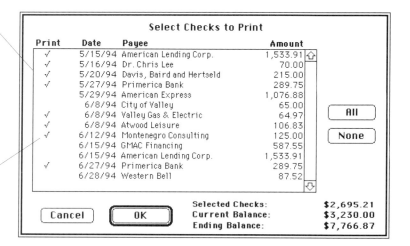

To mark a check to be printed, click the check. Quicken displays a checkmark in the Print column when you've selected a check to be printed. If you accidentally mark a check that you do not want to print, click the transaction again to deselect it.

9   **Click OK in the Print Checks window to open the printer dialog box.**

The settings in the printer dialog box vary for various printer types.

You can change the print quality options to decrease the time it takes Quicken to print your checks.

```
┌─────────────────────────────────────────────────────────────┐
│ ImageWriter                              7.0    ( Print )     │
│ Quality:      ○ Best      ⦿ Faster    ○ Draft                │
│ Page Range:   ⦿ All       ○ From:      To:      ( Cancel )    │
│ Copies:       1                                              │
│ Paper Feed:   ⦿ Automatic ○ Hand Feed                        │
└─────────────────────────────────────────────────────────────┘
```

10   **Select a Quality option.**

Option	Output	Printing speed	Notes
Best	Highest quality	Slowest	If you use CheckArt on your printed checks, you must select this option. See page 135.
Faster	High quality	Slower than Best; Faster than Draft	Try this option if Best takes too long to print.
Draft	Lower quality	Fastest	Doesn't print the fonts you've selected. Quicken chooses the font it can print the fastest.

11   **Click Print in the printer dialog box to start printing your checks.**

Stopping a print job

Press ⌘ .

If you notice a problem while your checks are being printed, stop the printing process by pressing the command key and the period key together. If your printer continues to print, turn its power switch off.

Examining printed checks

After the checks have finished printing, Quicken needs to know if your checks printed correctly.

If all the checks printed correctly, click Yes. Until you click Yes, unprinted checks in the register that you've selected to print have Print in the Number field. After you click Yes, Quicken inserts check numbers in the Number field.

If any of the checks did not print correctly, click No.

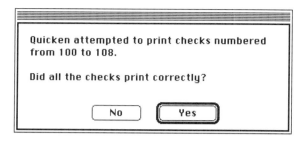

Quicken attempted to print checks numbered from 100 to 108.

Did all the checks print correctly?

No   Yes

1   Examine the printed checks.

2   If the checks printed correctly, click Yes.

Quicken inserts check numbers in the Number field of the printed checks in the register. You are finished printing.

3   If any of the checks did not print correctly:

- Quicken asks you to type the number of the first unprinted or incorrectly printed check. Type the number of the first check that printed incorrectly (or did not print) and click OK.

- Examine your printer to see if the checks jammed or the printer ran out of checks. If the text on the checks in your printer is not aligned correctly, you may need to adjust the check printing settings. See "Correcting continuous-feed check alignment" on page 126.

4   Start printing again after you've fixed the problem:

- Choose Print Checks from the File menu.

- Select an option to specify the checks you want to print.

- Click Print in the printer dialog box.

Reprinting checks

With Quicken, you can easily reprint any check at any time, for any reason. You can also fill in any number of copies in the Print Checks window to print multiple copies of checks.

The procedure below also works to print checks that you may have entered into the register instead of the Write Checks window.

1   In the register, select the transaction for the check you want to reprint.

2   Select the check number and type print **over the check number.**

(If you have QuickFill turned on, all you have to type is p.)

Quicken replaces the check number with Print in the Number field and considers the check ready to print.

Typing **print** in the Number field turns a check that has already been printed into a check that you can print again.

| 6/12 | PRINT | Humberg's Landscaping | 650 | 00 | | | 4,054 | 33 |
| 1994 | | Household:Garden June 94 | | | | | | |

You'd usually use the Write Checks window to enter checks that you plan to print and the Register window to enter handwritten checks. If you have already entered a check that you want to print into the register, type **print** into the empty Number field and click Record.

3   Click Record.

4   Print the check as usual, paying special attention to entering the correct number in the Starting Check Number field.

Adding art to checks

CheckArt is a Quicken feature that lets you print graphic images, text, logos, or any image you want on your checks. The image, referred to as *CheckArt*, can be 1 inch high and 5 inches wide on regular and voucher checks, and 0.5 inch high by 2.5 inches wide on wallet-size checks.

CheckArt always prints in the top left corner of your checks, where your name and address usually appear.

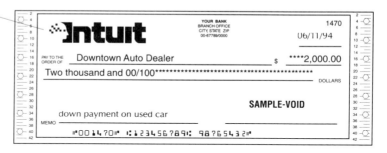

If you plan to use CheckArt to print your name and address on every check, be sure to specify "Without Name and Address" on the check order form when ordering checks. For information about ordering checks, see Appendix A, *Ordering supplies and other Intuit products,* beginning on page 387.

◆ **Create the image.**
See "Creating the CheckArt image" on this page.

◆ **Copy the image to a sample check.**
See "Copying CheckArt to your checks" on page 133.

◆ **Place the image on a sample check displayed on your screen.**
See "Positioning CheckArt on your checks" on page 134.

Creating the CheckArt image

You can create a CheckArt image using many different sources. These sources include:

- The clip art collection that comes with HyperCard
- Public domain and commercial clip art libraries
- Images you create using drawing programs like MacPaint or MacDraw
- Scanned images

The image must be in PICT (Paint or Draw) format from a program such as MacPaint. Although Quicken does not accept text or images created in a word processor or EPS (PostScript) files, you can copy an image created in a Post Script program such as Adobe Illustrator, Aldus Freehand, or TypeStyler into a PICT file. Select the image, press Option-Copy, and paste it into a PICT (Paint or Draw) file.

Copying CheckArt to your checks

Once you've created the image you want to use as CheckArt, you're ready to copy it to a sample check.

If you're used to working with the Finder or MultiFinder, you can simply copy the original image from the source program and paste it into the CheckArt window without using the Scrapbook. Go to "Positioning CheckArt on your checks" on page 134.

If you're not used to working with the Finder or MultiFinder, you need to paste the image into the Scrapbook. Before doing so, be sure you have the Scrapbook Desk Accessory installed in your system. For more information on the Scrapbook, see the Desk Accessories chapter of your *Macintosh System Software User's Guide*.

1   **Start the program that you used to create the image.**

2   **Open the file that contains the image you want to use for CheckArt.**

Or press ⌘ C

3   **Select the image you want and choose Copy from the Edit menu to copy it to the clipboard.**

4   **Choose Scrapbook from the Apple (⬮) menu.**

Or press ⌘ V

5   **Choose Paste from the Edit menu.**

When you paste the image into the Scrapbook, the word PICT should appear here; PICT is the only file type compatible with CheckArt.

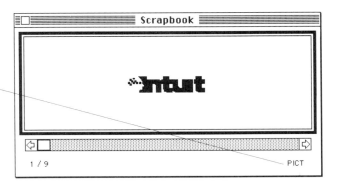

6 Start Quicken and open your checking account.

7 Choose Scrapbook from the Apple (🍎) menu.

8 Scroll through the Scrapbook until you see the image you want to use as CheckArt.

Or press ⌘ C

9 Choose Copy from the Edit menu to copy the image to the Clipboard.

10 Close the Scrapbook.

Positioning CheckArt on your checks

When the CheckArt image is on the clipboard, you're ready to place it on your checks.

1 Start Quicken and open your checking account if it's not already open.

2 Choose Check Printing from the Settings menu.

3 Click the CheckArt button.

Quicken displays a sample check with a blank rectangle in the top left corner.

Or press ⌘ V

4 Choose Paste from the Edit menu to paste the image from the Clipboard into the blank rectangle.

If the image is too large, Quicken automatically scales it to fit.

Select the Don't Print checkbox when you want to keep CheckArt from printing on your checks.

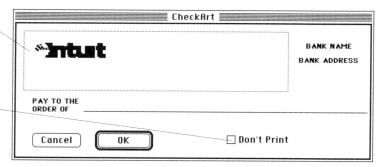

5 Reposition the image by dragging it with the mouse.

6 Click OK.

You've now added CheckArt to the current checking account. To use the same CheckArt with another checking account, open that account and repeat the steps on page 133.

You cannot modify your CheckArt with Quicken. To modify the image, you must go back to the program you used to create it. Modify the image there, and then repeat the steps in "Copying CheckArt to your checks" on page 133.

Printing checks with CheckArt

Once you've added CheckArt to the current checking account, you're ready to print checks with CheckArt.

You don't need to follow any special instructions to print your checks with CheckArt. See "Printing checks on continuous-feed printers" on page 122 or "Printing checks on page-oriented printers" on page 112.

If you have a continuous-feed printer, select Best print quality when you print checks. CheckArt does not print well if you select Faster print quality and does not print at all if you select Draft print quality.

Solving check printing problems

Common check printing problems and their solutions are described in the following table.

If you continue to have problems printing checks, see your printer manual or call Intuit's Technical Support group. (See "Phone numbers" on page 408.)

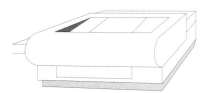

Problem	Your printer doesn't print.
Solution	Check the printer connections: • Make sure your printer is turned on and is online. • Make sure the cable connection between the printer and the Macintosh is secure. • Open the Chooser and make sure that the correct printer is selected.

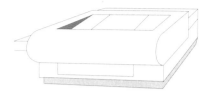

Problem Your printer was working fine when you printed your checks the last time. You haven't changed any settings, and you can print documents using other software, but when you try to print checks in Quicken:
- The print is misaligned, or
- Gibberish appears on the checks, or
- The print dialog box doesn't appear at all.

Solution If you printed checks without problems one day, and nothing works the next day, your printer driver is probably damaged. Reinstall the printer driver according to the instructions on page 111.

Problem Text on the first check printed on a continuous-feed or page-oriented printer prints in the right place but text on subsequent checks creeps up or down.

Solution You can adjust the vertical alignment of your text in the memo field. See "Adjusting check alignment" on page 138 and then see "Vertical positioning problems" on page 139.

Problem Text in the memo field prints too high or too low on checks.

Solution You need to change the Lines Per Check setting in Quicken. See "Adjusting check alignment" on page 138 and "Vertical positioning problems" on page 139.

Problem Text on the first check prints too high or too low.

Solution If you are printing continuous-feed checks and haven't already printed a sample check and adjusted its alignment, see "Correcting continuous-feed check alignment" on page 126.

If you are printing continuous-feed checks and have already printed a sample check *and* adjusted its alignment using the pointer line or if you are printing page-oriented checks, you need to change the Fine Tuning setting that Quicken assumes as the top of the check. See "Adjusting check alignment" on page 138 and "Vertical positioning problems" on page 139.

Problem   All text prints too far left or too far right on checks.

Solution   If text on *continuous-feed* checks prints too far left or right, reposition checks horizontally. Move checks to the right or left manually, moving the paper clamps as necessary.

If text on *page-oriented* checks prints too far left or right, you need to adjust the horizontal alignment of text in each field. See "Adjusting check alignment" on page 138 and then see "Horizontal positioning problems" on page 140.

Problem   One or more individual check fields start printing too far to the left or right.

Solution   You can adjust the horizontal alignment of text in specific fields. See "Adjusting check alignment" on page 138 and then see "Horizontal positioning problems" on page 140.

Problem   Numbers in the $ (amount) field start printing in the right place but are so long that they are cut off on the right.

Solution   You can adjust the horizontal alignment of the numbers in the $ (amount) field. See "Adjusting check alignment" on page 138 and then see "Horizontal positioning problems" on page 140.

Problem   The spelled-out check amount is so short that it doesn't fill out the line.

Solution   You can adjust the horizontal alignment of text in the spelled-out check amount field. See "Adjusting check alignment" on page 138 and then see "Horizontal positioning problems" on page 140.

Problem   The text on a check from a partial page of checks starts printing too high or too low and continues to print too high or too low on the next checks.

Solution   You can adjust the vertical alignment for a partial page of checks. See "Adjusting check alignment" on page 138 and then see "Partial-page positioning problems" on page 140.

Adjusting check alignment

In most cases, you won't need to do anything special to print checks.

If you have a non-Apple, page-oriented printer, you may need to use the information in this section, but only if you have read and followed the instructions for printing checks in this chapter and still have trouble with the position of text on printed checks.

You can make fine adjustments to the location of text on your check. You might find this necessary if certain fields don't print in quite the right place. Once you get your checks to print correctly, you don't have to do anything special the next time to print checks with the same alignment.

> You can adjust the positioning of text in individual fields on an Intuit check, but you cannot rearrange the order of the fields to match those on a non-Intuit check.

1 Refer to the printed check to decide which field and line positions need adjusting.

2 Choose Check Printing from the Settings menu and click Positioning in the Check Printing Settings dialog box.

Change the Fine Tuning setting to adjust the top-to-bottom position of all the text on a check and the top-to-bottom position of text in the Memo field. A negative number moves the text up; a positive number moves the text down.

In these vertical settings, 72 pixels equal approximately one inch, and 12 pixels equal approximately one line.

Change the Horizontal settings to adjust the side-to-side position of text in individual fields and text that seems too short or too long for a particular field.

Change the Partial Page settings to adjust the top-to-bottom position of all the text on a check printed as a partial page.

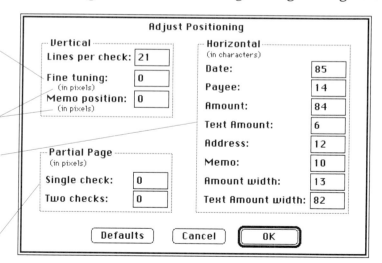

3 See the tables on the next pages for specific solutions to problems with the location of text on your check.

4 Enter new settings for the positions you want to change and click OK.

Vertical positioning problems	Solutions
All the text in the first check prints in the right places, but the text on the next check "creeps up" and prints too high.	Increase the number of lines in the vertical Lines Per Check setting.
All the text in the first check prints in the right places, but the text on the next check "creeps down" and prints too low.	Decrease the number of lines in the vertical Lines Per Check setting.
The text on the first check starts printing too high.	Adjust the setting that Quicken assumes as the top of the check. Increase the number of pixels in the Fine Tuning setting to move all the text on the check down. *A positive number moves it down.*
The text on the first check starts printing too low.	Adjust the setting that Quicken assumes as the top of the check. Decrease the number of pixels in the Fine Tuning setting to move all the text on the check up. *A negative number moves it up.*
The memo text on a check prints too high.	Increase the number of pixels in the Memo Position setting to increase the distance between the Memo field and the top of the check. *A positive number increases the distance.*
The memo text on a check prints too low.	Decrease the number of pixels in the Memo Position setting to decrease the distance between the Memo field and the top of the check. *A negative number decreases the distance.*

Horizontal positioning problems	Solutions
One or more individual check fields start printing too far to the left.	Increase the number of characters in the horizontal Date, Payee, $ (amount), Text Amount, or Memo setting to increase the distance between the text in that field and the left edge of the check.
One or more individual check fields start printing too far to the right.	Decrease the number of characters in the horizontal Date, Payee, Amount, Text Amount, Address, or Memo setting to decrease the distance between the text in that field and the left edge of the check.
Check amount starts printing in the right place, but is cut off on the right.	Decrease the number of characters in the Amount Width setting to force Quicken to fit the amount into a shorter space. Ten characters is the minimum.
Spelled-out check amount starts printing in the right place, but doesn't fill the line.	Increase the number of characters in the Text Amount Width setting to make the spelled-out amount longer.

Partial-page positioning problems	Solutions
The text on a check from a partial page of checks starts printing too high.	Adjust the setting that Quicken assumes as the top of the check. Increase the number of pixels in the Single Check or Two Checks setting, depending on whether you're trying to print one check or two checks.
The text on a check from a partial page of checks starts printing too low.	Adjust the setting that Quicken assumes as the top of the check. Decrease the number of pixels in the Single Check or Two Checks setting, depending on whether you're trying to print one check or two checks.

Balancing your checkbook

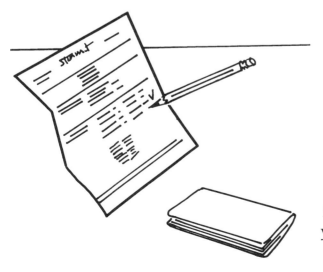

When your bank statement arrives, use Quicken to balance your checkbook, or "reconcile."

The goal of reconciliation is to bring your Quicken records into agreement with your bank records.

Quicken allows you to reconcile to the degree of accuracy that works for you. You can track down every cent if you prefer, but Quicken does not require you to balance to the penny.

About balancing Quicken accounts

When your bank statement arrives, follow the basic steps listed here to reconcile your account. Quicken reconciles one statement at a time. If you have accumulated two or more statements that need reconciling, start with the earliest statement and reconcile each one individually.

◆ **If this is the first time you've reconciled a Quicken account, check to see if you need to enter more transactions or revise the opening balance amount of this account.**
See "Balancing a Quicken account for the first time" on this page.

◆ **Start reconciling by entering information from your current bank statement.**
See "Starting reconciliation" on page 144.

◆ **Mark the transactions that have cleared your bank account in the Reconcile window.**
See "Marking cleared transactions" on page 146.

◆ **Compare the totals of cleared items in the Reconcile window with those on your bank statement.**
See "Completing reconciliation" on page 149.

◆ **(Optional) Create and print a reconciliation report.**
See "Completing reconciliation" on page 149.

Balancing a Quicken account for the first time

When you set up your Quicken bank account, you should have entered the ending balance from your last bank statement into the Deposit field of the Opening Balance transaction. If you mistakenly entered an amount different from the ending balance on the last bank statement, you need to change the amount of the Opening Balance transaction.

The first time you balance your account may take some extra time. After you find the point where Quicken and the bank agree on the amount of money in your account, reconciling your account each month should be fast and easy.

Before you can reconcile your account accurately for the first time, you need to do two things:

1 **Enter all uncleared transactions in your Quicken account.**

For bank accounts, these are all transactions that have not cleared the bank or shown up on previous bank statements.

In most cases you'll be reminded to enter all uncleared transactions because the transactions appear on the bank statement when you're trying to reconcile. You can also enter these transactions in the register as you find them during reconciliation.

2   **Make sure that the amount in the Deposit field of the Opening Balance transaction in the account is correct.**

If you used an amount other than the ending balance from your most recent bank statement when you set up your Quicken account, you may have problems reconciling. Go to the register now and change the amount in the Deposit column of the Opening Balance transaction.

Your opening balance . . .

Suppose, for example, the ending balance on the bank statement for your checking account was $200.52 on December 31, 1992. You started using Quicken on January 12, 1993. You used the ending balance from your December bank statement as the Opening Balance deposit in your Quicken checking account.

Then you entered transactions from your paper check register from January 1 to 12 into Quicken. From January 12 on, you entered all transactions into Quicken every few days as they occurred.

and checks that were outstanding when you started with Quicken

In February, you receive your January 31, 1993 bank statement. You see two checks (totaling $80) that you wrote in December 1992 that had not yet cleared the bank in December. Now they have cleared the bank, so they appear on the January bank statement. You didn't enter those checks in Quicken at the time you set up the checking account because they occurred before December 31.

Even though those two checks were written before the date of the Opening Balance transaction in Quicken, you need to enter them into Quicken's register. (You would not enter any other checks that you wrote in December if they had already cleared the bank in December.) If you don't enter these two transactions from December, Quicken will not be able to account for the missing $80 when you are finished reconciling.

Where the balances go . . .

You take the ending balance from your most recent bank statement and enter that amount in the Opening Balance Deposit field when you set up your Quicken account.

Quicken uses the Opening Balance deposit amount you entered in the account as the Previous Balance amount in the Reconcile Startup window.

When your next bank statement arrives, enter the ending balance from it in the Reconcile Startup window.

Starting reconciliation

Your first step in reconciling your account is to enter information from your bank statement.

If the balance shown on your most recent bank statement is different from Quicken's current balance for the account, do not assume that the bank balance is current. You've probably entered transactions into Quicken after the bank prepared your statement. You may also have checks or other transactions from earlier months that have not yet cleared the bank. Be sure to enter these transactions in the register now if you have not already done so.

1 Make sure the register for the account you want to reconcile is active.

2 Choose Reconcile from the Activities menu.

If this is the first time you are reconciling this account, Quicken uses the amount you entered for the Opening Balance transaction in your Quicken check register as the amount it displays in the Previous Balance field.

For example, say you started using Quicken in March 1993. The most recent bank statement you had at that time was dated February 19. You entered the ending balance amount from the February 19 statement as the Opening Balance transaction in your Quicken check register (271.53). Then you entered transactions as they occurred throughout March. Now you have received your March 19 bank statement and you want to balance it with your Quicken records. When you begin to reconcile this account, Quicken displays the 271.53 in the Previous Balance field.

Quicken displays the Reconcile Startup window with an amount already calculated in the Previous Balance field. The amount in Quicken's Previous Balance field should be the same as the previous balance on your bank statement.

```
▤☐▤▤▤▤▤▤▤ Checking: Reconcile Startup ▤▤▤▤▤
  Enter the following information from your bank statement:

   Previous Balance:        7,203.12

   New Balance:             6,789.65

  If you enter a service charge or interest, Quicken will add it to your account.
                         Date       Amount        Category
   Service Charge:       6/13/94        8.00   Bank Charges
   Interest Earned:      6/13/94        1.42   Interest Income

              [ Cancel ]        [[  OK  ]]
```

If this is not the first time you have reconciled this account, the amount in the Previous Balance field represents the total of all reconciled transactions in the Quicken register for this account. In the register, all reconciled transactions (including the Opening Balance transaction) are marked with a bold checkmark in the Cleared column.

3 Compare the previous balance amount shown on your bank statement with the amount shown in the Previous Balance field in the Reconcile Startup window.

Your bank statement might call the previous balance the "beginning" or "opening" balance.

The amount in the Previous Balance field should be the same as the previous balance on your bank statement.

If the amount displayed in the Previous Balance field does not match the previous balance on your bank statement for this account, you need to resolve this issue before you continue reconciling. The previously reconciled balance might differ for one of the reasons described in the table below.

Your situation	How to resolve the difference in the Previous Balance field
You are balancing your Quicken account for the first time.	Quicken uses the amount of the Opening Balance transaction in your check register as the amount in the Previous Balance field in the Reconcile Startup window (page 144). When you set up the Quicken account, you may have entered the wrong amount in the Deposit field of the Opening Balance transaction. See "Balancing a Quicken account for the first time" on page 142.
The ending balance of last month's bank statement is different than the starting balance on this month's statement.	One of the bank statements may be in error. Contact your bank to resolve the problem. The bank will correct the error with an adjustment that will appear on your next statement. For now, change the Previous Balance amount and let Quicken make the adjustment for you as described in "Letting Quicken adjust for differences" on page 151. This adjustment will appear as an already cleared item in the check register, so your account will be off by the same amount next month when you reconcile. Let Quicken make another adjustment when you finish reconciling the next statement.
You have started reconciling with your most recent bank statement, but you have not reconciled each of the previous months' statements.	You should reconcile one month at a time, starting with the earliest monthly statement. However, if you have skipped several months and don't want to balance each bank statement, see "Catching up if you skipped balancing your checkbook" on page 154.
You were using Quicken and reconciling your bank account, then you started recording earlier transactions in Quicken.	For example, say it's July. You started recording transactions in Quicken in May and subsequently reconciled your account for May and June. Then you went back and recorded transactions starting in January so that you could create reports, graphs, and budgets based on the full year's transactions. After entering these earlier items, you noticed that the ending balance in the check register was incorrect. So you updated the date and amount of the original Opening Balance transaction that Quicken recorded in the register when you set up your account in May. See "Adding earlier transactions to Quicken" on page 155.

4   **Find the new balance on your bank statement and enter it in the New Balance field in the Reconcile Startup window.**

Your bank statement might call the ending balance amount the "current" or "ending" balance.

5   If any service charges are listed on your bank statement and you haven't already entered them into your Quicken register, enter the date of the service charge in the Date field, and then enter the total amount in the Service Charge field.

6   Enter an expense category for the Service Charge amount.

Quicken remembers the category you use (such as Bank Charges) and inserts it in the Category field the next time you reconcile.

7   If your statement shows interest earned for your bank account and you haven't already entered it in your Quicken register, enter the date when the interest was earned in the Date field, and then enter the amount in the Interest Earned field.

8   Enter an income category for the Interest Earned amount.

Quicken remembers the category you use (such as Interest) and inserts it in the Category field the next time you reconcile.

9   When you've finished entering information in the Reconcile Startup window, click OK.

Quicken immediately adds the Service Charge and Interest Earned transactions to the account register and displays the Reconcile window. If you click Cancel instead of OK, the Service Charge and Interest Earned transactions remain in your register. You do not need to enter them again when you return to reconciling this account, unless you delete them from your register.

Marking cleared transactions

Your next step in balancing this account is to mark all *cleared* transactions. A cleared transaction is one that has been processed by the bank and is listed on your bank statement. The Reconcile window contains a list of all uncleared transactions you've entered in the register for the Quicken account you are reconciling.

1   Compare the transactions listed on your bank statement with those listed in the Reconcile window.

Look for each transaction in the Reconcile window that is also listed on your bank statement. Verify that the transaction amount matches the amount listed on the bank statement.

2 **If you find a transaction in the Reconcile window that matches a transaction on the bank statement, click the transaction to mark it as cleared.**

Quicken displays checks and other withdrawals first. Deposits are at the bottom of the Reconcile window.

Use the scroll bar to move up or down and view more transactions.

If the transaction appears on your bank statement, click the transaction to mark it as cleared. A checkmark appears in the left column of the Reconcile window. If you make a mistake, click the transaction again to unmark it.

If you want to see more information about an uncleared transaction listed here, double-click the transaction. Quicken opens the register and selects the transaction.

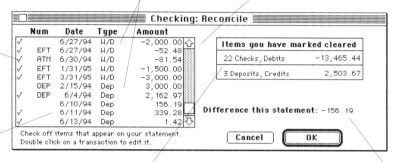

Quicken keeps a running record of the number of items and the total amounts you've marked as cleared.

As you check off cleared transactions, Quicken displays their total as the difference for this statement.

3 **If you find a transaction listed on your bank statement that is not shown in the list of uncleared transactions, enter it now in the check register.**

Or press ⌘ R

- Choose Register from the View menu to move to the register.

Or press ⌘ N

- Choose New Transaction from the Edit menu to move to a blank transaction at the end of the register.

- Enter information for the missing transaction.

- Click in the √ (cleared) field of the new transaction to mark it as cleared.

- Click Record to record the transaction in the register.

- Add any other missing transactions to the register now.

- Click back in the Reconcile window or choose Reconcile from the Activities menu to return to the list of items you are marking.

Quicken updates the Reconcile window to show the new transaction you just entered in the register.

4 If you find transactions that contain incorrect amounts or other errors, correct them now in the register.

- Double-click the transaction in the Reconcile window.

  Quicken opens the register and selects the transaction.

- Correct the error in the register.

- Click in the √ (cleared) field of the new transaction to mark it as cleared.

- Click Record to record the change.

- Click back in the Reconcile window or choose Reconcile from the Activities menu to return to the list of items you are marking.

To move from a selected transaction in the Reconcile window to the same transaction in the register, double-click the transaction. Quicken displays the register with the transaction selected.

For example, if your bank statement lists a transaction for 52.48, but you entered 54.28 into Quicken, you can correct the typo in the Quicken register. (Don't assume that different amounts between your Quicken records and the bank statement are your own data entry errors. Banks make mistakes too.)

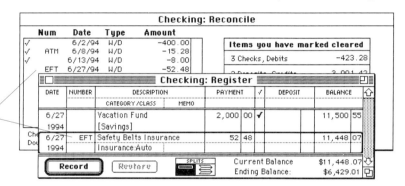

5 Continue to mark all cleared transactions, and then see "Completing reconciliation" on page 149 to finish balancing your account.

What's the difference between √ and ✓ in the √ (cleared) column?

If you return to the register while you are still reconciling your account with your bank statement, you'll see thin checkmarks in the √ field of all transactions you've just marked as cleared in the Reconcile window.

√ means that *you* have marked the transaction as cleared.

If a transaction has not been cleared at the bank, leave the √ (cleared) field blank until you receive your bank statement and begin to reconcile.

After you finish marking all transactions as cleared in the Reconcile window and click OK to show that your account is balanced, Quicken turns the thin checkmarks into bold checkmarks to signify that the "cleared" transactions are now "reconciled."

✓ means that *Quicken* has reconciled the transaction.

You can manually mark transactions as cleared or reconciled in the register at any time. You might also need to manually "unclear" or "unreconcile" some transactions that you cleared or reconciled incorrectly:

- Click in the √ (cleared) field to mark a transaction as cleared.

- Click in the √ (cleared) field again to delete the √.

- Option-click in the √ (cleared) field to mark a transaction as reconciled.

- Option-click in the √ (cleared) field again to delete the ✓.

Completing reconciliation

When you've finished checking off cleared transactions, look at the difference amount or amounts in the Reconcile window. Compare the amount or amounts in your Reconcile window with the three situations described on this page and the next page.

If the amount in the Difference This Statement field is zero *and* if Quicken does not display a field named Previous Difference, you've reconciled the current bank statement successfully. Click OK to complete reconciliation.

If there is a Previous Difference, it appears here above the Difference This Statement field. (This illustration does not show the Previous Difference field.)

If a Previous Difference field is displayed here, you have reconciled the current bank statement successfully, but you still need to resolve the difference. See "Letting Quicken adjust for differences" on page 151.

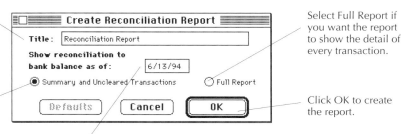

If the Difference amount is zero and if there is no Opening Balance Difference amount displayed above the Cleared Balance, you've balanced your account successfully.

Now you know that the balance in your Quicken check register is accurate as of your most recent bank statement. If you examine the check register after you click OK, you'll find a bold checkmark in the Cleared field next to each transaction. The transactions you marked as cleared (√) are now reconciled (✓).

When you successfully complete balancing your account, you may want to create a reconciliation report. (You can create a reconciliation report at any other time too.) Choose Business from the Reports menu, and then double-click Reconciliation. To see a sample report, see "Reconciliation" on page 317.

(Optional) Change the report title.

(Optional) Select Summary and Uncleared Transactions to see detail for every reconciled transaction in addition to summary information.

Select Full Report if you want the report to show the detail of every transaction.

Click OK to create the report.

(Optional) Change the date if you want the report to state your reconciled balance as of a different date than today. For example, you might want a reconciliation report that ends on the last day of your accounting period, even if your bank statements arrive mid-month.

Solving balancing problems

If your account doesn't balance, the difference is usually due to one or both of the following reasons: an incorrect number of payment or deposit items checked off as cleared, or incorrect dollar amounts on some items. If the Difference amount is not zero, your account doesn't balance for the current bank statement period.

The amount displayed in the Difference This Statement field is a running comparison of the total items marked cleared in Quicken and the total items shown on the bank statement. In this example, there's a -538.53 difference between the check register and the bank statement.

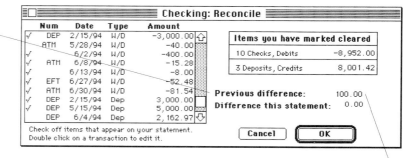

Checking: Reconcile

Num	Date	Type	Amount
√	6/2/94	W/D	-400.00
√ ATM	6/8/94	W/D	-15.28
√	6/13/94	W/D	-8.00
√ EFT	6/27/94	W/D	-52.48
√ ATM	6/30/94	W/D	-81.54
√ DEP	2/15/94	Dep	3,000.00
√ DEP	5/15/94	Dep	5,000.00
DEP	6/4/94	Dep	2,162.97
	6/13/94	Dep	1.42
DEP	6/18/94	Dep	2,162.97

Check off items that appear on your statement.
Double click on a transaction to edit it.

Items you have marked cleared

| 10 Checks, Debits | -8,952.00 |
| 2 Deposits, Credits | 8,000.00 |

Difference this statement: -538.53

[Cancel] [OK]

Problem   If the amount in this field is not zero, you have not balanced your account.

Solutions   Find the difference between your check register and the bank statement and correct it. See "Finding and correcting differences" on page 152.

OR   Click OK and let Quicken modify your account balance to agree with the bank's by recording an adjustment transaction. See "Resolving a nonzero difference" on page 151.

If the amount in the Difference This Statement field is zero, but there is a Previous Difference amount displayed above the Difference This Statement field, you have reconciled the current bank statement successfully, but you still need to resolve the *Previous Difference* amount. This amount is the difference between the total of the previously reconciled items in the register and the opening balance shown on the current bank statement.

If you changed the amount in the Previous Balance field when you entered information in the Reconcile Startup window, the difference shows up in the Reconcile window as the Previous Difference.

Checking: Reconcile

Num	Date	Type	Amount
√ DEP	2/15/94	W/D	-3,000.00
√ ATM	5/28/94	W/D	-40.00
√	6/2/94	W/D	-400.00
√ ATM	6/8/94	W/D	-15.28
√	6/13/94	W/D	-8.00
√ EFT	6/27/94	W/D	-52.48
√ ATM	6/30/94	W/D	-81.54
√ DEP	2/15/94	Dep	3,000.00
√ DEP	5/15/94	Dep	5,000.00
DEP	6/4/94	Dep	2,162.97

Check off items that appear on your statement.
Double click on a transaction to edit it.

Items you have marked cleared

| 10 Checks, Debits | -8,952.00 |
| 3 Deposits, Credits | 8,001.42 |

Previous difference: 100.00
Difference this statement: 0.00

[Cancel] [OK]

Problem   If there is a Previous Difference amount displayed, you need to resolve the difference.

Solution   You may have already tried to resolve this problem described in step 3 on page 144. Click OK, and then see "Resolving a previous difference" on page 151.

Letting Quicken adjust for differences

You might decide to ignore the difference between your check register and the bank statement. Ignoring the difference is appropriate if the amount is small and you feel it is not worth your time to track it down. If you want to resolve the difference yourself and balance to the penny, see "Finding and correcting differences" on page 152.

Quicken always asks you to confirm a change to a previously reconciled transaction. If you have already ruled out other possible errors, you may have inadvertently changed or deleted a previously reconciled transaction. Continue with reconciliation and have Quicken record an adjustment transaction when reconciliation is complete.

If you decide to ignore a difference, let Quicken enter an adjustment for the amount of the difference. That way you'll be starting with accurate totals the next time you reconcile your account.

Resolving a nonzero difference

If there is no Previous Difference amount to resolve, but the difference is not zero, Quicken tells you the amount of the discrepancy and asks if you want to resolve the difference.

Click Cancel if you want to return to the Reconcile window and track down the difference yourself.

Click Update Balance if you want Quicken to record an adjustment transaction in the register equal to the difference between your cleared items and the bank statement. You can delete the adjustment transaction later if you find the error that resulted in the difference.

> The total of the items you have marked is $84.60 more than the total of the items shown on your statement. You may have Quicken decrease your balance by this amount or click Cancel to go back to reconciling.
>
> [Cancel] [**Update Balance**]

Resolving a previous difference

If there is a Previous Difference amount to resolve, Quicken asks if you want to resolve the difference.

Click Cancel if you want to return to the Reconcile window and track down the difference yourself.

Click No to complete reconciliation without adjusting for the Opening Balance Difference. Do this if you want to resolve the discrepancy yourself.

Click Yes if you just want Quicken to enter an adjustment transaction. Do this if you do not want to resolve the discrepancy yourself.

> The total of the previously cleared items in your register does not match the previous statement balance.
>
> Would you like Quicken to create an adjustment to make your records agree with the statement?
>
> [Cancel] [No] [**Yes**]

Finding and correcting differences

You can find the differences between your Quicken account and the bank statement in a systematic way.

Finding a problem with the number of items

1 Count the number of debit items on your bank statement and compare that number with the number of "Checks, Debits" items you've marked in the Reconcile window.

2 Count the number of credit items on your bank statement and compare that number with the total number of "Deposits, Credits" items you've marked in the Reconcile window.

Check here to see the total number and dollar amount of items that you have checked off.

Debits include checks, transfers out of the account, ATM withdrawals, service charges and fees, and automatic payments.

Credits include direct deposits, transfers into the account, ATM deposits, and interest earned.

	Num	Date	Type	Amount
√		6/2/94	W/D	-400.00
√	ATM	6/8/94	W/D	-15.28
√		6/13/94	W/D	-8.00
√		6/27/94	W/D	-2,000.00
√	EFT	6/27/94	W/D	-52.48
√	ATM	6/30/94	W/D	-81.54
√	EFT	1/31/95	W/D	-1,500.00
√	EFT	3/31/95	W/D	-3,000.00
	DEP	2/15/94	Dep	3,000.00
	DEP	6/4/94	Dep	2,162.97

Checking: Reconcile

Items you have marked cleared

14 Checks, Debits   -10,816.75
0 Deposits, Credits   0.00

Difference this statement: -11.17

Check off items that appear on your statement.
Double click on a transaction to edit it.

Cancel   OK

If you know the problem is the number of debits, look only at payment transactions; if you know the problem is the number of credits, look only at deposit transactions. If the count does not agree, you may have a problem with the number of debits or credits marked as cleared.

The bank may summarize transactions that you've listed separately in your register.

For example, if you made several deposits on a single day, the bank might indicate the total sum of deposits for that day rather than listing each deposit separately.

Similarly, you may summarize transactions in your register, such as bank charges, that the bank itemizes. Some statements count the number of credits for you; others list interest earned and ATM deposits separately.

Some statements count the number of debits for you; others list service charges and ATM withdrawals separately.

3 Check to see if you:

- Missed recording an item in the check register
- Missed marking an item as cleared
- Mistakenly marked an item as cleared
- Entered any transactions twice
- Entered a deposit as a payment or a payment as a deposit
- Forgot to enter a check number. Scroll down in the list to the withdrawals (W/D) to see if you can find the check amount there instead of at the top of the list with all the other checks.

Finding a problem with the dollar amount of items

If there's no problem with the number of items marked as cleared, there may be a problem with the dollar amount of the items.

Check to see if you entered an amount incorrectly in the account register.

Make sure that you didn't transpose the amount of a transaction when you entered it (for example, you entered 34.56 instead of 43.65).

Compare the dollar amount of the Checks, Debits total in the Reconcile window with the dollar amount of debits shown on your bank statement. If the totals do not agree, you know you have a problem with the dollar amount of debits.

Compare the dollar amount of the Deposits, Credits total in the Reconcile window with the dollar amount of credits shown on your bank statement. If the totals do not agree, you know you have a problem with the dollar amount of credits.

If you know the problem is the dollar amount of debits, look only at payment transactions; if you know the problem is the dollar amount of credits, look only at deposit transactions.

Compare all amounts shown in the list of cleared transactions with the amounts shown on your statement. If you find an incorrect amount, return to the transaction in the account register (double-click the transaction) and correct the amount.

Check to see if you entered an amount incorrectly in the Reconcile Startup window.

Make sure you have entered the correct new balance from your bank statement into the New Balance field in the Reconcile Startup window. Your bank statement might call the ending balance amount the "current" or "ending" balance.

Check to see if the bank made a mistake by processing a transaction for a different amount than you wrote it for.

Adjust the balance by entering a transaction (or let Quicken make the adjustment for you as described in "Letting Quicken adjust for differences" on page 151). Then contact your bank. The bank will make an adjustment that will appear on your next statement.

Because this adjustment will appear as an already cleared item in the check register, your account will be off by the same amount at the end of the next reconciliation. Let Quicken make another adjustment when you finish reconciling the next statement.

Catching up if you skipped balancing your checkbook

In some circumstances, you need to enter transactions that have already cleared the bank, or mark transactions as previously cleared. This is different from checking off transactions as cleared while you are reconciling.

For example, if you have used Quicken for a number of months and have just decided that you want to reconcile. You may be starting to reconcile with your June bank statement after entering transactions in Quicken since January of the same year.

You can approach reconciliation in two ways: the recommended, best way and the second-best way.

The best way to catch up

Balance each month separately, starting with your earliest (January) statement and continue through your most recent (June) statement.

Follow the steps in "Starting reconciliation" on page 144, continue with the steps in "Marking cleared transactions" on page 146, and then in "Completing reconciliation" on page 149 for each month before starting to reconcile the statement for the next month.

The second-best way to catch up

You might not want to go back and reconcile your Quicken account against the bank statements for each of the previous months.

It's possible to balance all the unreconciled bank statements at the same time. Your records might not be as accurate as they would be if you reconciled each month separately. The second-best method follows.

1   **Choose Reconcile from the Activities menu.**

2   **Do not change the Previous Balance field in the Reconcile Startup window.**

3   **In the New Balance field of the Reconcile Startup window, enter the ending balance from your most recent bank statement and click OK.**

You would use the amount from the June bank statement in this example.

4 **In the Reconcile window, mark the transactions shown on all the bank statements for the period covered by your Quicken check register.**

See "Marking cleared transactions" on page 146.

5 **Finish reconciling.**

See "Completing reconciliation" on page 149.

If there is an amount other than zero in the Difference This Statement field, you or your bank may have made errors. If the difference is fairly small, you can have Quicken enter an adjustment transaction when it completes the reconciliation. Then your records will match the next time you reconcile your account. If the difference is large and you cannot account for it, you may want to ask your bank to determine which balance is accurate.

Adding earlier transactions to Quicken

If you've used Quicken to record and reconcile transactions, you may want to add earlier transactions to your Quicken bank account so you can create more comprehensive reports, graphs, and budgets. To keep the information in your account accurate, you need to follow the steps below.

In the following example, we assume that you started entering transactions in June. When you set up the Quicken bank account, you used the ending balance from your May statement as the opening balance for the Quicken account. You've already reconciled your June bank statement. Now you want to go back and add earlier transactions starting on January 1.

1 **Make note of the ending balance in your Quicken register before you begin to enter earlier transactions.**

2 **Change the date and amount of the Opening Balance transaction in the Quicken register to reflect the opening balance on the first date for which you are about to enter transactions.**

For best results, enter the beginning balance from the first bank statement you want to reconcile.

Suppose your opening balance transaction is currently dated June 1 and is in the amount of $450. Your January bank statement, which covers the period from December 14 to January 14, shows a beginning balance of $210. So, change the date of the Opening

Balance transaction in the check register to December 14 and the amount to $210.

3 Enter all the earlier transactions starting January 1 in your check register, just as you would enter any current transaction.

Don't worry about any transactions that occurred in the period between the beginning date of the January bank statement (December 14) and the first date for which you entered transactions (January 1). You'll take care of those transactions when you update the reconciled balance in step 5.

4 When you have finished entering transactions, the ending balance in the register should be the same as it was when you started.

If balance is not the same, you have made an error. You'll fix any errors in the next step.

5 Reconcile all the transactions that you entered for previous months (January to May).

Balance each month separately, starting with your earliest (January) statement. Follow the steps in "Starting reconciliation" on page 144, continue the steps in "Marking cleared transactions" on page 146, and then in "Completing reconciliation" on page 149 for each month before starting to reconcile the statement for the next month.

6 Now you can go on and reconcile for the current month (June).

The total of reconciled transactions in your register now includes all the transactions that appeared on your bank statements from January to June.

Saving time with memorized transactions

Every month you handle recurring transactions, such as utility bills and paycheck deposits. Quicken can memorize them for repeated use.

Using QuickFill to complete transactions

Quicken is preset to use QuickFill. If QuickFill isn't turned on, choose General from the Settings menu and click the Use QuickFill checkbox. (Turn off QuickFill by clearing this checkbox.)

Quicken automatically fills in transaction fields when you type a few characters, saving you time and keystrokes. We call this feature QuickFill. When you start typing in the following fields, Quicken fills in names from an appropriate list:

In this field	QuickFill recalls items from these lists
Payee field	Memorized transaction list Register window* (except portfolio and mutual fund accounts)
Category field	Category and transfer list Class list
Security field	Security list (portfolio and mutual fund accounts)
Goal field	Goal list (portfolio and mutual fund accounts)
Action field	Action list (portfolio and mutual fund accounts)
Type field	Type list (portfolio and mutual fund accounts)

For more information about using QuickFill in portfolio and mutual fund accounts, see "Entering investment transactions in the register" on page 251.

Recalling a recorded or memorized transaction

You can enter a new transaction quickly by recalling another transaction. When you recall a transaction, you let Quicken automatically fill in the fields of your new transaction with information from the transaction you recalled. The other transaction may be one that has already been recorded in the register* of the account you're working in or has been memorized for repeated use (see "Memorizing a transaction" on page 161 for information on memorized transactions).

Or press ⌘ N

1 In the register or the Write Checks window, choose New Transaction from the Edit menu to select a new transaction.

---

*   If you upgraded from a previous version of Quicken for Macintosh or transferred data from DOS Quicken, QuickFill can recall from the register only the transactions that you have entered into Quicken 4 for Macintosh.

2 Start typing a name in the Payee field.

As you type the first letters of the name, Quicken fills in matching payee names until the correct name appears in the Payee field.

DATE	NUMBER	DESCRIPTION		PAYMENT	✓	DEPOSIT		BALANCE	
		CATEGORY/CLASS	MEMO						
1/20 1994		Valley Gas & Electric						1,124	32

Quicken scans for a matching payee name, first in the memorized transaction list and then in the register. If more than one memorized or recorded transaction begins with the characters you typed, Quicken enters the first name.

3 When Quicken displays the payee you want, you can:

- Click in another field of the transaction or press Tab to recall the entire memorized or recorded transaction (except for the date and check number) for that payee name

  OR

- Control-click in another field of the transaction or press Control-Tab to recall just the payee name.

4 (Optional) Enter any changes you want to make to the transaction.

You can change any of the information that Quicken filled in automatically.

5 Click Record.

Filling in category and class information

You can use QuickFill to fill in category, class, and account names when you create a new transaction or edit an existing transaction.

1 Click the Category field in a new transaction.

Or if you're editing an existing transaction, select all of the text in the Category field.

2 Start typing a category name.

Quicken fills in names from the category and transfer list that match the characters you type. You can start typing a category name or a transfer account name.

3 When Quicken displays the category you want, you can:

- Press Tab to accept that name

  OR

- Type a colon (:) to begin entering a subcategory for that category.

DATE	NUMBER	DESCRIPTION		PAYMENT	√	DEPOSIT	BALANCE
		CATEGORY /CLASS	MEMO				
1/20		Valley Gas & Electric					1, 124 32
1994		Utilities:Gas & Electric					

Type the letters "ut" to display the category name "Utilities."

To enter a subcategory, type a colon as soon as you see the category you want.

Type the letter "g" after the colon to display the subcategory name "Gas & Electric."

4 Start typing a subcategory name until Quicken fills in the correct name.

5 To enter class information, type a slash character (/) and the first letter of the class name.

Quicken displays the class name after the slash.

6 Type enough letters to display the correct class name.

If you want a subclass, type a colon (:) and start typing the subclass name until Quicken fills in the correct name.

To enter categories or classes that are not in a list (that is, you are entering them into Quicken for the first time), type the new name in the Category field. When you press Tab, Quicken asks if you want to set up the new name in the list or select from the list. Click the Set Up button and set up the category as described in "Setting up categories and subcategories" on page 47.

Memorizing a transaction

When you memorize a transaction, Quicken saves a copy of the transaction in a separate list that you can use with any account (except portfolio and mutual fund accounts, in which you cannot memorize transactions nor recall memorized transactions). Quicken memorizes any split or address information you've entered, but it does not save the date or check number.

1   Select the transaction you want to memorize in the register or scroll to it in the Write Checks window.

Or press ⌘ N

Or if the transaction does not yet exist, choose New Transaction from the Edit menu to select a new transaction in the register or the Write Checks window and enter the new transaction information.

If the amount of a recurring payment transaction varies each time, you can memorize the transaction with no amount, and then enter an amount when you recall the transaction.

Your category assignment determines whether the memorized transaction is a payment or a deposit: an expense category defines a payment, while an income category defines a deposit.

DATE	NUMBER	DESCRIPTION		PAYMENT	√	DEPOSIT		BALANCE	
		CATEGORY/CLASS MEMO							
1/20		County Water Company		35	00			2,902	93
1994		Utilities:Water Acct. #987-10...							
1/22		Steve's paycheck				2,239	43	5,142	36
1994		*split*							
1/25		SDC Employees' CU		289	62			4,852	74
1994		*split* Loan #123-45...							
2/1		Lunch money for the kids							
1994		Dining							

Checking: Register

[**Record**] [**Restore**]   SPLITS   Current Balance: $2,937.93
                                            Ending Balance: $4,852.74

Or press ⌘ M

2   Choose Memorize from the Edit menu.

Quicken memorizes the information in the transaction. If a transaction with the same payee is already in the memorized list, Quicken asks if you want to replace it with the new transaction or add the new transaction.

3   If you entered a new transaction in step 1, click Record if you want to record it or click Restore if you want to delete it.

If you want to memorize a loan payment transaction, you should set up the loan to be tracked by Quicken instead. Quicken's loan feature creates a special memorized loan payment that calculates the interest and principal amounts automatically, and keeps track of the loan balance as well. See Chapter 17, *Tracking loans,* beginning on page 279.

Recalling a memorized transaction manually

If you choose to work with QuickFill turned off, you can still "manually" recall a memorized transaction to enter it in the register or the Write Checks window of any Quicken account.

1 If the memorized transaction you want to recall is a payment or deposit, open the register of the account you want to use. If the memorized transaction is a check with an address, open the Write Checks window of the account.

Or press ⌘ T

2 Choose Memorized Transactions from the View menu.

Quicken lists memorized transactions in alphabetical order by payee.

Select the transaction you want and click Use.

Or double-click the transaction to recall it.

Payee/Description	Amount	Memo	Type
40 AmeriBank	-40.00	$40 ATM withdrawal	Pmt
County Water Company	0.00		EPmt
Great Northern Bank	-2,177.35	Loan #CC52090	Chk
Lunch money for the kids	0.00		Pmt
SDC Employees' CU	-289.62	Loan #123-45-6789-01	Chk
Steve's paycheck	2,425.00		Dep
Valley Gas & Electric	0.00	SRN50-90	Chk

Use   Edit   Delete

If you recall a "Chk" in the register instead of the Write Checks window, Quicken enters the transaction as a payment and not a printable check.

3 Select the memorized transaction you want and click Use.

To select more than one transaction, shift-click the ones you want. (To unselect a selected transaction, shift-click it.)

4 (Optional) Review the transaction and make any changes or additions you want.

5 Click Record to record the transaction as usual.

If you want to print the list of memorized transactions, choose Print Memorized Transactions from the File menu.

Changing or deleting a memorized transaction

You can change the information in a memorized transaction, including total amount, payee, transaction type, address, category, amounts assigned to splits, cleared status, and so on.

You can also delete a memorized transaction from the list if you no longer want to recall it.

Although memorized loan payments appear in the memorized transaction list, you can change or delete these payments from the loan list only. See "Editing a loan" on page 293 and "Deleting a loan" on page 294.

Changing a memorized transaction

Or press ⌘ T

1   Choose Memorized Transactions from the View menu.

Or press ⌘ E

2   Select the transaction you want to change and click Edit.

If you want Quicken to insert the memorized transaction in the Write Checks window, be sure to click the Check button in the lower right corner of the window.

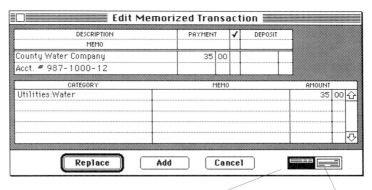

Button for a handwritten payment or deposit   Check button

If you click the Check button, the memorized transaction changes into a check that you can print in Quicken.

3   Edit any of the transaction information in the Edit Memorized Transaction window.

This is the Edit Memorized Transaction window for a printable check.

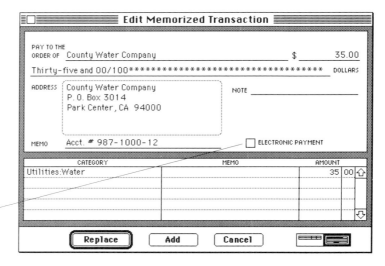

This checkbox appears only if you have enabled electronic payments. For more information on electronic payments, see Chapter 12, *Paying bills electronically,* beginning on page 171.

4 Either click Add to create a new memorized transaction without removing the original, or click Replace to remove the original memorized transaction and replace it with the new version.

Deleting a memorized transaction

Or press ⌘ T

1 Choose Memorized Transactions from the View menu.

Or press ⌘ D

2 Select the transaction you want to delete and click Delete.

3 Click Yes to confirm that you want to delete the transaction permanently.

Using transaction groups

Transaction groups are groups of recurring transactions that you pay or add to your account at the same time.

A transaction group may consist of a single transaction or many transactions. For example, one transaction group may have a single transaction in it—the paycheck you receive every two weeks. Another transaction group may include a mortgage payment, phone bill, electric bill, and car payment because these payments are all due near the beginning of each month.

Quicken lets you group these transactions and schedule a date for when you want them entered. You can have Quicken enter the group into the register automatically or simply remind you that the date has arrived.

When you tell Quicken to enter the group, Quicken enters all of the transactions into the register for you. This automatic group entry saves you time and keystrokes, yet you retain complete control. Once Quicken has entered the transactions, you can edit them, changing information such as amounts, or deleting any that you don't need to pay.

To be included in a transaction group, a transaction must already be memorized. (See "Memorizing a transaction" on page 161.)

Setting up a transaction group

1   **Choose Transaction Groups from the View menu.**

Quicken lists the transaction groups in alphabetical order and shows you their due dates if you've scheduled them.

Click New to create a transaction group.

Or press ⌘ N

2   **Click New.**

Quicken displays the Set Up Groups window.

3 Enter a name for the transaction group and choose a destination account.

Enter a descriptive name up to 20 characters long.

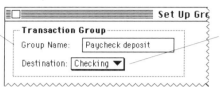

Quicken will recall the group of transactions into the register of the account that you choose from this list. (But when you recall the group, Quicken gives you the opportunity to choose a different account.)

4 (Optional) Specify reminder settings if you want to recall the group on a scheduled date or on a regular basis.

You can choose a frequency from the popup menu to indicate how often you want Quicken to schedule the group. If the group doesn't have a regular frequency, choose None.

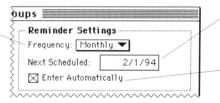

If you choose a frequency, enter the date of the next time you want to recall the group.

If you enter a next scheduled date, select this checkbox to have Quicken enter the transactions into the register automatically on that date.

For example, if today is 1/16/94 and you want to recall the group on the first of every month, choose a frequency of Monthly and enter a next scheduled date of 2/1/94. As another example, suppose you want Quicken to automatically enter a transaction group just once on 6/30/94. Choose a frequency of None, enter a next scheduled date of 6/30/94, and select the Enter Automatically checkbox.

After the next scheduled date, Quicken schedules the group according to the frequency you chose.

If you selected the Enter Automatically checkbox, see "How Quicken treats an automatically entered transaction group" on page 167. If you want to be reminded when a transaction group is due, see "Using Billminder" on page 169.

5 Select the memorized transactions you want to include in the group.

Select a transaction to include in the group by clicking it to mark it. (To unmark a transaction, click it again.)

Tip: To change the type of a memorized transaction (or edit it in any other way), double-click the transaction in this list.

If you want to create printable checks by recalling a transaction group, be sure that Chk appears in this column for those memorized transactions. (Quicken reads Chk as "printable check.")

6   **Click Create to create the group and add it to the transaction group list.**

Recalling a transaction group

1   **Choose Transaction Groups from the View menu.**

2   **Select the transaction group you want and click OK.**

Quicken will enter the transactions in the register of this account unless you choose a different account from the popup menu.

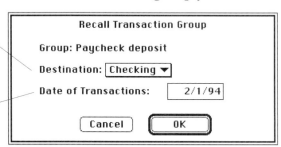

Recall Transaction Group

Group: Paycheck deposit

Destination: ⌷Checking ▼⌷

Date of Transactions: ⌷ 2/1/94 ⌷

⌷ Cancel ⌷   ⌷ OK ⌷

The scheduled due date, if there is one, is the date Quicken uses when it enters the transactions in the destination account.

3   **Verify that the destination account is correct and click OK to enter the group.**

Quicken enters all the transactions in the register of the account you selected or into the Write Checks window if the transactions are checks to be printed.

You may need to add the amount (if you memorized the transaction without an amount) or change the amount (if you memorized the transaction with an amount).

If the transactions are checks, you can print them in the same way you would print any Quicken check.

How Quicken treats an automatically entered transaction group

When you start Quicken, it checks the transaction group list for any group that needs to be automatically entered since the last time you used Quicken. It enters the group in the destination account (no "on the fly" changes for automatically entered groups), and then increases the scheduled date by one frequency period. If the new scheduled date is earlier than today's date, Quicken repeats the automatic entry and date increase until the scheduled date is after today's date.

Changing or deleting a transaction group

Once you have set up a transaction group, you can add transactions to it, change the transaction group information, or delete the group at any time.

Changing a transaction group

1 **Choose Transaction Groups from the View menu.**

Or press ⌘ E

2 **Select the group you want to change and click Edit.**

3 **Make any changes you want to the information in the Edit Group window.**

You can skip one scheduled entry of a group by increasing the Next Scheduled date by one frequency period.

See "Setting up a transaction group" on page 165 for information about the fields in the window.

4 **Click Change.**

Deleting a transaction group

1 **Choose Transaction Groups from the View menu.**

Or press ⌘ D

2 **Select the group you want to delete and click Delete.**

Caution:
When you delete a transaction group, you remove it permanently from your Quicken file. The memorized transactions included in the group remain in the memorized transaction list. However, if you delete a memorized transaction from the memorized transaction list, Quicken automatically removes it from the transaction group.

3 **Click Yes to confirm that you want to delete the group permanently.**

Using Billminder

Quicken's Billminder feature can remind you when you have checks to print, electronic payments to transmit to CheckFree, and transaction groups to enter.

How Billminder works

- Billminder can remind you of upcoming bills when you turn on your computer or start Quicken.

- The next time you turn on your computer or start Quicken, if you have any checks to print, electronic payments to transmit, or scheduled transaction groups that are due, you'll see the Billminder window.

Billminder displays messages like this one when you start your computer.

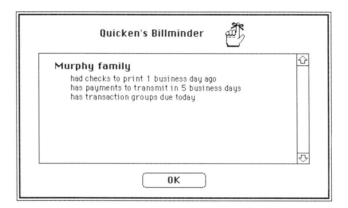

When you start Quicken, Billminder displays messages like this one.

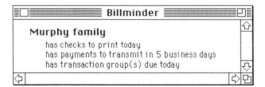

- If the current file has scheduled transaction groups that are due, Quicken opens the transaction group list and selects those groups.

  Double-click on any of the groups to recall all of them. Or shift-click a group to clear it.

- Each time you open a file, Quicken gives you an opportunity to recall any scheduled groups that are due or overdue in that file. If you want to skip one scheduled entry of a group, edit the transaction group. See "Changing a transaction group" on page 168.

Changing Billminder settings

1 Choose Billminder from the Settings menu.

Enter a number of business days between 0-30.

```
                    Billminder Settings

   Day(s) in advance to remind you of postdated checks
   and scheduled transaction groups (0-30):            [ 7 ]

   ┌─Quicken will remind you of your bills ─────────────────┐
   │  ☒ When you turn on your computer                      │
   │  ☒ When you start Quicken                              │
   └────────────────────────────────────────────────────────┘

                      [ Cancel ]   [  OK  ]
```

To turn off Billminder, clear both of these checkboxes.

2 Enter the number of business days in advance that you want Quicken to remind you of upcoming bills.

If you use Quicken	Set business days in advance to
Daily (except weekends)	0 days
At least every other day	1 day
At least once every three days	2 days
At least weekly	5 days
At least once every two weeks	10 days
At least once a month	30 days

3 Select the checkbox(es) indicating when you would like Billminder to remind you of upcoming bills.

Or turn off Billminder by clearing both checkboxes.

4 Click OK to save the new settings.

Once Billminder is turned on, it automatically checks all your Quicken files for upcoming bills each time you start your computer. If Billminder finds transaction groups due, checks to print, or payments to transmit, it lists them and shows you the location of the files that contain them.

Paying bills electronically

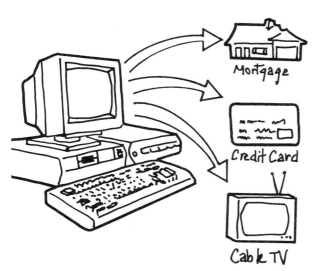

CheckFree lets you pay bills electronically, using your personal computer and a modem. This service is offered by the CheckFree Corporation of Columbus, Ohio, the nation's leading provider of electronic payment services.

You enter your bills directly into Quicken and then tell Quicken to send the information to CheckFree.

About CheckFree

The CheckFree payment service* provides convenience and security. It's convenient because you don't need stamps or envelopes and you don't have to print and sign checks. It's secure because you have a CheckFree "Personal Security Code" and you control access to this number. You enter all data offline and your financial records reside only in your computer.

Many small businesses use CheckFree; however, it is not specifically designed for business use. (For example, it can't pass invoice numbers through to merchants.) CheckFree works for any household with a computer, modem, and Quicken. If you are undecided about the benefits of paying bills through CheckFree, give it a try. The first month is free. See the CheckFree brochure, which includes a sign-up form, included in your Quicken package. (If you need an additional sign-up form, contact Intuit Customer Service at the phone number listed on page 408.)

How CheckFree works

When you use Quicken to pay bills through CheckFree, you start a series of events.

1 **You enter an "electronic payment" transaction in Quicken, much as you enter transactions in the register or in the Write Checks window.**

Your transaction includes the payment date.

2 **Using your modem and the communications options in Quicken, you transmit your payment instructions to CheckFree before the payment date.**

See page 181 for payment scheduling guidelines.

3 **Quicken dials the CheckFree Processing Center and transmits your instructions.**

Quicken tells you that the transmission was successful and updates your check register as soon as transmission is complete. The CheckFree Processing Center returns a confirmation number for each transaction, which Quicken stores in the register.

---

* You can use CheckFree for payments in the United States regardless of where you transmit from. The bank account used for CheckFree must also be in the United States. CheckFree is an independently owned company.

4   The CheckFree Processing Center makes the payment.

Some merchants are set up to receive electronic payments, and others receive a printed check. See the table on page 183 for details.

5   You receive verification of the payment both in your bank statement and in the statement you receive from the merchant (if the merchant ordinarily sends statements).

If you've never used CheckFree before

Check off these preliminary steps before you follow the rest of the instructions in this chapter.

1   Set up service with CheckFree.

You can't send electronic payments until CheckFree has processed your signed CheckFree sign-up form and voided check. Service begins immediately after CheckFree processes your sign-up form and enters you as a subscriber to the service for a monthly fee. As of the date of this manual, the fee is $9.95, plus added charges for more than 20 monthly transactions (see the information booklet). The first month of service is free.

2   Get the CheckFree confirmation package and have it handy.

CheckFree sends you a package to confirm that you are set up for service. The confirmation package also contains information that you will need when you set up Quicken for electronic payments, as well as additional information about CheckFree services and rates.

3   Equip your computer with a Hayes-compatible modem.

You can use any Hayes-compatible modem that works at 300, 1200, 2400, or 9600 baud*. (A baud is a unit of speed.) Note which port you (or your dealer) attached your modem to. Consult your computer dealer or the modem user manual for help with these tasks.

If you need a modem, CheckFree sells one for $99.00, plus $4.00 shipping. To order a modem, call CheckFree at 800-882-5280.

---

*   If you will be using a modem at 9600 baud, you must contact CheckFree Corporation to obtain a special local access telephone number. Call CheckFree's Customer Service Department (see the phone number on page 408) after you have received your confirmation package

If you're already using CheckFree to pay bills

If you've been using CheckFree with a previous version of Quicken for Macintosh, continue using Quicken and CheckFree as always. All the information and data you have entered are retained as you begin using Quicken 4 for Macintosh.

If you've been using CheckFree with either Quicken for DOS or Quicken for Windows, you can continue using Quicken and Check-Free *except* for setting up fixed payments and receiving electronic mail from CheckFree. However, you should contact CheckFree Corporation before you switch to Quicken for Macintosh to ensure a smooth transition. (See page 408 for the phone number to Check-Free's Customer Service Department.)

If you've been using CheckFree with Quicken for DOS, Quicken for Windows, or any other CheckFree-capable software, follow these important preliminary steps:

1   **Back up your CheckFree data.**

2   **Use your current CheckFree-capable software to print the list of merchants you have set up on CheckFree. Then delete every one of the merchants. Be sure to transmit these deletions to the CheckFree Processing Center.**

    If you do not delete these merchants, the CheckFree Processing Center may make errors in processing your payments. Note that any pending payments scheduled for the next few business days are already in process at CheckFree and will *not* be stopped by your deletions. Any payments dated in the future are deleted, so you must reschedule them with Quicken.

3   **If necessary, update your Quicken register by importing the historical data from your CheckFree register. You can use Quicken to import transactions (but not merchant names) from CheckFree software.**

    Instructions for importing historical data from CheckFree into Quicken are in Help. (Press ⌘ ? and then click Topics. Click "Check-Free," and then click "Importing data from a CheckFree 3.0 file.")

    Quicken 4 for Macintosh imports only CheckFree files that are created with version 3.0 of the CheckFree software.

    After you use Quicken even once to make payments, CheckFree Corporation will no longer permit you to process payments using another CheckFree-capable product. Other CheckFree-capable products and Quicken are not designed to be used alternately or concurrently. You'll learn how to record the monthly CheckFree service charge on page 175.

4   **Get the confirmation letter that you received from the CheckFree Corporation when you subscribed to the service.**

The confirmation letter contains information you used to set up the CheckFree software; you need that information now to set up Quicken for electronic payments. If you can't find the confirmation letter, copy this information from the CheckFree-capable software setup screens to the appropriate Quicken electronic payment setup screens.

Handling the CheckFree service charge

You pay a monthly service charge to use CheckFree, which the CheckFree Corporation automatically charges to your bank account. You will see this charge on your bank statement.

Do not use electronic payments to pay CheckFree Corporation directly for the service charge.

To keep your Quicken register up to date for this charge, add the CheckFree charge to the Service Charge field in the Reconcile Startup window. (See "Starting reconciliation" on page 144.)

Alternately, set up the fee as a memorized transaction and add it to a monthly transaction group. (See "Using transaction groups" on page 165.) Recall the transaction group each month. Then you can adjust the amount if necessary when you reconcile your check register against your bank statement.

Setting up your modem to transmit electronic payments

With Quicken, you can send electronic payment instructions directly to CheckFree. When you install Quicken, the electronic payment option is not turned on, but you can set up your modem and turn on electronic payment capability for your file at any time.

If you already use your modem to download electronic statements for IntelliCharge, skip this procedure. You can use your modem with no additional setup to transmit electronic payments.

1 Choose Modem from the Settings menu.

Click the icon for the correct port.

Choose the correct speed for your modem.

Click the Tone Dialing button if you have a touch-tone (pushbutton) phone. Click the Pulse Dialing button if you have a rotary dial phone.

Enter the telephone number CheckFree gives you. Do not include the area code if you are within that area.

Modem Settings	OK
	Cancel

Modem Port:

Modem Speed: 2400 baud ▼

⦿ Tone dialing ◯ Pulse dialing

Local access telephone number: 555-1234

Initialization String: (optional)

You can customize Quicken's modem settings to handle special requirements of your modem. To find out what codes you need, look in the manual that came with your modem for the correct configuration codes to enter in the Initialization String field.

2 Select the modem port, modem speed (baud rate), and dialing type you want to use.

3 Enter the telephone number you received from CheckFree in your confirmation package.

Quicken uses your modem to dial this number exactly as you enter it here. Include any special sequence of digits or characters required (for example, *70 to turn off call waiting before you dial the number). You can also include a comma to indicate a pause, or multiple commas if you need a longer pause between digits.

4 (Optional) Skip the Initialization String field unless you need to customize your modem initialization.

Your modem user's guide lists the codes that your modem needs. (Most modem commands must begin with the prefix AT.)

5 Click OK.

Now you can set up a bank account for electronic payments.

Setting up an account for electronic payments

After you have set up your modem, you can set up electronic payments for the bank account you specified when you filled out the CheckFree sign-up form.

CheckFree allows you to use one bank account with one CheckFree account. You can have as many as five CheckFree bank accounts in a single Quicken file. If you need to use more than one bank account with CheckFree, contact CheckFree Customer Service at the phone number listed on page 408.

1   Choose Enable Electronic Payments from the Settings menu.

Select the bank account you want to set up for electronic payments.

Select this checkbox.

Enter the phone number (including the area code) at which CheckFree Customer Service can contact you in case of a problem. You don't have to type punctuation characters such as hyphens or parentheses.

Enter the CheckFree Account Number that you provided in your sign-up form. (In most cases, this number is your Social Security number.)

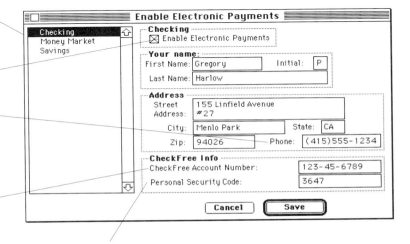

Enter the Personal Security Code listed in your confirmation package.

2   Select the bank account that you want to set up for electronic payments and then select the Enable Electronic Payments checkbox.

3   Enter your name, address, and CheckFree information.

4   Click Save to save your changes.

Quicken marks the account name in the list with a lightning bolt to show that you've enabled electronic payments.

If you decide later you will no longer make electronic payments, select the account from the list and clear the Enable Electronic Payments checkbox. Then notify CheckFree Corporation in writing that you are canceling service.

5   Close the Enable Electronic Payments window.

You are ready to set up merchants by adding them to the merchant list. See "Setting up merchants" on page 178.

Setting up merchants

For Quicken to record an electronic payment, you must first add the merchant to the merchant list. (A "merchant" can be any business, organization, or individual to whom you make payments.)

You have to add a specific merchant to the merchant list only once; all accounts in a Quicken file share that same list. You can add merchants before you begin writing electronic payments or as you write payments.

1   Choose Merchants from the View menu.

Or press ⌘ N

2   Click New.

Enter the name of the merchant you want to pay. If you have two customer accounts with the same merchant, you may want to set up that merchant twice: once for each account number. Merchant uniqueness is determined by merchant name *and* account number.

You can enter an optional merchant description to distinguish two merchant entries with identical names on the list. This information is not passed along to CheckFree and is for your use only.

Enter the merchant's address, phone number, and account number accurately. CheckFree uses this information to ensure that your payment is routed to the correct merchant. (In some cases, CheckFree may need the address to mail your payment to the merchant.)

```
╔════════════════ Set Up Merchants ════════════════╗
  Merchant:              County Water Company
  Description:
  Street Address:        P. O. Box 52090

  City:                  Menlo Park
  State:                 CA              Zip:   94026
  Payee's Phone Number:  (415)555-7890
  Account Number:        RA300XP

                         ( Cancel )   (( Create ))
╚═══════════════════════════════════════════════════╝
```

Enter the phone number you would call if you had a billing question, beginning with the area code. CheckFree must have the correct phone number to route your payments correctly.

Enter the number the merchant uses to identify you (account number, policy number, or loan number). If you don't know the number, enter your last name. The merchant needs the account number to credit your account for the payment.

3   Enter information in the Set Up Merchants window.

4   Click Create to record the information.

You can continue to set up merchants or go on to entering payments.

5   (Optional) To print the list of merchants you have set up, choose Print Merchants from the File menu.

Entering electronic payments

Entering electronic payments in the register or Write Checks window is very similar to entering any other kind of payment. See "Entering electronic payments in Write Checks" on this page or "Entering electronic payments in the register" on page 180.

Entering electronic payments in Write Checks

After you have set up a merchant, each time you want to send a payment to that merchant, you enter the payment in your Quicken account. (If you prefer to enter electronic payments in the register instead of in the Write Checks window, see "Entering electronic payments in the register" on page 180.)

1 Choose Open Account from the File menu, and then choose the CheckFree bank account.

Or press ⌘ J

2 Choose Write Checks from the Activities menu.

3 Select the Electronic Payment checkbox to display the screen in electronic payment format.

Quicken automatically postdates any electronic payment by five business days from today. You can change the date to postdate this check even further. See "Scheduling electronic payments" on page 181.

Enter a merchant name or choose it from the merchant list.

When you have electronic payment set up for an account and select the Electronic Payment checkbox, Quicken clearly labels the window.

Quicken does not transmit the contents of the Memo field to CheckFree. The information in the memo field is for your records.

You can clear the Electronic Payment checkbox if you want to write and print a paper check next.

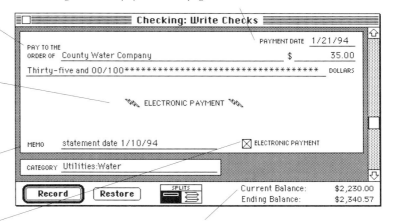

The Current Balance does not include postdated transactions; the Ending Balance does. (All electronic payments must be postdated by at least five business days.)

4 In the Date field, enter the payment date.

Quicken automatically postdates any electronic payment by five business days from today. You can change the date to postdate this check even further. See "Scheduling electronic payments" on page 181.

5 **In the Pay to the Order Of field, enter the merchant name.**

If you type the name of a merchant who is not in the merchant list, Quicken lets you select from the list or set up a new merchant.

6 **Fill in the $ Amount, Memo, and Category fields as usual.**

7 **Click Record to record the payment.**

Quicken records the payment in the check register with SEND in the Number field. Quicken does not transmit the payment until you tell it to. (See "Transmitting electronic payments" on page 183.)

Entering electronic payments in the register

You can enter electronic payments in the register instead of in the Write Checks window. Open the register and enter the transaction using the information in steps 4 through 6 of the previous procedure. Type S (for SEND) in the Number field to indicate to Quicken that this is an untransmitted electronic payment. Record the payment as usual.

A lightning bolt marks a transmitted electronic payment.

As soon as you type an S, Quicken fills in the rest of the Number field. SEND means the transaction *will be* transmitted.

		Checking: Register						
DATE	NUMBER	DESCRIPTION		PAYMENT	√	DEPOSIT	BALANCE	⬆
		CATEGORY/CLASS	MEMO					
12/17 1993	⚡	Primerica Bank [Quicken Visa]		183 34			468 07	
12/28 1993	SEND	County Water Company Utilities:Water		100 00			368 07	

Duplicate payments

CheckFree will not process a payment that appears to be a duplicate of a previous payment (a payment that has the same merchant, amount, and payment date). Although you will receive a confirmation number for the duplicate payment, only the previous payment will be processed. If you want to send a duplicate payment, change the amount or payment date slightly.

Scheduling electronic payments

Using CheckFree does not mean you can pay your bills at the last moment. Quicken and CheckFree require lead time between the date you transmit your payment instructions and the date your payment is due.

The first time you make a payment to each merchant, use the following table to determine how to schedule the payment.

Quicken and CheckFree require that you transmit the payment at least five business days before the payment date.

In addition to the five business days between the transmission date and the payment date, Intuit advises you to schedule the payment date to each *new merchant* five business days in advance of the due date. The additional five days allow you to see how promptly the merchant was able to process the payment.

Date	Definition	Calculation
Transmission date	Date you send payment instructions from Quicken to CheckFree	Five business days before the payment date, ten business days before the due date
Payment date	Date that you've entered in the Date field in Quicken; it's the date the merchant receives payment from CheckFree	Five business days before the due date
Due date	Due date on the statement from the merchant	

For example, suppose you have a bill due on November 16, 1993. *If this is the first electronic payment to the merchant*, you transmit the payment on November 2, ten business days before the due date.

November 1993

The transmission date is November 2, five business days before the payment date.

The merchant receives payment from CheckFree on the payment date, November 9, five business days before the due date.

The due date of the bill is November 16.

1	②	3	4	5	6	7
8	⑨	10	11	12	13	14
15	⑯	17	18	19	20	21
22	23	24	25	26	27	28
29	30					

Shaded areas on this calendar are nonbusiness days.

If a payment is due on or after a holiday such as Thanksgiving, be sure you still allow a minimum of five business days between the transmission date and the payment date.

To decide how to schedule your future payments, examine the next statement from the merchant to see how promptly the merchant was able to process the payment. If you need to adjust the schedule for your next payment, see the guidelines on page 182. The latest possible date you can transmit a payment from Quicken to Check-Free is five business days before the bill is due.

Guidelines to avoid late payments

Enter the correct telephone number, account number, and address for the merchant when you set up a merchant in Quicken.

After you have made several payments to a merchant, use the following table to determine when to transmit the payment to CheckFree.

After you have made several payments to the merchant and you determine how quickly the merchant can process a CheckFree payment, you may want to decrease the length of time between the payment date and the due date. You might even treat the payment date and the due date as the same date if you know that a particular merchant always processes the payment from CheckFree immediately.

You cannot decrease the length of time required between the transmission date and the payment date (five business days).

Date	Definition	Calculation
Transmission date	Date you send payment instructions to Check-Free	Five business days before the payment date (can be no less than five business days, but may be more)
Payment date	Date that you've entered in the Date field in Quicken; it's the date the merchant receives payment from CheckFree	Five business days before the due date (if the merchant always processes the payment immediately, the payment date may be the same day as due date)
Due date	Due date on the statement from the merchant	

Memorizing and recalling electronic payments

You memorize a recurring electronic payment just as you memorize any other transaction. For example, you may want to memorize a payment to a particular merchant with category, memo, and split information.

If you memorize a transaction in the check register, Quicken memorizes it as an electronic payment if the Number field contains either SEND or the lightning bolt symbol.

If you recall a memorized electronic payment in the check register or recall it in the Write Checks window and review it later in the check register, you'll see SEND in the Number field.

When you recall a memorized electronic payment, Quicken postdates it five business days. Similarly, when you recall a transaction group containing electronic payments, Quicken postdates the electronic payments five business days. It recalls any regular transaction in the group with the current or specified date.

For more information on memorizing transactions, recalling memorized transactions, and transaction groups, see Chapter 11, *Saving time with memorized transactions,* beginning on page 157.

Transmitting electronic payments

The transactions you transmit to CheckFree can include payments, changes to the merchant list (merchants that are edited, added, or deleted), stop payment orders, and inquiries or messages to the CheckFree Processing Center.

You should view a summary of payment and payment-related transactions before you transmit them. Then transmit payments to CheckFree at least five business days before bills are due.

The way the CheckFree Processing Center makes the payment depends on the merchant you're paying.

Payment method	Description
Electronic-to-check	CheckFree mails a check on your behalf to the merchant and then receives funds electronically from your bank on the payment date you specified. Your bank statement will list the merchant name, payment amount, and date for this type of transaction, instead of attaching a canceled check as a receipt.
Laser draft	CheckFree mails a check drawn on your bank account to the merchant. The check contains information such as your account number and address. If your checks are returned with your bank statement, this laser-printed check from CheckFree will be returned like any other paper check.
Direct electronic transfer of funds	If the merchant is set up to receive electronic payments via one of CheckFree's payment networks, CheckFree initiates an electronic payment directly from your bank account to the merchant's bank account. Your bank statement will list the merchant name, payment amount, and date for this type of transaction, instead of attaching a canceled check as a receipt.

Previewing and transmitting payments

1 **Open the bank account set up for CheckFree.**

2 **Choose Transmit from the Activities menu, and then choose Payments.**

Quicken marks each payment to be transmitted. Click to unmark any payment you don't want to send now. (When you're ready to send that payment, click to mark it.)

These are updates you have made to the merchant list since the last time you transmitted payments to CheckFree. Whenever you add, delete, or edit a merchant, the action appears in this list. CheckFree uses all these changes you make in Quicken to update your CheckFree records.

You cannot modify payments and merchant list updates from here. Click Cancel if you need to make such changes.

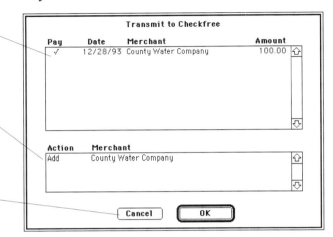

3 **Unmark any payment that you do not want to send now.**

4 **If the transactions are correct, click OK.**

Quicken initializes the modem and dials the CheckFree Processing Center. As it transmits, Quicken displays messages indicating progress. If you see an error message, try the procedure again. See "Solving CheckFree problems" on page 190.

> Intuit recommends that you back up your Quicken data file after you transmit payments or updates to CheckFree. Making a backup copy of your data takes only seconds to do and protects you against accidental loss of data. See "Backing up your Quicken data file" on page 63.

Unposted payments

You should allow at least 10 business days from the payment date for a merchant to post your payment. If a merchant does not post your payment within this period, you should:

- Call the merchant directly. In most cases, the payment will be posted by the time you call and any questions can be cleared up easily. If this is not the case, follow the next step.

• Contact CheckFree Customer Service (see page 408 for the phone number). Provide a merchant contact name and phone number, and CheckFree will provide proof of payment remittance to your merchant. If the posting problem is due to a CheckFree error, Check-Free resolves the situation directly with your merchant (including paying any late fees up to a maximum of $50).

Getting transmission status information

Quicken keeps status information for every electronic payment you transmit. This information includes the transmission date, payment date, merchant account number, and confirmation number that CheckFree sends back to Quicken for each transmission.

1   **Select the transaction in the check register.**

2   **Choose Get Payment Info from the Activities menu.**

Stopping electronic payments

After Quicken transmits an electronic payment, you can stop payment on the transaction if you don't wait too long. On the basis of the five days it can take CheckFree to make a scheduled payment, Quicken determines whether you are likely to be able to stop the payment and tells you if it's clearly too late.

1   **Select the transaction in the check register.**

2   **Choose Transmit from the Activities menu, and then choose Stop Payment Request.**

Quicken tells you when the payment is scheduled to be made. If it is possible to stop payment, Quicken asks if you want to do so. If it's too late to stop the payment or the payment has not yet been transmitted, Quicken lets you know.

Timing is critical: Quicken determines whether you can still stop a payment, taking into account the usual five days between the transmission date and the payment date. CheckFree Corporation does not assess a charge for stop payments performed in this manner.

If Quicken tells you that it is too late to stop the payment, you can contact CheckFree by phone and request a stop payment. **CheckFree assesses an additional fee to stop payments manually.** See the "How to Get the Most from CheckFree" booklet enclosed in the CheckFree confirmation package for details.

3 Click Yes if it's still possible to stop the payment.

Quicken immediately transmits your request to CheckFree. Messages inform you of the progress of the transmission. If the transmission is successful, Quicken marks the payment VOID in the register and records the stop payment confirmation number received from CheckFree. To see the confirmation number, select the transaction in the check register and choose Get Payment Info from the Activities menu.

Editing or deleting a merchant

Edit a merchant if you want to change any information about the merchant. Delete a merchant if you will no longer be making electronic payments to the merchant. Use this table to determine whether you can edit or delete a merchant.

Action	No untransmitted payments, no pending payments	Payments Untransmitted	Payments Pending (transmitted but not paid)
Can you edit merchant information?	Yes	Yes	Yes (see also the example below)
Can you delete the merchant from the merchant list?	Yes	No	No

When you edit or delete merchants in Quicken, you must transmit these changes to CheckFree to update your CheckFree records. If you want these changes to apply to a payment, you must transmit the update five business days before the payment date.

The following example illustrates how the five-business-day lead time affects pending payments.

You transmit a payment for American Express on November 2.

You specified a payment date (the date that American Express receives payment from CheckFree) of November 16.

November 1993

1	2	3	4	5	6	7
8	9	10	11	12	13	14
15	16	17	18	19	20	21
22	23	24	25	26	27	28
29	30					

Suppose you edit the merchant information for American Express.

If you want the updated merchant information to apply to your payment, you must transmit the update by November 9. Any updates received after that date will not affect the payment.

(Shaded areas on this calendar are nonbusiness days, which are weekends and holidays.)

Editing merchant information

1 Choose Merchants from the View menu.

2 Select the name in the merchant list.

Or press ⌘ E

3 Click Edit.

4 Enter the changes you want and then click Change.

5 (Optional) Repeat steps 2 through 4 for any other merchants you want to edit.

6 Open the bank account set up for CheckFree.

7 Choose Transmit from the Activities menu, and then choose Payments.

8 (Optional) If you have any untransmitted payments that you don't want transmitted, clear the checkmark from those payments.

9 Click OK.

Quicken transmits your merchant updates and any untransmitted payments that you wanted to transmit.

Deleting a merchant

1 Choose Merchants from the View menu.

2 Select the name in the merchant list.

Or press ⌘ D

3 Click Delete.

4 Click OK to confirm that you want to delete the merchant.

Communicating with CheckFree

You can send electronic messages directly to CheckFree by making payment inquiries or by sending electronic mail. If you want to speak with a CheckFree customer service representative, see the telephone numbers on page 408.

Inquiring about electronic payments

CheckFree knows nothing about a payment until you transmit it to them. To get information about an untransmitted payment, you can view it in the check register or preview it as part of a transmission.

You can find out the status of a transaction that you've already transmitted to CheckFree; just be sure today is later than the transaction's payment date. CheckFree responds to your inquiry by U.S. mail.

1   Select the payment in the check register.

2   Choose Transmit from the Activities menu, and then choose Payment Inquiry.

Quicken shows you the date the transaction was transmitted, the payment date, the transmission status, the merchant account number, and the confirmation number.

3   Check to make sure this transaction is the one you want to inquire about.

If it is, click Yes to display the Transmit Payment Inquiry dialog box.

4   Specify the type of inquiry and action already taken, and then type any other information in the text area.

You can type up to three 60-character lines, if you want.

As you type, don't press Return. Instead, when the cursor approaches the end of the line, let Quicken move the cursor to the next line.

5   Click OK to send the inquiry to CheckFree.

Sending electronic mail

You can send CheckFree a message that is not specific to a payment.
CheckFree responds to your message by U.S. mail.

**1   Choose Transmit from the Activities menu, and then choose
Message.**

You can type up to ten 60-character
lines here.

As you type, don't press Return.
Instead, when the cursor approaches
the end of the line, let Quicken move
the cursor to the next line.

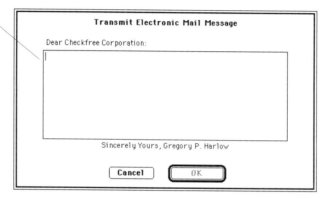

2   Type your message in the text area.

3   Click OK to send your message.

Solving CheckFree problems

If you have trouble transmitting to CheckFree, wait a minute or two and try transmitting again. The CheckFree system may simply have been busy when you first tried to transmit. If that doesn't work, try the troubleshooting steps in this section one by one. After each step, try transmitting until you transmit successfully.

Do this	Here's how
Check that you've set up your modem correctly.	See "Setting up your modem to transmit electronic payments" on page 176.
Check all hardware connections at both ends.	Check the modular phone plugs, modem cable, and power cords to be sure they are securely plugged in and the power is on.
Check the modem switch settings, if any.	Your modem user's manual describes the function of each switch on the modem.
	With the modem turned off, set the switches to originate a call (not to answer), to respond to DTR ("data terminal ready"), and to recognize commands.
Eliminate telephone line noise.	Turn off call waiting by including its disable code in the service number (see the service number example in the next step).
Dial the service number yourself.	Your service number is supplied by CheckFree for your particular modem speed and geographic location. Dial the number that the modem dials to be sure that you're getting a dial tone and that when you dial the service number, the CheckFree Processing Center answers with a high-pitched tone.

Code to turn off call waiting (*70) — Digit for a long-distance call (1)

*70, 1, 800 555 1111

Pauses (commas) — Area code and fictional telephone number

Do you have to wait to get an outside line or do you have to add extra digits?

Write down the sequence of digits, characters, and pauses you dialed. An example of a character is an asterisk (*), which many phone systems use as a signal for a special phone feature.

Translate what you've written down into the sequence of numbers, commas, and characters you need to enter in the Local Access Telephone Number field of the Modem Setup dialog box. (Use a comma for each pause, or several commas for longer pauses. For example, if you need to dial 9 to get an outside line and then need to wait a second to hear a dial tone, enter 9 and then enter a comma in this field.)

More steps on next page.

Do this	Here's how
Change one of the settings in the Modem Setup dialog box.	See "Setting up your modem to transmit electronic payments" on page 176.
	Change the setting for tone or pulse dialing.
	Try this step only if you are getting no response at all from your modem: select a different modem port to see if you've been using the wrong port.
	Change the setting for the modem speed (baud rate) and check that the access number is correct for the modem speed. If possible, change to a slower speed.
	In the Initialization String field, you may need to include a different sequence of commands for Quicken to send to the modem before dialing the service number. Enter any special letters, digits, and other characters to be sent to the modem. To find out what codes you need, look in the modem user's manual. (Most modem commands must begin with the prefix AT.)
Change a setting on your computer.	Remove any INITs from your System Folder.
If your modem appears to be operating correctly, but the CheckFree Processing Center does not respond, call CheckFree Customer Service.	Call CheckFree Customer Service at the phone number listed on page 408. Do **not** call Intuit with these questions; we have no control or knowledge in these areas.

Tracking credit card transactions

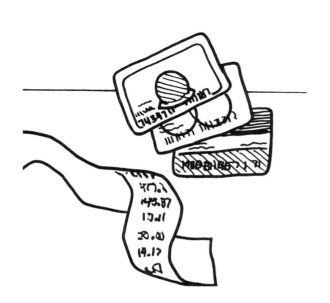

Credit card expenses are often an integral part of personal and business finances. Quicken lets you choose how to handle your credit cards: use either a Quicken bank account or a separate Quicken credit card account.

You can also automate entering transactions into a credit card register with a special Quicken credit card and IntelliCharge. Each month, you either receive an electronic statement disk in the mail or download your statement by modem. IntelliCharge updates your register in seconds (even assigning categories to transactions) and writes a check for the credit card bill.

When to use Quicken credit card accounts

Credit card accounts are useful if you want detailed records of your credit card transactions or if you pay your credit card charges over time. Use the following information to determine the best way to use Quicken to track your credit card transactions and payments.

Preferences for keeping records	Account to use	Actions to take
You want to keep records of only a few individual credit card transactions, and you usually pay your credit card bills in full.	Bank account	Record the check that pays the bill in your Quicken bank account. Split the transaction if you want to categorize particular credit card charges or groups of charges. See "Tracking credit card transactions in Quicken bank accounts" on this page. This is the fastest way to handle credit cards. However, this method doesn't track your outstanding credit card balance.
You want to keep records of some (but not all) credit card transactions, and you pay your credit card bills over time.	Credit card account	In each credit card account, enter only those transactions you want to keep a record of. (You can use your charge slips, or work from your monthly credit card statement.) Create one transaction covering all the charges you don't want to take the time to enter. This method lets you keep detailed records of selected transactions without taking the time to enter every credit card transaction.
You want to keep a record of every credit card transaction *and* know your outstanding credit card balance at all times.	Credit card account	Enter each credit card transaction in the account from your charge slips as you make purchases throughout the month. The credit card register shows your card balance and the available credit remaining on the card. Use Quicken to update your credit card statement and pay your bill. See "Reconciling credit card accounts" on page 198.
You want to keep a record of every credit card transaction, but you don't want to take the time to enter transactions in the account. You don't need to check your outstanding credit card balance in Quicken more than once a month.	Credit card account with IntelliCharge	Use IntelliCharge to update your credit card account *automatically* every month. See "Using IntelliCharge" on page 201.

Tracking credit card transactions in Quicken bank accounts

If you usually pay your credit card bills in full and you have only a few credit card expenses that you want to record, it's fastest to track these expenses in your Quicken bank account. With this method, you track some or all of your credit card purchases by entering multiple categories in a split transaction when you write a check to pay your bill.

In this example, suppose your credit card statement lists transactions for gifts and clothing. You also need to pay a finance charge.

1 **Enter the payment as usual in either the Write Checks or Register window except for the category.**

2 **Click the right side of the Splits button.**

The total amount of the check appears in the first line of the split.

3 **Categorize the first line as "Gifts," and replace the original amount in the first line with the amount you spent on gifts.**

(See "Assigning categories to transactions" on page 82.) You can classify credit card transactions with classes as well as categorize them with income and expense categories. For example, if you use a credit card for both business and personal expenses, you might want to use a class called Business to identify business-related charges.

When you leave the Amount field, Quicken calculates the remainder and inserts it in the next Amount field.

4 **Categorize the second line as "Clothing," and replace the amount in the second line with the amount you spent on clothing.**

Quicken includes the expenses for gifts, clothing, and finance charges when you create any report or graph based on categories.

When you leave the Amount field, Quicken calculates the final remainder and inserts it here. This is your finance charge.

5 **Categorize the remainder in the third line as "Finance Charges."**

6 **Click Record to record the transaction.**

Although this example assigned specific categories to all purchases, you may not want to categorize all of your purchases. In such cases, don't leave those purchases uncategorized. Instead, group them in a split that you categorize as "Miscellaneous" to avoid getting uncategorized amounts in reports.

Using regular credit card accounts

A Quicken credit card account is very similar to a Quicken bank account. If you've used a Quicken bank account, you already know most of what you'll need to use a credit card account.

◆ **Set up the account.**
See "Setting up additional Quicken accounts" on page 36 to set up a credit card account for each card you use.

◆ **Save your transaction slips when you charge an item, and enter the transactions as they occur throughout the month.**
See "Entering credit card transactions" on this page.

◆ **Update your account with the credit card statement.**
See "Updating regular credit card accounts" on page 198.

◆ **Pay your credit card bill.**
See "Paying credit card bills" on page 200.

Entering credit card transactions

To enter transactions in the credit card register you can:

● Save your transaction slips when you charge an item and enter the transactions as they occur throughout the month.

This method provides you with your current credit card balance at all times. It also lets you double-check your charges against those listed on your credit card statement.

● Wait until you receive your monthly statement and enter the transactions from the statement.

If you don't need to know your balance throughout the month, this method is easy to use.

If you want to keep a record of every credit card transaction, but you don't want to take the time to enter transactions in Quicken and you don't need to know the outstanding credit card balance more than once a month, consider using IntelliCharge. IntelliCharge updates your credit card account *automatically* every month. See "Using Intelli-Charge" on page 201.

• Create transfers between the credit card account and other Quicken accounts. You use transfers to track the movement of money from your bank account to your credit card account (bill payments, for example), or from your credit card account to your bank account (overdraft protection through your credit card account, for example).

• Keep track of the credit limit, or line of credit, remaining in the account.

To open the register for a credit card account, open the account list and choose the account name.

This type of transfer payment is recorded automatically with Quicken's bill-paying feature. The account name tells you in what account Quicken recorded the check. To pay the credit card bill, see page 200.

The √ (cleared) column displays a ✓ (a bold checkmark) for transactions you have reconciled with your monthly credit card bill.

Instead of the Payment and Deposit columns of the check register, the credit card register has Charge and Payment columns. Use the Charge column for amounts you have charged, finance charges, and other fees. Use the Payment column to record bill payments or a credit to your account.

Categorize your credit card charges. That way, you'll see credit card expenses categorized in income and expense reports and graphs.

Ending Balance is your outstanding balance. Credit Remaining is your credit limit for the account less the Ending Balance amount. (The credit limit for this account is $5,000.)

Visa: Register

DATE	DESCRIPTION		CHARGE		√	PAYMENT		BALANCE	
	CATEGORY/CLASS	MEMO			?				
12/22	Primerica Bank				✓	592	04	123	04
1993	[Checking]								
12/23	Wal-Mart		51	27	✓			174	31
1993	Household								
12/23	Gift Horse 400 St Joseph		9	03	✓			183	34
1993	Gifts								
1/5	Jesper Helweg, DDS		350	00				533	34
1994	Medical&Dental								

Record   Restore   SPLITS

Ending Balance: $533.34
Credit Remaining: $4,466.66

This example shows a home equity line of credit being tracked in a credit card account.

Charges to this line of credit are made by writing drafts (much as you would write a check for a bank account).

In this example, the draft number was noted in the description, but you could note it in the Memo field instead.

Line of credit: Register

DATE	DESCRIPTION		CHARGE		√	PAYMENT		BALANCE	
	CATEGORY/CLASS	MEMO			?				
1/15	Opening Balance				✓			0	00
1994	[Line of credit]								
2/1	Ken Chiu Construction (Draft #1001)		5,350	00	✓			5,350	00
1994	[House]	bathroom remodel							
2/24	Service Charge		32	10	✓			5,382	10
1994	Mortgage Int								
3/8	Great Northern Bank					350	00	5,032	10
1994	[Checking]	Home equity LOC #05							

Record   Restore   SPLITS

Ending Balance: $5,032.10
Credit Remaining: $14,967.90

Updating regular credit card accounts

To make sure that your credit card account contains accurate information, you should reconcile it each month with your credit card statement. Such reconciliation also allows you to take advantage of certain Quicken features:

- You don't have to enter every credit card charge. Instead, Quicken can record a single adjustment transaction that covers all the charges that you choose not to record individually.

- Quicken automatically records a transaction for any finance charge to your credit card account.

- If you have a bank account, Quicken automatically records any credit card payment.

Reconciling credit card accounts

You update your Quicken credit card statement much as you balance your Quicken bank account against your bank statement. You mark transactions as cleared and enter any missing transactions you want to keep a record of. Reconcile one monthly statement at a time, the oldest statement first. Then pay your bill.

1   Open the credit card account.

2   Choose Reconcile from the Activities menu.

Enter the information from your own credit card statement.

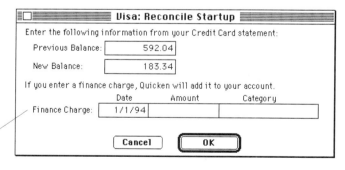

If you enter a finance charge, Quicken will record a transaction for that amount.

3   In the Previous Balance and New Balance fields, enter the beginning and ending balance (or "balance due") from your credit card statement.

4   In the Finance Charge Date field, enter the date of the credit card statement.

5 In the Finance Charge Amount and Category fields, enter the total finance charges from your credit card statement, and categorize the amount with an expense category.

6 Click OK to see a list of uncleared items.

Click an item that appears on your credit card statement to mark it as cleared. To remove the checkmark, click the item again.

When the Difference This Statement amount is zero, you've checked off every item that appears on the statement.

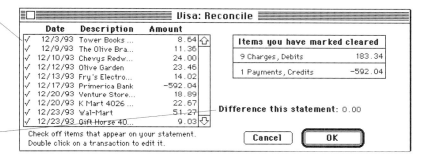

7 Click each transaction shown in the list of uncleared transactions that is also listed on your credit card statement.

8 If you find transactions listed on your statement that are missing from the list of uncleared items, press ⌘ R to enter them now in the register.

You can enter each of the missing transactions in the register. (If you choose this method, click the √ (cleared) column in the register for each transaction you enter. This step marks the transaction as cleared, saving you the effort of locating and marking the transaction in the Reconcile window.)

Or, if you prefer, Quicken can combine these new charges into a single adjustment transaction when you finish reconciling your statement.

9 When you have finished marking items as cleared, check the Difference This Statement amount.

Reconciling a credit card account is basically the same as reconciling a bank account at this point. See "Completing reconciliation" on page 149.

10 After you complete reconciliation, click Yes if you want Quicken to create a transaction for paying your credit card bill.

If you click Yes, Quicken displays the Pay Credit Card Bill dialog box. See "Paying credit card bills" on page 200 to pay your bill.

Paying credit card bills

As the final step in reconciling your credit card statement, Quicken can write a check to print with Quicken or record a handwritten check in the check register.

Select the account name. Quicken records the payment in the checking account as a transfer to the credit card account.

Select Handwritten if this check will not be printed with Quicken.

Select Electronic if you use CheckFree and plan to transmit the check electronically.

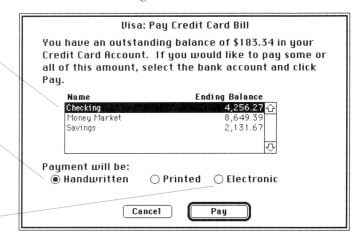

1   **Select the name of the checking account from which you plan to write the check.**

2   **Specify whether you are planning to write the check manually, print it with Quicken, or transmit it electronically.**

3   **Click Pay to enter the payment and the transfer information in the Write Checks or Register window.**

    After Quicken records the payment, it selects the payment transaction in the Write Checks window or the check register.

4   **Complete the transaction with a payee, memo, and address (for a printable check), and then click Record.**

    Quicken remembers the payment information and uses it the next time you make a payment on this credit card.

Intuit recommends that you back up your Quicken data file after you have reconciled your credit card account. Making a backup copy of your data takes only seconds to do and protects you against accidental loss of data. See "Backing up your Quicken data file" on page 63.

Using IntelliCharge

IntelliCharge makes it easy to manage credit card accounts: it enters and categorizes transactions in your register, reconciles your account, and creates your payment transaction for you.

IntelliCharge reads transactions from an electronic credit card statement, adds the charges and payments to your register, and categorizes the transactions automatically. You receive the electronic statement on a floppy disk through the mail or by modem through CompuServe (although no CompuServe membership is necessary).

To use IntelliCharge, you must have a Quicken credit card. If you would like to apply for a Quicken credit card, see the application included in your Quicken package. (If you need another application, call Intuit Customer Service at the phone number listed on page 408 under "To get an application form for: Quicken credit card.")

◆ **Set up the account to use IntelliCharge.**
   See "Setting up a credit card account to use IntelliCharge" on this page.

◆ **Let IntelliCharge update your account.**
   See "Updating credit card accounts with IntelliCharge" on page 205.

◆ **Let IntelliCharge pay your bill.**
   See "Paying credit card bills with IntelliCharge" on page 210.

Setting up a credit card account to use IntelliCharge

1 **Set up a credit card account for your Quicken credit card.**

See "Setting up additional Quicken accounts" on page 36 to set up the account.

2   Choose Enable IntelliCharge from the Settings menu.

Select the credit card account to use with IntelliCharge.

Select this checkbox to use IntelliCharge with the selected account.

Enter the number of your Quicken credit card.

If you will receive your electronic statement by modem, click this button...

...and enter the Social Security number that you used on your credit card application...

...and then enter a password of your choice that is from four to eight alphanumeric characters long.

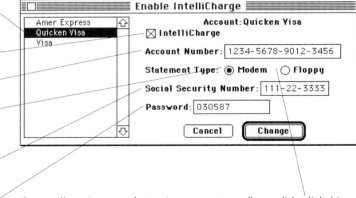

If you will receive your electronic statement on a floppy disk, click this button. (This action dims the Social Security Number and Password fields, which are for modem users only.)

If you decide you no longer want to receive electronic statements, you should cancel your Quicken credit card account. The bank requires you to pay the delivery fee for electronic statements as long as your account is open.

3   Select the credit card account that you just created and then select the IntelliCharge checkbox.

4   If you will receive your electronic statements by modem, select Modem as the statement type, and then enter your Social Security number and a password.

IntelliCharge uses your Social Security number (as well as your account number) to identify which electronic statements are yours. The password prevents unauthorized access to your electronic statement.

When you download your first electronic statement, IntelliCharge sets up your password with CompuServe. You can change this password at any time. IntelliCharge will set up the new password with CompuServe the next time you download a statement.

5   Click Change to save your changes.

Quicken marks the account name in the list with a lightning bolt to show that IntelliCharge is enabled.

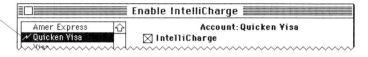

6   Close the Enable IntelliCharge window.

If you will receive your electronic statements by modem, you still may need to set it up. see "Setting up your modem to use Intelli-Charge" on page 203.

Setting up your modem to use IntelliCharge

If you already use CheckFree to pay your bills electronically, skip this procedure. You can download electronic statements with no additional setup.

1 **Choose Modem from the Settings menu.**

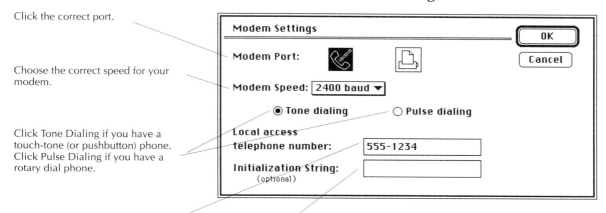

Click the correct port.

Choose the correct speed for your modem.

Click Tone Dialing if you have a touch-tone (or pushbutton) phone. Click Pulse Dialing if you have a rotary dial phone.

Enter your local access number for CompuServe. Do not include the area code if you are within that area.

You can customize Quicken's modem settings to handle special requirements of your modem. To find out what codes you need, look in the manual that came with your modem for the correct configuration codes to enter in the Initialization String field.

2 **Select the modem port, modem speed (baud rate), and dialing type you want to use.**

You do not need a CompuServe membership to use IntelliCharge. Just follow this step to get the access number.

3 **Enter a telephone number in the Local Access Telephone Number field.**

To get the local access number for CompuServe, where Quicken downloads your personal statement information from, call **1-800-848-8980**. At the prompt, press 2.

The system asks first for the phone number *from which you will be calling*, and then for the speed of your modem. It then gives you the access number nearest to you.

Quicken uses your modem to dial the number exactly as you enter it in the field. Include any special sequence of digits or characters required (for example, *70 to turn off call waiting before you dial the telephone number). You can also include a comma to indicate a pause, or multiple commas if you find you need a longer pause between digits. If the access number includes an area code, do not use the area code if you are within that area.

If you have problems with your modem, try troubleshooting with the tips in "Solving CheckFree problems" on page 190. Even if you do not use CheckFree to pay your bills electronically, the tips in that section may help you to set up and use your modem correctly.

4 **(Optional) Skip the Initialization String field unless you need to customize your modem initialization.**

Your modem user's guide lists the codes that your modem needs. (Most modem commands must begin with the prefix AT.)

5 **Click OK.**

After you have set up your account, you need to wait until it is time to download your IntelliCharge statement. See "Updating credit card accounts with IntelliCharge" on page 205 when it is time to get your IntelliCharge statement.

Entering data in your credit card account

You don't need to enter your Quicken credit card transactions because IntelliCharge will enter them automatically when you update your account.

Intuit strongly recommends that you do not enter transactions manually. IntelliCharge works best when you let it do the work for you.

(If you still decide to enter transactions manually, see "How Intelli-Charge updates your manually entered transactions" on page 211.)

Updating credit card accounts with IntelliCharge

Each month, Intuit either mails you an IntelliCharge statement disk or makes an electronic statement file available for you to download by modem. The disk or file contains all the transactions for your credit card that occurred in the current statement period. These transactions include credit card purchases, finance and cash advance charges, credits from merchants, and payments. (You'll also receive a paper statement containing these same transactions from the bank that provides your Quicken credit card.*)

Intuit does not provide an electronic statement if there was no activity on your Quicken credit card account during the billing period or your account is closed, except for a closing statement. (The bank sends a paper statement whether or not there was activity during the billing period.)

Caution:
Get your IntelliCharge statement either from a disk or by modem only once a month. Do not update your account more than once with the same statement or you'll end up with duplicate transactions in your register.

Getting your IntelliCharge statement from a disk

1   **Open the Quicken credit card account.**

2   **Choose Get IntelliCharge Data from the Activities menu.**

3   **Insert your IntelliCharge statement disk in your floppy drive and select the electronic statement.**

Select the electronic statement and then click Open.

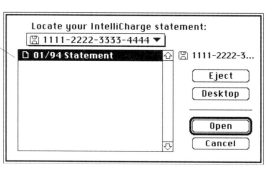

* Your paper and electronic statements should always match. However, if there is ever any discrepancy between your paper and electronic statements, the bank always considers the paper statement to be correct. Contact Intuit Technical Support if such a discrepancy occurs. See "Phone numbers" on page 408.

4   Click Open.

See "Checking transactions in the electronic statement" on page 208 to continue with the updating process.

Getting your IntelliCharge statement by modem

Your electronic statement is available for you to download at approximately the same time as you receive your paper statement in the mail.

Before you download your first electronic statement, wait until the paper statement arrives to save yourself repeated modem calls.

1   Be sure your modem is turned on (if it is external) and the phone line is plugged in.

2   Open the Quicken credit card account.

If you have problems with your modem, try troubleshooting with the tips in "Solving CheckFree problems" on page 190. Even if you do not use CheckFree to pay your bills electronically, the tips in that section may help you to set up and use your modem correctly.

3   Choose Get IntelliCharge Data from the Activities menu.

In most cases, Quicken dials the local access telephone number* and downloads your statement file. (Getting your statement by modem takes a few moments longer the first time you do it.)

But if you did not record the transactions from your previous electronic statement (that is, if you clicked Cancel instead of OK in the Intellicharge Statement window), Quicken doesn't download a new statement file. Instead, Quicken gets the previous statement file, which was saved on your hard disk. After you update your credit card account with the previous statement file, you can use this procedure again to get the new statement file.

If you see an error message on screen instead of the electronic statement, go to the table in "If you have problems downloading your statement" on page 207 for more information.

Once your statement file is completely downloaded, IntelliCharge saves the file on your hard disk. You will need this disk file if you ever need to redo an update. See "Redoing an update" on page 214.

See "Checking transactions in the electronic statement" on page 208 to continue with the updating process.

---

*   Your local telephone company charges you for the phone call when you download your statement, but in most cases the call is a local one.

If you have problems downloading your statement

If you get an error trying to download your statement, the information in the following table may help you solve your problem.

Error message	Possible reasons and solutions
The IntelliCharge processing center does not recognize your Social Security number or account number. Either you entered one of these numbers incorrectly, or your first statement is not ready yet. If you entered the numbers correctly, wait a few days and try again.	Are you sure you signed up for modem delivery? If you're not sure, call the bank to verify your delivery format (See "Phone numbers" on page 408). If you have not received your first paper statement yet, wait until it arrives before you try downloading your electronic statement again. Be sure the Social Security number you used on your credit card application and the account number from your credit card are correctly entered in the Enable IntelliCharge window (see page 201).
Quicken was unable to dial the IntelliCharge number. Be sure your modem is correctly connected, and you have the correct IntelliCharge phone number. The number may be busy.	The phone number may be busy. Wait a few minutes and try again. Verify that you are using the current local access number. To check this number, call CompuServe (see page 203); have your phone number for downloading and modem baud rate handy. If you are within the area code of a local access number, do not include that area code when you enter the seven-digit phone number. Some areas require a 1 in front of the seven-digit number. If your building requires an "outside line" number (for example, 9), insert this number before your local access number.
This month's statement is not yet available. We apologize for the delay. Please try again tomorrow.	If you have not received your paper statement yet, wait until it arrives before you try downloading your electronic statement again. Have you recently switched to disk delivery? If so, then you can no longer get statements by modem. Be sure to change the statement type to Floppy in the Enable IntelliCharge window (see page 201). If you had no activity on your credit card this month, you won't receive an electronic statement.
An error occurred while configuring your IntelliCharge account. Please try again. OR Quicken was unable to set up the password you entered for your account. Please try again.	IntelliCharge may have had problems because of noise on the phone line. See "Solving CheckFree problems" on page 190 for tips about eliminating phone line noise.

Checking transactions in the electronic statement

As it's getting your electronic statement, IntelliCharge tries to categorize each transaction in the statement. (See "How Intelli-Charge categorizes your transactions" on page 212.) When it has finished, IntelliCharge shows you the statement onscreen.

1   **If IntelliCharge tells you it was unable to categorize all of the transactions in the electronic statement, click OK in the message dialog box.**

You will be able to assign categorizes to these transactions yourself as you review the statement. See step 3 of this procedure for instructions.

2   **Review the transactions in the IntelliCharge Statement window.**

The onscreen statement is similar to the paper statement you receive from the bank, with the addition of categories assigned to transactions.

IntelliCharge was unable to assign a category to this transaction. To assign (or change) a category, select the transaction, press ⌘ L to open the category list, and then double-click the category you want.

A credit or a payment appears as a negative number in the Amount column. This is a payment.

This transaction is marked for special attention. To mark a transaction, select it and then click Mark. These actions insert a question mark in the left column.

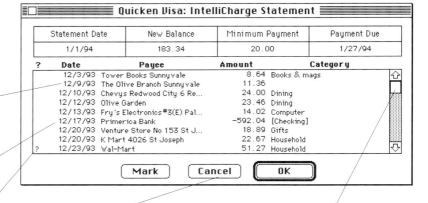

To cancel the IntelliCharge update without saving your category assignments or recording any transactions, click Cancel. To redisplay the IntelliCharge Statement window, see "Getting your IntelliCharge statement from a disk" on page 205 or "Getting your IntelliCharge statement by modem" on page 206.

Use the scroll bar to see the rest of the transactions in the statement.

3   **(Optional) To assign or change a category, select the transaction, press ⌘ L to display the category list, and then double-click the category that you want from the list.**

IntelliCharge remembers all of the category assignments to improve its ability to categorize your transactions automatically. See "How IntelliCharge categorizes your transactions" on page 212 for more information.

4 **(Optional) To mark a transaction for special attention, select it and then click Mark.**

You may want to mark a transaction to:

- Verify or change the payee information

- Split the transaction

- Assign a class

- Enter text in the Memo field of the transaction

- Compare it with your credit card receipt or charge slip and possibly dispute it (See "Handling Quicken credit card disputes" on page 211 for more information.)

For each transaction you mark, IntelliCharge places a question mark (?) in the left column of the IntelliCharge Statement window. When you record the transactions in the credit card register, IntelliCharge displays a marked transaction with a question mark in the ? (marked) field (see the illustration in step 5).

5 **Click OK when you have finished reviewing the statement to record the transactions.**

- If your credit card account has an outstanding balance, IntelliCharge displays the Pay IntelliCharge Bill dialog box to help you enter your payment transaction. See "Paying credit card bills with Intelli-Charge" on page 210.

- If your credit card account has no outstanding balance, you'll see your credit card register.

IntelliCharge records the transactions in the credit card register with bold checkmarks to show they have been reconciled.

You can identify a marked transaction by the question mark here. See page 212 for instructions on using Find (⌘ F) to locate marked transactions in the register.

DATE	DESCRIPTION	CHARGE	√	PAYMENT	BALANCE	
	CATEGORY/CLASS MEMO		?			
12/20 1993	K Mart 4026 St Joseph Household	22 67	√		123 04	
12/23 1993	Wal-Mart Household	51 27	√ ?		174 31	
12/23 1993	Gift Horse 400 St Joseph Gifts	9 03	√		183 34	
1/5 1994						

Quicken Visa: Register

Record | Restore | SPLITS | Current Balance: $592.04 | Ending Balance: $183.34

Intuit recommends that you back up your Quicken data file after you have updated your credit card account with IntelliCharge. Making a backup copy of your data takes only seconds to do and protects you against accidental loss of data. See "Backing up your Quicken data file" on page 63.

Paying credit card bills with IntelliCharge

1 Enter information in the Pay IntelliCharge Bill dialog box.

Select the name of the bank account from which you will pay the bill.

Click a button to indicate whether you will pay your bill with a handwritten check (a register entry), a check you print from Quicken, or an electronic payment (only if you have set up a bank account to use with CheckFree).

Click this button to pay an amount other than the minimum or outstanding balance.

Then, after you click OK, enter the amount you paid into the payment transaction. IntelliCharge remembers this amount the next time you pay your bill.

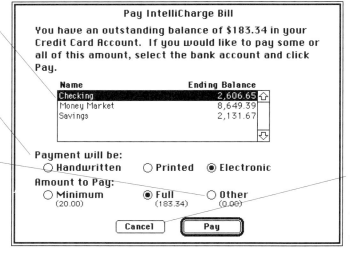

Pay IntelliCharge Bill

You have an outstanding balance of $183.34 in your Credit Card Account. If you would like to pay some or all of this amount, select the bank account and click Pay.

Name	Ending Balance
Checking	2,606.65
Money Market	8,649.39
Savings	2,131.67

Payment will be:
○ Handwritten   ○ Printed   ● Electronic

Amount to Pay:
○ Minimum   ● Full   ○ Other
(20.00)   (183.34)   (0.00)

[Cancel]   [Pay]

If you don't want to enter a payment transaction now, click Cancel.

2 Click Pay.

If you are paying with a manually written check, Quicken displays the register for the bank account so you can enter your payment transaction.

If you are paying with a check printed with Quicken or through CheckFree, Quicken displays the Write Checks window.

If you pay your bill electronically with CheckFree, the payment date is either five business days before the due date shown on the statement, or five business days from today, whichever is later.

3 Make any necessary changes to the transaction in the register or the Write Checks window.

4 Click Record.

You have finished updating your account for this month.

If you receive your electronic statement on a disk, Intuit recommends that you save your latest disk until you back up your Quicken data file. If you receive your electronic statement by modem, Quicken automatically saves all of your statements on your hard disk. These old statements may come in handy if your Quicken data file gets damaged and you need to redo an IntelliCharge update. See "Redoing an update" on page 214.

How IntelliCharge updates your manually entered transactions

If you have entered any transactions manually in the credit card register, IntelliCharge attempts to match exactly the amount of your transaction with a transaction amount from the electronic statement. (IntelliCharge matches charges only to charges and payments only to payments.)

When it's successful, IntelliCharge displays your transaction, and not the matching transaction from the electronic statement, in the Statement window. IntelliCharge also marks your transaction in the register with a bold checkmark in the √ (cleared) column once you've completed the update. (A bold checkmark in your Intelli-Charge register means that the transaction appeared on your credit card statement.)

But when IntelliCharge is unsuccessful, it does nothing to your transaction in the register, since the matching transaction may appear on a future electronic statement.

Caution:

If you enter a transaction manually but the amount differs from what is on the electronic statement, IntelliCharge will not match the transaction and your balance will not be correct. Because of this possibility, Intuit strongly recommends that you not enter transactions manually. Let IntelliCharge enter the transactions.

Handling Quicken credit card disputes

You can use IntelliCharge to help single out a charge that you don't recognize or an amount that does not match the charge amount on your credit card receipt.

1   **Mark the disputed item with a question mark (?) in the left column of the IntelliCharge Statement window.**

2   **Click OK in the IntelliCharge Statement window to record the disputed item and all the other transactions in the register.**

3 Locate each disputed transaction in the register so you can review it.

Do not delete or change the disputed transaction! For whatever reason the charge has appeared on your credit card statement, you must notify the bank and follow the bank's instructions to dispute the charge. If the charge was an error, a credit will appear on a subsequent statement disk to correct the balance of your account.

To locate marked transactions in a credit card register:

Or press ⌘ F

- Choose Find from the Edit menu.

- Leave the Find field blank, and choose Marked "?" from the Search popup menu. (This menu item is available only when the credit card account is set up to use IntelliCharge.)

- Click Next or Previous to search forward or backward in the register for a marked transaction.

4 Call the bank immediately about the disputed charge.

Check the Revolving Loan Agreement and Disclosure Statement that you received from the bank, or consult the back of your paper credit card statement to find out how the bank advises you to dispute a transaction. The bank's telephone number is on page 408.

5 Notify the bank *in writing* of the disputed item.

How IntelliCharge categorizes your transactions

The first time that IntelliCharge updates your register with transactions from your electronic statement, it categorizes the transactions according to Quicken's standard category list.

After your first IntelliCharge update, you can change the categories assigned to particular transactions at any time. When you make changes, you automatically teach IntelliCharge how you would like transactions categorized in the future.

IntelliCharge *learns* how you want to categorize transactions with a particular payee, so the next time it records a transaction with the same payee, it uses the same category.

IntelliCharge uses the payees in your transactions to learn how to categorize them. When categorizing a new transaction from the electronic statement, IntelliCharge first searches your Quicken credit card account register for a matching payee.

If IntelliCharge finds this	It does this
No matching payee	Assigns a category to the new transaction from its own list of credit card categories. Each transaction in your IntelliCharge statement was assigned a standard credit card industry code number for the payee. IntelliCharge maps these codes to Quicken category names. For example, IntelliCharge assigns the Quicken category "Medical" to a credit card transaction you charged to "Joseph D. Jacobs, MD."
A transaction with a matching payee	Copies the category information from the most recent transaction with a matching payee.
A split transaction with a matching payee	Copies the category information from the first line of the split transaction.

Keep IntelliCharge in mind when you make changes to past transactions. If you change the information in the Payee field after IntelliCharge records the transactions in your register, it will not be able to match payees and categories correctly the next time you update your register.

IntelliCharge's use of payee information may also affect your decision as to whether to remove previous years' transactions from your accounts for archival purposes. When you remove transactions, IntelliCharge may not be able to match payees and categories the next time you update your register.

Redoing an update

If your Quicken data file becomes damaged and you must now use a backup data file, you can redo IntelliCharge updates to bring your credit card account up to date quickly.

You'll need to redo an update if you made your backup file prior to the last time you updated your credit card account. For example, suppose your Quicken data file was damaged on January 15, 1994, but you backed up your file on January 1, 1994. If you updated your credit card account between January 1 and January 15, you would need to redo your IntelliCharge update (most likely with your 1/94 statement) after you restored your Quicken data file.

1 If you receive statements on floppy disks, skip to step 4.

2 (Modem only) Choose Enable IntelliCharge from the Settings menu. Then select your IntelliCharge credit card account, click Floppy, and click Change.

First, select your IntelliCharge credit card account from this list.

Next, click this button. (You'll be getting the statement from your hard disk where IntelliCharge saves old electronic statements.)

Finally, click Change.

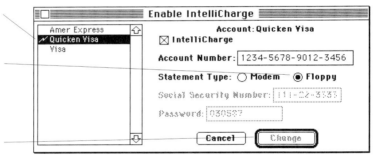

3 Open your IntelliCharge credit card account register.

4 Choose Get IntelliCharge Data from the Activities menu.

5 Open the electronic statement you need to redo.

If you are not sure which statement to open, start with the one whose month is the same as the month that you made your backup data file. For example, if your backup data file is dated January 1, 1994, open your 1/94 statement.

- **Floppy disk:** Insert the IntelliCharge statement disk in your floppy drive and double-click the electronic statement.

- **Modem**: Get the statement from the IntelliCharge Statements folder in your Quicken 4 Folder.

First, open the Quicken 4 Folder on your hard disk.

Second, double-click the IntelliCharge Statements folder.

Next, double-click the folder for the account that you want.

Finally, double-click the statement for the month that you want. If you need to redo more than one statement, start with the earliest month.

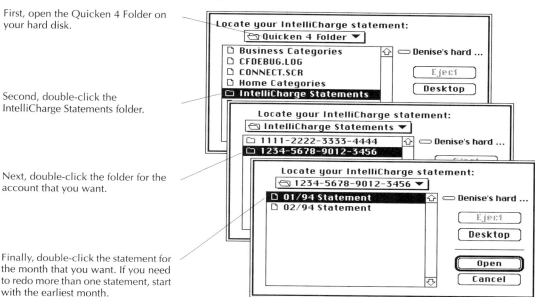

6   **If IntelliCharge warns you that it was expecting an earlier (or later) statement than the one you opened, click Cancel, and then repeat steps 5 and 6, but open the previous (or next) statement.**

7   **Review transactions in the IntelliCharge Statement window as you would normally do, and then click OK when you have finished.**

See page 208 for instructions.

8   **Enter information in the Pay IntelliCharge Bill dialog box and click OK.**

- If you have not yet paid the bill for this statement, see "Paying credit card bills with IntelliCharge" on page 210 for instructions.

- If you have already paid the bill, check your records for the amount you paid. Then enter the information as shown here and click Pay.

Select the bank account from which you paid the bill.

Click this button, even if you paid with a printed check or by electronic payment. IntelliCharge will enter a transaction for this payment in the register.

Note: If you had paid your bill with an electronic payment, you cannot recover the payment confirmation information in Quicken. Contact CheckFree Technical Support to recover this information. See "Phone numbers" on page 408.

Click this button. Then after you click OK, enter the amount you paid into the payment transaction.

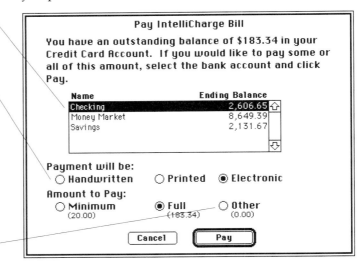

Pay IntelliCharge Bill

You have an outstanding balance of $183.34 in your Credit Card Account. If you would like to pay some or all of this amount, select the bank account and click Pay.

Name	Ending Balance
Checking	2,606.65
Money Market	8,649.39
Savings	2,131.67

Payment will be:
○ Handwritten   ○ Printed   ● Electronic

Amount to Pay:
○ Minimum   ● Full   ○ Other
(20.00)   (183.34)   (0.00)

[Cancel]   [Pay]

9 (Modem only) In the Enable IntelliCharge dialog box, select your IntelliCharge account, click Modem, and then click Change to re-enable modem delivery.

10 (Modem only) Close the Enable IntelliCharge dialog box.

Tracking cash transactions

You can record cash transactions in two different ways in Quicken. You can set up a separate Quicken cash account, or you can enter your cash spending right in your Quicken bank account.

Both methods allow you to categorize your cash expenses so that you can include them in reports, graphs, and budgets. The method you choose depends on how much detail you want about your cash spending.

When to use cash accounts

You can record cash transactions in two different ways in Quicken: You can set up a separate Quicken cash account and enter cash transactions there, or you can enter your cash transactions right in your Quicken bank account. Neither method requires you to account for every penny.

Set up and enter cash transactions in a Quicken cash account if you:

- want to keep detailed records of most or all of the cash transactions you make
- prefer to use cash instead of checks or credit cards
- are often paid in cash
- need to track petty cash for your small business

See "Setting up and using cash accounts" on page 221.

Enter cash transactions in a Quicken bank account if you want to categorize the income or expenses for only a few cash transactions. See "Entering cash transactions in bank accounts" on this page.

Entering cash transactions in bank accounts

If you want to track only a few important cash transactions and treat the rest as miscellaneous expenses or income, you don't need to set up a separate cash account. Instead, enter cash deposits and withdrawals in your Quicken bank accounts (checking, savings, or money market accounts) as usual.

When you enter an insignificant cash transaction in a Quicken bank account, assign a catchall category such as Cash Withdrawal or Cash Deposit to the transaction. In reports, graphs, and budgets, Quicken displays these insignificant transactions lumped together in the Cash Withdrawal or Cash Deposit category. See "Entering insignificant cash expenses in a Quicken bank account" on page 219 for an example.

When you enter an important cash transaction that you'd like to track more specifically in a Quicken bank account, split the transaction and assign a category more specific than Cash Withdrawal or Cash Deposit to that transaction. Assign categories to important cash transactions in your bank account so that Quicken includes them whenever you create reports, graphs, and budgets. "Important" may include tax-related transactions or transactions that involve receiving or spending large amounts. See "Entering important cash expenses in a Quicken bank account" on page 220 for an example.

Entering insignificant cash expenses in a Quicken bank account

Suppose you have a $500 bonus check and you want to deposit $400 of it in your checking account and keep $100 in cash. You don't want to track how you spend the $100.

1 **Open your checking account.**

Or press ⌘ N

2 **Choose New Transaction from the Edit menu.**

3 **In the Description field, enter the name of the company that gave you the bonus check.**

4 **In the Deposit field, enter $400 and press Tab.**

Or press ⌘ E

5 **Open the split transaction.**

6 **Assign the income category Bonus to the first line.**

(See "Assigning categories to transactions" on page 82.)

7 **Type the bonus amount ($500) over the amount in the first line ($400) and press Tab to move to the next line.**

When you leave the Amount field, Quicken calculates the remainder (−100.00) and inserts it in the next Amount field.

8 **Assign the expense category Cash Withdrawal to the second line.**

Quicken inserts the difference between the transaction amount and the amount you categorized as bonus income.

DATE	NUMBER	DESCRIPTION	PAYMENT	✓	DEPOSIT	BALANCE	
		MEMO					
6/13 1994		SDP			400 00		

CATEGORY/CLASS	MEMO	AMOUNT	
Bonus		500 00	
Cash withdrawal		−100 00	

Or press ⌘ E

9 **Close the split transaction.**

10 **Click Record to record the transaction.**

Entering important cash expenses in a Quicken bank account

Suppose you withdraw $200 from your checking account. Instead of assigning a category of Cash Withdrawal to the entire amount, you may want to track the $100 you gave to a charity and the $45 you paid for dinner in a restaurant. You do not want to want to track how you spent the remaining $55.

1   **Open your checking account.**

2   **Enter the cash withdrawal transaction for $200.**

Or you could select a cash withdrawal transaction that you entered in the register previously. Choose any transaction dated on or around the date of the cash expenses that will cover the amounts to which you want to assign categories.

Or press ⌘ E   3   **Open the split transaction.**

4   **Assign the expense category Charity to the first line of the split transaction.**

(See "Assigning categories to transactions" on page 82.)

5   **Type 100 over the amount in the first line and press Tab to move to the next line.**

When you leave the Amount field, Quicken calculates the remainder (100.00) and inserts it in the next Amount field.

6   **Assign the expense category Dining to the second line of the split transaction.**

7   **Type 45 over the amount in the second line and press Tab to move to the next line.**

When you leave the Amount field, Quicken calculates the remainder (55.00) and inserts it in the next Amount field.

8 **Assign the expense category Cash Withdrawal to the third line of the split transaction.**

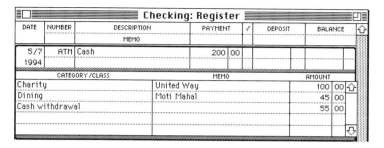

DATE	NUMBER	DESCRIPTION	PAYMENT	√	DEPOSIT	BALANCE	
		MEMO					
5/7 1994	ATM	Cash	200 00				

CATEGORY/CLASS		MEMO		AMOUNT	
Charity		United Way		100 00	
Dining		Moti Mahal		45 00	
Cash withdrawal				55 00	

Or press ⌘ E

9 **Close the split transaction.**

10 **Click Record to record the transaction.**

Setting up and using cash accounts

Use a cash account if you want to keep records of most or all of the cash transactions you make. If you need to keep records of only a few cash transactions, see "Entering cash transactions in bank accounts" on page 218.

◆ **Set up a cash account.**
See "Setting up additional Quicken accounts" on page 36 to set up a new account.

◆ **Open the account.**
Choose Open Account from the File menu and select the cash account or choose Accounts from the View menu, select the cash account, and click Open.

◆ **Enter transactions in the cash account.**
See "Entering transactions in a cash account" on page 222.

◆ **From time to time, update the balance of the account.**
By updating, you can keep the value of this account accurate even if you do not enter every single cash transaction. See "Updating your cash balance" on page 223.

Entering transactions in a cash account

Save the receipts and other records of your cash transactions and enter each one as a separate transaction.

If one cash receipt covers several items that you want to keep track of individually, split the transaction when you enter it in the cash account.

Although you don't have to enter transactions for all the cash you've spent, you should enter transactions that show all the cash you've received when you:

- record transfer transactions for cash withdrawals, deposit less-cash transactions from a bank account, or advances from your other accounts (See "Transferring money between accounts" on page 86.)
- you are paid in cash or given cash
- cash a check without depositing it in another account

Instead of the Payment and Deposit columns of the check register, the cash account register has Spend and Receive columns. Use the Spend column for purchases made with cash; use the Receive column to record increases in the amount of cash on hand.

To review entering transactions in a register, see page 80. The basic steps for entering transactions are the same for all account types.

The Description field specifies the store where you made the cash purchase.

Categorize all cash transactions so they'll be included in income and expense reports and graphs.

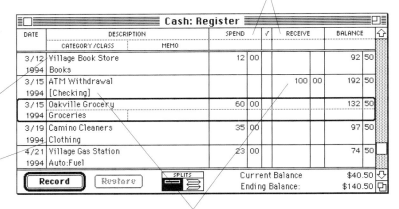

The cash account received cash as a transfer when an ATM withdrawal was recorded in a checking account. The name of the checking account is in the Category field.

Updating your cash balance

You don't need to balance your cash accounts in the same way you reconcile the register for your bank accounts. The main purpose of updating the balance in a cash account is to save you from having to enter every cash transaction. You enter only those cash transactions you want to track in the register. Then, when you update your cash balance, Quicken enters one adjustment transaction for the remaining amount of miscellaneous cash expenses.

1 **Choose Open Account from the File menu and select the cash account if it is not already open.**

2 **Choose Adjust Balance from the Activities menu.**

3 **Enter information in the Adjust Balance window.**

Enter the amount of cash you currently have on hand. Quicken compares this amount with the current balance in the account.

(Optional) Change the date.

(Optional) Enter a category for the adjustment transaction.

4 **Click OK.**

Quicken creates the balance adjustment transaction in the register.

Tracking assets and liabilities

Quicken's asset and liability accounts let you track such things as loan balances, lines of credit, accounts receivable, capital equipment, 401(k) retirement plans, and the tax basis of your home.

If you set up accounts for assets and liabilities, Quicken provides a home net worth report and a business balance sheet that each combine the balances from all your accounts for a complete financial picture.

When to use asset and liability accounts

Assets show what you own; *liabilities* show what you owe. The difference between your assets and your liabilities is your *net worth*. The balances in your bank and cash accounts represent part of your assets. The balances due on your credit cards represent part of your liabilities. But they may not give a total picture of your finances.

Use Quicken's portfolio and mutual fund accounts to track assets such as stocks, Individual Retirement Accounts (IRAs), and other investments.

Type of asset	Sample uses for asset accounts
Home tax cost basis	You can set up an asset account to track your home improvements over the years. Use your purchase price as the opening balance and record each improvement in the register as you make it. When you sell your home, accurate records may allow you to justify a higher tax basis and reduce your taxes.
Contents of your home	Create a home inventory to track furnishings, major appliances, audio and video equipment, jewelry, and other property that you keep in your home. Enter each item with its purchase date and price as a transaction in an asset account. If your property is damaged or stolen, your records can help to settle your claim with your insurer.
Capital equipment	Businesses can set up an asset account that tracks the value of all capital equipment as it is acquired and depreciation as it occurs.
Accounts receivable	Businesses can keep up-to-date A/R records in an asset account.
Loan notes you hold	You can track loans that you've lent. When you receive a payment, deposit it in the bank account that you normally would, but transfer the amount of the principal payment to your loan asset account. This account's balance shows the amount that is currently owed to you. Note: Quicken's feature for amortized loans simplifies this process. It automatically sets up the asset account and a memorized loan payment that you recall whenever you receive a payment. See Chapter 17, *Tracking loans*, beginning on page 279.

Type of asset	Sample uses for asset accounts
Prepaid medical expenses	If your employer helps you set aside pre-tax dollars for medical expenses, you can use an asset account as a holding account for tracking amounts withheld from your paycheck. See "Sample split transactions" on page 94 for information about transferring part of your paycheck to an asset account.

Type of liability	Sample uses for liability accounts
Loan balances	You can use liability accounts to keep track of loans you've taken out, such as car loans, home equity loans*, and mortgages. When you write a check to make a loan payment, transfer the amount of the principal payment to your loan liability account. Then you can see your up-to-date loan balance at any time. Note: Quicken's feature for amortized loans (including the types of loans listed above) simplifies this process. It automatically sets up the liability account and a memorized loan payment that you recall whenever you want to make a payment. See Chapter 17, *Tracking loans,* beginning on page 279.
Accrued liabilities	Businesses can use liability accounts for accrued liabilities, such as payroll taxes and income taxes payable. When you do your company's payroll, as part of the split transaction detail, transfer the payroll taxes portion of each check to a payroll liability account. This technique makes it easy for you to keep track of how much is due for payroll taxes.
Accounts payable	Businesses can keep up-to-date A/P records in a liability account.

*   If you have a home equity *line of credit,* use a credit card account to track it. Unlike liability accounts, credit card accounts track the amount credit available to you. See "Using regular credit card accounts" on page 196, and take special note of the illustration of the register for a home equity line of credit account on page 197.

Setting up and using asset and liability accounts

Quicken asset and liability accounts are very similar to Quicken bank accounts. If you've used a Quicken bank account, you already know most of what you need to use an asset or liability account.

◆ **Set up an asset or liability account.**
See "Setting up additional Quicken accounts" on page 36.

◆ **Enter transactions in the asset or liability account.**
See the illustrations on this page and on page 229.

◆ **From time to time, close inactive items in the account or update the value of the account.**
See "Updating the value of asset and liability accounts" on page 229.

Using the liability account register

This example shows a liability account set up for Social Security (FICA) payroll taxes collected for a household employee.

The Opening Balance shows the amount of Social Security tax owed at the time you set up the liability account.

Each month, the employer records a transaction for the employee's paycheck in the checking account. The transaction here is a transfer from that paycheck transaction in the checking account. Its amount is the sum of the Social Security tax withheld from the employee's pay plus the employer's Social Security contribution. This amount increases the total amount owed.

DATE	NUMBER	DESCRIPTION	INCREASE	√	DECREASE	BALANCE
		CATEGORY/CLASS MEMO				
12/31 1993		Opening Balance [Payroll-FICA]	326 46	√		326 46
12/31 1993		Internal Revenue Service [Checking] 4Q '93 Form 942			326 46	0 00
1/1 1994		Angela Goettsch [Checking] 12/93 childcare	108 82			108 82
2/1 1994		Angela Goettsch [Checking] 1/94 childcare	108 82			217 64
3/1 1994		Angela Goettsch [Checking] 2/94 childcare	108 82			326 46
3/31 1994		Internal Revenue Service [Checking] 1Q '94 Form 942			326 46	0 00

Payroll-FICA: Register

Record   Restore   SPLITS   Current balance $0.00

This transaction shows a quarterly tax payment recorded in the checking account as a transfer to the liability account. The amount appears in the Decrease column because it decreases the total amount owed.

The Current Balance is the amount of Social Security tax owed as of today.

Using the asset account register

These purchases of new capital equipment were recorded in a checking account as transfers to the Cap Equip asset account. The amounts appear in the Increase column because they increase the total value of the account. You set up a single asset account for a group of related assets.

Instead of the Payment and Deposit columns of the check register, the asset account register has Decrease and Increase columns. Use the Decrease column to record amounts that decrease the value of your asset; use the Increase column to record amounts that increase the value of your asset.

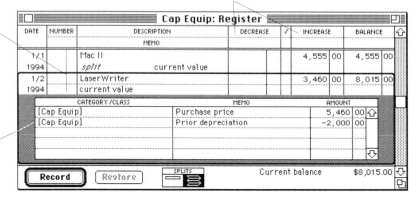

This depreciation transaction was recorded directly in the asset account register. The amount is negative in the Amount column because it decreases the value of the asset account.

Updating the value of asset and liability accounts

In asset and liability accounts, you don't have to reconcile the account in the same way you reconcile a checking account. Instead you can mark transactions that are closed or update the values of those that are still open.

Closing assets or liabilities

Closed items are those that are no longer active as assets or liabilities. For example, if you sell an asset listed in an asset account, such as an antique, or you pay off a loan listed in a liability account, that item is no longer part of your net worth. You won't want to include it in most reports; however, you don't want to delete it from your account, either. (In the event of an audit, you might want to produce a report that includes it.)

The solution is to mark closed items as cleared. Then you can restrict your report to uncleared items only. Open the asset or liability account and mark as cleared both the transaction for the purchase and for the sale of an item. (To mark a transaction as cleared, select it and then click its ✓ (cleared) field.) Use Find (⌘ F) to locate related transactions.

Updating the account balance

You can have Quicken make an adjustment to the balance in the account to update the current value of the account. For example, if you have an asset account for some real estate you own, you can tell Quicken to enter a transaction to update the current value of the property.

1   **Open the account.**

2   **Choose Adjust Balance from the Activities menu.**

3   **Enter the amount and date that represent the true balance of the account.**

For example, if you know that your property is worth $15,000, enter that amount. Quicken compares this amount with the current balance in the account and creates an adjustment transaction for the difference.

4   **(Optional) Enter a category name for the adjustment transaction.**

5   **Click OK to record the balance adjustment transaction in the register.**

Tracking investments

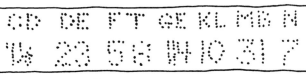

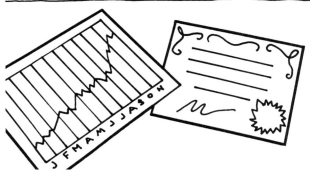

This chapter describes how to use Quicken to track your investments in stocks, bonds, mutual funds, and other investments that fluctuate in price.

Quicken shows you whether you are making or losing money on each investment and lets you compare the performance of your investments. At tax time, Quicken can report on investment income and capital gains for the year.

When to use an investment account

Quicken portfolio and mutual fund accounts help you keep track of investments that fluctuate in price, such as stocks, bonds, and mutual funds. We designed these accounts for investors who want to track their investment transactions, see the performance of investments, update current market values, and create tax reports.

When you record investment transactions in a portfolio or mutual fund account and enter current prices from time to time, Quicken shows you how much your investments are worth. Quicken investment reports and graphs give you all the information you need to analyze your investment portfolio.

To track an investment in a portfolio or mutual fund account, you must know the share price and dollar amount for each purchase or sale transaction. If you don't have this information (retirement plans often don't provide these details), use an asset account instead of a portfolio or mutual fund account.

It's also simpler to use an asset account if an investment has a constant share price or no share price and is not in a brokerage account with investments that do fluctuate. (See Chapter 15, *Tracking assets and liabilities*, beginning on page 225.) However, you may want to use a portfolio or mutual fund account to take advantage of Quicken's ability to calculate return on investment.

If you invest in	Use this type of account
Stocks, bonds, and mutual funds for which you want to track a cash balance (for example a collection of investments through brokerage firm)	Portfolio
A single mutual fund that has no cash balance	Mutual fund
Real estate investment trusts (REITs) or partnerships	Portfolio
Unit trusts	Portfolio
IRA accounts, Keogh accounts, or variable annuities	Portfolio
Cash management accounts (CMAs)	Bank for checking part of account, Portfolio for everything else (use transfers for purchases, dividends, and so on)

If you invest in	Use this type of account
Money market funds	Bank (if you write checks) Mutual fund (if you want the IRR—internal rate of return)
CDs, Treasury bills, collectibles, and precious metals	Portfolio or asset
Fixed annuities	Portfolio or asset
Employer retirement plans (401(k)✳, 403(b), pension)	Portfolio or asset
Real estate	Asset

✳ If your 401(k) gives you a statement that shows every purchase, with the number of shares and price for that purchase, you can use a portfolio account to track the 401(k). If your 401(k) does not give you a detailed statement that shows every purchase, you don't have enough information to use a portfolio account. Instead, use an asset account and adjust the balance when you get your statement. If you want to keep track of the different funds that make up your 401(k) but your statement doesn't provide enough information to use a portfolio account, use a separate asset account for each fund.

After you set up the portfolio or asset account for the 401(k), you can transfer amounts from your paycheck to the 401(k) account. See "Sample split transactions" on page 94 for an example of a deduction from a paycheck to an IRA account. Use the same technique to record a 401(k) deduction from your paycheck.

Here are some recommendations about how to group your securities within one or more Quicken investment accounts.

Security type	Recommendation
Brokerage accounts	Use a separate Quicken portfolio account for each actual brokerage account or other managed account you have.
	If you have a cash management type of account (CMA) with a broker, set up the checking part as a Quicken bank account. (You'll be able to print checks, track check numbers, and reconcile easily.) Set up a Quicken portfolio account for the rest of the investments in the brokerage account. You transfer money between the two Quicken accounts when you buy and sell investments or receive investment income.

Security type	Recommendation
IRAs, 401(k) accounts	Use separate Quicken portfolio accounts for your IRA and for your spouse's IRA. (Even if you do not have securities with fluctuating prices in your IRA, it's a good idea to set up your IRA as a Quicken portfolio account, as you may want to change the investments later.) This advice applies to other retirement plans that you manage directly, such as a Keogh plan. If you have more than one security in your IRA, put them in the same Quicken portfolio account, even if the securities are managed by, say, different mutual fund managers. If you transfer an IRA security from one manager to another, Quicken can still track the performance of your IRA as a whole.
Securities you hold directly	If you have a few individual securities you hold directly, you may wish to set each one up as a separate Quicken portfolio account. Then you can easily reconcile each account with its statement. On the other hand, you may prefer to lump the securities in a single Quicken portfolio account, especially if you have other portfolio accounts. Then you can subtotal these securities by account on reports and track them as a group.

Although Quicken can handle most common investment needs, its investment tracking does have limitations. Although it can import data from a file (for example Quicken can import prices saved from a Prodigy Quote Track list), Quicken does not currently retrieve prices on its own via modem. While Quicken provides basic tax reports, it doesn't keep track of changes in tax laws. Finally, Quicken doesn't track aspects of sophisticated transactions such as commodities trading or strike prices.

Deciding the investment account type (portfolio or mutual fund)

Quicken has two types of investment accounts: the portfolio account and the mutual fund account. When you set up the account, you designate the account type. The following table describes the differences between a portfolio account and a mutual fund account.

Type	Description
Portfolio account	Designed for one or more than one security.
	May have either a cash balance, as in a brokerage account, or no cash balance.
	The register displays the cash balance after every transaction and the current market value of the account. The register does not display the share balance (total number of shares) of individual securities within the account. (Quicken displays share balances of individual securities in the Portfolio window.)
	The advantage of the portfolio account is its flexibility. You can change the securities in it and leave cash in it.
Mutual fund account	Designed for a single mutual fund, not a family of funds. However, if you own shares in more than one mutual fund, you can set up a Quicken mutual fund account for each individual fund.
	Restricted to only one security. (You should not have two or more mutual funds in the same mutual fund account.)
	It has no cash in it, only shares of the security.
	The register displays the share balance (total number of shares) of the single security and the current market value of the security.
	The advantage of the mutual fund account is that certain procedures are streamlined. For example, when you write a check from your Quicken checking account to the mutual fund account, the transaction automatically appears in the mutual fund register as a purchase of shares.

Portfolio accounts and mutual fund accounts give you the same information about your investments. Quicken allows you to track income, capital gains, and performance of individual securities no matter what type of account they are in.

In addition to the uses listed on the previous page, you can also use a mutual fund account to track the value of one foreign currency. See "Managing foreign currency" on page 277.

Choosing an option for first-time setup

When you set up a new portfolio or mutual fund account, you have three options for setting up your opening balance (see page 236). We recommend the first option.

Options	Advantages	Disadvantages
Option 1: Enter all historical data. For each security in the account, enter the initial purchase and all subsequent transactions: • Name and type of security • Date, amount invested, and number of shares bought (or price per share) for initial purchase • All subsequent acquisitions (including reinvestments), sales and gifts, stock splits, and return of capital • All dividends, interest, and capital gains distributions for the current year • (Optional) All nonreinvested dividends, interest, and capital gains distributions for prior years (This data gives you a more complete value for the performance of your security for past years but does not affect Quicken's value for the cost basis.) • Price per share at the end of last year (and prior years, if available) and today	All Quicken reports are complete and accurate. If you sell a security, the capital gains report displays the purchase dates, amounts invested, and the realized gain, so you can use this report to prepare Schedule D tax information. All your investment records are in one convenient place, making it easier for you to analyze your investments and produce data for tax and other purposes.	You have to locate data for transactions that occurred in the past. You must spend time entering all prior transactions.

Options	Advantages	Disadvantages
Option 2: Set up for this year. Enter your investment holdings as of the end of last year. Then enter all investment transactions for each security since the beginning of this year. For each security in the account, enter: • Name and type of security • Number of shares owned at the end of last year • Price per share at the end of last year and today • All transactions (purchases, sales, dividends, reinvestments, and so on) for the current year	The information you need to gather goes back only to the end of last year and is probably easy for you to find. Data for the year is complete, so you can use the investment income report to prepare Schedule B tax information. Quicken produces accurate reports on performance, income, and changes in unrealized gain for time periods starting with the beginning of this year.	Quicken cannot give you an accurate value for total unrealized gain, which depends on the *cost basis* for the security.※ If you sell the security, the capital gains report does not display an accurate purchase date. Also, because the cost basis only dates back to the beginning of the year, the realized gain is not accurate.
Option 3: Set up fast. Enter your current investment holdings. For each security in the account, enter: • Name and type of security • Number of shares you now own • Current price per share	You can get started with the minimum amount of information to gather. You can start using the account right away to see whether you think it's worthwhile to gather and enter more information. Quicken produces accurate reports on performance, income, and changes in unrealized gain for time periods starting now.	Data for this year is incomplete, so you can't use the investment income report to prepare Schedule B tax information. You may have to wait a few months before your investment data is in the range where Quicken can display a valid investment performance report. Quicken cannot give you an accurate value for total unrealized gain, which depends on *cost basis* for the security.※ If you sell the security, the capital gains report does not display an accurate purchase date. Also, because you are starting from today, the realized gain is not accurate.

※ *Cost basis* is the IRS term for the amount of money you have invested in your shares. The IRS permits several different accounting methods to determine cost basis. Quicken uses the First In, First Out (FIFO) method. FIFO is the most popular method of calculating cost basis and is the standard method currently used by the IRS. Under the FIFO method, Quicken assumes that the shares you sold are the ones you've held the longest.

Setting up a portfolio account

A portfolio account is designed to track more than one security. To set up a portfolio account in Quicken, you need to do three things:

◆ Set up the Quicken portfolio account (below).

◆ Set up all the securities in the account (page 240).

◆ Set up the opening share balance (the number and value of shares you own) of each security in the account (page 241).

Setting up a Quicken portfolio account

1 Choose New Account from the File menu.

See "Deciding the investment account type (portfolio or mutual fund)" on page 235 for more information about the portfolio account type.

```
┌─────────────────── Set Up Account ───────────────────┐
│ ┌─ Account Type ─────────────────────────────────────┐│
│ │ ○ Bank Account              ○ Liability            ││
│ │   Use for checking, savings, or money    Use for items you owe, such as a loan ││
│ │   market accounts.                       or mortgage.  ││
│ │ ○ Cash                      ◉ Portfolio            ││
│ │   Use for cash transactions or petty cash.  Use for brokerage accounts, stocks, ││
│ │                                          or bonds. ││
│ │ ○ Asset                     ○ Mutual Fund          ││
│ │   Use for valuable assets such as your home.  Use for a single mutual fund. ││
│ │ ○ Credit Card                                      ││
│ │   Use for any credit card account.                 ││
│ └────────────────────────────────────────────────────┘│
│   Account Name:  Schwab                                │
│   Description:   111-222-333                           │
│   (optional)                                           │
│        [ Notes ]   [ Cancel ]   [ Create ]             │
└───────────────────────────────────────────────────────┘
```

2 Select Portfolio as the account type.

3 Enter a name for the account in the Account Name field.

Use the broker's name or a descriptive name such as "Schwab."

4 (Optional) Enter a description of the account.

You may use up to 30 letters, numbers, or spaces.

5 Click Create to set up the account.

Quicken opens the Portfolio window for this account. The Portfolio window is where you set up each security in the account. For example, if you are holding shares of two different stocks in a brokerage account and the cash balance in the brokerage account is invested in a money market fund, you might set up three securities: two for the stocks and one for the money market fund.

6   **Continue to "Setting up the securities in a portfolio account" on page 240.**

Where your investment data goes:

You set up a portfolio account in Quicken to track one or more securities. For example, you would set up a portfolio account to track a brokerage account with a cash balance.

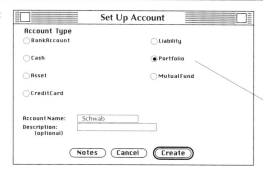

When you set up a portfolio account, Quicken opens the Portfolio window for the account. The Portfolio window is where you set up all the securities in the account.

You also use the Portfolio window to update security prices and view market values and prices for different dates.

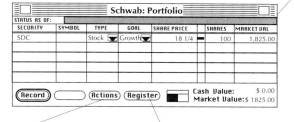

A

Schwab: Actions	
Transfer Money	Move cash from one account …
Buy	Buy shares with cash
Sell	Sell shares and receive cash
Misc. Income	Income from a miscellaneous …
Misc. Expense	Expense for various reasons
Move Shares In	Add shares to account without …
Move Shares Out	Remove shares from account …
Dividend	Receive cash from a dividend
Interest Income	Receive cash from interest …
Capital Gain Long	Receive cash from long-term …

B

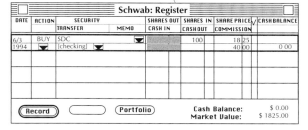

Two ways to enter transactions:

A - QuickForms

If you are new to Quicken or to investments, you can use QuickForms to enter investment transactions (Buys, Sells, Dividends, and so on).

B - The register

You can enter investment transactions directly into the account register once you are familiar with Quicken and with the different actions. The register is where you can view all the transactions that have been entered in the account.

As you record investment actions using QuickForms or the Action popup menu in the register, Quicken automatically updates the prices in the Portfolio window.

Setting up the securities in a portfolio account

Quicken opens the Portfolio window when you set up a portfolio account. The Portfolio window is where you set up all securities in the account. For now, don't worry about the date or share prices.

1 Enter the name of the first security in the Security field.

To delete a security, select the security and choose Delete Security from the Edit menu. You can delete a security only if you own zero shares.

If you want to see onscreen guides on what to enter in each field, choose Qcards from the Settings menu, and then select Investments and click OK.

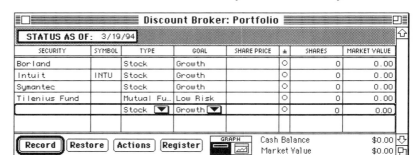

2 (Optional) Enter a symbol in the Symbol field if you plan to export or import price data from a file.

For more information about using symbols, see "Importing prices" on page 272.

The preset list of security types:
- Bond
- CD
- Mutual Fund
- Stock

Quicken can sort and subtotal investment reports and graphs by security type.

You cannot delete a type being used for any security

3 Choose the type appropriate for this security from the Type popup menu.

If none is appropriate, choose Edit from the Type menu and click New in the Types window. For example, you might add Money Fund, T-Bill, Tax-Free Bond, Option, REIT, Unit Trust, NYSE, NASDAQ, or AMEX. You can also use types or goals to identify taxable vs. tax-free income or securities in your children's names.

The preset list of investment goals:
- College Fund
- Growth
- High Risk
- Income
- Low Risk

Quicken can sort and subtotal investment reports and graphs by investment goal.

4 (Optional) Choose the investment goal appropriate for this security from the Goal popup menu.

If none is appropriate, choose Edit from the Goal menu and click New in the Goals window. For example, you may wish to add Retirement, Down Payment, Remodeling, Growth & Income, or Medium Risk. You may also use goals to designate industry groups (such as technology, energy, consumer products, and so on).

5 Click Record to save the new security.

Ignore the Share Price field for now.

Or press ⌘ N

6 Choose New Security from the Edit menu and repeat steps 1 through 5 for each security in this account.

Setting up the opening balance of each security

If you don't remember which option you decided to use for setting up the opening share balance, see "Choosing an option for first-time setup" on page 236.

If you don't enter a complete transactions history for a security, starting with the initial purchase or acquisition, Quicken cannot report accurate unrealized or realized gains. See page 274.

Most people will need to record a "Move Shares In" transaction for each security in the account. Move Shares In has two functions:

- It allows you to add shares you already own to a Quicken account.

- It also allows you to enter a purchase of shares for a date prior to when you started using Quicken, without deducting the money from a Quicken account.

1 Select a security in the Portfolio window and click the Actions button at the bottom of the window.

2 In the Actions window, double-click Move Shares In.

For option 1 (recommended), fill in the following information:

Enter the number of shares you purchased or acquired on this date. (See step 3 on page 242.)

Enter your actual initial cost per share (including commission, fees, and load), or leave this field blank. (See step 4 on page 242.)

```
☐☰ Discount Broker: Move Shares In ☰
Move Shares In          Date      6/1/90
      100  Shares Of   Borland      ▼
                       At      5.25
Memo: initial purchase
 Record    Cancel
```

Enter the date of your initial purchase or acquisition of the security.

If necessary, choose a security from this popup menu.

Alternatively, if you opened your real-world portfolio (brokerage) account AFTER you started using Quicken, you might want to start by transferring money from your Quicken bank account to your Quicken portfolio account. (Use the Transfer Money action to record the opening cash balance of the portfolio account as a transfer from your bank account.)

Then, use the Buy action to record a transaction for each initial purchase of a security instead of the Move Shares In action.

For option 2 (start this year), fill in the following information:.

Enter the number of shares you owned on 12/31 of last year. (See step 3 on page 242.)

Enter the cost per share (including commission, fees, and load) if you purchased the security all at one time, or leave this field blank. (See step 4 on page 242.)

```
☐☰ Discount Broker: Move Shares In ☰
Move Shares In          Date     12/31/92
      100  Shares Of   Borland      ▼
                       At      5.25
Memo: purchased 6/1/90
 Record    Cancel
```

Enter 12/31 of last year.

If necessary, choose a security from this popup menu.

For option 3 (start today), fill in the following information:

Enter the number of shares you now own. (See step 3 on page 242.)

Enter today's date.

```
┌─────────────────────────────────────────┐
│ ▣☐▤ Discount Broker: Move Shares In ▤▤▤ │
│                                           │
│  Move Shares In        Date      6/1/93   │
│  _____100  Shares Of  │Borland  │  ▼│    │
│                        At ____5.25        │
│  Memo: purchased 6/1/90                   │
│  ┌────────┐  ┌────────┐                   │
│  │ Record │  │ Cancel │                   │
│  └────────┘  └────────┘                   │
└─────────────────────────────────────────┘
```

Enter the cost per share (including commission, fees, and load) if you purchased the security all at one time, or leave this field blank. (See step 4 on page 242.)

If necessary, choose a security from this popup menu.

3   **In the Shares field, enter the number of shares you owned on the date in the Date field (up to four decimal places).**

Security type	Number of shares to enter
Stock or mutual fund	Actual number of shares
Bonds	Ten times the actual number of bonds (to match the way prices are quoted). Equivalently, enter one hundredth of the total face value of the bonds. For example, if you have two bonds with a total face value of $2,000, enter 20 in the Shares field.
Money market fund or CD	The total dollar value
Collectible	The number 1
Precious metal	The number of ounces

4   **In the "At" (Share Price) field, enter a share price in decimals or fractions.**

To enter a share price as a whole number plus a fraction, leave a space after the whole dollar amount, and use a slash (/) between the numerator and denominator. For example, enter 36 3/8.

Security type	Price to enter
Stock or mutual fund	Actual price per share
Bonds	One-tenth of the actual market value of each bond (to match the way prices are quoted)
Money market fund or CD	One dollar

Security type	Price to enter
Collectible	Total value
Precious metal	Price per ounce

5   **(Optional) In the Memo field, enter a memo.**

6   **Click Record to save the Move Shares In transaction.**

7   **Repeat steps 1 through 6 for each security in the account.**

8   **For options 1 and 2, use the actions in the Actions window to record subsequent transactions for each security according to the table on page 236 (purchases, sales, dividends, reinvestments, and so on).**

See "Recording your investment transactions" on page 249 for details about entering the most common investment transactions.

9   **Check the cash balance in the lower right corner of the Portfolio window.**

The cash balance in this brokerage account is invested in a money market fund (Tilenius MMF), so the remaining cash balance is zero (0.00).

The cash balance in the account. When you record a action, Quicken calculates the correct cash balance. If you have no cash in the account, the column displays zeros.

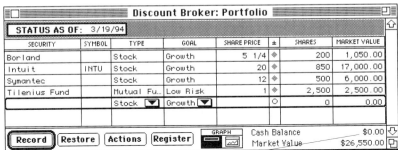

SECURITY	SYMBOL	TYPE	GOAL	SHARE PRICE	±	SHARES	MARKET VALUE
Borland		Stock	Growth	5 1/4	◈	200	1,050.00
Intuit	INTU	Stock	Growth	20	◈	850	17,000.00
Symantec		Stock	Growth	12	◈	500	6,000.00
Tilenius Fund		Mutual Fu...	Low Risk	1	◈	2,500	2,500.00
		Stock ▼	Growth ▼		○	0	0.00

Discount Broker: Portfolio — STATUS AS OF: 3/19/94

Record Restore Actions Register GRAPH Cash Balance $0.00
Market Value $26,550.00

The market value of the account is the number of shares times the most recently entered price.

- If the final amount displayed for the cash balance in this account is correct, your portfolio account is now set up. Skip ahead to "Updating the prices of your securities" on page 267.

- If the final amount displayed for the cash balance in this account is not correct, see "Setting up the cash balance in a portfolio account" next to continue.

Setting up the cash balance in a portfolio account

You might have a cash balance in your portfolio account. For example, you might have transferred some funds from a bank account, sold some securities, or received a cash dividend or interest. After you have entered all the transactions for your securities according to the first-time setup option you selected from the table on page 236, you can set up the correct cash balance for your account.

> **Optional MMF setup:** Usually, the cash balance of a brokerage account is swept periodically into a money market mutual fund that pays interest (this interest can be taxable or tax-exempt). If the cash balance in your portfolio account is invested in a money market fund (MMF), we recommend that you set up that MMF as a security like any other in the account. The Portfolio window for the account shows how much cash you have invested in the MMF, and you can enter dividends as you would for any other security. See "Entering dividends and interest" on page 257.

1   Choose Adjust Cash Balance from the Activities menu.

Quicken displays the Adjust Cash Balance window.

2   Enter the current cash balance and date for this account.

Quicken adds a balance adjustment transaction in the portfolio account register that makes your cash balance correct.

Your portfolio account is now set up. Quicken displays the market value of your account in the lower right corner of the Portfolio window and the register, based on the latest prices you supplied.

3   Update the prices in the Portfolio window.

- For options 1 or 2, you need to enter prices for the end of last year as well as for today. Then you can track unrealized (paper) gains or losses and performance for the current year.

- For option 3, you need to enter current prices for your securities.

See "Updating the prices of your securities" on page 267.

Setting up a mutual fund account

A mutual fund account is designed to track a single mutual fund with no cash balance. To set up a mutual fund account in Quicken, you need to do two things:

◆ Set up the Quicken mutual fund account (below)

◆ Set up the opening share balance—the number and value of shares you own (page 247).

Setting up a Quicken mutual account

1 **Choose New Account from the File menu.**

See "Deciding the investment account type (portfolio or mutual fund)" on page 235 for more information about the mutual fund account type.

```
━━━━━━━━━━━━━━━ Set Up Account ━━━━━━━━━━━━━━━
┌─ Account Type ──────────────────────────────────────────┐
│ ○ Bank Account                      ○ Liability          │
│   Use for checking, savings, or money   Use for items you owe, such as a loan │
│   market accounts.                      or mortgage.     │
│ ○ Cash                              ○ Portfolio          │
│   Use for cash transactions or petty cash.  Use for brokerage accounts, stocks, │
│                                         or bonds.        │
│ ○ Asset                             ● Mutual Fund        │
│   Use for valuable assets such as your home.  Use for a single mutual fund. │
│ ○ Credit Card                                            │
│   Use for any credit card account.                       │
└──────────────────────────────────────────────────────────┘
   Account Name:  [ Wichman Fund          ]
   Description:   [                        ]
   (optional)
        [ Notes ]   [ Cancel ]   [ Create ]
```

2 **Select Mutual Fund as the account type.**

3 **Enter a name for the account in the Account Name field.**

You'll probably want to use the name of the mutual fund. You may use up to 15 letters, numbers, or spaces.

4 **(Optional) Enter a description of the account.**

You may use up to 30 letters, numbers, or spaces.

5 **Click Create to set up the account.**

Quicken opens the Portfolio window for this account. The Portfolio window is where you enter the opening share balance of the account. See the illustration on page 246.

6 Continue to "Entering the opening share balance of a mutual fund account" on page 247.

Where your investment data goes:

You set up a mutual fund account in Quicken to track a single mutual fund with no cash balance.

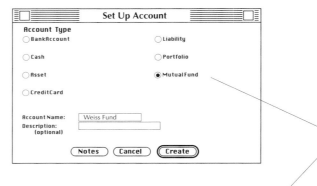

When you set up a mutual fund account, Quicken opens the Portfolio window for the account.

The Portfolio window is where you view and update the price history and market value for the fund.

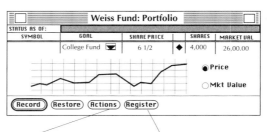

A

B

DATE	ACTN	TRANSFER MEMO	SHARES OUT CASH IN	SHARES IN CASHOUT	SHARE PRICE COMMISSION	√	SHARE BALANCE
4/10 1994	BUY	[Steve Checking]		265.376 1,678.26	6.250 19.66		265.376

Weiss Fund: Register

(Record) ( ) (Portfolio)   Cash Balance: 265.376   Market Value: $ 0.00

Two ways to enter transactions:

A - QuickForms

If you are new to Quicken or to investments, you can use QuickForms to enter investment transactions (Buys, Sells, Reinvested Dividends, and so on).

B - The register

You can enter investment transactions directly into the register once you are familiar with Quicken and with the different actions. The register is where you can view all the transactions that have been entered in the account.

As you record investment actions using QuickForms or the Action popup menu in the register), Quicken automatically updates the prices in the Portfolio window.

Entering the opening share balance of a mutual fund account

It you don't enter a complete transactions history for a security, starting with the initial purchase or acquisition, Quicken cannot report accurate unrealized or realized gains. See page 274.

If you don't remember which option you decided to use for setting up the opening share balance, see "Choosing an option for first-time setup" on page 236.

You need to record a "Move Shares In" transaction for your shares in this fund. Move Shares In has two functions:

- It allows you to add shares you already own to a Quicken account.

- It also allows you to enter a purchase of shares for a date prior to when you started using Quicken, without deducting the money from a Quicken account.

1 **Click the Actions button in the Portfolio window.**

2 **In the Actions window, double-click Move Shares In.**

3 **Fill in the Move Shares In window as shown for the setup option you want to use (option 1 is recommended).**

For option 1 (recommended), fill in the following information:

Enter the number of shares you purchased or acquired on this date.

Enter the date of your initial purchase or acquisition of these shares.

Enter your actual initial cost per share (including commission, fees, and load) or leave this field blank.

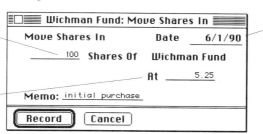

Alternatively, if you initially purchased this fund AFTER you started using Quicken, you might want to start by recording the purchase of the fund as a transfer from your bank account. (Use the Buy action to record the initial Buy transaction instead of the Move Shares action.) See "Transferring money to and from other accounts" on page 259.

For option 2 (start this year), fill in the following information:.

Enter the number of shares you owned on 12/31 of last year.

Enter 12/31 of last year.

Enter the cost per share (including commission, fees, and load) if you purchased the security all at one time, or leave this field blank.

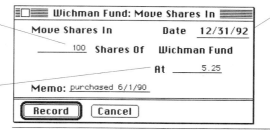

For option 3 (start today), fill in the following information:

Enter the number of shares you now own.

Enter today's date.

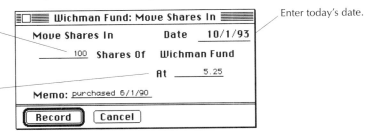

Enter the cost per share (including commission, fees, and load) if you purchased the security all at one time, or leave this field blank

4   Click Record to save the Move Shares In transaction.

Quicken records the price per share, multiplies the share price by the number of shares you own, and displays the result in the Market Value column of the Portfolio window.

In a mutual fund account, this column displays the number of shares you hold (to four decimal places). When you record a transaction, Quicken automatically calculates the correct total number of shares of the security you hold in the account.

The market value of the account.

Later on, after you have entered a few prices or investment actions, Quicken will display a graph here.

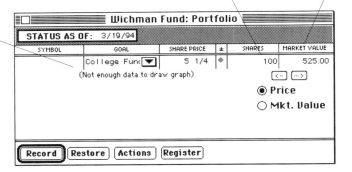

5   For options 1 and 2, use the actions in the Actions window to record subsequent transactions for this fund according to the table on page 236 (purchases, sales, dividends, reinvestments, and so on).

See "Recording your investment transactions" on page 249 for details about entering the most common investment transactions.

6   Update the market value of this fund in the Portfolio window.

- For options 1 or 2, you need to enter the price for the end of last year as well as for today. Then you can track unrealized (paper) gains or losses and performance for the current year.

- For option 3, you need to enter today's share price.

See "Updating the prices of your securities" on page 267.

Recording your investment transactions

This section describes how to record the most common investment transactions in a portfolio or mutual fund account. Before you begin recording investment transactions, see "Setting up a portfolio account" on page 238 or "Setting up a mutual fund account" on page 245.

Using QuickForms to enter investment transactions

1 **For help as you enter investment transactions, make sure investment Qcards are turned on before you start.**

To turn on investment Qcards, choose Qcards from the Settings menu. Then select Investments and click OK.

Or press ⌘ H

2 **Choose Portfolio from the View menu.**

3 **(Portfolio account option) Select the security for which you want to record an investment transaction.**

4 **Click Actions to display the Actions window.**

Click Actions to display the Actions window for this account.

You can also choose Actions (⌘ J) from the Activities menu to display the Actions window.

SECURITY	SYMBOL	TYPE	GOAL	SHARE PRICE	±	SHARES	MARKET VALUE
Borland		Stock	Growth	5 1/4	◆	200	1,050.00
Intuit	INTU	Stock	Growth	20	◆	850	17,000.00
Symantec		Stock	Growth	12	◆	500	6,000.00
Tilenius Fund		Mutual Fu...	Low Risk	1	◆	2,500	2,500.00
		Stock ▼	Growth ▼		○	0	0.00

Discount Broker: Portfolio
STATUS AS OF: 3/19/94

[Record] [Restore] [Actions] [Register]   GRAPH   Cash Balance $0.00
Market Value $26,550.00

5 **In the Actions window, double-click an investment action.**

See "Choosing investment actions" on page 250. Quicken displays the QuickForm for the action you chose.

If you're using a Quicken portfolio account, you have already used the Move Shares In action to record the opening share balance of each security in the account. If you're using a Quicken mutual fund account, you have already used the Move Shares In action to record the opening share balance of the fund.

6 **Follow the guidelines in the Qcards to fill in the investment action QuickForm, and then click Record.**

Quicken saves the transaction in the register for this account.

Choosing investment actions

You'll learn what action to choose for different investment transactions later in this section. See the page references in the table.

Action		Description	# of shares	Cost basis	Category⁂
Buy⁂	BUY	Buy security with cash (page 255).	Increases	Increases	—
Capital Gain Long⁂	CGL	Receive cash from long-term capital gains distribution (page 257).	—	—	• Long Cap Gain
Capital Gain Short⁂	CGS	Receive cash from short-term capital gains distribution (page 257).	—	—	• Short Cap Gain
Dividend⁂	DIV	Receive cash from dividend (page 257).	—	—	• Div Income
Interest Income⁂†	II	Receive cash from interest income (page 257).	—	—	• Int Income
Misc. Expense†	MISC	Pay for miscellaneous expense with cash.	—	—	Choose category from list
Misc. Income†	MISC	Receive cash from miscellaneous income.	—	—	Choose category from list
Move Shares In	MS	Add shares to account.	Increases	Increases	—
Move Shares Out	MS	Remove shares from account.	Decreases	Decreases	—
Reinvest Dividend	RD	Reinvest in additional shares of the security with money from dividend or income distribution (page 258).	Increases	Increases	• Div Income
Reinvest Interest	RI	Reinvest in additional shares of the security with money from interest distribution (page 258).	Increases	Increases	• Int Income
Reinvest Long	RL	Reinvest in additional shares of the security with money from long-term capital gains distribution (page 258).	Increases	Increases	• Long Cap Gain

Action		Description	# of shares	Cost basis	Category⌗
Reinvest Short	RS	Reinvest in additional shares of the security with money from short-term capital gains distribution (page 258).	Increases	Increases	•Short Cap Gain
Return of Capital※†	RC	Receive cash from return of capital.	—	Decreases	—
Sell※	SELL	Sell security and receive cash (page 255).	Decreases	Decreases	•Realized Gain or •Unrealized Gain
Stock Split	SS	Change number of shares as a result of stock split.	Increases (usually)	—	—
Transfer Money†	XFR	Transfer money in or out of this account.	—	—	Choose transfer account from list

⌗ Quicken adds investment categories to your category list when you add a portfolio or mutual fund account to your file. You cannot delete or edit these categories, which all begin with a "•" symbol. If you need to set up a new investment category for MISC actions, you can type Option-8 to insert a "•" at the beginning of the category name.

※ These actions can add cash to or remove cash from the current account, or they can involve a transfer of cash to or from another account. If you are using a mutual fund account, these actions *must* involve a transfer.

† These actions add cash to or remove cash from a portfolio account. They are not available in a mutual fund account because a mutual fund account cannot have a cash balance.

Entering investment transactions in the register

While you're learning how to enter investment transactions, use the investment action QuickForms described in "Using QuickForms to enter investment transactions" on page 249. Later, when you're familiar with entering investment transactions, you might find it faster to enter them directly in the account register.

1   **For help as you enter investment transactions, make sure investment Qcards are turned on before you start.**

To turn on transaction entry Qcards, choose Qcards from the Settings menu. Then select Investments and click OK.

The Qcards for entering investment transactions are the same as the Qcards for filling in an investment action QuickForm.

2 In the Date field, enter a date as you would in any register.

For a portfolio account, this column displays the cash balance in the account. When you record a transaction, Quicken calculates the correct cash balance. If you have no cash in the account, the column displays zeros.

The portfolio account register

Quicken outlines the name of the current field.

If a price for a stock or bond is not an exact multiple of 1/32, Quicken displays it as a decimal. If the number of shares is an exact integer, Quicken displays the number without decimals.

The mutual fund account register

If Quicken displays a row of asterisks (*****) in a register field, the number is too large for Quicken to display. Quicken displays dollar amounts between -$9,999,999.99 and $9,999,999.99. Outside of that range, Quicken keeps track of the amount but doesn't display it. (You can split a large transaction into two smaller transactions with amounts that Quicken can display.)

In a mutual fund account, this column displays the number of shares you hold (to four decimal places). When you record a transaction, Quicken automatically calculates the correct total number of shares of the security you hold in the account.

3 In the Action field, choose an action name.

See "Choosing investment actions" on page 250. With QuickFill turned on, you start typing an action name and Quicken fills in the rest automatically. Once you choose the action you want to use, Quicken blocks out transaction fields that are irrelevant to that action. For example, the Shares In field is relevant to a Buy action because you are adding shares for a security to the account, but the Shares Out field is irrelevant.

4 (Portfolio accounts only) In the Security field, choose the name of the security associated with the action or set up a new security in the Portfolio window for the account.

With QuickFill turned on, when you start typing a security name, Quicken fills in the rest automatically.

For actions that do not involve securities, Quicken replaces the Security field with a Description field.

5   **If you are entering an action that affects the share balance of an account, you enter amounts in any two of these fields:**

For actions that increase the share balance:

(Share Price × Shares In) ± Commission = Cash Out (dollar amount)

For actions that decrease the share balance:

(Share Price × Shares Out) ± Commission = Cash In (dollar amount)

Quicken knows that share price, number of shares, and dollar amount are related. If you fill in only two of the three quantities, Quicken will calculate the third quantity from the relationship.

> You can enter up to four decimal places in the Share Price field. For information about how Quicken displays the amounts that you enter, see "How Quicken displays amounts in the portfolio or mutual fund register" on page 254.

6   **For a Buy or Sell action, you might need to enter commissions and fees in the Commission field.**

After you enter the commission or fee, Quicken adjusts the dollar amount in the Cash In or Cash Out field.

Alternatively, Quicken can calculate the commission or fee automatically. Enter values for the price, number of shares, and a dollar amount that includes the commission. If the dollar amount doesn't equal the price times the number of shares, Quicken enters a value for the commission or fee. For example, if you enter a purchase of 100 shares at $15 per share and a total cost of $1600, Quicken enters a commission of $100 for the transaction.

7   **(Optional) Fill in the Memo field.**

8   **Some actions require an account name in the Transfer field.**

Sometimes you are entering a transaction that involves a transfer of cash from one account to another. With QuickFill turned on, Quicken fills in the rest of the account name for you.

See "Transferring money to and from other accounts" on page 259 for more about investment transfers.

9   **One action, MISC, allows you to enter a category and class in the Category field.**

When you use the Miscellaneous action, Quicken displays a Category field. Choose a category as you do in other account registers.

10   Click Record to record the transaction as usual.

How Quicken displays amounts in the portfolio or mutual fund register

The way Quicken displays amounts in the register varies by field.

Field	How Quicken display amounts
Share Price	Quicken keeps internal track of decimal prices to the nearest 0.00005 and normally displays them to the nearest 0.001. It displays exact integers without decimals. If there are more than four decimal places, Quicken cuts off the additional places.
Shares In/Out	Quicken displays the number of shares to four decimal places. It displays exact integers without decimals. It does not display zeros after the decimal point unless they are followed by nonzero digits. If there are more than four decimal places, Quicken cuts off the additional places. For example, Quicken truncates the number of shares 8.21678 to 8.2167.
Cash In/Out	Quicken displays dollar amounts to two decimal places. When it calculates the amount from the price and number of shares, it rounds to the nearest 0.01. For example, if you enter 40.3 shares at $8.26, Quicken rounds the dollar amount upward to $332.88.

At the end of each year, you may wish to adjust for the effects of rounding, to make the register match your statements. You can adjust the cash balance or the share balances of individual securities. See "Adjusting the cash or share balance" on page 278.

If Quicken displays a row of asterisks (*****) in a register field, the number is too large for Quicken to display. Quicken displays dollar amounts between -$9,999,999.99 and $9,999,999.99. Outside of that range, Quicken keeps track of the amount but doesn't display it. If you wish, you can split a large transaction into two smaller transactions with amounts that Quicken can display.

Buying and selling securities

For every purchase and sale transaction, you must know two of these three factors:

1) the number of shares
2) the price of the shares
3) the amount of the transaction.

When you buy a security with money you already have, you pay for it either with cash from the same account or with cash you transfer from another account, such as your checking account.

Similarly, when you're selling a security, you can keep cash from the sale in the same account or transfer it to another account.

		Transfer information selected:	
Action	**Desired Result**	**In a QuickForm**	**In the register**
BUY	Quicken subtracts the purchase amount from the cash balance of the current account.	"this account" (or blank)✠	"no transfer" (or blank)✠
BUY	Quicken subtracts the purchase amount from the cash balance of [Checking].	[Checking]✳	[Checking]✳
BUY	Cash balance of current account is unchanged.	[Current Account]✛	[Current Account]✛
SELL	Quicken adds the sale proceeds to the cash balance of the current account.	"this account" (or blank)✠	"no transfer" (or blank)✠
SELL	Quicken adds the sale proceeds to the cash balance of [Checking].	[Checking]✳	[Checking]✳
SELL	Cash balance of current account is unchanged.	[Current Account]✛	[Current Account]✛

✠   This choice is not available in a mutual fund account because a mutual fund account cannot have a cash balance.

✳   In this table, "[Checking]" represents a generic transfer to or from any other account.

✛   In this table, "[Current Account]" represents the name of your current account.

See "Transferring money to and from other accounts" on page 259 for specific tips about recording purchase transactions in Quicken.

Commissions. If there is an explicit commission added to the purchase or subtracted from the sale proceeds, enter it in the Commission field.

Loads. A *load* (sometimes called a *front-end load*) is a commission built into the purchase price of a mutual fund or other security. A load fund has two share prices: a "Buy" or "Offer" price, and a "Sell" or net asset value (NAV) price. Enter the purchase of a load fund at the "Buy" price with no additional commission.

The true market value of your investment is based on the Sell or NAV price. If you want to correct the market value, update the price of the fund (see "Updating the prices of your securities" on page 267) using the NAV price. The difference between the market value and what you paid is the load.

A *back-end load* is a commission built into the selling price. Funds with these loads have a net asset value (share price) greater than the selling price. Enter the sale of such a fund using the actual selling price.

Accrued Interest. When you buy a bond after its original date of issue, you usually have to pay *accrued interest* to the previous owner. Accrued interest is interest the bond has already earned but not yet paid out.

- Use a Buy action to enter the bond purchase transaction without including accrued interest.

- Use the Misc. Expense action to enter the payment of accrued interest as a separate transaction. (If you are working in the register, use the MISC action.) Enter the security name in the Security field, the dollar amount in the Cash Out field, and the expense category "•Accrued Int" in the Category field.

- If you paid the accrued interest out of another Quicken account, enter a third transaction to show a cash transfer equal to the accrued interest. Use the Transfer Money action (XFR) and enter the source account.

Entering dividends and interest

For reinvested dividends or interest, including interest that stays in a CD or dividends that stay in a money market fund, see "Entering reinvestments" on page 258.

When you enter the receipt of cash from dividends or interest, tell Quicken whether the cash is staying in the account or being transferred out. Use the Dividend action (DIV) or the Interest Income action (II).

		Transfer information selected:	
Action	**Desired result**	**In a QuickForm**	**In the register**
DIV or II	Quicken adds the dividend or interest income to the cash balance of the current account.	"this account" (or blank)⊞	"no transfer" (or blank)⊞
DIV or II	Quicken adds the dividend or interest income to the cash balance of [Checking].	[Checking] ✳	[Checking] ✳
DIV or II	Cash balance of current account is unchanged.	[Current Account] ✚	[Current Account] ✚

⊞ This choice is not available in a mutual fund account because a mutual fund account cannot have a cash balance.

✳ In this table, "[Checking]" represents a generic transfer to or from any other account.

✚ In this table, "[Current Account]" represents the name of your current account.

For dividend income from a money market fund that is the cash balance of a brokerage account, use the Dividend action and enter the name of the money market fund in the Security field.

An *income distribution* is money a mutual fund pays you as a result of dividends and interest it receives from the securities within the fund. Treat it like dividends in Quicken.

Entering capital gains distributions from mutual funds

A *capital gains distribution* is money paid to you by a mutual fund as a result of capital gains the fund earns by selling securities within the fund. The fund usually informs you whether the distribution is for *short-term* or *long-term* capital gains. (You may receive both at the same time. If the fund doesn't tell you whether a capital gains distribution is short-term or long-term, assume it's long-term.) Under United States tax law at the time of this printing, short-term capital gains distributions are treated the same as dividends. Use the Capital Gain Long (CGL) or Capital Gain Short (CGS) action.

		Transfer information selected:	
Action	Result	In a QuickForm	In the register
CGL or CGS	Quicken adds the cash from the capital gains distribution to the cash balance of the current account.	"this account" (or blank)✠	"no transfer" (or blank)✠
CGL or CGS	Quicken adds the cash from the capital gains distribution to the cash balance of [Checking].	[Checking]✳	[Checking]✳
CGL or CGS	Cash balance of current account is unchanged.	[Current Account]✚	[Current Account]✚

✠ This choice is not available in a mutual fund account because a mutual fund account cannot have a cash balance.

✳ In this table, "[Checking]" represents a generic transfer to or from any other account.

✚ In this table, "[Current Account]" represents the name of your current account.

For capital gains distributions reinvested in new shares, see "Entering reinvestments" next.

Entering reinvestments

A *reinvestment* is the purchase of additional shares of a security with money paid to you by that security as dividend or interest income (Reinvest Dividend or Reinvest Interest) or capital gains distribution (Reinvest Long or Reinvest Short). (For a CD or money market fund, you are buying new shares at a share price of one dollar.)

Reinvestments work like two transactions: Dividend and Buy. Reinvestments increase your cost basis because each reinvestment counts as a purchase of shares.

Redeeming shares for IRA custodial fees

In a mutual fund account set up as an IRA or other retirement account, the fund custodian may redeem shares as a custodial fee.

For redemption of shares as a custodial fee, use the Sell action. Enter the share price and the dollar amount (Total Cost in the Sell action QuickForm, Cash In in the register). Also enter the dollar amount of the fee in the Commission field to make the net amount of the transaction zero. Enter the name of the account itself as the destination account for a transfer.

Transferring money to and from other accounts

If you have never created a transfer before, see "Transferring money between accounts" on page 86.

Some actions can involve a transfer of cash between the investment account and another account. Some examples:

- If you write checks by hand to pay for a security in a portfolio account, record a Buy action in the portfolio account with a transfer from a checking account. Then go to the checking account and fill in the check number on the checking account side of the transfer.

Use the Buy action to record the purchase.

Enter the name of the source bank account.

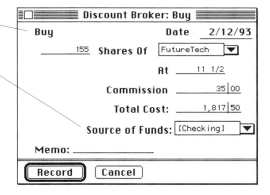

Quicken records the Buy transaction in the portfolio account register.

Here's the checking account side of the Buy transaction. Fill in the check number here.

- If you print checks using Quicken or use electronic payments to purchase securities, enter the payment in the checking account with a transfer to the portfolio account. You'll have to go to the portfolio register to change the Transfer Money action to a Buy action and add the security name (if needed), price, and number of shares.

This is the checking account side of the transfer. Select it and press ⌘ [to see the other side of the transfer.

DATE	NUMBER	DESCRIPTION		PAYMENT		√	DEPOSIT	BALANCE	
		CATEGORY/CLASS	MEMO						
2/14 1993	PRINT	Discount Brokers, Inc. [Discount Broker]		2,500 00				6,916 19	

Checking: Register

This Transfer Money transaction is the portfolio account side of the transfer. You need to change the action to Buy. Then enter the name of the security you're buying, the Share Price, and the Shares In amount.

DATE	ACTION	DESCRIPTION		SHARES OUT	SHARES IN	SHARE PRICE	√	CASH BALANCE	
		TRANSFER	MEMO	CASH IN	CASH OUT	COMMISSION			
2/14 1993	XFR ▼	Discount Brokers, [Checking ▼]			2,500 00			2,500 00	

Discount Broker: Register

- If you're buying a security in a mutual fund account, Quicken knows that you have only one security. When you enter the payment in your checking account with a transfer to the mutual fund account, Quicken records the transaction as a Buy in the mutual fund register and fills in the number of shares (Shares In) based on the most recent price known to Quicken. Thus, you'll probably choose to record the transaction from your checking account.

This is the checking account side of the transfer. Select it and press ⌘ [to see the other side of the transfer.

DATE	NUMBER	DESCRIPTION		PAYMENT		√	DEPOSIT	BALANCE	
		CATEGORY/CLASS	MEMO						
2/14 1993	PRINT	Janus Fund [Janus Fund]		2,500 00				6,916 19	

Checking: Register

Here's the mutual fund side of the transfer. Quicken sets it up as a Buy transaction and fills in the number of shares based on the most recent price you entered. You need to enter the Share Price and the Cash Out amount.

DATE	ACTION	TRANSFER		SHARES OUT	SHARES IN	SHARE PRICE	√	SHARE BALANCE	
		MEMO		CASH IN	CASH OUT	COMMISSION			
2/14 1993	BUY ▼	[Checking]			133.833 2,500 00	18.680 0 00		267.572	
4/14 1993	MS	[Janus Fund]		200				67.572	

Janus Fund: Register

- If you're transferring cash out of a portfolio account, enter a Transfer Money transaction in the portfolio account register. You can enter more information about the transaction in this register.

Giving and receiving securities

When you give or receive shares of a security, without using cash, Quicken treats the transaction differently than it treats a purchase or sale.

- If you're giving shares that are now in a Quicken account, use the Move Shares Out action to record the number of shares (but no price or dollar amount).

  Quicken reduces your number of shares and records a sale with a capital gain of zero, without adding cash to any account.

  If you're transferring the shares to another Quicken account, enter a separate transaction for receipt of the shares in the register of the second account.

- If you're receiving shares, use the Move Shares In action. The Move Shares In action increases your number of shares without subtracting cash from any Quicken account. Enter the number of shares received and the actual initial cost per share (including commission, fees, and load). The way you figure the cost depends on whether you're receiving the shares as a gift or as an inheritance:

  Inherited shares. The cost basis of inherited shares is generally the value of the shares on the date that the decedent died or alternative valuation date. When you receive the inherited shares, record the cost per share on that date.

  Gift shares. The cost basis of shares you received as a gift depends on the value of the shares on the date of the gift and the price that the giver paid for the shares, as well as your sale price if you sell the shares. When you receive the gift shares, record the cost per share when the giver originally purchased the shares.

  Consult your tax advisor about any additional rules that may apply to determining your gain or loss.

Entering stock splits and stock dividends

Stock splits. When a company declares a *stock split*, you are given additional shares. Each share is now worth less than it was before the split, but the total market value of all your shares is unchanged. (In a *reverse split*, you receive fewer shares than you have now.)

If you have more than one transaction for the security on the same day, Quicken places the stock split ahead of the other transactions. For example, if you had 100 shares before a two-for-one split, and you sell 100 shares on the day of the split, Quicken knows you still have 100 shares remaining.

When you record a stock split, Quicken recalculates your average cost per share and recalculates the price. Quicken doesn't change transactions previously recorded in the register.

- For a stock split, use the Stock Split action. (If you are in the Portfolio window, click the Actions button and double-click Stock Split. If you are working in the Register window, type ss in the Action field.)

This example is a 2-for-1 split.

To take another example, if you received one additional share for every three old shares, you would have four (or three plus one) for every three you had before, so the Split Ratio would be 4-for-3.

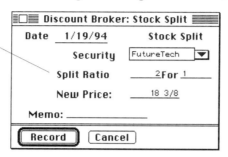

Discount Broker: Stock Split

Date	1/19/94	Stock Split
	Security	FutureTech
	Split Ratio	2 For 1
	New Price:	18 3/8
Memo:		

Record   Cancel

Stock dividends. A *stock dividend*, which is rare, is a dividend in the form of additional shares ***instead of cash***. Most stock dividends are nontaxable. The company issuing the stock dividend will inform you whether it is taxable.

A stock dividend is ***not*** the same as a cash (normal) dividend issued by a company nor is it the same as a reinvested cash dividend.

- Enter a nontaxable stock dividend as a stock split. For the ratio of new shares to old shares, add 1 to the number of dividend shares given per existing share. For example, if you receive 0.05 share per existing share, use 1.05 to 1 as the ratio of new shares to old shares.

- Enter a taxable stock dividend as a reinvested dividend.

Buying on margin

A *margin loan* is money you borrow from a broker to pay for a security you're buying. You don't have to tell Quicken you have a margin loan. (If you buy a security and don't have enough cash for it in your account, Quicken displays a negative cash balance.) Alternatively, you may want to set up a liability account for the loan.

- To record interest you pay on the margin loan, use the Misc. Expense action to record a margin interest transaction. (Use the MISC action if you are working in the register.) Assign the category •Int Expense to the margin interest transaction.

- If you have set up a liability account for the loan, use the Transfer Money action to record the amount you are borrowing at the time, and enter the liability account name in the action QuickForm Source of Funds field (or in the register Transfer field). (Enter another Transfer Money transaction when you pay off the loan.)

Buying and redeeming U. S. savings bonds

The U. S. government issues Series EE bonds in various face value denominations. You buy a Series EE bond at a discount from its face value. Interest is paid only when a bond is redeemed. The interest from a Series EE bond is exempt from state and local taxes, and no federal tax is due until the bond is redeemed.

- When you buy a Series EE bond, use this format:

In this example, the buyer purchased 1 Series EE bond with a face value of $1000.

(To match the way bond prices are quoted, you divided the price by 10 and multiplied the number of shares by 10.)

The purchase price was $500 because it was purchased at half face value. The security name is

US $1000 6% 1/23

This means "face value $1000, Series EE Bond, maturity date 1/2023."

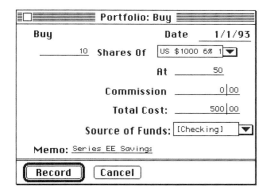

- When you redeem the savings bond (at or before maturity), enter the purchase price as the sales price in the Sell transaction. The difference between the purchase price and the redemption price is taxable interest. Use the Interest Income action to record the remainder of the proceeds as interest income.

If you use the cash method of accounting, as most individual taxpayers do, you generally report the interest on U. S. savings bonds when you receive it. If you use the accrual method of accounting, you must report interest on U. S. savings bonds each year as it accrues. To record the annual accrual of interest, use the method described for recording taxable interest in "Recording zero-coupon bonds" on page 265.

Redeeming T-bills

When you buy a T-bill, you buy it at a discount from its face value. When you sell it, part of the proceeds is interest you've earned while holding the bill.

- To record interest received when you sell, use the Interest Income action.

- Subtract the interest received from the total you receive. Enter the difference as the dollar amount (Net Proceeds) for the sale transaction.

Entering a return of capital or principal

A *return of capital* is money paid to you as total or partial repayment of the money you invested. Return of capital differs from a sale in that you are not the one who initiates the return of capital. For example, a mortgage-backed security (such as a Ginnie Mae) returns capital when the underlying mortgages pay off principal, which is passed on to you. A unit trust returns capital as it sells the bonds within the trust. Note that return of capital, which is not a taxable event, is different from capital gains distribution.

- For a return of capital or principal, use the Return of Capital action.

  Quicken reduces the cost basis of the security by the amount of the return of capital. If you have purchased shares of the security on different dates, Quicken reduces the cost basis of each set of shares in proportion to the number of shares in each set. You will see the adjusted cost basis of each set of shares in the capital gains report after you sell the shares.

  If you use the Return of Capital action with a *negative* amount, you *raise* the cost basis and decrease the cash balance in your account.

Recording zero-coupon bonds

You buy a zero-coupon bond at a discount. While you hold it, its value increases due to the interest it earns. Even though you don't receive this interest (until you sell), it is reported to you every year on a Form 1099-OID as taxable interest.

• To record interest shown on a Form 1099-OID, use the Interest Income action.

• To record the subsequent increase in value of the bond, use the Return of Capital action to record a second transaction. Enter a dollar amount equal to the *negative* of the interest. (The negative Return of Capital amount increases your cost basis. It thus reduces unrealized gain if you sell the bond or update to the current market price of the bond.)

Handling tax-free bond income

If you have a tax-free bond for which you want to record income, set up a new "TaxFree Int" category. When you receive a non-taxable dividend, use the Misc. Income action to record a transaction for the dividend. (If you are working in the register, use the MISC action.) Assign the "TaxFree Int" category to the transaction to separate your tax-free income from regular interest income.

Selling short

A *short sale* is the sale of a security you don't own. You deliver to the purchaser shares you borrow from your broker. You hope to buy the security later at a lower price to pay back your broker.

• For a short sale, use the Sell action.

• When you buy the security later, use the Buy action. Quicken calculates your gain or loss on the entire process at that time. The gains from short sales do not appear in capital gains reports. Use the investment income report to see your gains on short sales.

In investment performance reports, the average annual total return for short sales (a Sell followed by a Buy) as a negative value.

If you're selling short a security you already own in the same account (with the intention of buying additional shares), create different lots for the security. See "Using security lots" on page 273.

If you have a short sale that you want to appear in a capital gains report, you need to close out the short sale with a Buy at the original sales amount. Then enter a Buy at your actual purchase price and enter a second Sell transaction at the original sales amount.

This is your original short sale.

This transaction closes out the short with no gain/loss.

This is the buy that closed out your position. Enter it first so the trade can appear in the capital gains report.

This transaction closes out your trade, showing the profit in the capital gains report.

DATE	ACTION	SECURITY / **TRANSFER** MEMO	SHARES OUT / CASH IN	SHARES IN / CASH OUT	SHARE PRICE / COMMISSION	√	CASH BALANCE
4/1 1993	SELL	High-Tek / short sale	100 / 10,000 00		100 /		10,000 00
4/7 1993	BUY	High-Tek / no gain/loss		100 / 10,000 00	100 /		0 00
4/7 1993	BUY	High-Tek / close position		100 / 9,000 00	90 /		-9,000 00
4/7 1993	SELL	High-Tek / ●Reali… close trade	100 / 10,000 00		100 /		1,000 00
4/7 1993 ▼	BUY	▼				0 00	

Portfolio: Register

Entering options (puts and calls)

Treat an option like a security but give it a distinctive name (such as "XYZ put Aug 40"). If you sell an option you don't already own, Quicken treats it like a short sale. If an option you bought or sold expires worthless, enter the opposite action (Sell or Buy) for the option at a price of zero to close your position. Quicken then records a realized gain or loss. If you exercise a call, close your position with a Sell transaction for the call. When entering the purchase of the underlying security, include the cost of the call as a fee paid (to correct the cost basis).

Updating the prices of your securities

In the Portfolio window for an account, Quicken displays share prices and market values for all the securities in the account. You can update share prices daily if you like. (Quicken keeps track of one price per day.) Quicken uses new prices to recalculate the market values of the securities and the account.

Viewing and changing prices in the Portfolio window

When you first open a portfolio or mutual fund account, Quicken displays the Portfolio window. In the Portfolio window, Quicken displays prices and market values for the securities in the account "as of" the most recent prior date for which you recorded a price. If you want to look at prices and market values "as of" a different date, change the date in the "As Of" field.

Change this date to view share prices and market values "as of" a different date.

STATUS AS OF:	3/19/94	
SECURITY	SYMBOL	TYPE
Borland		
Delta		
Syntex		

Quicken uses the following symbols in the column after the Share Price field in the Portfolio window (see the illustration of the Portfolio window on page 268):

Share Price Symbol	Means
◆ (diamond)	This price is an estimate (Quicken uses the most recent share price you've entered for this security).
↑ or ↓	This price represents an increase or decrease over the previous known share price.
▬ (bar)	This price is the same as the last price entered for this security.
○ (circle)	No prices have been entered yet for this security.

1   Choose Portfolio from the View menu.

Market value equals the share price times the number of shares. Quicken cannot display a market value greater than $9,999,999. Quicken displays a row of asterisks (******) when the market value is greater than that amount.

The Portfolio window lists all securities for this account.

The only value that you can edit is the share price.

To delete a security, select it and press ⌘ D. You cannot delete a security when you have an open position for it (that is, when you own any shares).

```
▤□▥           Discount Broker: Portfolio           ▥□▤
  STATUS AS OF:  3/19/94
  SECURITY    SYMBOL    TYPE      GOAL     SHARE PRICE  ±   SHARES   MARKET VALUE
 Borland               Stock    Growth        5 1/4  ◈     200      1,050.00
 Intuit       INTU     Stock    Growth          20   ◈     850     17,000.00
 Symantec              Stock    Growth          12   ◈     500      6,000.00
 Tilenius Fund         Mutual Fu… Low Risk       1   ◈   2,500      2,500.00
                       Stock ▼  Growth▼             ○       0          0.00

 [ Record ] [ Restore ] [ Actions ] [ Register ]  GRAPH  Cash Balance      $0.00
                                                 ▭ ⌲     Market Value  $26,550.00
```

To see a graph of the price and market value of the selected security in a portfolio account, click Graph.

2   Change the "As Of" date to the date for which you wish to enter share prices.

	Press this key	
To go to this date	**In the Date field**	**In any other field**
Next day	+ (Plus)	Option-Plus
Previous day	− (Minus)	Option-Minus
Latest known price for the selected security	Option-Shift-Plus	Option-Shift-Plus
Earliest known price for the selected security	Option-Shift-Minus	Option-Shift-Minus
Next known price for the selected security	>	Option->
Previous known price for the selected security	<	Option-<

3   Select a security and enter the price for the "As Of" date.

Press + or − to change the price in the selected Share Price field to the next 1/8 (or 0.125).

For information about entering share prices for different kinds of securities, see page 242.

4   **Click Record to record the newly entered price.**

If this security has a symbol, Quicken updates any additional securities with the same symbol. For information about adding a symbol to a security, see "Setting up the securities in a portfolio account" on page 240.

5   **(Optional) To see a graph of the price or market value of the selected security, click Graph. Quicken will display a graph if you have entered more than one price for the security.**

Click an arrow to see the price history for the previous or next 12 months (if you have that much data entered into Quicken).

Click on a date in the graph to see the exact share price for that date.

You can also click in the graph and drag to the right or left to change the "As Of" date. The date in the small window under the Price/Market Value options shows what the "As Of" date will be when you release the mouse button.

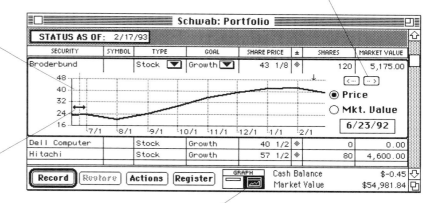

Click here to graph the price history for the selected security.

6   **(Optional) To print the contents of this window, choose Print Portfolio from the File menu.**

Removing a price in the Portfolio window

You may enter a price incorrectly and want to delete it. Or you might want to delete a price that shows up in an investment report or graph. Here's how to find the price in question and delete it:

•   If you know the date of the price you want to delete, use any of the techniques illustrated above to scroll to or jump to the date for that price. Then go to the Share Price field for that date, erase the price or enter 0 (zero), and click Record.

•   If you don't know the date of the price you want to delete, press > to review all prices entered after the current "As Of" date or press < to review all prices entered before the current "As Of" date.

Deleting a security in the Portfolio window

There is no need to delete an unused security in Quicken. However, you might want to delete a security for reasons such as these:

- You've been tracking a security that you don't own to see how it does and you lose interest in that security. (See "Tracking indexes and securities you don't own" on page 276.)

- You want to start over for any reason. (You usually don't have to delete the security to start over. It's probably simpler to edit the existing security name and price history in the Portfolio window.)

- You've been using Quicken for many years. Your portfolio contains many securities that you used to own, but don't own anymore. You decide to archive some of the old investment history to a backup file on a floppy disk and delete it from your working file.

You can delete a security as long as you don't have an open position in that security (that is, as long as you own zero shares for the security).

Deleting the security will not delete any transactions associated with the security. Any transactions associated with the deleted security will have a blank in the Security field. If you want to keep the transaction history in the register, you probably should keep the security, too. (Otherwise, investment reports and graphs from the older period will display no security names and will be difficult to decipher.)

1   Open the Portfolio window for the account.

2   Select the security you wish to delete.

Or press ⌘ D   **3   Choose Delete Security from the Edit menu.**

Analyzing your investments

Quicken takes the information you provide about your investments and produces summaries, reports, and graphs so you can see what you have and how well you're doing.

To get	Look in
Number of shares, market value, and price history of all securities in the account	Portfolio window for a portfolio account (page 267)
Share balance (number of shares), market value, and price history of the fund	Portfolio window for a mutual fund account (page 267)
Share balance and market value of the fund	Mutual fund account register or Portfolio window
Cash balance and market value of the account	Portfolio account register or Portfolio window
Number of shares of a security	Portfolio value report (page 306)
Market value (balance) of one or more accounts	
Market value (balance) of one or more securities	
Current cost basis of a security	
Unrealized gain or loss for one or more securities	
Realized gain or loss for one or more securities	Capital gains report (page 299)
Average annual total (IRR) return for one or more securities	Investment performance report (page 302)
Income and expenses for one or more securities or accounts	Investment income report (page 301)
Monthly portfolio value by security, type, goal, or account	Investment performance graph (page 348)
Average annual total return by security, type, goal, or account	
Market value of a security	

Importing prices

You can import security price data from a text file (for example, prices saved to a file from a Prodigy Quote Track list). The text file must have one symbol/price/date per line, delimited by either commas or double spaces (using only one type of delimiter per line).

Quicken matches up the prices it imports based on the *symbol*, not the *name*, of the security. If you wish to import prices, you need to add symbols to the securities in your Portfolio window.

These import formats are all acceptable. Note that Quicken can handle quotation marks:

ABC, 123.456

ABC, 123.456, 12/31/93

ABC   123.456   12/31/93

"ABC", 123.456, "12/31/93"

"ABC", "123.456", "12/31/93"

Delimit data on a line with either double spaces or commas. Use only one type of delimiter per line. Quicken will ignore single spaces.

Importing a price file into Quicken

1 **From the Portfolio window for an account, choose Import Prices from the File menu.**

2 **Select the file that contains the price data and click Open.**

Saving prices from a Prodigy Quote Track list to a file

For more information about using Prodigy quotes, open the Prodigy ABOUT menu and select the appropriate topic.

1 **In Prodigy, [Jump]:** QUOTE TRACK **and follow the onscreen instructions for creating or viewing a Quote Track list.**

2 **Choose REPORT SETUP from the FILE menu.**

3 **Set up the Quote Track Report Settings window like this:**

Range:	Entire List
Report Type:	Closing Prices
Destination:	File

4 **In the File Settings window, select the following options:**

Delimited (*.CSV)—You can use the name QTRACKØ1.CSV or change it.

No Column Headings

5 **Click Save and Print to create or update the destination file you specified.**

If the file already exists, Prodigy asks whether you want to write over it or add these quotes to it.

6 **If you have more Quote Track lists, you can view them and print to the same file without resetting the report options.**

Using security lots

One reason to use different lots of the same security is when you're selling a portion of your shares and want to identify which shares you're selling. (Unless told otherwise, Quicken assumes you're selling the ones you bought earliest.)

Or, you may sell short a security you already own in the same account, and you want Quicken to know that the short sale is for a different lot of shares.

When you create a new lot with the same symbol as an existing lot, Quicken gives it the same price history as the older lot.

When you update the share price of a security in the Portfolio window, Quicken updates any additional securities that have the same symbol. (See "Updating the prices of your securities" on page 267 for more information about viewing and changing prices in the Portfolio window.)

Creating a different lot for an existing security

1   **Set up a security with the same name but add a number after the name.**

2   **Use the same symbol for the security in both lots.**

Quicken recognizes lots of the same security by the symbol. If you don't have a symbol for the first security, edit it to give it one.

The symbol is the same for each lot. If you want to, you can edit the first security name to add a 1, so you'll recognize that it too is a separate lot.

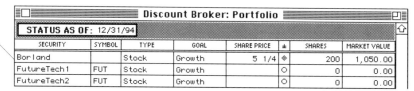

SECURITY	SYMBOL	TYPE	GOAL	SHARE PRICE	±	SHARES	MARKET VALUE
Borland		Stock	Growth	5 1/4	◆	200	1,050.00
FutureTech1	FUT	Stock	Growth		○	0	0.00
FutureTech2	FUT	Stock	Growth		○	0	0.00

Discount Broker: Portfolio
STATUS AS OF: 12/31/94

3   **If necessary, revise earlier transactions for the security in the register by substituting the new lot in the Security field.**

Entering prior history for investments

The more information you give Quicken about your investments, the more complete and accurate your reports and summaries will be. You may have set up a new investment account by entering a rough estimate of what you paid for the securities. You may have omitted dividends or capital gains distributions that you received since buying the securities.

To get	Tell Quicken
Accurate market values for a specified date	Price and number of shares of securities owned on that date
Accurate average annual total return for a specified time period	Price and number of shares on **day before** beginning of period and on last day of period
	All transactions during the period
Accurate capital gains summary (realized short-term and long-term gain or loss) for a specified time period	Number of shares and cost basis on date at least one year before beginning of period for all securities you have sold
	All purchases and sales (including stock splits, reinvestments, and return of capital) from that date to end of period
Accurate income and expense summary for a specified time period	All transactions during the period
	Number of shares owned and price per share at beginning and end of period (if you're including unrealized gains)

If you set up your investment account using Option 2 or 3 (see page 236), you might decide later to go back and enter a complete transaction history for your securities (Option 1). If you want to enter a complete transaction history for a security, the first step is to revise the Move Shares In transaction that you entered for that security.

Revising the initial Move Shares In transaction for a security

1   Select the Moves Shares In transaction for the security in the account register.

2   (Optional) Revise the date to the initial date of acquisition.

3   Enter your actual initial cost per share (including commission, fees, and load) in the Share Price field.

4   Revise the number of shares in the Shares In field.

5   Click Record to record the revised transaction.

The revised transaction appears in the register in the correct sequence for the new date.

Entering transactions for dates in the past

1   Enter additional transactions at the end of the register, but change the date that Quicken defaults to.

Quicken puts each new transaction in order by date.

2   If a transaction such as a Dividend or Sell involves a transfer of cash out of the account, or a Buy transaction involves a transfer of cash into the account, use a self-transfer transaction to avoid changing the cash balance in this account or any other.

To create a self-transfer transaction choose "this account" from the Destination of Funds menu (or Source of Funds menu) in the investment action QuickForm. If you are working in the register, insert the name of the current account in the Transfer field.

Use this procedure for both types of investment accounts. In a portfolio account, these types of self-transfer transactions have no effect on the cash balance.

3   If you want to enter a simple transfer of cash into or out of a portfolio account, use the Transfer Money action (XFR) to record a self-transfer transaction.

An XFR transaction with the name of the current account in the Transfer field increases or decreases the cash balance in the account.

4   After you've entered the transactions from the past, the cash balance in the account may be incorrect. Adjust it by choosing Adjust Cash Balance from the Activities menu. See "Adjusting the cash or share balance" on page 278.

Tracking indexes and securities you don't own

You may want to track one or more of the popular stock indexes, such as the Dow Jones Industrial Average or Standard & Poor's 500 stock index. Or you might want to track the price of a security you don't own. You have two options:

Option	How to set it up
Track prices only	Add the index or security to the Portfolio window for an existing portfolio account. For an index, you might want to set up a security type called "Index."
Track both prices and performance	Set up a portfolio account called "Index" or "What If", and set up the indexes or securities you want to track in that account.

1 **Open the Portfolio window for the account in which you want to track the index or security.**

2 **In the "As Of" field, enter the date from which you are beginning to track.**

3 **Set up the name, type, and goal of the first index or security you want to track.**

You don't really need a symbol unless you plan to import prices for the index or security from a file.

4 **Enter the index value or security price in the Share Price field.**

If you watch the price of a mutual fund you don't own, be aware that the price may drop because of income or capital gains distributions. When a fund makes a distribution, the share price is reduced by an equal amount (in addition to any changes caused by changes in market value of the underlying securities in the fund).

Managing foreign currency

If you have investments or other types of accounts in a country other than the United States, you need a way to manage foreign currency and keep track of changing exchange rates. You can use a Quicken mutual fund account to track holdings in a foreign currency.

1 Set up a Quicken mutual fund account for the account that you hold in a foreign currency.

If you don't know how to set up a mutual fund account, see page 245.

For example, you could set up an account with the name "U.K. Savings" for a bank account in the U.K.

Quicken opens the Portfolio window for the new account.

2 In the Portfolio window, enter the current exchange rate in the Share Price field.

For example, suppose the current rate to convert U.K. pounds to U.S. dollars is 1.5. You would enter 1.5 in the Share Price field.

3 Use the Buy or Move Shares In action to record an opening balance transaction for the account. Enter the balance of the account in the Shares In field.

4 When you earn interest in the account, record a Reinvest Interest transaction.

For the number of shares, enter amounts in U.K. pounds.

Enter the current exchange rate in the Share Price field.

This is the opening balance of the account.

Record a Reinvest Interest transaction when you earn interest on the account.

When you transfer funds between a Quicken bank account and the foreign currency account, Quicken automatically records a Buy or Sell transaction.

DATE	ACTION	TRANSFER / MEMO	SHARES OUT / CASH IN	SHARES IN / CASH OUT	SHARE PRICE / COMMISSION	√	SHARE BALANCE
1/1 1994	BUY	[U.K. Savings] Opening Balance		21,000 31,500|00	1 1/2		21,000
1/15 1994	RI	•Int Income		50 76|00	1.520		21,050
2/15 1994	RI	•Int Income		55 86|35	1.570		21,105
2/28 1994	BUY	[Checking]		2,000 3,080|00	1.540 0|00		23,105

U.K. Savings: Register

[Record] [Restore] [Portfolio]

Share Balance 23,105
Market Value $35,581.70

The share balance displays the current balance in U.K. pounds.

The market value displays the current balance in U.S. dollars.

5 (Optional) Keep track of the current exchange rate in the Portfolio window for the account.

Reconciling investment accounts

When you get a statement from your broker, mutual fund, or other financial adviser, you can reconcile your account with the statement.

Reconciling a portfolio or mutual fund account is similar to reconciling other Quicken accounts. You reconcile portfolio and mutual fund accounts the same way, except that you reconcile a cash balance in one and a share balance in the other. If you've been reconciling your other Quicken accounts, follow the same procedures. See "Starting reconciliation" on page 144 for more information.

After you've reconciled the cash balance in a portfolio account, go to the Portfolio window (⌘ H). If you haven't already entered the share prices from the statement, you have a chance to do so now.

> A mutual fund account that includes a stock split transaction cannot be reconciled. Use Adjust Share Balance to update the account to match your statements.

Adjusting the cash or share balance

If you don't want to use the Reconcile command, you can still adjust the cash balance in a portfolio account or the share balance of a mutual fund account to match what appears on your statement.

To adjust the share balance of a particular security in a portfolio account, use the Move Shares In action or Move Shares Out action.

1 **Choose Adjust Cash Balance from the Activities menu in a portfolio account. (For a mutual fund, choose Adjust Share Balance from the Activities menu).**

2 **Enter the date for the adjustment and the correct value for the new cash or share balance.**

For a portfolio account, the cash balance adjustment appears in the register with the action Transfer Money (XFR). For a mutual fund account, the share balance adjustment appears in the register with the action Move Shares (MS). The memo for the adjustment transaction is "Balance Adjustment."

Tracking loans

You can track loan amortization with Quicken.

By tracking a loan, you can stay up to date on the amount of interest you've paid on it for tax purposes and how its outstanding balance affects your net worth.

Quicken can handle many different loan features, including variable interest rates, balloon payments, and negative amortization. You can also use Quicken to track payments you receive for a loan.

Tracking loan amortization

Quicken can track how your loan is *amortized*, or paid off, with each payment you make. Quicken keeps you informed of the amount of interest you've paid on the loan and of the loan's outstanding principal.

If you've tracked loan amortization manually, you know how tedious it can be: Because each payment always covers a different proportion of interest and principal, a memorized transaction can't do the job for you completely – even if you pay the same amount every time. But Quicken can automate the tracking for you.

How Quicken tracks your loan

- **When you set up a loan for amortization**, Quicken creates two items that work in tandem to track your loan: a special memorized loan payment and a principal account.

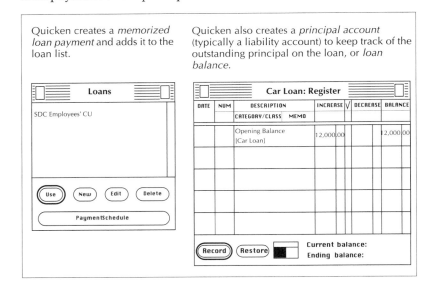

Quicken creates a *memorized loan payment* and adds it to the loan list.

Quicken also creates a *principal account* (typically a liability account) to keep track of the outstanding principal on the loan, or *loan balance*.

• **When it's time to make a payment on your loan**, you recall the memorized loan payment into the account that you're paying from. What makes the memorized loan payment special is that it automatically calculates the proportion of interest and principal when you recall it.

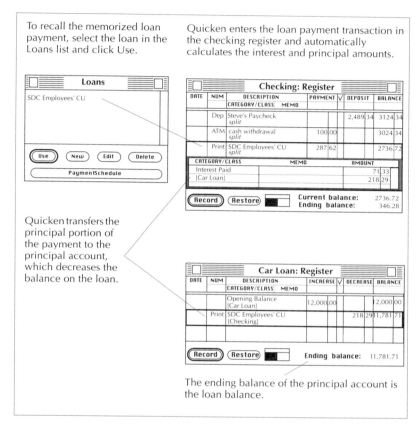

To recall the memorized loan payment, select the loan in the Loans list and click Use.

Quicken enters the loan payment transaction in the checking register and automatically calculates the interest and principal amounts.

Quicken transfers the principal portion of the payment to the principal account, which decreases the balance on the loan.

The ending balance of the principal account is the loan balance.

For more information about memorized transactions, see Chapter 11, *Saving time with memorized transactions*, beginning on page 157. For more information about liability accounts, see Chapter 15, *Tracking assets and liabilities*, beginning on page 225.

Setting up a loan

When you set up a loan, you enter information about your loan and lender. Quicken creates a memorized loan payment and the principal account based on your information.

Set up the loan using information that reflects the loan's current status. (To ensure accuracy, refer to the loan statement for the most recent payment.) Then Quicken will track the loan beginning with the next payment.

Quicken can handle a variety of loan features, which are described in the section starting on page 285. You may find it useful to refer to that section, both before you set up your loan and during loan setup.

1   Choose Loans from the View menu.

If you are setting up your first loan, skip to step 3.

2   Click New.

The loan list is where you go to set up a new loan, edit or delete an existing loan, or select a loan for which you want to enter a payment.

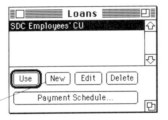

Click this button to set up a new loan.

3   In the Set Up Loan window, select the type of loan you are setting up and specify whether you want Quicken to confirm the loan payment before recording.

If you hold a loan note, click this button.

Select this checkbox if any of these items apply:

- You want to review or possibly change payment information each time you recall the loan payment.

- The loan has a variable interest rate.

- The loan has negative amortization.

- You plan to make prepayments of principal either occasionally or in varying amounts.

4   Fill in the Set Up Loan window with the scheduled payment, annual interest rate, total years, and payments per year.

As you fill in the fields, press Tab to move to the next field.

Enter the amount you currently pay toward principal and interest. Do not include other charges, such as impound or escrow payments.

Enter the current interest rate on the loan.

If you know the current balance on the loan, enter a number that's at least as large as the number of years remaining on the loan (the original loan term is a convenient number to enter). Be sure to enter the current balance in step 5.

If you don't know the current balance, enter the exact number of years remaining on the loan. (If your loan has a balloon payment, enter the number of years remaining in the amortization period.) See below for more information.

Enter the number of scheduled payments made per year.

Type of Loan	
● Borrowing	○ Lending

Loan Info

Scheduled payment:	1,933.91
Annual interest rate:	8.625 %
Total years:	30.00
Payments per year:	12
Loan amount:	248,641.75

Payment Coupon...

When you press Tab after filling in a field, Quicken calculates a loan amount based on the information you entered. This amount will be used as the current balance unless you change it in step 5.

Note: Your lender may use a different calculation method from Quicken.

If you know the current balance on the loan, the number you enter in the Total Years field needn't be accurate, only sufficiently large. But if you don't know the current balance, accuracy is important, as you'll use the loan amount that Quicken calculates as your current balance.

The following tips will help you enter an accurate number in the Total Years field:

- Use this formula to calculate the number of years remaining if you know how many payments you've already made and you've neither prepaid any principal nor had any interest-rate changes since the beginning of the loan:

  original loan term − (# payments made / # payments per year)

  For example, if you've already made 15 monthly payments on a 30-year loan: 30 − (15 / 12) = 30 − 1.25 = 28.75 years remaining.

- Calculate a decimal value to represent a number of months or weeks as a partial year.

  For months, divide the number of months by 12. For example, if you have 11 years and 4 months remaining on your loan, enter 11.33.

  For weeks, divide the number of weeks by 52. For example, if you have 14 years and 26 weeks remaining on your loan, enter 14.5.

5   **Enter the rest of the information in the Set Up Loan window.**

Enter the expense category you want to use to track interest paid on the loan.

Enter a name for the account you want to use to track the loan balance. (If the liability or asset account already exists, see "Existing principal accounts" on page 289 for additional information.)

If you know the current balance, enter it here.

If you don't know the current balance, leave the amount that Quicken calculated in this field.

Enter the date of your next payment.

Leave the Payments Made field at zero.

If your loan has a balloon payment, select this checkbox. Then see "Balloon payments" on page 286.

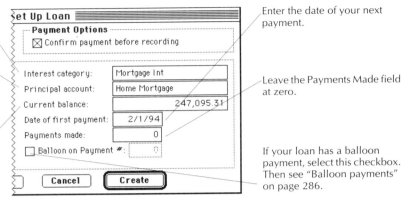

Set up your loan as though it begins with your next payment (that is, set the Date of First Payment field to the date of your next payment, and the Payments Made field to zero).

6   **Click Payment Coupon.**

7   **Fill in the Payment Coupon window.**

Enter the name of the lender here.

If you include amounts for impounds or escrow in addition to principal and interest, enter the total payment in the $ Amount field. Then Quicken will enter the additional amounts to the split transaction.

If you will be printing a check for the payment, click the Printed option and then enter the lender's address.

You can enter a memo for the payment.

After you enter the total payment in the $ Amount field above, you can categorize the additional amounts in the split transaction. If you have more than one amount to categorize, see "Splitting transactions" on page 92.

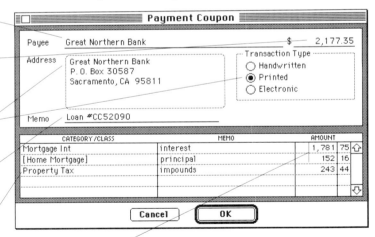

Ignore these amounts during setup. Quicken will calculate the correct amounts of interest and principal at the time you make a payment.

8   **Click OK to return to the Set Up Loan window.**

9   **Click Create in the Set Up Loan window.**

Quicken creates a memorized loan payment transaction and adds it to the loan list. See "Making a loan payment" on page 291 for instructions on recalling this transaction. (Quicken also adds the loan payment transaction to the memorized transaction list so that you can include the loan payment in a transaction group. Using a transaction group is a great way to ensure that you enter payments on time. See "Using transaction groups" on page 165.)

If you are interested in working out "what if" scenarios with your loan, we recommend that you use the loan calculator. See "Calculating loan payments and principal" on page 381.

Handling different types of loans

Quicken can handle many different types of loan features and setup requirements. For example, you can use Quicken to track adjustable-rate loans or loans on which you make additional prepayments of principal.

You'll find a set of guidelines for setting up each feature and requirement here (see the list below). Each set of guidelines tells you how to fill in fields in the Set Up Loan or Payment Coupon window. For fields not listed in a set of guidelines, follow the instructions in "Setting up a loan" starting on page 282. If your loan involves several different features (for example, an adjustable-rate loan with negative amortization), you can follow all of the guidelines that apply to your loan.

- "Adjustable-rate loans" on page 286
- "Balloon payments" on page 286
- "Negative amortization" on page 287
- "Zero-interest loans" on page 287
- "Additional prepayments of principal" on page 288
- "Loans for which you receive payments" on page 289
- "Existing principal accounts" on page 289

Adjustable-rate loans

An adjustable-rate loan has a variable interest rate. When the rate changes, the scheduled payment amount also changes.

Field in Set Up Loan window	Guidelines on what to enter
Scheduled payment	Current payment amount
Annual interest rate	Current interest rate
Confirm payment before recording	Select this checkbox. Then when your interest rate changes, you'll be able to enter the new rate and payment amount when you recall the loan payment transaction.

Balloon payments

A loan with a balloon payment is amortized over one period (that is, the payment is calculated based on this period), but is repaid over a considerably shorter period. At the end of the repayment period, the loan balance is due. For example, if you have a "30 due in 7" loan, your payment is amortized over 30 years. But at the end of seven years, you must either pay off the loan balance or refinance your loan.

Field in Set Up Loan window	Guidelines on what to enter
Total years	Number of years remaining in the amortization period as of the date of the first loan payment you plan to record in Quicken
Balloon on Payment #	Select this checkbox and enter the number of the final payment. Calculate this number by multiplying the number of years remaining in the payment period by the number of payments per year.

For example, if you borrowed a "30 due in 7" loan 2 1/2 years ago and you make monthly payments on the loan, you would enter 27.5 in the Total Years field and 54 (= (7 − 2.5) × 12) in the Balloon On Payment # field.

In some balloon payment loans, each payment covers only the accrued interest (no principal), and the original loan amount is due at the end of the repayment period. For such an "interest-only" loan, do not use Quicken's loan tracking feature. Instead, create a regular memorized transaction for the payment and categorize the entire amount as interest. See "Memorizing a transaction" on page 161 to create a regular memorized transaction.

Negative amortization

If your loan has negative amortization, your actual payment is less than the amortized payment (that is, the amount you pay doesn't cover the interest and principal due for a given payment). If your actual payment doesn't completely cover the interest (and none of the principal), the unpaid interest is added to the loan balance.

Field in Set Up Loan window	Guidelines on what to enter
Scheduled payment	The amount on which the loan amortization was initially based
Annual interest rate	For some types of negative amortization loans, the payment amount is fixed, but the interest rate varies. If your loan works this way, enter the interest rate on which the loan amortization was initially based.
Confirm payment before recording	Select this checkbox. Then you'll be able to enter your actual payment or your new interest rate when you recall the memorized loan payment.

Zero-interest loans

If you have a zero-interest loan, you do not incur any interest expenses. Your entire payment (excluding other charges such as impound payments) is principal.

Field in Set Up Loan window	Guidelines on what to enter
Annual interest rate	Zero (0)
Interest category	Leave this field blank.

Additional prepayments of principal

If you include an additional prepayment of principal with your scheduled payment, the prepayment is applied entirely to principal. By making prepayments, you will pay off the loan balance sooner and pay less interest altogether than if you pay only the scheduled payment amount.

- **For consistent prepayments** (that is, you include the same prepayment amount with every scheduled payment):

Field in Payment Coupon window	Guidelines on what to enter
$ Amount	Add the prepayment amount to the scheduled payment. For example, if your payment amount is $1575 and you always prepay $225, you enter $1800 in the $ Amount field of the payment coupon.
Split transaction	Categorize this amount as a transfer to the principal account. For example, if your principal account is named "Home Mortgage," you enter [Home Mortgage] as the category in the split transaction for the prepayment amount.
(Optional) Split transaction memo	Enter a note that this amount is a prepayment. Then you'll be able to identify regular prepayments you've made on your loan by creating a report that is restricted by memo (the text of your note) and category (the name of your principal account).

- **For occasional or variable-amount prepayments:**

Field in Set Up Loan window	Guideline on what to enter
Confirm payment before recording	Select this checkbox. Then you'll be able to enter your actual payment or your new interest rate when you recall the memorized loan payment.

You can also make prepayments of principal between scheduled loan payments. See "Making prepayments between scheduled payments" on page 292.

Loans for which you receive payments

If you hold a loan note and receive payments on a loan, you can set up your loan for amortization in Quicken. For such a "lending loan," Quicken creates a memorized loan deposit (instead of a payment) and uses an asset account (instead of a liability account) as the principal account whose balance shows how much the borrower still owes you.

Window	Field	Guidelines on what to enter
Set Up Loan	Type of loan	Click the Lending button.
Payment Coupon	Payee	Name of the borrower

Existing principal accounts

If you have been manually tracking a loan in Quicken (that is, you've been entering payments for the loan by copying the principal and interest amounts from your loan statement into the split transaction of the payment, and tracking the principal in a liability or asset account), you can still use your existing principal account with the memorized loan payment. Quicken will use the ending balance of your principal account as the current loan balance on which it bases its amortization calculations.

Before you set up the loan, be sure that in your principal account register, the ending balance and the date of the last transaction correctly reflect your most recent payment.

Field in Set Up Loan window	Guideline on what to enter
Principal account	Name of existing principal account

Viewing a loan's payment schedule

You can view a payment schedule to see how your loan progresses with each future payment. (The schedule does not show you past payments.) You can also print the payment schedule if you like.

1   Choose Loans from the View menu.

2   Select the loan whose payment schedule you want to view.

3   Click Payment Schedule.

For each payment, Quicken shows the scheduled payment date, the payment number (where Pmt 1 is the next payment), the amounts of principal and interest based on the current interest rate, and the loan balance after the payment is made

Quicken shows you the current interest rate and balance of the loan.

Date	Pmt	Principal	Interest	Balance
			8.625%	248,640.00
2/1/94	1	146.81	1,787.10	248,493.19
3/1/94	2	147.87	1,786.04	248,345.32
4/1/94	3	148.93	1,784.98	248,196.39
5/1/94	4	150.00	1,783.91	248,046.39
6/1/94	5	151.08	1,782.83	247,895.31
7/1/94	6	152.16	1,781.75	247,743.15
8/1/94	7	153.26	1,780.65	247,589.89
9/1/94	8	154.36	1,779.55	247,435.53
10/1/94	9	155.47	1,778.44	247,280.06
11/1/94	10	156.58	1,777.33	247,123.48

Great Northern Bank Payment Schedule

Scroll the window to see the rest of the schedule.

4   (Optional) To print the entire schedule, choose Print Payment Schedule from the File menu.

If you would like to know the total amount of interest paid on the loan as of each payment, use the loan planner. Such information may be useful in estimating this year's mortgage interest payments for Form W-4 calculations. See "Estimating this year's mortgage interest payments" on page 382.

Making a loan payment

When it's time to make a regularly scheduled payment on your loan, you recall the memorized loan payment. When you record the payment, Quicken recalculates the interest and principal amounts of the payment and updates the loan balance.

1   **Open the register or the Write Checks window for the bank account from which you will make the loan payment.**

2   **(Optional) If QuickFill is turned on, start typing the lender's name. When you see the full name, press Tab to recall the memorized loan payment. Then skip to step 5.**

3   **Choose Loans from the View menu.**

4   **Select the loan for which you want to enter a payment, and then click Use.**

5   **(Optional) If you have set up your loan for payment confirmation, review or change any information necessary for this payment, and click OK to enter the payment transaction.**

If you selected the payment confirmation checkbox when you set up the loan, you'll see this window.

If this amount doesn't match the actual balance on your loan, enter the correct amount.

If you have an adjustable-rate loan and the interest rate has changed as of this payment, enter the new rate and scheduled payment.

Changes you make to the three fields above affect the payment schedule and all future payments. See "How changes to the loan payment affect future payments and schedules" next for details.

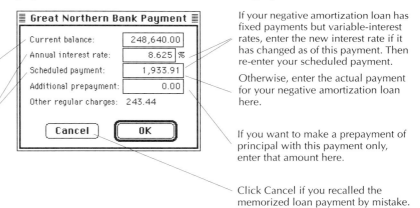

If your negative amortization loan has fixed payments but variable-interest rates, enter the new interest rate if it has changed as of this payment. Then re-enter your scheduled payment.

Otherwise, enter the actual payment for your negative amortization loan here.

If you want to make a prepayment of principal with this payment only, enter that amount here.

Click Cancel if you recalled the memorized loan payment by mistake.

6   **Click Record in the register or the Write Checks window to record the loan payment transaction.**

When you make the total number of payments scheduled for this loan, Quicken reminds you that this is the last payment. After you make the last payment, you will not be able to recall the memorized loan payment again.

If you recalled the memorized loan payment by mistake, delete the transaction from the register (⌘ D). Quicken restores the loan balance and the number of payments made automatically.

How changes to the loan payment affect future payments and schedules

This table explains what happens when you change the fields in the Payment Confirmation window (step 5 on page 291).

If you change this field	This happens
Current balance	Quicken adjusts the balance and interest for the loan in the payment schedule. Quicken also adds a balance adjustment transaction to the principal account that increases or decreases the current balance.
Annual interest rate	Quicken adjusts the scheduled payment amount and current interest rate for this payment and all future payments.
Scheduled payment	Quicken uses the amount you enter as the new scheduled payment amount *for this payment and all future payments.*
	If you increase the scheduled payment, Quicken increases the principal amount for each payment, and reduces either the final payment or the number of payments remaining in the schedule.
	If you decrease the scheduled payment, Quicken decreases the principal amount for each payment. Quicken does not increase the number of payments remaining in the schedule. Instead, it creates a balloon payment as the final payment.
Additional prepayment	Quicken increases the principal amount *for this payment only,* and reduces either the final payment or the number of payments remaining in the schedule

Making prepayments between scheduled payments

If you make a payment on your loan between scheduled payments, the entire payment is a prepayment of principal. For this type of payment, do not recall the memorized loan payment. Instead, create a regular transaction in the account from which you are making the payment, and enter the name of the principal account as a transfer account in the Category field of the transaction.

You can also set up your loan to include prepayments of principal with your scheduled payment. See "Additional prepayments of principal" on page 288.

Editing a loan

Edit a loan if you need to change any of the loan setup information except for changing the principal account name. See "Editing account information" on page 40 to rename an account.

1 Choose Loans from the View menu.

Or press ⌘ E

2 Select the loan whose information you want to change, and then click Edit.

Quicken shows you the Edit Loan window with your current loan information.

3 Make your changes to the loan or payment coupon information.

See the instructions for filling in the Set Up Loan and Payment Coupon windows starting on page 282. (You'll actually enter your changes in the Edit Loan window, which contains the same fields as the Set Up Loan window.)

Caution:
Once you have recalled loan payments, do not change the number in the Payments Made field. Quicken won't be able to do the amortization calculations correctly if you change this number.

---

4 When you have finished making your changes, click Change in the Edit Loan window.

If your loan is set up for payment confirmation, you can also change certain information when you recall the memorized loan payment, including the scheduled payment, interest rate, and the current balance. You can use the preceding procedure to set up your loan for payment confirmation.

Deleting a loan

Delete a loan from the loan list when you have finished paying off the loan. When you delete a loan, Quicken removes it from the loan list, the memorized transaction list, and any transaction groups that include it. However, Quicken does not delete the loan's principal account, as you may want to keep the account for your records; see "Deleting an account" on page 42 for instructions.

1 **Choose Loans from the View menu.**

Or press ⌘ D

2 **Select the loan you want to delete, and then click Delete.**

3 **Click Yes to confirm the deletion.**

Estimating year-to-date loan interest

You may want to know how much interest you've paid on the loan since the beginning of the year for tax purposes. You can estimate the year-to-date interest by creating a report that summarizes your loan's interest payments. (You can estimate interest payments for the entire year using the loan planner if you have a fixed-rate loan and have not made prepayments of principal. See page 382.)

1 **Choose Personal Finance from the Reports menu.**

2 **Scroll the report list until you see the Summary report, and then double-click it.**

3 **Click the Show Options button, and then fill in the Create Summary Report window as shown below.**

You can enter a different title.

Choose this item from the Date popup menu.

Set up these restrictions:

- Account: the account from which you make loan payments.
- Category: the interest expense category that you specified when you were setting up your loan.
- Payee/Description: your lender.

For more information, see "Changing report restrictions" on page 331.

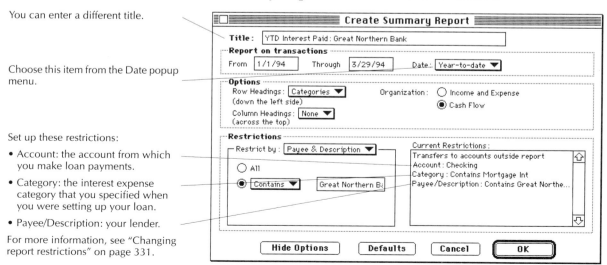

• 294 •

4   **Click OK to create the report.**

This summary report was created from the settings shown in step 3.

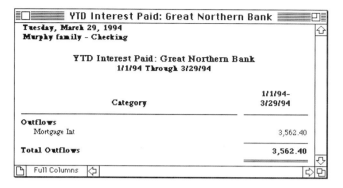

```
YTD Interest Paid: Great Northern Bank

Tuesday, March 29, 1994
Murphy family – Checking

              YTD Interest Paid: Great Northern Bank
                     1/1/94 Through 3/29/94


                                                    1/1/94–
                          Category                  3/29/94

Outflows
    Mortgage Int                                    3,562.40

Total Outflows                                      3,562.40

 Full Columns
```

Refinancing a loan

If you refinance a loan that you've been tracking in Quicken, follow this procedure to set up the new loan and "pay off" the old loan. (To help you determine whether you should refinance, see "Calculating the cost of refinancing a loan" on page 383.)

1   **Set up your new loan.**

Enter the new loan information as shown in "Setting up a loan" on page 282.

Be sure to:

- Enter the original loan term of the new loan in the Total Years field.

- Enter a name for the new principal account that's different from the old principal account.

- Enter the original amount of the new loan in the Current Balance field.

- Set up the payment coupon (not shown here). See page 284 for more information.

```
                         Set Up Loan
┌─ Type of Loan ──────────────┐  ┌─ Payment Options ───────────┐
│  ● Borrowing   ○ Lending    │  │ ☐ Confirm payment before recording │
└─────────────────────────────┘  └─────────────────────────────┘
┌─ Loan Info ─────────────────────────────────────────────────┐
│ Scheduled payment:     1,791.03   Interest category:  Mortgage Int  │
│ Annual interest rate:    7.750 %  Principal account:   Refi Mortgage │
│ Total years:            30.00     Current balance:         250,000.00 │
│ Payments per year:         12     Date of first payment:    5/1/94 │
│ Loan amount:        250,000.00    Payments made:                 0 │
│                                   ☐ Balloon on Payment #:       0 │
└─────────────────────────────────────────────────────────────┘
       [ Payment Coupon... ]    [ Cancel ]    [ Create ]
```

2 **Edit the Opening Balance transaction in the new principal account register to create a split that "pays off" the old loan and categorizes or transfers any remaining amounts.**

This is the register of the principal account for the new loan.

Change the description from "Opening Balance" to the name of the new lender. This change makes the transfer transactions more meaningful.

This split pays off the outstanding balance on the old loan. It does this by transferring the balance of the old principal account to the new principal account. (The next illustration shows the transfer transaction in the old principal account register.)

The new loan amount covers the closing costs of the loan. Categorize this expense in the split.

DATE	NUMBER	DESCRIPTION	INCREASE	√	DECREASE	BALANCE
		MEMO				
3/29		J. R. Lindsay & Company	250,000 00	√		250,000 00
1994		new mortgage				

Refi Mortgage: Register

CATEGORY	MEMO	AMOUNT
[Home Mortgage]		247,589 89
Refinance	closing costs	200 00
[Checking]	cash out	2,210 11

Record   Restore   SPLITS   Current balance $250,000.00

If the new loan is greater than the old loan balance plus closing costs, you may receive a check from the lender for the difference. In this example, the check was deposited in the checking account.

This is the register of the principal account for the old loan.

Home Mortgage: Register

DATE	NUMBER	DESCRIPTION	INCREASE	√	DECREASE	BALANCE
		CATEGORY / MEMO				
1/1 1994		Opening Balance [Home Mortgage]	247,895 31	√		247,895 31
2/1 1994		Great Northern Bank [Checking] Loan #CC52090			152 16	247,743 15
3/1 1994		Great Northern Bank [Checking] Loan #CC52090			153 26	247,589 89
3/29 1994		J. R. Lindsay & Company [Refi Mortgage] new mortgage		√	247,589 89	0 00

This is the transfer transaction from the new loan's principal account. It pays off the balance of the old loan.

Record   Restore   SPLITS   Current balance $0.00

3 **Delete the old loan from the loan list.**

See "Deleting a loan" on page 294.

Sample reports

Once you've entered transactions, Quicken can automatically create reports based on transactions in one or more of your accounts. These reports can help you examine your finances in detail.

Look through this chapter for examples of Quicken's standard personal finance and business reports. The next chapter explains how to create them.

Personal finance reports

This section briefly describes each standard personal finance report. To create a personal finance report, choose Personal Finance from the Reports menu and double-click on the report you want.

Budget

The budget report compares actual income and expenses against budgeted income and expenses by month (or by any other period).

This example is based on the initial report options. You can change the format of the report or the data selected for the report—see the next chapter.

The Actual column contains the amounts for categories used in transactions that fall within the date range for the report column.

A positive value means your Actual amount was more than your Budget amount.

The Budget column contains the amounts you entered in the Set Up Budgets window (see page 352).

The Diff column is the difference between what you budgeted and what you actually spent or received.

These are transfers from asset, liability, and investment accounts to bank, cash, and credit card accounts.

Budget Report
1/1/93 Through 1/31/93

Category	1/1/93 Actual	– Budget	1/31/93 Diff
Inflows			
Interest Income	0.42	0.00	0.42
Salary	18,508.35	18,508.00	0.35
From Auto Loan	0.00	0.00	0.00
From Mortgage	0.00	0.00	0.00
From Sally's 401k	0.00	0.00	0.00
From Steve's IRA	0.00	0.00	0.00
Total Inflows	**18,508.77**	**18,508.00**	**0.77**
Outflows			
Auto:			
Fuel	90.31	100.00	-9.69
Repairs	35.00	140.00	-105.00
Total Auto	125.31	240.00	-114.69
Clothing	426.63	400.00	26.63
Education	0.00	50.00	-50.00
Entertainment	76.50	100.00	-23.50
Gifts	21.57	0.00	21.57
Groceries	319.54	320.00	-0.46
Household	155.99	0.00	155.99
Mortgage Int	1,417.48	1,420.00	-2.52
Taxes:			
FICA	1,097.90	1,000.00	97.90
FWH	4,127.10	4,100.00	27.10
SDI	65.74	70.00	-4.26
Total Taxes	5,290.74	5,170.00	120.74
Telephone	87.52	75.00	12.52
Utilities:			
Electricity	64.97	60.00	4.97
Water	0.00	45.00	-45.00
Total Utilities	64.97	105.00	-40.03
To Auto Loan	210.63	210.00	0.63
To Mortgage	116.43	120.00	-3.57
To Sally's 401k	98.61	100.00	-1.39
To Steve's IRA	100.00	100.00	0.00
Total Outflows	**8,511.92**	**8,410.00**	**101.92**
Overall Total	**9,996.85**	**10,098.00**	**-101.15**

Initial options for this report*

Column Headings:	Month
Organization:	Cash flow
In budget reports, include:	Budgeted categories only
Restrictions:	
Accounts	Selected (bank, cash, credit card)
Transfers:	To accounts outside report

* To control which categories appear in budget reports, see "Changing global report settings" on page 323.

These are transfers to asset, liability, and investment accounts from bank, cash, and credit card accounts.

This is your net savings for the month. If the number is positive, you earned more than you spent. If the number is negative, you spent more than you earned.

This example is based on the initial report options. You can change the format of the report or the data selected for the report—see the next chapter.

Capital gains

A capital gains report shows long-term and short-term capital gains for securities sold during a specified time period. (For capital gains distributions from a mutual fund, use the investment income report.)

To get an accurate capital gains report, you must tell Quicken the date or dates you bought the shares you sold, and the actual cost basis of those shares. If you haven't already done so, you can enter this information in the portfolio or mutual fund register after you make the sale. See "Entering prior history for investments" on page 274. If you enter the sale of a security with a zero cost basis in Quicken, you should enter the historical information to get an accurate capital gains report on the sale.

If you sold only part of your shares of a security in an account, Quicken assumes that the shares you sold are the ones you've held the longest. If you have designated other shares as the ones you sold, use separate lot numbers to identify the shares. See "Using security lots" on page 273.

Quicken does not distinguish "wash sales" from other sales. (A "wash sale" is a sale at a loss within 30 days of acquiring the same security. Special tax rules apply.)

Initial options for this report	
Subtotal by:	Short- vs. long-term
Maximum short-term gain holding period:	365 days
Restrictions:	
Accounts	Current

Capital Gains Report
1/1/93 Through 3/31/93

Security	Shares	Bought	Sold	Sales Price	Cost Basis	Gain/Loss
Dell Computer	200	6/23/92	2/5/93	8,006.81	3,202.31	4,804.50
Hitachi	80	6/15/92	3/9/93	4,950.33	4,919.50	30.83
Total Short Term				12,957.14	8,121.81	4,835.33

After creating this report, you can export the report to a file to use in tax preparation software. See "Creating tax summary reports" on page 374.

To use this report for Schedule D (after you've entered all prior history for any security you've sold), subtotal by short-term vs. long-term gain. Select only those accounts that have taxable capital gains (for example, exclude IRAs).

This example is based on the initial report options. You can change the format of the report or the data selected for the report—see the next chapter.

Category

A category report summarizes income and expenses by category. A category report usually excludes transfer transactions that occur between the accounts included in the report (that is, between bank, cash, and credit card accounts). For example, Quicken does not include a transfer of funds from checking to savings.

Quicken groups income categories with any transfers *from* accounts not included in the report.

Quicken groups expense categories with any transfers *to* accounts not included in the report.

Category Report
1/1/93 Through 3/31/93

Category	1/1/93–3/31/93
Inflows	
Bonus	3,000.00
Salary	48,441.71
Total Inflows	**51,441.71**
Outflows	
Auto:	
Fuel	181.31
Repairs	165.98
Total Auto	347.29
Books	281.14
Clothing	2,626.60
Dining	630.45
Entertainment	517.37
Gifts	461.97
Groceries	1,066.15
Household	849.64
Mortgage Int	4,252.44
Taxes:	
FICA	2,939.54
FWH	10,810.46
SDI	197.22
Total Taxes	13,947.22
Telephone	277.07
Utilities:	
Electricity	353.73
Water	57.50
Total Utilities	411.23
Vacation	332.31
To Auto Loan	636.10
To Mortgage	349.29
To Sally's 401k	230.09
To Steve's IRA	300.00
Total Outflows	**27,516.36**
Overall Total	**23,925.35**

Initial options for this report (based on the summary report)

Row Headings:	Category
Column Headings:	None
Organization:	Cash flow*
Restrictions:	
Accounts	Selected (bank, cash, credit card)
Transfers:	To accounts outside report

* Compare to the summary report on page 307. It is organized by income and expense, which means that transfers are grouped together at the end of the report.

These are transfers to asset, liability, and investment accounts from bank, cash, and credit card accounts.

Investment income

The investment income report shows dividend income (taxable and tax-exempt), interest income (taxable and tax-exempt), capital gains distributions, realized gain or loss, unrealized gain or loss (as an option), and margin interest and other investment expenses during a specified time period.

If you want to use this report to gather information for Schedule B, be sure you've entered all investment transactions for the year. Select only those accounts for which you must report income (for example, exclude IRAs). Subtotal by security. Create one report for all your reportable income, both taxable and tax-exempt. Then create a second report, using filters to include only securities that generate reportable but tax-exempt income. Again, subtotal by security. Do not select the option to include unrealized gains.

This example is based on the initial report options. You can change the format of the report or the data selected for the report—see the next chapter.

Initial options for this report (based on the summary report)

Column Headings:	None
Organization:	Cash flow
Include unrealized gains:	No
Restrictions:	None

The categories with • are standard Quicken investment categories. See "Choosing investment actions" on page 250 for information about which categories are associated with which investment actions.

The balance forward (Bal Fwd) items in this report are the result of redeeming mutual fund shares for IRA custodial fees, as described in "Redeeming shares for IRA custodial fees" on page 259.

Investment Income Report
1/1/92 Through 12/31/92

Category	1/1/92– 12/31/92
Inflows	
•Div Income	1,287.85
•Int Income	0.19
•Long Cap Gain	250.99
•Realized Gain	320.02
•Short Cap Gain	368.80
From Checking	28,542.11
From Mather-Sally	2,221.73
From Mather-Steve	2,226.09
From Olde	4,813.08
From Schwab One MMF	14,000.01
From Vanguard MMF	62,675.04
From Vanguard ST	3,000.00
From Vanguard Star	505.63
Bal Fwd-Fidelity 0551	-10.00
Bal Fwd-Mather-Steve	-12.00
Total Inflows	**120,189.54**
Outflows	
Invest Exp	30.33
Outflows - Other	0.00
To Fidelity 0551	2,221.73
To New Asia Fund	2,226.09
To Fidelity 0767	3,000.00
To Schwab	4,813.08
To Schwab One MMF	14,000.00
To Vanguard Index	505.63
Total Outflows	**26,796.86**
Overall Total	**93,392.68**

This example is based on the initial report options. You can change the format of the report or the data selected for the report—see the next chapter.

Investment performance

The investment performance report shows the average annual total return of your securities during a specified time period. This return takes into account dividends, interest, and other payment you receive as well as increases and decreases in the market value of your securities. Generally, if the average annual return on an investment is 10%, that investment is performing as well as a bank account that pays 10% interest.

When the average annual total return is greater than 10,000% or less than -99.9%, or when the timing of cash flows prevents Quicken from calculating a figure, Quicken displays a message that one or more calculations appear as N/A (not available).

The average annual total return is the internal rate of return (IRR) for your investment. It equals the discount rate at which all the cash flows associated with the investment have a net present value of zero.

Initial options for this report	
Subtotal by:	Security
Restrictions:	None

Investment Performance Report
1/1/92 Through 12/31/92

Date	Acct	Action	Description	Investments	Returns	Avg. Annual Tot. Return
All American S...						
12/31/91			Beg Mkt Value	0.00		
8/13/92	Schwab	BUY	1,000 All American S...	1,309.50		
11/17/92	Schwab	SELL	500 All American Semi		678.25	
12/31/92			End Mkt Value		750.00	
Total All Ameri...				1,309.50	1,428.25	30.50%
Broderbund						
12/31/91			Beg Mkt Value	0.00		
6/15/92	Schwab	BUY	120 Broderbund	2,849.40		
12/31/92			End Mkt Value		5,100.00	
Total Broderbund				2,849.40	5,100.00	190.80%
Dell Computer						
12/31/91			Beg Mkt Value	0.00		
6/23/92	Schwab	BUY	300 Dell Computer	4,803.47		
9/17/92	Schwab	SELL	100 Dell Computer		2,763.00	
12/31/92			End Mkt Value		9,600.00	
Total Dell Com...				4,803.47	12,363.00	749.10%

This example is based on the initial report options. You can change the format of the report or the data selected for the report—see the next chapter.

Initial options for this report (based on the transaction report)	
Subtotal by:	Don't Subtotal
Organization	Cash flow
Include unrealized gains:	No
Restrictions:	None

Investment transactions

The investment transactions report shows you how transactions during a specified time period have affected either the market value or the cost basis of your investments and the cash balance in your investment accounts.

If you do not include unrealized (paper) gains, the report shows the change in cost basis of your investments between the beginning and the end of the period. On the other hand, if you select the option of including unrealized gains, the report shows the change in the market value of your investments between the beginning and the end of the period.

You may subtotal the report by period, account, category, security, security type, or investment goal.

For each transaction, the Investment Value column shows the change in cost basis of the security if unrealized gains are not included, or the change in market value if unrealized gains are included. The balance is the current cost basis or market value of all the securities.

For each transaction, the Cash + Investment column shows the sum of the amounts in the Cash and Investment Value columns.

Investment Transactions Report
1/1/93 Through 3/31/93

Date	Action	Secur	Categ	Price	Shares	Comms...	Cash	Investment Value	Cash + Investment
1/9/93	XFR	-Cash-	[Checking]				6,000.00		6,000.00
1/14/93	BUY	Schwab C...		1	6,000		-6,000.00	6,000.00	
1/15/93	RD	Schwab C...		1	4		-4.00	4.00	
			●Div Income				4.00		4.00
2/5/93	SELL	Dell Com...		40 1...	200	93.19	3,202.31	-3,202.31	
			●Realized Gain				4,804.50		4,804.50
2/8/93	XFR	-Cash-	[Checking]				2,300.00		2,300.00
2/8/93	MISC	-Cash-	Computer				50.00		50.00
2/10/93	BUY	Schwab C...		1	2,350		-2,350.00	2,350.00	
2/16/93	RD	Schwab C...		1	18		-18.00	18.00	
			●Div Income				18.00		18.00
2/16/93	BUY	Schwab C...		1	8,006.81		-8,006.81	8,006.81	
3/1/93	XFR	-Cash-	[Checking]				2,000.00		2,000.00
3/1/93	XFR	-Cash-	[Schwab One ...				3,382.21		3,382.21
3/9/93	SELL	Hitachi		62 1...	80	49.67	4,919.50	-4,919.50	
			●Realized Gain				30.83		30.83
Total 1/1/93 – 3/31/93							10,332.54	8,257.00	18,589.54

A reinvested dividend shows up as a buy transaction on one line, followed by a Dividends transaction on the next line (a reinvested dividend counts as a buy and a dividend). In general, complex transactions appear on several lines, with one line for each component of the transaction.

The Cash column shows the change in the cash balance of your account or accounts as a result of each transaction.

This example is based on the initial report options. You can change the format of the report or the data selected for the report—see the next chapter.

Quicken lists income transactions first, unless no income transactions occurred during the report date range.

Quicken lists expense transactions after income transactions, followed by transfers between accounts and balances forward. (In this example, no income transactions occurred during the report date range.)

Itemized categories

An itemized category report lists transactions from all your accounts, grouped and subtotaled by category.

Itemized Category Report
2/1/93 Through 2/8/93

Date	Acct	Num	Description	Memo	Category	✓	Amount
Inc/Exp							
Expenses							
Clothing							
2/1/93	Checki...	131	Macy's	New Jac...	Clothing	✓	-129.87
2/1/93	Quicke...		Classy Clothes	Catalina...	Clothing	✓	-59.82
Total Clothin							-189.69
Dining							
2/5/93	Cash		Joe's Burgers		Dining	✓	-10.00
2/5/93	Quicke...		Harvey's		Dining	✓	-23.00
Total Dining							-33.00
Groceries							
2/6/93	Cash		Mary Manor		Groceries	✓	-60.00
2/8/93	Checki...	132	Central Mar...		Groceries	✓	-89.90
Total Groceri							-149.90
Household:							
Garden and							
2/1/93	AMX		Payless Drugs	primro...	Household:...	✓	-22.54
Total Gard							-22.54
Total Househ							-22.54
Utilities:							
Water							
2/8/93	Checki...	5053	City of Valle...		Utilities:W...	✓	-28.75
Total Wate							-28.75
Total Utilitie							-28.75
Total Expenses							-423.88
Total Inc/Exp							**-423.88**

Initial options for this report (based on the transaction report)

Subtotal by:	Category
Organization:	Income and expense
Show split detail	No
Show totals only:	No
Sort by check number:	No
Show missing checks	No
Restrictions:	None

This example is based on the initial report options. You can change the format of the report or the data selected for the report—see the next chapter.

Initial options for this report	
Report at intervals of:	None
Restrictions:	None

If your bank accounts include any unprinted or postdated checks, Quicken adds them to your bank balance and also lists them as a liability.

If you want Quicken to include "Checks Payable" (unprinted checks) under "Assets" and "Liabilities," be sure to enter an ending date for the report that is later than any of your postdated checks in the register.

If you have set up portfolio or mutual fund account accounts, the net worth report shows the market value of your investments based on the most recent prices you entered prior to the report date. Also, the balances for these accounts include unrealized gains.

This section includes all asset accounts.

This section includes all liability accounts.

The OVERALL TOTAL shows your net worth, which Quicken calculates as the difference between your assets and your liabilities.

Net worth

A net worth report calculates your net worth on the basis of all accounts in the current Quicken data file.

Net Worth Report
As of 3/1/93

Acct	3/1/93 Balance
Assets	
Cash and Bank Accounts	
Checking	369.95
Vanguard MMF	1,481.11
Total Cash and Bank Accou	1,851.06
Investment	
401k-Sally	10,422.88
401k-Steve	9,271.43
Janus Fund	2,376.83
New Asia Fund	2,289.77
Olde	17,688.82
Schwab	59,185.35
Scudder	5,471.81
Vanguard Health	2,111.55
Vanguard Index	2,296.64
Vanguard ST	3,050.32
Total Investments	114,165.40
Other Assets	
House	260,000.00
Total Other Assets	260,000.00
Total Assets	**376,016.46**
Liabilities	
Credit Cards	
First Card-Sall	5,082.49
First Card-Stev	392.66
Total Credit Cards	5,475.15
Other Liabilities	
mortgage 1	203,779.60
mortgage 2	26,000.00
Total Other Liabilities	229,779.60
Total Liabilities	**235,254.75**
Overall Total	**140,761.71**

Portfolio value

A portfolio value report shows the value of each of your securities on a specified date. The portfolio value report shows unrealized gain in dollars (instead of as a percentage), and has options for subtotaling by account, security type, or investment goal.

Most recent price per share. Quicken marks estimated prices with an asterisk (*). (Quicken estimates the price if you haven't updated the price for the date of the report.)

Your cost basis for the security. Quicken displays 0.00 if you did not enter the cost basis of the security.

Unrealized (paper) gain or loss in dollars.

Market value on the date of the report.

Number of shares (to the nearest 0.01).

Portfolio Value Report
As of 3/31/93

Security	Shares	Curr Pri...		Cost Basis	Gain/Loss	Balance
All America...	500.00	1 1/2	*	654.75	95.25	750.00
Borland	510.00	4.300	*	1,680.15	512.85	2,193.00
Broderbund	120.00	40 1/4	*	2,849.40	1,980.60	4,830.00
Delta	100.00	106 7/8	*	10,961.81	-274.31	10,687.50
EIF-Equity I...	130.65	15.630	*	2,038.69	3.37	2,042.06
EXF-Equity ...	828.87	12.630	*	10,045.38	423.25	10,468.63
IBM	50.00	54 3/8	*	4,068.25	-1,349.50	2,718.75
Intl Stock F...	240.41	8.890	*	2,252.86	-115.58	2,137.28
Intuit	850.00	30	*	17,000.00	8,500.00	25,500.00
Janus Fund	133.74	18.680	*	2,376.83	121.41	2,498.24
Microsoft	100.00	83 3/8	*	7,004.00	1,333.50	8,337.50
New Asia Fund	167.33	12.600	*	2,289.77	-181.47	2,108.30
New Income ...	281.65	9	*	2,541.66	-6.82	2,534.84
Schwab CA ...	20,554.04	1	*	20,554.04	0.00	20,554.04
Scudder	393.95	13.030	*	5,471.81	-338.60	5,133.21
Symantec	220.00	10 5/8	*	4,581.70	-2,244.20	2,337.50
TeleMex	150.00	49 5/8	*	7,424.25	19.50	7,443.75
Vanguard He...	60.72	34.010	*	2,111.55	-46.63	2,064.92
Vanguard In...	70.59	40.970	*	2,296.64	595.40	2,892.04
Vanguard ST	291.19	11.010	*	3,050.32	155.66	3,205.98
Vanguard Star	0.00	12.470	*	0.00	0.00	0.00
Verifone	100.00	23 1/4	*	2,174.50	150.50	2,325.00
-Cash-	17,972.11	1		17,972.11	0.00	17,972.11
Total Invest...				131,400.47	9,334.18	140,734.65

Initial options for this report

Subtotal by:	Don't subtotal
Restrictions:	None

This example is based on the initial report options. You can change the format of the report or the data selected for the report—see the next chapter.

Summary

A summary report summarizes transactions from your accounts by category or whatever else you choose for the row headings. Unlike a transaction report, it does not show individual transactions. Several other reports are based on the summary report (for example, the category, investment income, A/P by vendor, A/R by customer, cash flow, and job/project reports).

A summary report groups income and expense items in separate sections, followed by transfers and balances forward, unless you select the cash flow report organization option (see "Changing report formats" on page 328).

Initial options for this report	
Row Headings:	Categories
Column Headings:	None
Organization:	Cash flow
Restrictions:	
Accounts	Selected (bank, credit card, cash)
Transfers	To accounts outside report

Quicken groups all transfers to and from the current account.

A summary report usually displays category or class descriptions rather than category or class names, but you can change the report to display names; see "Changing global report settings" on page 323. If a category or class has no description, Quicken displays the category or class name.

Summary Report
1/1/93 Through 3/31/93

Category	1/1/93- 3/31/93
Inc/Exp	
Income	
Bonus	3,000.00
Salary	48,441.71
Total Income	51,441.71
Expenses	
Auto:	
Fuel	181.31
Repairs	165.98
Total Auto	347.29
Books	281.14
Clothing	2,626.60
Dining	630.45
Entertainment	517.37
Gifts	461.97
Groceries	1,066.15
Household	849.64
Mortgage Int	4,252.44
Taxes:	
FICA	2,939.54
FWH	10,810.46
SDI	197.22
Total Taxes	13,947.22
Telephone	277.07
Utilities:	
Electricity	353.73
Water	57.50
Total Utilities	411.23
Vacation	332.31
Total Expenses	26,000.88
Total Inc/Exp	**25,440.83**
Transfers	
To Auto Loan	-636.10
To Mortgage	-349.29
To Sally's 401k	-230.09
To Steve's IRA	-300.00
Total Transfers	**-1,515.48**
Overall Total	**23,925.35**

This example is based on the initial report options. You can change the format of the report or the data selected for the report—see the next chapter.

Tax schedule

A tax schedule report lists those transactions with categories assigned to tax schedule line items, grouped and subtotaled by tax form name and line item.

See "Assigning line items from tax forms and schedules to categories" on page 364 for information about assigning categories to a tax form and line item.

Initial options for this report (based on the transaction report)
Restrictions:
Category: Tax-related only

After creating this report, you can export the report to a file to use in tax preparation software. See "Exporting Quicken data to tax preparation software" on page 377.

Tax Schedule Report
1/1/93 Through 3/31/93

Date	Acct	Num	Descrip...	Memo	Categ...	✓	Amount
Schedule A							
<u>Cash charity cor</u>							
1/8/93	Checki...	DEP	Steve's P...	Unite...	Charity	✓	-13.22
1/13/93	Checki...	125	TGRK		Charity	✓	-150.00
1/22/93	Checki...	DEP	Steve's P...	Unite...	Charity	✓	-13.22
3/15/93	Checki...	DEP	Steve's P...	Unite...	Charity	✓	-13.22
3/15/93	Checki...	DEP	Steve's P...	Unite...	Charity	✓	-13.22
3/31/93	Checki...	DEP	Steve's P...	Unite...	Charity	✓	-13.22
3/31/93	Checki...	DEP	Steve's P...	Unite...	Charity	✓	-13.22
Total Cash chari							-229.32
<u>Home mortgage :</u>							
1/15/93	Checki...	5047	American...	inter...	Mortg...	✓	-1,417.48
2/15/93	Checki...	5054	American...	inter...	Mortg...	✓	-1,417.48
3/15/93	Checki...	5061	American...	inter...	Mortg...	✓	-1,417.48
Total Home mor							-4,252.44
Schedule B							
<u>Interest income</u>							
1/15/93	Checki...	EFT	Interest ...		Intere...	✓	0.42
2/22/93	Checki...	EFT	Interest ...		Intere...	✓	0.42
3/11/93	Checki...	EFT	Interest ...		Intere...	✓	0.42
Total Interest ir							1.26
W-2							
<u>Salary</u>							
1/2/93	Checki...	DEP	Sally's P...		Salary	✓	3,541.67
1/8/93	Checki...	DEP	Steve's P...		Salary	✓	3,941.67
1/15/93	Checki...	DEP	Sally's P...		Salary	✓	3,541.67
1/22/93	Checki...	DEP	Steve's P...		Salary	✓	3,941.67
1/29/93	Checki...	DEP	Sally's P...		Salary	✓	3,541.67
2/12/93	Checki...	DEP	Sally's P...		Salary	✓	3,541.67

This example is based on the initial report options. You can change the format of the report or the data selected for the report—see the next chapter.

If you set up a file with Quicken's standard home category list, tax-related categories are already marked for you in the list. If you have set up your own categories, you need to mark the ones that are related to the tax forms you want to fill out. See "Setting up categories and subcategories" on page 47 for instructions.

Quicken lists expense transactions after income transactions, followed by Transfers and Balance Forward transactions, if Quicken finds any within the date range for the report.

A Balance Forward transaction is a self-transfer transaction. A self-transfer transaction has the name of the current account in the Category field.

Examples of self-transfer transactions are Opening Balance transactions and balance adjustment transactions.

Tax summary

A tax summary report lists tax-related transactions from all your accounts, grouped and subtotaled by category.

Tax Summary Report
1/1/93 Through 3/31/93

Date	Acct	Num	Description	Memo	Category	✓	Amount
Inc/Exp							
Income							
Interest Incom							
1/15/93	Checki...	EFT	Interest Ear...		Interest I...	✓	0.42
2/22/93	Checki...	EFT	Interest Ear...		Interest I...	✓	0.42
3/11/93	Checki...	EFT	Interest Ear...		Interest I...	✓	0.42
Total Interest							1.26
Salary							
1/2/93	Checki...	DEP	Sally's Payc...		Salary	✓	3,541.67
1/8/93	Checki...	DEP	Steve's Payc...		Salary	✓	3,941.67
1/15/93	Checki...	DEP	Sally's Payc...		Salary	✓	3,541.67
1/22/93	Checki...	DEP	Steve's Payc...		Salary	✓	3,941.67
1/29/93	Checki...	DEP	Sally's Payc...		Salary	✓	3,541.67
2/12/93	Checki...	DEP	Sally's Payc...		Salary	✓	3,541.67
2/26/93	Checki...	DEP	Sally's Payc...		Salary	✓	3,541.67
3/12/93	Checki...	DEP	Sally's Payc...		Salary	✓	3,541.67
3/15/93	Checki...	DEP	Steve's Payc...		Salary	✓	3,941.67
3/15/93	Checki...	DEP	Steve's Payc...		Salary	✓	3,941.67
3/26/93	Checki...	DEP	Sally's Payc...		Salary	✓	3,541.67
3/31/93	Checki...	DEP	Steve's Payc...		Salary	✓	3,941.67
3/31/93	Checki...	DEP	Steve's Payc...		Salary	✓	3,941.67
Total Salary							48,441.71
Total Income							48,442.97
Expenses							
Charity							
1/8/93	Checki...	DEP	Steve's Payc...	United...	Charity	✓	-13.22
1/13/93	Checki...	125	TGRK		Charity	✓	-150.00
1/22/93	Checki...	DEP	Steve's Payc...	United...	Charity	✓	-13.22
3/15/93	Checki...	DEP	Steve's Payc...	United...	Charity	✓	-13.22
3/15/93	Checki...	DEP	Steve's Payc...	United...	Charity	✓	-13.22
3/31/93	Checki...	DEP	Steve's Payc...	United...	Charity	✓	-13.22
3/31/93	Checki...	DEP	Steve's Payc...	United...	Charity	✓	-13.22
Total Charity							-229.32
Mortgage Int							
1/15/93	Checki...	5047	American Le...	interest	Mortgage ...	✓	-1,417.48
2/15/93	Checki...	5054	American Le...	interest	Mortgage ...	✓	-1,417.48
3/15/93	Checki...	5061	American Le...	interest	Mortgage ...	✓	-1,417.48
Total Mortgage							-4,252.44

Initial options for this report (based on the transaction report)

Subtotal by:	Category
Organization:	Income and expense
Show split: detail	No
Show totals only:	No
Sort by check number	No
Show missing checks:	No
Restrictions:	
Category	Tax-related only

This example is based on the initial report options. You can change the format of the report or the data selected for the report—see the next chapter.

Transaction

A transaction report lists transactions from one or more registers. Unlike a summary report, it shows individual transactions. Several other reports are based on the transaction report (for example, the itemized category, tax summary, and tax schedule, reports).

Initial options for this report	
Subtotal by:	Don't subtotal
Organization:	Income and expense
Show split detail:	No
Show totals only:	No
Sort by check number:	No
Show missing checks:	No
Restrictions:	None

Transaction Report
1/1/93 Through 3/20/93

Date	Acct	Num	Description	Memo	Category	✓	Amount
Balance 12/31/92							0.00
1/1/93	AMX		Opening Bal...		[AMX]	✓	0.00
1/3/93	AMX		Atwood Leis...		Recreation...	✓	-506.83
1/5/93	AMX		Cook's Esso		Auto:Fuel	✓	-15.28
1/12/93	AMX		Electronics ...		Computer:...	✓	-145.01
1/14/93	AMX		Target (cred...	waffle ...	Gifts:Chris...	✓	32.46
1/14/93	AMX		Garden Grill	John a...	Dining:Lun...	✓	-47.57
1/20/93	AMX		Emporium	split		✓	-124.57
1/20/93	AMX		Chevron		Auto:Fuel	✓	-17.03
1/21/93	AMX		Sam's Resta...	Steve ...	Dining:Lun...	✓	-34.67
1/22/93	AMX		Fish Market		Dining:Din...	✓	-24.33
1/23/93	AMX		Park Restau...		Dining:Din...	✓	-85.00
1/23/93	AMX		Orchard Sup...	spring...	Household:...	✓	-115.49
1/24/93	AMX		The Tied Hou...		Dining:Din...	✓	-62.00
1/25/93	AMX		Oil Changer		Auto:Maint...	✓	-22.25
1/30/93	AMX		Hacienda		Dining:Din...	✓	-53.00
1/31/93	AMX		American Ex...		[Checking]	✓	1,083.32
1/31/93	AMX		Macy's	Clinique	Personal:B...	✓	-15.70
2/1/93	AMX		Spring Garden	Sally ...	Dining:Lun...	✓	-24.00
2/1/93	AMX		Payless Drugs	primr...	Household:...	✓	-22.54
2/4/93	AMX		Disneyland t...		Entertain...	✓	-57.50
2/4/93	AMX		Annaheim In...		Entertain...	✓	-55.37
2/4/93	AMX		Target		Personal:E...	✓	-41.61
2/4/93	AMX		China Closet	Kim	Gifts:Birth...	✓	-48.43
2/4/93	AMX		French Mar...		Dining:Bre...	✓	-15.89
2/4/93	AMX		Avis rental ...		Vacation	✓	-332.31
2/4/93	AMX		FunFactory	sweats...	Gifts:Other	✓	-43.94
2/12/93	AMX		Valley Sprin...		Dining:Din...	✓	-43.00
2/12/93	AMX		Garden Grill	suzanne	Dining:Lun...	✓	-32.09
2/13/93	AMX		Pat's		Dining:Bre...	✓	-31.00
2/15/93	AMX		Payless Drugs	saline ...	Personal:E...	✓	-23.10
2/15/93	AMX		Smith and H...		Household:...	✓	-67.04
2/15/93	AMX		Orchard Sup...		Household:...	✓	-45.99
2/15/93	AMX		Blue Sky Cafe		Dining:Bre...	✓	-18.14
2/18/93	AMX		Airport Gifts		Gifts	✓	-21.98
2/22/93	AMX		Ethan Allan	dining ...	Household:...	✓	-1,687.02
2/22/93	AMX		Mumtaj		Dining:Din...	✓	-32.05
2/28/93	AMX		American Ex...		[Checking]	✓	1,076.88
3/5/93	AMX		China Outlet	Kitche...	Household	✓	-132.67
3/14/93	AMX		Country Gou...	Sally ...	Dining:Lun...	✓	-23.53
3/16/93	AMX		Emporium	table ...	Household:...	✓	-32.45
3/18/93	AMX		Holt Renfrew	spring...	Clothing	✓	-347.78
3/20/93	AMX		Eaton's Galle...	Painting	Household	✓	-235.00
1/18/93	Auto ...		Opening Bal...		[Auto Loan]	✓	-11,868.71
1/27/93	Auto ...		Primerica B...	Accoun...	[Checking]	✓	210.63
2/27/93	Auto ...		Primerica B...	Accoun...	[Checking]	✓	212.03
1/1/93	Cash		Opening Bal...		[Cash]	✓	50.00
1/5/93	Cash		ATM Withdr...		[Checking]	✓	300.00

•
•
•
•
•

This end of this report summarizes your Total Inflows, Total Outflows, and Net Total

Business reports

This example is based on the initial report options. You can change the format of the report or the data selected for the report—see the next chapter.

This section briefly describes each standard business report. To create a business report, choose Business from the Reports menu and double-click on the report you want.

A/P by vendor

An accounts payable (or A/P) report summarizes the dollar amount of all the unprinted checks in your bank accounts by payee name.

If you are not using Quicken to print checks, the A/P report still works if you enter all your payables as printable checks. When you pay the bill, go back to the register and record the actual check number in the Number field (type over the word "print").

Initial options for this report (based on the summary report)	
Row Headings:	Payees
Column Headings:	Month
Organization:	Income and expense
Restrictions:	
Accounts	Bank, cash, and credit card
Transaction Type:	Unprinted checks

Accounts Payable Report
3/1/94 Through 4/30/94

Payee	3/94	4/94	Overall Total
Chris Jacobson	0.00	-961.15	-961.15
First Statewide Bank	0.00	-2,641.60	-2,641.60
Richard Long	0.00	-1,058.20	-1,058.20
Valley Real Estate	0.00	-400.00	-400.00
Overall Total	**0.00**	**-5,060.95**	**-5,060.95**

This example is based on the initial report options. You can change the format of the report or the data selected for the report—see the next chapter.

A/R by customer

The accounts receivable (or A/R) report summarizes uncleared transactions in all your Quicken asset accounts by payee. You might want to restrict the report to the asset account for receivables. (See "Selecting items to include in a report" on page 335.)

Initial options for this report (based on the summary report)	
Row Headings:	Payees
Column Headings:	Month
Report organization:	Income and expense
Restrictions:	
Accounts:	Selected (asset)
Cleared:	Uncleared

Accounts Receivable Report
3/1/94 Through 4/30/94

Payee	3/94	4/94	Overall Total
Ace Computer Sales	-592.78	0.00	-592.78
Balloon Adventures	-722.25	0.00	-722.25
Blaine Associates	1,417.75	1,037.90	2,455.65
Computer Waves	-130.54	1,926.00	1,795.46
Engineering Control	-1,502.30	920.20	-582.10
Osborne Studios	-144.45	2,874.02	2,729.57
Reynolds Markets	2,316.55	0.00	2,316.55
Robinson Shoes	1,257.25	2,889.00	4,146.25
Tower Concerts	957.65	0.00	957.65
Overall Total	**2,856.88**	**9,647.12**	**12,504.00**

Initial options for this report	
Report at intervals of:	None
Restrictions:	None

Balance sheet

A balance sheet is a snapshot of the assets, liabilities, and equity (or capital) of a business as of a specific date.

Balance Sheet
As of 4/15/94

Acct	4/15/94 Balance
Assets	
Cash and Bank Accounts	
First Statewide	
Ending Balance	27,343.71
plus: Checks Payable	5,060.95
Total First Statewide	32,404.66
Total Cash and Bank Accounts	32,404.66
Other Assets	
AR	16,158.17
Cap Equip	9,960.00
Total Other Assets	26,118.17
Total Assets	**58,522.83**
Liabilities & Equity	
Liabilities	
Checks Payable	5,060.95
Credit Cards	
American Exp	0.00
Total Credit Cards	0.00
Other Liabilities	
AP	1,695.00
Payroll–FUTA	320.00
Payroll–FWH	0.00
Payroll–FICA	2,554.88
Payroll–MCARE	597.60
Owner's Equity	6,000.00
Sales Tax	3,802.70
Payroll–SWH	230.32
Payroll–SUI	160.00
Total Other Liabilities	15,360.50
Total Liabilities	20,421.45
Equity	38,101.38
Total Liabilities & Equity	**58,522.83**

This section includes all asset accounts.

If your bank accounts include any unprinted or postdated checks, Quicken adds them to your bank balance and also lists them as a liability as "Checks Payable.".

This section includes all liability accounts.

Quicken calculates equity as the difference between your total assets and liabilities.

Budget

This report is identical to the budget report on page 298.

Cash flow

This report is identical to the category report (see page 300). Note that cash flow reporting and cash-basis accounting are independent ideas: you do not have to use cash-basis accounting to create a cash flow report.

Income statement

An income (profit and loss) statement summarizes the revenue and expenses of a business by category (first income, then expenses).

This example is based on the initial report options. You can change the format of the report or the data selected for the report—see the next chapter.

Initial options for this report (based on the summary report)	
Row Headings:	Categories
Column Headings:	None
Organization:	Income and expense
Restrictions:	
Transfers:	To accounts outside report

If you run your business using cash-basis accounting, you want your income to show up when you receive it, not when you issue invoices. Use a cash flow report instead of an income statement for income and expense reporting.

Income Statement
1/1/94 Through 4/15/94

Category	1/1/94–4/15/94
Inc/Exp	
Income	
Design	36,404.25
Interest Inc	311.04
Production	20,529.83
Total Income	57,245.12
Expenses	
Ads	977.87
Auto:	
Gas	279.81
Insurance	301.73
Leasing	417.12
Service	59.95
Tickets	23.00
Total Auto	1,081.61
Computer	163.48
Contractor	1,010.00
Depreciation	950.00
Federal Express	580.07
Insurance	559.05
L&P Fees	348.25
Mailing Lists	658.00
Meals & Enter	217.02
Office	240.20
Paper	1,639.45
Payroll:	
Comp FICA	1,277.44
FUTA	320.00
Gross	20,602.96
Medicare	298.80
SUI	160.00
Total Payroll	22,659.20
Photocopying	293.39
Photostats	306.70
Postage	337.32
Printing	6,253.91
Ref. Materials	116.66
Rent Paid	1,600.00
Telephone	347.73
Total Expenses	40,339.91
Total Inc/Exp	**16,905.21**

Itemized categories

This report is identical to the itemized category report on page 304.

Job/project

A job/project report summarizes your income and expenses for each job, property, client, project, department, or other Quicken class. The following report summarizes income and expenses for two projects. To get a report like this, you must set up each project name as a class; then categorize all project-related transactions with an income or expense category and identify them with project names (classes). (See "Setting up categories and subcategories" on page 47 for information about setting up classes.)

If you manage properties and have set up properties as class names, you can use this report to report on income and expenses by property.

Initial options for this report (based on the summary report)	
Row Headings:	Categories
Column Headings:	Class
Organization:	Income and expense
Restrictions:	None

```
                        Job/Project Report
                       1/1/94 Through 3/31/94

                                                          Overall
       Category        Job 1       Job 2       Job 3       Total
  Inc/Exp
    Income
      Design         2,900.00    6,342.50    3,602.00   12,844.50
      Production       753.80    1,319.95    1,234.85    3,308.60

    Total Income     3,653.80    7,662.45    4,836.85   16,153.10

    Expenses
      Federal Express   56.35      81.39       77.54      215.28
      Paper             47.96      27.80      109.41      185.17
      Photocopying       0.00      48.95       57.44      106.39
      Photostats        18.85       4.95       13.90       37.70
      Printing         105.50     467.95       80.00      653.45

    Total Expenses     228.66     631.04      338.29    1,197.99


  Total Inc/Exp      3,425.14    7,031.41    4,498.56   14,955.11
```

If you have any transactions that have not been assigned to classes, Quicken will display an "Other" column. You can restrict the report to transactions that have been assigned to classes, or select specific classes to be included in the report. See "Changing report restrictions" on page 331.

The example on page 316 is based on the initial report options. You can change the format of the report or the data selected for the report—see the next chapter.

Payroll

The payroll report summarizes income and expenses by category and has a separate column for each payee. The payroll report is set up so it is limited to those transactions with category or transfer account names that start with the word "Payroll." That is, the report is restricted to transactions categorized with payroll categories and transfers to payroll liability accounts.

In the payroll report, the TRANSFERS TO columns show decreases in your accrued payroll liabilities. For example, each time you record a FICA payment in your checking account, Quicken automatically transfers the amount to the Payroll-FICA account, where it decreases the balance you owe.

In the payroll report, the TRANSFERS FROM columns show increases in your accrued payroll liabilities. For example, each time you record a paycheck, Quicken automatically transfers the FICA contribution amount from your checking account to the Payroll-FICA account, where it increases the balance you owe. Use memorized payroll transfers to track your liability for items like FUTA, SUI, Federal Withholding, FICA, and so on.

How transfers show up in payroll reports

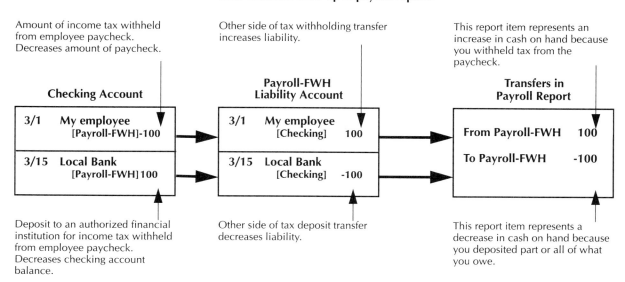

Amount of income tax withheld from employee paycheck. Decreases amount of paycheck.

Other side of tax withholding transfer increases liability.

This report item represents an increase in cash on hand because you withheld tax from the paycheck.

Checking Account

| 3/1 | My employee [Payroll-FWH]-100 |
| 3/15 | Local Bank [Payroll-FWH]100 |

Payroll-FWH Liability Account

| 3/1 | My employee [Checking] 100 |
| 3/15 | Local Bank [Checking] -100 |

Transfers in Payroll Report

| From Payroll-FWH | 100 |
| To Payroll-FWH | -100 |

Deposit to an authorized financial institution for income tax withheld from employee paycheck. Decreases checking account balance.

Other side of tax deposit transfer decreases liability.

This report item represents a decrease in cash on hand because you deposited part or all of what you owe.

This row shows gross wages.

Payroll Report
1/1/94 Through 3/31/94

Category	Chris Jacobs...	First Statew...	Richard Long	Overall Total
Inc/Exp				
Expenses				
Payroll:				
FICA	534.17	0.00	583.59	1,117.76
FUTA	140.00	0.00	140.00	280.00
Gross	8,615.39	0.00	9,412.20	18,027.59
Medicare	124.95	0.00	136.50	261.45
SUI	70.00	0.00	70.00	140.00
Total Payroll	9,484.51	0.00	10,342.29	19,826.80
Total Expenses	9,484.51	0.00	10,342.29	19,826.80
Total Inc/Exp	**-9,484.51**	**0.00**	**-10,342.29**	**-19,826.80**
Transfers				
To Payroll-FWH	0.00	-2,311.40	0.00	-2,311.40
From Payroll-FUTA	140.00	0.00	140.00	280.00
From Payroll-FWH	1,141.28	0.00	1,170.12	2,311.40
From Payroll-FICA	1,068.34	0.00	1,167.18	2,235.52
From Payroll-MCARE	249.90	0.00	273.00	522.90
From Payroll-SWH	86.94	0.00	114.59	201.53
From Payroll-SUI	70.00	0.00	70.00	140.00
Total Transfers	**2,756.46**	**-2,311.40**	**2,934.89**	**3,379.95**
Overall Total	**-6,728.05**	**-2,311.40**	**-7,407.40**	**-16,446.85**

Initial options for this report (based on the summary report)

Row Headings:	Categories
Column Headings:	Payee
Organization:	Income and expense
Restrictions:	
Category:	Contains PAYROLL

This column shows the total increase in your accrued payroll liabilities.

This example is based on the initial report options. You can change the format of the report or the data selected for the report—see the next chapter.

The first section of the report summarizes the Quicken transactions you reconciled with your last bank statement.

Reconciliation

You can create a report that summarizes your latest Quicken reconciliation activity.

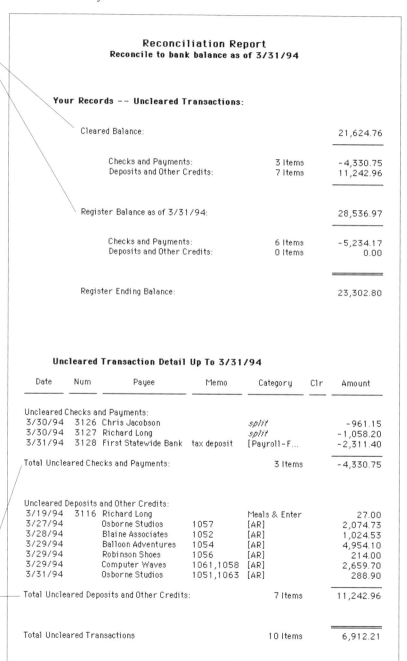

Reconciliation Report
Reconcile to bank balance as of 3/31/94

Your Records -- Uncleared Transactions:

Cleared Balance:		21,624.76
Checks and Payments:	3 Items	-4,330.75
Deposits and Other Credits:	7 Items	11,242.96
Register Balance as of 3/31/94:		28,536.97
Checks and Payments:	6 Items	-5,234.17
Deposits and Other Credits:	0 Items	0.00
Register Ending Balance:		23,302.80

Uncleared Transaction Detail Up To 3/31/94

Date	Num	Payee	Memo	Category	Clr	Amount
Uncleared Checks and Payments:						
3/30/94	3126	Chris Jacobson		*split*		-961.15
3/30/94	3127	Richard Long		*split*		-1,058.20
3/31/94	3128	First Statewide Bank	tax deposit	[Payroll-F...		-2,311.40
Total Uncleared Checks and Payments:				3 Items		-4,330.75
Uncleared Deposits and Other Credits:						
3/19/94	3116	Richard Long		Meals & Enter		27.00
3/27/94		Osborne Studios	1057	[AR]		2,074.73
3/28/94		Blaine Associates	1052	[AR]		1,024.53
3/29/94		Balloon Adventures	1054	[AR]		4,954.10
3/29/94		Robinson Shoes	1056	[AR]		214.00
3/29/94		Computer Waves	1061,1058	[AR]		2,659.70
3/31/94		Osborne Studios	1051,1063	[AR]		288.90
Total Uncleared Deposits and Other Credits:				7 Items		11,242.96
Total Uncleared Transactions				10 Items		6,912.21

The second section of the report lists the transactions in the account that you have not yet reconciled. These transactions include any items that have not been cleared at the bank. They are usually transactions that occurred between the date the bank prepared your statement and the date you received the statement.

Summary

This report is identical to the summary report on page 307.

Transaction

This report is identical to the transaction report on page 310.

Creating reports

Quicken provides report templates you can use to define your own reports. You can customize any report by changing titles, settings, options, and filters.

This chapter explains how to create and customize reports, how to memorize a customized report set up for repeated use, and how to investigate the transactions that make up the report.

Creating reports

You follow the same basic steps to create all Quicken reports. This section shows you how to produce any standard report.

1 Choose Personal Finance or Business from the Reports menu.

2 In the Personal Finance Reports window or Business Reports window, double-click the report you want to run.

Quicken displays a Create Report window.

This is the Create Report window for a category report. Depending on the report you are creating, Quicken might need a single date instead of a date range, or no date at all.

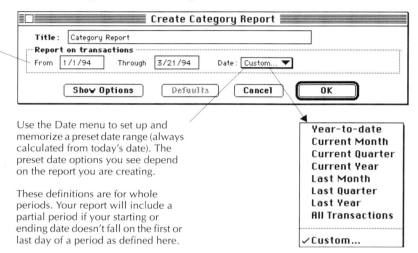

Use the Date menu to set up and memorize a preset date range (always calculated from today's date). The preset date options you see depend on the report you are creating.

These definitions are for whole periods. Your report will include a partial period if your starting or ending date doesn't fall on the first or last day of a period as defined here.

3 (Optional) Change the title for the report.

4 (Optional) Change the date range for the transactions to be included in the report.

Unless you change the dates, the starting date is the first day of this year and the ending date is today. If the report is an "as of" report (for example, a net worth report), the closing date is today.

You can enter dates in numbers (MM/DD/YY) or choose a preset date range from the Date popup menu. Preset date ranges are calculated from today's date. For example, if today is February 15, 1994 and you select the date template "Last Month," Quicken calculates an actual date range of January 1 to January 31, 1994.

5 (Optional) Click Show Options to change the report format or to restrict the report to certain accounts, categories, classes, payees, amounts, and so on.

Quicken displays the Create Report window. See page 321.

Use these options to change the report format. These options vary depending on the report you are creating. See "Changing report formats" on page 328.

Use these restrictions to limit the transactions in your report by any criteria you like. See "Changing report restrictions" on page 331.

Click Hide Options to return to the Create Report window with dates and title only.

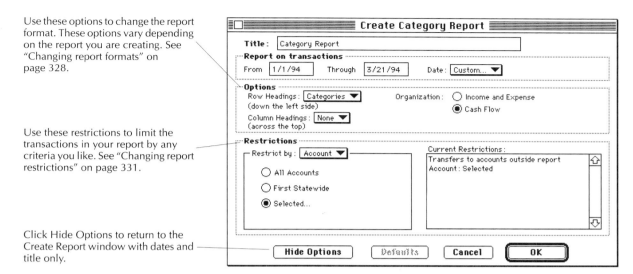

6 **Click OK to start the report.**

Quicken searches the current file for transactions that meet the criteria of the report and then displays the report on the screen. The search may take some time, depending on the size of your accounts and the complexity of the report criteria.

7 **(Optional) You can resize report column widths in the report by dragging anywhere between the column heading and the first line of report text.**

The mouse pointer changes to a double-pointed arrow when it passes over the area that you can drag to resize.

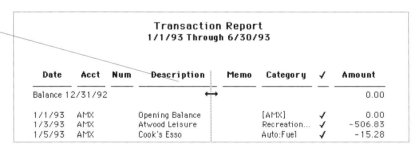

8 **(Optional) To print the report, choose Print Report from the File menu.**

For more information about printing reports, see page 326.

9 **(Optional) To save the report to a file, choose Export Report from the File menu.**

For more information about exporting reports, see page 325.

Updating reports

You can always leave a report open while you make several different kinds of changes. For example, you can change

- Transaction data in one or more account registers
- Budget amounts in the Set Up Budgets window
- Securities data in the Portfolio window for an investment account
- Report settings or report fonts from the Settings menu

When you make any of these changes, Quicken updates all open reports. However, if a report is very large and you need to make a series of changes, you might want Quicken to update the report once, when you have finished making changes. To control when Quicken updates (recalculates) the report data, turn off automatic recalculation.

1   Choose Auto Recalculation from the Reports menu to turn it off.

When Auto Recalculation has no checkmark next to it, Auto Recalculation is turned off.

2   Make the changes you want to transactions, budget amounts, securities, report settings, or report fonts.

3   Click the Recalculate button in the lower left corner of the report output window (next to the Page Preview button).

Page Preview button. See page 326.

Click Recalculate to update the report.

When you click Recalculate, Quicken updates the current report. It does not update any other windows. When the report is updated, Quicken dims the Recalculate button.

Changing global report settings

The settings in the Report Settings window affect every report that you create. For example, you can change the way Quicken lists category, class, and account information in reports. (By default, Quicken reports list the description—if a description exists—of a category, class, or account instead of the name.)

1   **Choose Report Settings from the Settings menu.**

```
                     Report Settings

┌─Show Category/Class────────┐  ┌─Show Account──────────┐
│ ● Description              │  │ ● Description         │
│ ○ Name                     │  │ ○ Name                │
│ ○ Both                     │  │ ○ Both                │
└────────────────────────────┘  └───────────────────────┘

┌─In transaction reports, show─┐ ┌─In Budget Reports, include──────┐
│ ○ Memo                      │  │ ● Budgeted categories only       │
│ ○ Category                  │  │ ○ Budgeted or non-zero actuals   │
│ ● Both                      │  │ ○ All categories                 │
└─────────────────────────────┘  └──────────────────────────────────┘

              [ Defaults ]  [ Cancel ]  [  OK  ]
```

Click Defaults to return report settings to the state they were in when you installed the program.

2   **Select the setting or settings you want to change.**

Report setting	Selection	Results
Show Category/Class:	Description Name Both	Shows the category/class description only. Shows the category/class name only. Shows both the name and description.
Show Account:	Description Name Both	Shows the account description only. Shows the account name only. Shows both the name and description.
In transaction reports, show:	Memo Category Both	Shows memo information only. Shows category information only. Shows both memo and category information.
In budget reports, include:	Budgeted categories only	Includes only categories for which you have entered amounts in the Set Up Budgets window.
	Budgeted or non-zero actuals	Includes only categories for which you have entered amounts in the Set Up Budgets window and categories that you have already used in transactions. Includes every category in the category and transfer list.
	All categories	

3   **Click OK to save the changes you made.**

Changing report fonts

You can change the font for any section of a report. For example, you might want the title of a report to display and print in Geneva 12-point Bold. In this example, Geneva is the font name, 12 is the size, and Bold is the style.

The preset report fonts are customized to the printer currently selected by the Chooser, to the best of Quicken's knowledge. For example, Times is the default font for a LaserWriter, and Geneva for an ImageWriter.

1   Choose Report Fonts from the Settings menu.

The name of the selected report section.

A sample of the selected text format.

```
                        Report Fonts

        Section                    Text Format
        Data                       Times, 10, Plain
        Header (Page Num, Date, etc.)   Times, 10, Bold
        Section Headers/Totals     Times, 10, Bold
        Subtitle                   Times, 10, Bold
        Title                      Times, 12, Bold
        Row Headers                Times, 10, Plain
        Column Headers             Times, 10, Bold

        Font:  [ Times ▼ ]
        Size:  [ 10 ▼ ]          [ Sample ]
        Style: [ Plain ▼ ]

              [ Defaults ]   [ Cancel ]   [ OK ]
```

2   Select the name of a report section.

Quicken highlights the section name and the current text format for that section. Notice how a sample of the current text format for the section appears in the Sample box.

3   Choose a font name from the Font popup menu.

If all the report sections currently share the same font name (for example, Geneva) and you select a different font name for one section, Quicken asks whether you want to change the fonts for all the sections.

4   Choose a size from the Size popup menu.

5   Choose a text style from the Style popup menu.

6   Click OK.

Saving a report to disk

When you save the data in a Quicken report to a file, you select one of two file formats. A third file format, MacInTax, is available for the tax schedule report and the capital gains report only.

1 From the report output window, choose Export Report from the File menu.

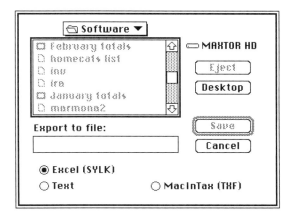

2 Enter a name for the file in the Export to File field.

3 Select a file format: SYLK, Text, or TXF.

- Select Text if you want to import the file into an application such as a word processor.

- Select Excel (SYLK) if you want to import the file into a spreadsheet application such as Microsoft Excel.

- Select MacInTax (TXF) if you want to import the file into MacInTax and or a similar tax preparation application.

4 Click Save.

Quicken exports the report data to the file format you chose.

For more information about exporting tax information from Quicken tax schedule or capital gains reports to MacInTax, see Chapter 22, *Preparing your income taxes,* beginning on page 361.

Printing reports

Print a report when you want a paper copy of the report you see on the screen. Before you print, you might want to change the report fonts as described in "Changing report fonts" on page 324.

1 Choose Print Report from the File menu.

2 Click OK in the printer dialog box.

> Tip: If your report starts printing at the center of the page, make sure US Letter is selected in Page Setup, NOT Computer Paper.

Previewing page breaks in a report

To preview page breaks in a report, click the Page Preview button.

This dotted line indicates a printed page break.

	Net Worth Report				

Sunday, March 21, 1993
Smith Finances – All Accounts

Net Worth Report
As of 4/30/93

Acct	1/1/93 Balance	1/31/93 Balance	2/28/93 Balance	3/31/93 Balance	4/30/93 Balance
Assets					
Cash and Bank Acc					
Cash	50.00	420.50	12.50	74.50	0.50
Checking	3,230.00	5,691.34	7,496.22	10,932.30	9,716.19
Savings	314.86	3,814.86	3,814.86	6,814.86	8,814.86
Total Cash and Ba	3,594.86	9,926.70	11,323.58	17,821.66	18,531.55
Investment					
Chandler Sec	2,376.83	2,376.83	4,568.06	4,557.49	4,557.49
Marmona Fund	0.00	0.00	0.00	969.58	969.58
Sally's IRA	10,224.65	10,593.40	10,787.94	10,981.45	11,181.45
Steve's IRA	0.00	100.00	100.00	279.35	279.35
Total Investments	12,601.48	13,070.23	15,456.00	16,787.87	16,987.87
Other Assets					
House	352,800.00	352,800.00	352,800.00	352,800.00	352,800.00
Sally's 401k	4,731.11	4,929.72	5,095.46	5,161.20	5,226.94
Total Other Assets	357,531.11	357,729.72	357,895.46	357,961.20	358,026.94
Total Assets	**373,727.45**	**380,726.65**	**384,675.04**	**392,570.73**	**393,546.36**
Liabilities					
Credit Cards					
AMX	0.00	152.95	1,719.07	1,677.63	1,399.51
Quicken Visa	1,541.89	1,000.00	1,000.00	1,048.56	1,048.56
Total Credit Cards	1,541.89	1,152.95	2,719.07	2,726.19	2,448.07
Other Liabilities					
Auto Loan	0.00	11,658.08	11,446.05	11,232.61	11,017.74
Mortgage	197,213.97	197,097.54	196,981.11	196,864.68	196,748.25
Total Other Liabil	197,213.97	208,755.62	208,427.16	208,097.29	207,765.99
Total Liabilities	**198,755.86**	**209,908.57**	**211,146.23**	**210,823.48**	**210,214.06**
Overall Total	**174,971.59**	**170,818.08**	**173,528.81**	**181,747.25**	**183,332.30**

Full Columns

Click the Page Preview button to display or hide the dotted lines that indicate printed page breaks.

After you click the Page Preview button, Quicken adds a dotted line or lines in the report window to indicate printed page breaks. To remove the dotted lines, click the Page Preview button again.

There are several things you can do to change the page breaks in a report. You can use any or all of the following techniques:

- If the report columns are too wide to fit on a single sheet of paper, you can resize the report column widths by dragging anywhere between the column heading and the first line of report text (as illustrated in step 7 on page 321). The report below is the same as the report shown on page 326; the report column widths have been narrowed so that all the columns print on a single page.

This report is the same as the report on page 326. The column widths in this report have been narrowed so that all the columns fit on one sheet of paper.

```
▤☐▯                   Net Worth Report                        ▯☐
Sunday, March 21, 1993                                           ⇧
Smith Finances - All Accounts

                        Net Worth Report
                         As of 4/30/93

                 1/1/93      1/31/93     2/28/93     3/31/93     4/30/93
     Acct        Balance     Balance     Balance     Balance     Balance

Assets
  Cash and Ban
    Cash            50.00      420.50       12.50       74.50        0.50
    Checking     3,230.00    5,691.34    7,496.22   10,932.30    9,716.19
    Savings        314.86    3,814.86    3,814.86    6,814.86    8,814.86

  Total Cash an  3,594.86    9,926.70   11,323.58   17,821.66   18,531.55

  Investment
    Chandler S   2,376.83    2,376.83    4,568.06    4,557.49    4,557.49
    Marmona          0.00        0.00        0.00      969.58      969.58
    Sally's IR  10,224.65   10,593.40   10,787.94   10,981.45   11,181.45
    Steve's IR       0.00      100.00      100.00      279.35      279.35

  Total Investn 12,601.48   13,070.23   15,456.00   16,787.87   16,987.87

  Other Assets
    House      352,800.00  352,800.00  352,800.00  352,800.00  352,800.00
    Sally's 40   4,731.11    4,929.72    5,095.46    5,161.20    5,226.94

  Total Other A 357,531.11  357,729.72  357,895.46  357,961.20  358,026.94

Total Assets   373,727.45  380,726.65  384,675.04  392,570.73  393,546.36

Liabilities
  Credit Cards
    AMX              0.00      152.95    1,719.07    1,677.63    1,399.51
    Quicken Vi   1,541.89    1,000.00    1,000.00    1,048.56    1,048.56

  Total Credit C 1,541.89    1,152.95    2,719.07    2,726.19    2,448.07

  Other Liabili
    Auto Loan        0.00   11,658.08   11,446.05   11,232.61   11,017.74
    Mortgage   197,213.97  197,097.54  196,981.11  196,864.68  196,748.25

  Total Other L 197,213.97  208,755.62  208,427.16  208,097.29  207,765.99

Total Liabi...  198,755.86  209,908.57  211,146.23  210,823.48  210,214.06

Overall Total   174,971.59  170,818.08  173,528.81  181,747.25  183,332.30  ⇩
☐  Full Columns  ⇦                                                  ⇨▯
```

Click the Full Columns button to reset column widths any time after you resize the report window.

- You can choose Page Setup from the File menu and switch from Portrait to Landscape orientation. Landscape means that your report prints lengthwise on the paper.

- For some printers, you can choose Page Setup from the File menu and reduce the printed report to less than 100%, or switch the print orientation from portrait to landscape. You can enter a reduction percentage in the Reduce or Enlarge field to eliminate or minimize page breaks. For an ImageWriter, you can select the reduce 50% option.

- You can choose Report Fonts from the Settings menu and change the fonts for all or some of the sections in your report. For example, Times prints smaller than most other fonts at similar point sizes. See "Changing report fonts" on page 324 for more information.

- For transaction reports, you can exclude the memo or category column of the report. See "Changing global report settings" on page 323.

Changing report formats

Report formats determine how Quicken organizes and presents the information in your report. You can change the format of any Quicken report.

To change the format of a report, click Show Options in the Create Report window.

Use the options in this section to change the report format. These options vary depending on the report you are creating.

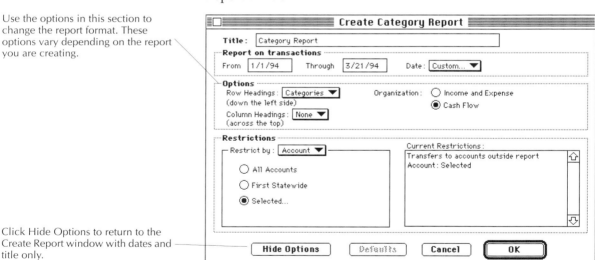

Click Hide Options to return to the Create Report window with dates and title only.

We describe options for reconciliation reports separately. (See "Completing reconciliation" on page 149.)

The table on page 329 lists all report format options alphabetically. The choices available for each format option vary by report type.

Name of format option	Selection	Results
Assign Tax Categories (tax schedule report)	See page 364	Creates a link between the Quicken categories and standard categories used by tax preparation software.
Column Headings (budget, cash flow, category, summary, A/P by vendor, A/R by customer, income statement, job/project, and payroll reports)	None Period Category Class Payee Account	Creates a separate column for each item. If you choose None, Quicken creates a report with a single column. For information about how Quicken calculates periods of time, see "How Quicken defines report periods" on page 331.
(investment income reports)	None Period Account Security Security Type Investment Goal Category	These are the column heading options for the investment income report.
Include unrealized gains (balance sheet, capital gains, investment income, investment transactions, net worth reports)	Selected	Generates additional transactions (in the investment transaction report) or income/inflow lines (in the investment income report) to represent the impact of price increases and decreases for securities.
	Not selected	Quicken does not include unrealized gains.
Maximum short-term holding period (capital gains report)	Any number of days	Quicken computes your short-term capital gains on the basis of the number of days you enter here.
Organization (budget, cash flow, category, investment income, investment transactions, itemized categories, summary, tax summary, transaction, A/P by vendor, income statement, job/project, and payroll reports)	Income and Expense	Totals income, expense, and transfer transactions in separate sections of your report.
	Cash Flow	Groups and totals inflows and outflows (including expenses and transfers out of the account). For example, if you have an asset account called "House," and you treat home improvement transactions as transfers to that account, choosing cash flow basis lets you treat those transfers as spending, giving you a more accurate picture of your total expenditures.
Report at intervals of (net worth and balance sheet reports)	None	Includes one total for account balances based on the ending date you enter at the top of the window.
	Period	Creates a column and totals account balances for each week, two weeks, half month, month, quarter, half year, or year.

Name of format option	Selection	Results
Row Headings (cash flow, category, summary, A/P by vendor, A/R by customer, A/R by vendor, income statement, job/project, and payroll reports)	Category Class Payee Account	Creates a row for each category, class, payee, or account.
Show missing checks (itemized categories, tax summary, and transaction reports))	Selected	Lists check numbers that are missing or duplicated in the series of check numbers for each account.
	Not selected	Does not list missing or duplicated check number.
Show split detail (itemized categories, tax summary, and transaction reports)	Selected	Includes the detail from the Split Transaction window.
	Not selected	Does not include the detail from the Split Transaction window. However., if you restrict categories or classes, Quicken automatically reports split transactions detail too.
Show totals only (itemized categories, tax summary, and transaction reports)	Not selected	Lists all the transactions that meet the criteria you've specified.
	Selected	Displays only the total dollar amount of transactions that meet the criteria you've specified.
Sort by check number (itemized categories, tax summary, and transaction reports)	Not selected	Sorts transactions first by account type, then by account name, and then by date.
	Selected	Sorts transactions first by account type, then by account name, and then by check number.
Subtotal By (itemized categories, tax summary, and transaction reports)	Don't Subtotal Period Category Class Payee Account	Groups and totals transactions by the item you choose. (See "How Quicken defines report periods" on page 331.) If you choose Don't Subtotal, Quicken doesn't subtotal amounts in the report. You can subtotal a budget report by period only.
(capital gains, investment performance, investment transactions, and portfolio value reports)	Don't Subtotal Period Account Security Security Type Investment Goal Short- vs. long-term	These are the subtotal options for investment reports only. Not all options apply to all investment reports. Available for capital gains reports only.

How Quicken defines report periods

You can subtotal certain reports by period. Refer to this table if you have any question about a specific period.

Period	Quicken definition
Week	Starts on Sunday, runs through Saturday
Two weeks	Starts on Sunday, runs for 14 days (ends on Saturday)
Half month	Runs from the 1st through the 15th or from the 16th through the last day of the month
Month	Starts on the 1st of the month, ends on the last day of the month
Quarter	Includes three consecutive calendar months, starting with January 1, April 1, July 1, or October 1
Half year	Starts on the starting date and ends on the last day of the month five months later; for example, January 2 through June 30, February 2 through July 31, March 3 through August 31
Year	Starts on the starting date, runs for 365 days (366 days for leap year)

Changing report restrictions

Report restrictions further define or limit the transactions to be included in your reports. You can tell Quicken what must be true about a transaction for it to be included in a report.

For example, you can tell Quicken to include only transactions with a specific payee or only transactions with a specific payee that have been reconciled and cleared in your accounts. You can have Quicken report only on payments from your accounts or only on deposits. You can even print a report limited to tax-related categories.

Restricting the items in a report

1   **Follow steps 1 to 4 in "Creating reports" on page 320 to choose a report type and set the date range.**

2   **If you don't see all the options in the Create Report window, click Show Options.**

Use these options to change the report format. These options vary depending on the report you are creating. See "Changing report formats" on page 328.

Select the item you want to restrict in the report here.

Quicken displays the options for the item you selected above. These are the options for restricting by account.

Click Hide Options to return to the Create Report window with dates and title only.

Create Category Report

Title: [Category Report]

Report on transactions
From [1/1/94]   Through [3/21/94]   Date: [Custom... ▼]

Options
Row Headings: [Categories ▼]   Organization: ○ Income and Expense
(down the left side)   ● Cash Flow
Column Headings: [None ▼]
(across the top)

Restrictions
Restrict by: [Account ▼]

○ All Accounts
○ First Statewide
● Selected...

Current Restrictions:
Transfers to accounts outside report
Account: Selected

[Hide Options]   [Defaults]   [Cancel]   [OK]

3 **Select the item you want to restrict from the popup menu.**

Quicken displays the options for the item you selected under the menu. Quicken also shows all existing restrictions on this report in the "Current Restrictions" list to the right.

4 **Select an option for the item you selected.**

The table on page 332 shows all the options for restricting items in a report. Investment items are available only for investment reports.

5 **Click OK when you are ready to run the report.**

Name of item to restrict	Selection	Results
Account	All	Includes transactions from all accounts in the current Quicken file.
	Current account	Includes transactions in the current account (or the last current account).
	Selected	Includes only transactions from the accounts you select. When you select this option, Quicken displays the Select Accounts window. See "Selecting items to include in a report" on page 335.
Amount	Any amount	Includes all transaction amounts.
	Equal	Includes amounts equal to the amount you enter.
	Greater	Includes amounts greater than the amount you enter.
	Greater or equal	Includes amounts greater than or equal to the amount you enter.
	Less	Includes amounts less than the amount you enter.
	Less or equal	Includes amount less than or equal to the amount you enter.

Name of item to restrict	Selection	Results
Category	All	Includes transactions with any or no category information.
	Exact Contains Starts with Ends with	Includes categories that match the text you enter exactly. Includes categories that contain the text you enter. Includes categories that begin with the text you enter. Includes categories that end with the text you enter.
	Selected	Includes only transactions assigned to the categories you select. When you select this option, Quicken displays the Select Categories window. See "Selecting items to include in a report" on page 335.
	Tax-related only	Includes only transactions that have been applied to tax-related categories.
Check Number	All Checks No Checks Checks Numbered From ___ Through	Includes all transactions. Excludes transactions with numbers or PRINT in the Number field. Includes only checks within the range of numbers you specify.; for example, from 1 through 5.
Class	All	Includes transactions with any or no class information.
	Exact Contains Starts with Ends with	Includes classes that match the text you enter exactly. Includes classes that contain the text you enter. Includes classes that begin with the text you enter. Includes classes that end with the text you enter.
	Selected	Includes only transactions assigned to the classes you select. When you select this option, Quicken displays the Select Classes window. See "Selecting items to include in a report" on page 335.
Cleared	Uncleared	Includes only uncleared transactions. Uncleared transactions have nothing in the √ (cleared) field.
	Cleared (√)	Includes only cleared transactions. Cleared transactions have a thin checkmark in the √ (cleared) field.
	Reconciled (✓)	Includes only reconciled transactions. Reconciled transactions have a bold checkmark in the √ (cleared) field.
Investment Goal (investment reports only)	All	Includes all investment goals.
	Exact Contains Starts with Ends with	Includes goals that match the text you enter exactly. Includes goals that contain the text you enter. Includes goals that begin with the text you enter. Includes goals that end with the text you enter.

Name of item to restrict	Selection	Results
Memo	All	Includes only transactions for that memo in the report.
	Exact	Includes memos that match the text you enter exactly.
	Contains	Includes memos that contain the text you enter.
	Starts with	Includes memos that begin with the text you enter.
	Ends with	Includes memos that end with the text you enter.
Payee & Description	All	Includes only transactions for that payee in the report.
	Exact	Includes payees that match the text you enter exactly.
	Contains	Includes payees that contain the text you enter.
	Starts with	Includes payees that begin with the text you enter.
	Ends with	Includes payees that end with the text you enter.
Security (investment reports only)	All	Includes all securities.
	Exact	Includes securities that match the text you enter exactly.
	Contains	Includes securities that contain the text you enter.
	Starts with	Includes securities that begin with the text you enter.
	Ends with	Includes securities that end with the text you enter.
	Selected	When you click OK from the Create Report window, Quicken displays the Select Security to Include window. See "Selecting items to include in a report" on page 335.
Security Type (investment reports only)	All	Includes all security types.
	Exact	Includes types that match the text you enter exactly.
	Contains	Includes types that contain the text you enter.
	Starts with	Includes types that begin with the text you enter.
	Ends with	Includes types that end with the text you enter.
Transaction Type	Payments	Includes payments only (including checks). For nonbank accounts, payments are decreases to cash and other asset accounts, and increases to credit card and other liability accounts.
	Deposits	Includes deposits only.
	Unprinted Checks	Includes unprinted checks only.
	Untransmitted Payments	Includes untransmitted electronic payments only (available only if electronic payments are enabled).
Transfers	All Transfers	Includes all transfers in the report.
	No Transfers	Excludes all transfers in the report.
	Transfers to accounts outside report	Excludes transfers between accounts that are included in the report. Essentially, these are transfers that cancel each other out in the report.

Selecting items to include in a report

In the table on pages 332-334, four items have a "Selected" option:

- accounts
- categories
- classes
- securities

When you click the Selected option for accounts, investment actions, categories, or classes, Quicken displays a window where you can select the items you want Quicken to include in the report.

For example, if you click the Selected option for categories, Quicken displays the Select Categories window.

You can select "–No category–" if you want to report to include transactions that have not been assigned to a category.

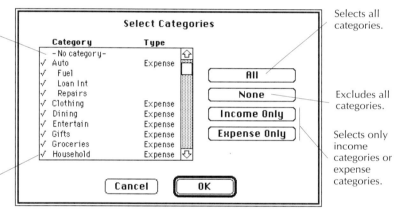

Selects all categories.

Excludes all categories.

Selects only income categories or expense categories.

Click on a category or subcategory to mark or unmark it. Quicken includes all categories or subcategories marked with a check in the report.

When you click OK, Quicken returns to the Create Report window. When you run the report, Quicken includes only those transactions assigned to the categories you selected.

> You can also select account names at the end of the list to include only selected transfers.

The technique to restrict a report to selected accounts, classes, or securities is the same as the technique to restrict a report to selected categories.

Using wildcard characters to restrict reports

When you use payee, memo, category, class, security, security type, or investment goal information to restrict the transactions in a report or search for a transaction, you can use special *wildcard* characters in text fields to narrow the search. The following chart shows some examples of how wildcards can change your report.

Wildcard	Description
.. (two periods)	Finds a match that contains unspecified characters where you type .. (at the beginning, in the middle, or at the end of the text you type).
? (question mark)	Finds a match with one unspecified character
~ (tilde)	Excludes all matches for the text that follows. For example, If you type ~.. (a tilde and two periods), Quicken excludes all transactions except those that are empty in the specified field.

Case doesn't matter, and Quicken ignores any spaces before or after the phrase you type.

Example	The report includes	The report does not include
~tax	rent, utilities	tax, Tax, TAX, taxable, tax deduction, Tax:-State, surtax, new tax loss
t..x	trix, tx, tkx, t——x, tax, Tax, TAX	taxable, tax deduction, Tax:State, surtax, new tax loss, rent, utilities
t?x	tkx, tax, Tax, TAX	trix, tx, t——x, taxable, tax deduction, Tax:-State, surtax, new tax loss, rent, utilities
..	tax, rent, utilities, and so on	*blank*
~..	*blank*	tax, rent, utilities, and so on

The table on pages 332-334 describes the Starts With, Ends With, and Exact search options for categories, classes, investment goals, memos, payees and descriptions, securities, and security types.

Investigating items in reports using QuickZoom

You can use QuickZoom to examine the transaction detail in the following types of reports: budget reports, investment performance reports, summary reports (A/P by vendor, A/R by customer, cash flow, category, income statement, investment income, job/project, and payroll), and transaction reports (itemized categories, tax summary, and tax schedule).

1   Select an amount in the report and double-click it.

Quicken displays a detail report, which is a list of the transactions that make up that amount. (Or, if you use QuickZoom in a transaction report, Quicken displays the register.)

For example, if you are curious about the individual transactions represented by an amount in a category report, you can double-click the amount to see a list of the transactions that make up that amount.

You can QuickZoom an item when the mouse pointer turns into a magnifying glass.

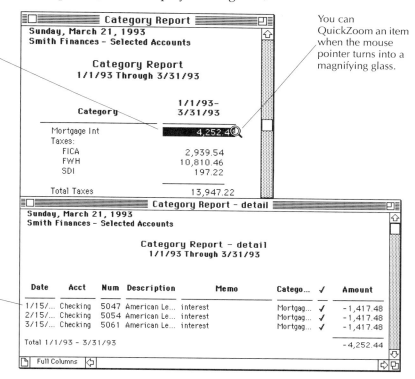

If you want to examine or change a transaction, double-click it to go to the account register with that transaction selected.

2   (Optional) To examine a transaction in the register or make any changes, double-click the transaction.

Quicken displays the register and selects the transaction. If you make any changes to transactions, Quicken updates the report immediately.

> QuickZoom is a handy way to track down and assign categories to uncategorized amounts in a summary report. Uncategorized amounts show up as "Other" in Quicken reports.

Memorizing and recalling reports

Once you change the format and restrictions for a report, you can memorize the changes so you can recall the report using the same report instructions time after time. This feature is most useful for reports that use restrictions. You can also change a memorized report and then rememorize it with the changes.

Quicken does *not* memorize budget amounts or the printer settings because they are not part of the report.

Memorizing reports

1   Create and display a report as described in "Creating reports" on page 320.

If you resize any report columns, Quicken will memorize those, too.

Or press ⌘ M

2   Choose Memorize from the Edit menu.

When you memorize a report, you must type a report title. If you use the same title again, Quicken warns that you are about to overwrite an existing memorized report.

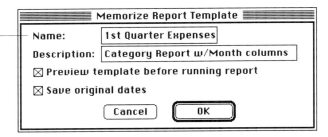

3   Enter a title for the memorized report.

4   Choose an option for report dates.

Preview template before running report. If you select this option, you will always see the Create Report window for this report and have an opportunity to make changes before you run the report. If you don't select this option, Quicken will always run the report immediately.

Save original dates. If you select this option, Quicken memorizes the actual dates that were used in the report. If you don't select this option, Quicken will use the preset starting and ending dates that appear in the Create Report window when you recall the report.

5   Click OK to memorize the report.

Quicken adds the report to the Memorized Reports window.

Recalling reports

After you have memorized a report, you can recall it. When you recall a report, it's really the report definition you are recalling (including the format and restrictions you've specified).

Or press ⌘ M

1 Choose Memorized from the Reports menu.

Quicken displays the Memorized Reports window.

2 Double-click the report you want to use.

If you selected the Preview Template Before Running Report checkbox when you memorized this report, Quicken displays the usual Create Report window, so you can change the recalled report instructions if you want. When you are satisfied with the instructions, Quicken searches for transactions and prepares the report as usual.

If you did not select the Preview Template Before Running Report checkbox when you memorized this report, Quicken runs the report immediately, without displaying a Create Report window. To restore the Preview option for a report, memorize it again and select the Preview Template Before Running Report checkbox.

If you change the instructions for a memorized report, you can rememorize it with the same title or you can give the altered report a new title and memorize it again. If you don't rememorize a report whose definition you have changed, it retains the original definition the next time you recall the report.

3 Click OK.

Quicken searches for transactions and displays the report.

- To change a memorized report, double-click it in the Memorized Reports window, change the instructions in the Memorized Reports window, and then rememorize the report with the same title.

Or press ⌘ D

- To delete a memorized report, select it in the Memorized Reports window and choose Delete Memorized Report from the Edit menu.

Creating graphs

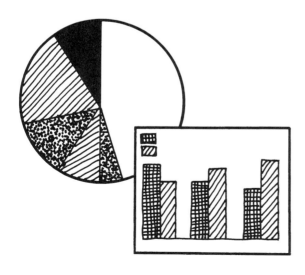

As well as viewing numbers in an account register or a report, you can display your Quicken data as pie charts and bar graphs. Graphs help you visualize your entire financial picture quickly.

Create graphs to help analyze your income and expenses, compare your income and expenses to your budget, determine your net worth, and evaluate the performance of your investments.

About graphs

Graphs are helpful if you're looking for a visual summary of your finances. If you need more detailed information about an item you see in a graph, you can get it quickly using the QuickZoom feature to move to another, more detailed graph.

Quicken creates four types of graph:

- income and expense (page 345)
- budget variance (page 346)
- net worth (page 347)
- investment performance (page 348)

Creating graphs

1   Choose Graphs from the Reports menu.

2   Enter information in the Create Graph window.

Choose the type of graph you want to create.

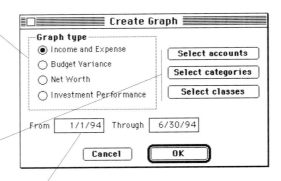

(Optional) Click the Select buttons if you'd like to restrict the accounts, categories, classes, or securities that appear in the graph. You can restrict accounts, categories, and classes in income and expense, budget variance, and net worth graphs. You can restrict accounts and securities (not shown here) in investment performance graphs. Select items to restrict the same way you select them in reports. See "Selecting items to include in a report" on page 335.

(Optional) Change the dates in the date range. You can create graphs for all the data you have entered in Quicken, but it's best to limit the date range. Graphs may be too cluttered and difficult to understand if you enter a date range much longer than a year.

3   Click OK to create the graph.

Understanding the parts of a graph

Quicken is preset to display two graphs in one window (except for the single net worth graph) unless your Macintosh has a small screen. If your Macintosh has a larger screen but you prefer to view the graphs in separate windows, you can change the display setting. See "Changing graph settings" on page 349.

Graphs are also preset to display in three dimensions. It should take Quicken about the same length of time to create a graph as it takes to create a comparable report. If it takes a long time to create graphs, either limit the date range of the graph or display graphs in two dimensions instead of three dimensions. See "Changing graph settings" on page 349.

Each segment of a graph is shaded with a different color (or pattern if you do not have a color monitor).

If you shrink a graph window, Quicken decreases the size of the graphs and text displayed in it.

The title of each individual graph is right above the graph. You can change the way the titles and other text are displayed and printed. See "Changing graph fonts" on page 349.

Legends identify the meaning of each bar, line, or pie slice. A legend is located to the right of each graph.

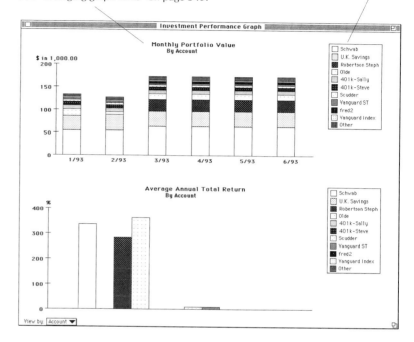

Understanding the information in a graph

Quicken totals any subcategories you may have (for example, auto:fuel, auto:maintenance, and auto:insurance) and displays only the category (for example, auto) in graphs.

Whenever you see the arrow cursor turn into a magnifying glass, you can QuickBrowse the exact value of the element that is below the magnifying glass. Click and hold down the mouse button.

In bar graphs, Quicken displays dollar amounts on the y-axis. Months or categories are on the x-axis for income and expense, budget variance, and net worth graphs. (Months, accounts, investment types, goals, or securities are on the x-axis for investment performance graphs.)

In pie charts, if you have more than ten categories, Quicken displays the largest ten categories first.

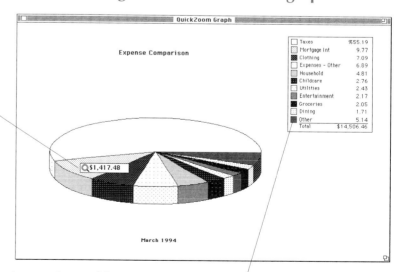

It groups the rest of the categories in the eleventh slice of the pie called "Other." To see the rest of your categories in a pie chart, double-click the "Other" slice in the pie chart or double-click "Other" in the legend.

Investigating items in graphs using QuickZoom

You can investigate the information you see in a graph in more detail. As with Quicken reports, you can QuickZoom from a graph to examine transaction details in a report.

QuickZoom is a handy way to track down and assign categories to any uncategorized amounts that appear in a graph. Quicken displays uncategorized transactions as Income-Other or Expenses-Other.

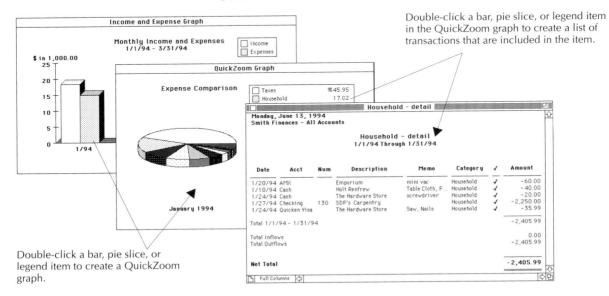

Double-click a bar, pie slice, or legend item in the QuickZoom graph to create a list of transactions that are included in the item.

Double-click a bar, pie slice, or legend item to create a QuickZoom graph.

1 **Select any pie slice, bar, or legend item in the graph and double-click it.**

Quicken displays a QuickZoom graph, which shows more detail about the pie slice, bar, or amount you selected.

2 **(Optional) To examine an item in the QuickZoom graph further or to make any changes to a transaction that appears in the QuickZoom graph, double-click the item.**

Quicken displays a detail report, which is a list of the transactions that make up the item. (Or, if you use QuickZoom in a transaction graph, Quicken displays the register and selects the transaction.)

3 **(Optional) To examine a transaction in the register or to make any changes to a transaction that appears in the detail report, double-click the transaction in the detail report.**

Quicken displays the register and selects the transaction. If you make any changes, Quicken updates the open graphs immediately.

Analyzing income and expenses

Income and expense graphs can help you spot spending patterns, highlight your top ten expenses, warn about overspending, and provide comparisons of historical data.

Quicken creates these graphs using the categories you assign when you enter transactions. Quicken ordinarily includes the value of any subcategory within its parent category; however, you can create a graph with a filter that includes only one particular subcategory. See "Changing report restrictions" on page 331.

Income and expense graphs help you answer these financial questions:

- Is my income changing over time?
- Is my income covering my expenses?
- Where does my money come from?
- Where does my money go?

The first graph, monthly income and expenses, compares income and expense over time.

This example shows that expenses were greater than income in June. Income and expenses fluctuate from month to month in this household.

The net savings and expense comparison graph is the second income and expense graph.

If your income was greater than your expenses in the time period covered, this pie chart shows your top ten expenses relative to (as a percentage of) your *total income.* Quicken displays the difference between your income and expenses as "Net Savings." The Net Savings slice represents the amount of money that you had but did not spend.

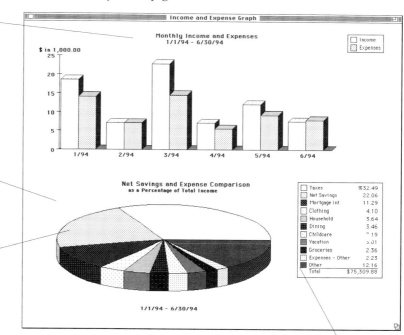

If your expenses were greater than your income in the time period covered by the graph, this pie chart will show your top ten expenses as a percentage of your *total expenses* and the Net Savings slice will not appear in the graph.

If you see a dollar amount instead of a percentage in the legend, this means that you have entered a transaction with either a positive amount for an expense category or a negative amount for an income category. (For example, if you return some clothing, you enter the expense category Clothing, but you enter the amount of the credit as a deposit instead of a payment.)

When you double-click Other in the legend or the pie, Quicken creates a QuickZoom graph of the next ten highest expense categories.

Understanding budget variance

Budget variance graphs compare actual spending and income with budgeted spending and income. Quicken calculates the difference in dollars between the two so you can see how you are actually doing compared to your budget.

You can create budget variance graphs that quickly alert you to potential problem areas such as expenses that are over budget or income that is under budget. Determining how successfully you budgeted this year can help you prepare next year's budget. (If you have not already set up and entered amounts into your budget, Quicken cannot create budget variance graphs. See Chapter 21, *Budgeting your income and expenses,* beginning on page 351.)

Budget graphs help you answer these financial questions:

- Am I staying within my budget from month to month?
- How well do I estimate what I will earn and spend?
- In what categories do I overspend or underspend?

Favorable means that either actual income was more than budgeted income or actual expenses were less than budgeted expenses. *Unfavorable* means that actual income was less than budgeted income or actual expenses were more than budgeted expenses.

The first budget variance graph, actual vs. budgeted net income, shows actual net income less budgeted net income.

This example shows a favorable budget variance in the first quarter.

The actual vs. budgeted categories graph shows the five categories that are farthest from budget (both over and under).

Income categories appear above the x-axis. Expense categories appear below it.

Using the information in this graph, you can pursue the reasons for overspending or under-earning by category.

Based on what you learn, you may be able to budget better for these categories in the next six months or next year.

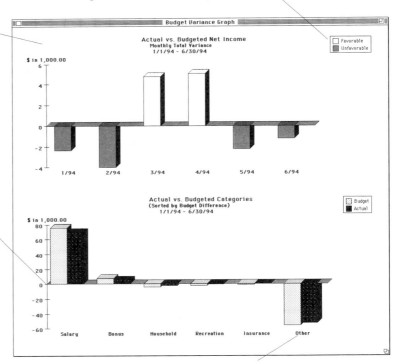

If you have entered budget amounts for more than five categories, Quicken displays the five categories with the largest difference between the budget amount and the actual amount. It groups the rest of the categories in the sixth bar called "Other." To see the rest of your categories in a bar chart, double-click the "Other" bar.

Analyzing net worth

Net worth graphs are similar to income and expense graphs, except they use account balances rather than category data. Net worth graphs are also similar to net worth reports or balance sheets you may create in Quicken.

Create net worth graphs to show the balance of your credit cards or other debts and your bank accounts or other assets over time, or to show if your net worth is changing.

Net worth graphs help you answer these financial questions:

- Do I own more than I owe?
- In what assets do I have most of my money?
- What are my largest debts?
- How is my net worth changing over time?

The monthly assets, liabilities, and net worth graph displays one graph (instead of two) in the window.

The graph shows your assets in bars above the x-axis and your liabilities in bars below the x-axis. Your net worth is the difference between your assets and liabilities. This example shows that net worth is positive (above zero) and increasing slightly over the first half of the year.

You can double-click an asset bar to see an asset comparison graph as of that month. The QuickZoom graph shows a breakdown of your individual assets as a percentage of your total assets.

Or double-click a liability bar to see a liability comparison graph as of that month to see a breakdown of your individual liabilities as a percentage of your total liabilities.

Double-click a pie slice in the QuickZoom graph to create a list of transactions that are included in the item.

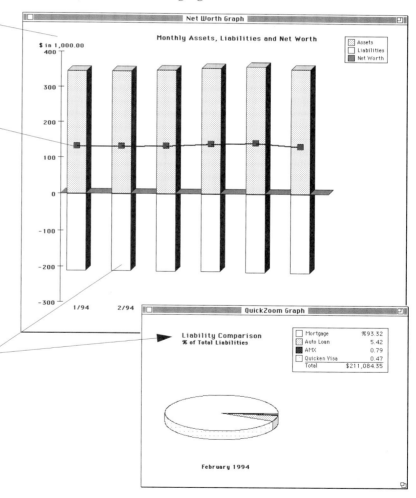

Evaluating investment performance

Investment performance graphs display information that helps you to evaluate your investment portfolio. You can also view graphs of the price or market value of a selected security for the previous six months. See "Viewing and changing prices in the Portfolio window" on page 267.

Four portfolio value graphs summarize the market value of each security you own, either by type (such as bond, CD, or mutual funds), goal (such as college, retirement, growth, or income), security (such as IBM, Exxon, AT&T), or Quicken investment account (such as Steve's IRA, Sally's IRA, or Merrill Lynch).

The average annual total return graph is a measure of how well your securities are performing.

Investment performance graphs help you answer these financial questions:

- Is my portfolio value increasing?
- How is my portfolio allocated?
- How are my stocks and bonds doing?

The monthly portfolio value graph summarizes the market value of each security you own.

The average annual total return graph measures how well your securities are performing. Taller bars indicate better performance.

The monthly portfolio value graph is summarized by security in this example. To change how the graph is summarized (by type of security, goal, security, or account), select your choice from the popup menu here.

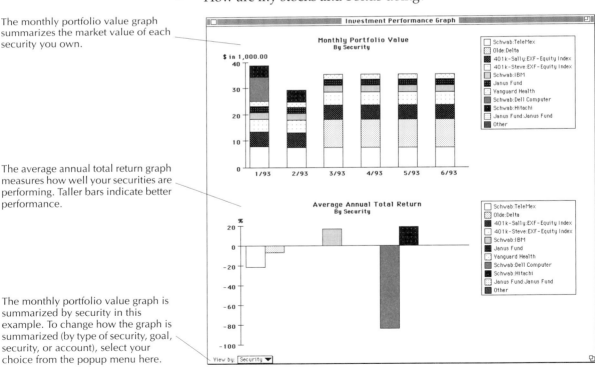

Changing graph settings

The settings in the Graph Settings dialog box affect how Quicken displays every graph that you create.

If you are using a color monitor and some of the colors in your graphs are very similar to other colors, turn up the brightness or contrast on your monitor. Each color becomes vivid and distinct.

1   Choose Graphs from the Settings menu.

Select 2-Dimensional if your computer takes a long time to display three-dimensional graphs.

Select this preference to display each graph in a window instead of two graphs per window. (If your Macintosh has a small monitor, Quicken turns on this preference automatically.)

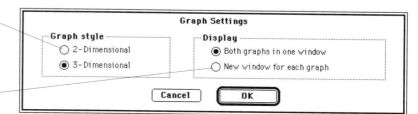

2   Select the settings you want to use.

3   Click OK to save the changes you made.

Changing graph fonts

You can change the font for any section of a graph. For example, you might want the title of a graph to display and print in Helvetica 14-point Bold. In this example, Helvetica is the font name, 14 is the size, and Bold is the style.

1   Choose Graph Fonts from the Settings menu.

The name of the selected graph section.

The preset graph fonts are customized to the printer currently selected by the Chooser, to the best of Quicken's knowledge. For example, Times is the preset font for a LaserWriter, and Geneva for an ImageWriter.

A sample of the selected text format.

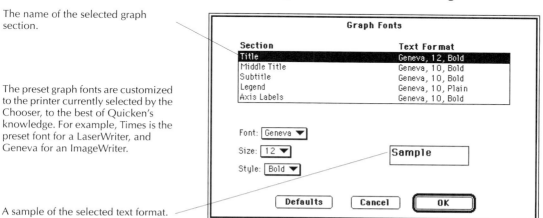

2   Select the name of a graph section.

Quicken highlights the section name and the current text format for that section and displays a sample of the current text format for the section in the Sample box.

3   Choose a font name from the Font popup menu.

If all the graph sections currently share the same font name and you select a different font name for one section, Quicken asks whether you want to change the fonts for all the sections.

4   Choose a size from the Size popup menu.

5   Choose a text style from the Style popup menu.

6   Click OK to save the changes you made.

Printing graphs

When you print a graph, Quicken uses the settings you've selected for graph fonts. See "Changing graph fonts" on page 349.

Your printer needs sufficient memory to print a graph successfully at a resolution of 300 dpi (dots per inch) or higher.

1   Make sure your printer is turned on, online, and loaded with paper.

2   Create the graph you want to print.

3   Choose Print Graph from the File menu.

Quicken opens the printer dialog box.

4   Click Print in the printer dialog box.

Quicken prints the graph. A printed graph typically looks a little different than the onscreen graph.

Budgeting your income and expenses

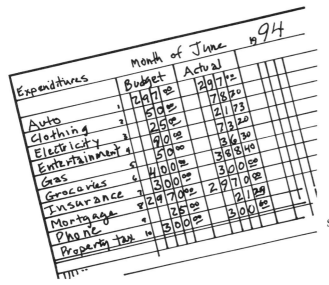

You can use Quicken to budget all of your income and expenses or just a few of them.

After you enter budget amounts for your income and expenses into Quicken's budget spreadsheet, you can create reports and graphs to compare your actual income and expenses against your plan.

Setting up a budget

When you set up a budget in a Quicken file, you set monthly budget amounts for some or all of the categories and subcategories you use. (You can also set budget amounts for transfers.) You can enter and change monthly budget values at any time.

Quicken organizes the budget according to your income and expense categories. Before you set up a budget, you might like to set up new categories or evaluate how well your current categories are providing you with the information you need in reports and graphs.

Quicken can create only one budget per file. The starting point for every Quicken budget is the beginning of the calendar year; you cannot set up a budget in Quicken for the fiscal year.

◆ **Set up home or business income and expense categories.**
 See "Setting up categories and subcategories" on page 47.

◆ **Categorize transactions.**
 See "Assigning categories to transactions" on page 82.

◆ **Display the budget.**
 See below.

◆ **Enter amounts for categories into the budget.**
 See "Entering amounts in the budget" on page 354 and "Editing amounts in the budget" on page 357.

◆ **Create budget reports or graphs.**
 After you've estimated your income and expenses, you're ready to create budget reports or graphs to see what you've actually earned and spent compared to your budget. See "Creating budget reports and graphs" on page 358.

Displaying the budget

To open and display the budget so that you can review it or enter amounts into it:

1   **Choose Budget from the Planning menu.**

Quicken displays the budget spreadsheet illustrated on the next page (the Set Up Budgets window).

2   **(Optional) Change the layout of the budget.**

To display the budget amounts by quarter or by year instead of by month, choose Quarter or Year from the View By popup menu. You can change the layout of the budget at any time without worrying about how the change will affect your budget amounts.

If you enter budget amounts by quarter or by year, and then switch back to monthly budget amounts, Quicken distributes the budget amounts evenly across the months in the period, with any remainder included in the first month. For example, if you budgeted $301 for the first quarter of the year and changed the layout to the monthly format, Quicken distributes $100.34 to January and $100.33 each to February and March.

Quicken uses the categories from your category and transfer list to format your budget. You cannot delete categories from the budget. If you want to change the way your category and transfer list is organized, see "About categories" on page 44.

Your income categories appear in this column at the top of the list of categories as inflows. Your expense categories appear below as outflows.

The total budgeted amounts for each category are in the Totals column on the right side of the window (not shown). Depending on the size of your Macintosh monitor, you may need to scroll horizontally to see the Totals column. Depending on the number of categories you use, you may need to scroll vertically to see all the categories.

Category	Jan	Feb	Mar	Apr	May	Jun
From Sally's 401k	0.00	0.00	0.00	0.00	0.00	0.00
From Sally's IRA	0.00	0.00	0.00	0.00	0.00	0.00
From Savings	0.00	0.00	0.00	0.00	0.00	0.00
From Steve's IRA	0.00	0.00	0.00	0.00	0.00	0.00
From Weiss Fund	0.00	0.00	0.00	0.00	0.00	0.00
Total Inflows	**24,312.00**	**17,359.00**	**16,147.00**	**13,945.00**	**17,938.00**	**11,948.00**
Outflows						
Auto:						
Fuel	100.00	100.00	100.00	100.00	100.00	100.00
Maintenance	50.00	50.00	50.00	50.00	50.00	50.00
Parking	10.00	10.00	10.00	10.00	10.00	10.00
Registration	0.00	120.00	0.00	0.00	0.00	0.00
Repairs	140.00	130.00	100.00	100.00	100.00	100.00
Total Auto	300.00	410.00	260.00	260.00	260.00	260.00
Bank Charges	20.00	20.00	20.00	20.00	20.00	20.00
Books	50.00	50.00	50.00	50.00	50.00	50.00
Charity	180.00	0.00	50.00	0.00	200.00	0.00
Total Budget Inflows	**24,312.00**	**17,359.00**	**16,147.00**	**13,945.00**	**17,938.00**	**11,948.00**
Total Budget Outflows	**18,656.00**	**13,500.00**	**18,810.00**	**12,779.00**	**12,905.00**	**11,241.00**
Difference	**5,656.00**	**3,859.00**	**-2,663.00**	**1,166.00**	**5,033.00**	**707.00**

QuickBudget | Fill Row | View by : Month

Click to have Quicken automatically enter amounts into the budget based on actual amounts from your existing Quicken data (page 354).

Although the budget is limited to one year, QuickBudget can use more than one year's worth of data to automatically create the budget.

Click to copy a selected amount to all fields to the right in the same row (page 357).

Click to set the time period by which you want to display or print your budget.

Quicken calculates and displays the total budgeted amounts for all categories in the area below the bold line at the bottom of the budget.

Quicken displays the difference between the amount you have budgeted for income (total budget inflows) and the amount you have budgeted for expenses (total budget outflows) in the Difference field at the bottom of the window.

A negative number in the Difference field means that you have budgeted to spend more than you have budgeted to earn for that month.

Entering amounts in the budget

You can have Quicken create a budget automatically using the QuickBudget feature, or you can start from scratch to enter data manually into a budget.

Entering amounts in the budget automatically with QuickBudget

QuickBudget uses data that you've already entered into your account registers. You can extract these amounts from any time period in the current Quicken file and then have QuickBudget insert the amounts in the current year's budget automatically.

QuickBudget inserts realistic amounts that you've already spent or earned for each category. You can then edit those amounts to reflect changes in your financial situation, or adjust the amounts for inflation.

If the budget is displayed by month, Quicken enters the average amount in every month. If the budget is displayed by quarter or year, Quicken enters three or twelve times the monthly average in every period.

If you've been using Quicken for a long time, your historical data helps you to plan for your future income and expenses.

If you're a new Quicken user, the small number of transactions you have already entered into Quicken might not provide enough data to make a QuickBudget meaningful.

1   **Choose Budget from the Planning menu.**

Quicken displays the budget spreadsheet.

2   **Click QuickBudget.**

The QuickBudget button is in the bottom left corner of the budget.

3 Enter information in the Automatically Create Budget window.

(Optional) Change the date range. The preset dates include all transactions from the previous calendar year.

Click a Fill In Budget For option to show Quicken how to copy the amounts:

- Click All categories if you want Quicken to create a QuickBudget for all categories.

- Click Selected if you want Quicken to create a QuickBudget for only the categories you choose. Quicken displays the Select Categories window. Select categories the same way you select them for reports. See "Selecting items to include in a report" on page 335.

- Select the Overwrite Non-zero Amounts checkbox if you are sure you want Quicken to replace amounts that you may already have entered.

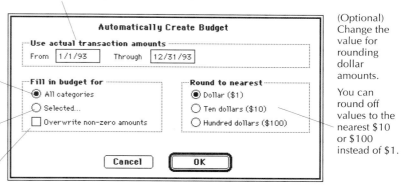

(Optional) Change the value for rounding dollar amounts.

You can round off values to the nearest $10 or $100 instead of $1.

Caution:

If you select the Overwrite non-zero amounts checkbox, Quicken will replace any budget amounts you have already entered manually with new amounts it calculates from your actual data. Clear the checkbox if you want to save the amounts you entered previously.

4 Click OK to copy data from your accounts into the budget.

Quicken overwrites any budget amounts you entered with data from your accounts.

Entering amounts in the budget manually

Although this is a slower, methodical method for entering data into the budget, you begin with a clean slate. You can enter the amounts you would like to spend or earn without being influenced by previous actual amounts.

1 Choose Budget from the Planning menu.

Quicken displays the budget spreadsheet.

2 To enter an amount you want to budget for a category, select an amount and type a new amount over it, and then press Tab to move to the next field in the row, or press Return to move to the next category in the column.

Pressing Enter or Return enters the amount into the budget. For information about shortcuts for entering and changing budget amounts, see "Editing amounts in the budget" on page 357.

3   **When you have finished entering budget amounts, close the spreadsheet.**

Quicken automatically saves the new or edited amounts you entered.

Budgeting for transfers

Quicken displays the names of all your accounts under both Inflows and Outflows in the budget in case you want to budget amounts for transfers as well as income and expense categories. For example, you might want to budget for items such as mortgage payments and transfers to 401(k) and IRA accounts.

You don't have to budget transfer amounts, but budgeting transfers can give you a more complete picture of your cash flow. For example, if you want to budget a monthly transfer of $200.00 from checking to savings, you should enter 200 for Inflows from [Checking] and the same amount for Outflows to [Savings].

Enter or edit transfer amounts in the budget just as you would budget income and expense amounts.

Copying budget amounts from one file to another

All the accounts in one Quicken file share the same budget. You can copy budget amounts from one Quicken file to another by exporting the amounts to a separate file, and then importing the separate file with the amounts into the second Quicken file.

The steps to copy budget amounts from one Quicken file to another are the same as those to copy categories from one Quicken file to another, except that you start by choosing Budget from the Planning menu. Then choose Export Budgets from the File menu. See "Copying categories from one file to another" on page 53.

Editing amounts in the budget

Budget amounts for each category can be the same for each month. Or, if your income and expenses for a category change, you may want to enter different budget amounts for different months in the year. For example, if you pay property taxes twice a year, you can budget the amount only in the two months in which you make payments.

To do this	Do this
Copy the budget amount from the current field to all fields to the right in the same category	Select the amount you want to copy and click Fill Row
Erase all budget amounts and start with a blank budget	Enter a zero into the first field of a row and click Fill Row to copy zeros into each field in the row
Copy the budget amount in one field to the next field on the right	Type ' or " (quote)

Use the following keys to move around the budget spreadsheet while you are entering or editing budget amounts.

Press	To move
Tab	Right one column in the same category
Shift+Tab	Left one column in the same category
Up Arrow	Up one category in the same column
Down Arrow	Down one category in the same column
Return	Down one category in the same column
Home	To the top of the budget spreadsheet
End	To the bottom of the budget spreadsheet
Click the horizontal scroll bar	Left or right by one screen
Click the vertical scroll bar	Up or down by one screen

Printing the budget

When you print the budget spreadsheet, Quicken uses the same settings you selected for printing reports. It prints the text in your budget using the report text (body) font settings. See "Changing report fonts" on page 324 to change the font settings.

1   **Make sure your printer is turned on, online, and loaded with paper.**

2   **Choose Budget from the Planning menu.**

    Quicken displays the budget spreadsheet.

3   **(Optional) To display and print budget amounts by quarter or by year instead of by month, choose Quarter or Year from the View By popup menu.**

4   **Choose Print Budget from the File menu.**

    Quicken prints the budget spreadsheet.

Creating budget reports and graphs

To use budget reports and graphs, you must first categorize your transactions (see "Assigning categories to transactions" on page 82) and enter budget amounts for those categories that you wish to track (see "Entering amounts in the budget" on page 354).

Creating a budget report

A budget report compares the money you spend and receive each month with your budgeted amount for each category, subtotaled by month. Quicken calculates the difference between the actual and budgeted amounts for each category so you can see exactly where you met your budget, where you were over or under the amounts you budgeted, and by how much. All bank, cash, and credit card accounts are included. You can include other accounts in the budget report by changing the restrictions.

Budget amounts in reports are always in a monthly format, no matter what time periods you specify in the report. If you choose time periods other than monthly, Quicken automatically adjusts budget amounts accordingly. For example, if you subtotal a report by quarter, Quicken totals the budget amounts for the three months in each quarter when it creates the report.

Budget reports are organized like cash flow reports, which list transfers from other Quicken accounts under Inflows and transfers to other Quicken accounts under Outflows.

You can see a sample budget report on page 298.

1   **Choose Home or Business from the Reports menu, and then choose Budget.**

2   **(Optional) Change the dates to cover the time period you want.**

You might want to change the report ending date from the preset date (today) to the end of this month.

3   **(Optional) Click Show Options to change any of the report options.**

4   **Click OK to create the report.**

Quicken compares the income and expense amounts in the registers with the budgeted amounts that you entered.

To print the budget report, see page 326.

To change the fonts in the budget report, see page 324.

To memorize a custom budget report setup for repeated use, see page 338.

Other reports useful for budgeting

Quicken has two other reports that may help with your budgeting:

- The category report shows you how much you've spent in each category, how much you've earned, and your net savings. Use it when you want to see your monthly spending trends or when you want to review exactly how you've been spending your money. For an example of a category report, see "Category" on page 300.

- An itemized category report lists all the transactions in your accounts, subtotaled by category. See "Itemized categories" on page 304.

Creating a budget variance graph

Quicken uses the budget data you enter to create a budget variance graph. Budget variance graphs compare actual spending and income with budgeted spending and income. Quicken calculates the difference in dollars between the two so you can see how you are actually doing compared to your budget.

You can see a sample budget variance graph in "Understanding budget variance" on page 346.

1   **Choose Graphs from the Reports menu.**

2   **Click Budget Variance.**

3   **(Optional) Change the dates to cover the time period you want.**

    You might want to change the graph ending date from the preset date (today) to the end of this month.

4   **(Optional) Click the Select buttons to restrict the graph.**

5   **Click OK to create the graph.**

    To print the budget graph, see page 350.

    To change the fonts in the budget graph, see page 349.

Preparing your income taxes

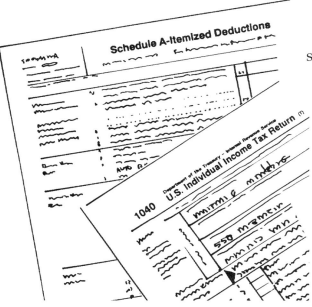

Quicken can simplify the preparation of your federal and state income tax return and related tax schedules. Using Quicken helps whether you use tax preparation software, prepare your returns manually, or gather the information to turn over to a tax preparation service.

You can produce a tax schedule report and capital gains report that list the exact amounts to fill in your tax forms and schedules. You can also export the reports to tax preparation software such as MacInTax and TurboTax ProSeries for Macintosh.

Preparing your income taxes

Filing income tax returns takes time because you first need to understand what is required, then you need to calculate and enter the amounts of your income and deductions. However, if you assign tax information to your Quicken categories, Quicken can calculate the amounts for you. If you assign tax information to Quicken categories and categorize your transactions throughout the year, you can create the reports you need at the end of the year in seconds.

You can further simplify the process of computing your taxes by transferring Quicken data directly to tax preparation software, eliminating the need to reenter financial information. See "Transferring Quicken data to tax preparation software" on page 377.

In Quicken, you use categories to organize transactions into types of income or expense. Many categories you assign to transactions are not tax-related. For example, whether you assign the category Clothing or Telephone to a transaction usually makes no difference to your taxes.

But some categories are tax-related: for example, Charity, Dividend Income, Medical, and Mortgage Interest. Income from charity goes on a line in Schedule A, income from dividends goes on the line "Dividend income" of Schedule B, and so on.

There are two different types of tax information that you can attach to your Quicken categories. Determine how you should assign tax information to your categories according to your tax situation.

Option	Your tax situation	Sample tax reports
Mark categories as tax-related	• Your taxes are fairly straightforward, *and* • You don't want to use tax preparation software, *and* • You need the general, high-level type of information that a tax summary report provides	See "Tax summary" on page 309 for a sample report.
Assign a specific line item from tax forms and schedules to categories	• You want to use tax preparation software, *or* • You need the specific, detailed type of information that a tax schedule report provides	See "Tax schedule" on page 308 and "Capital gains" on page 299 for sample reports.

Marking categories as tax-related

If you mark your categories as tax-related, you can create a tax summary report. (See "Tax summary" on page 309.)

Mark categories as tax-related if:

- your taxes are fairly straightforward, *and*
- you don't want to use tax preparation software, *and*
- you need the general, high-level type of information that a tax summary report provides.

If a category is not tax-related, do not mark it as tax-related.

◆ **Mark the Quicken income and expense categories you use as tax-related.**
Follow the procedure below for each category you want to mark.

◆ **Assign categories to transactions as usual.**
See "Entering transactions with tax time in mind" on page 373.

◆ **Create a tax summary report.**
See "Creating tax summary reports" on page 374.

Or press ⌘ L

1 Choose Categories & Transfers from the View menu.

If the category is not already in the list, create a new category. See "Setting up categories and subcategories" on page 47.

2 Select the category or subcategory that is tax-related.

Or press ⌘ E

3 Click Edit.

4 Select the Tax-related checkbox.

If you want to create tax summary reports, select the Tax-related checkbox.

Categories you mark as tax-related are in the current file. If you have several Quicken data files (for example, one file for your personal finances and one for your small business), you may need to enter tax information separately in the category and transfer list of each file.

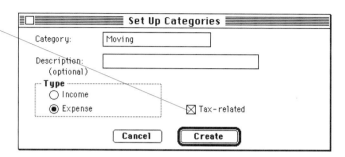

5 Click Change.

Assigning line items from tax forms and schedules to categories

If you assign line items from tax forms and schedules to categories, you can create a tax schedule report and a capital gains report. (See "Tax schedule" on page 308 and "Capital gains" on page 299 for sample reports.)

Assign line items from tax forms and schedules to categories if:

- You want to use tax preparation software, *or*
- You need the specific, detailed type of information that a tax schedule report provides.

Quicken's preset lists of home and business categories already have tax information assigned to them, but you need to make sure that the assignments are correct for your situation.

If you create your own categories from scratch or add categories to Quicken's standard categories, you must assign line items from tax forms and schedules for each new tax-related category you create. If a category is not tax-related, do not assign a line item from tax forms and schedules to the category.

These procedures are for a tax filer with only one W-2 form (one wage earner with one employer) and only one Schedule C. If your Quicken data file contains personal finances for both you and your spouse or for both your personal finances and your business finances, you need to set up and assign classes to tax-related transactions, and assign a different copy number to each class. Or if you have more than one W-2 form or Schedule C or more than one rental property or farm, you must also assign a different copy number to each copy of the form. See "Assigning copy numbers to forms and schedules" on page 371.

◆ **Assign line items from tax forms and schedules to categories according to your situation.**
See "Assigning line items to main categories" on page 365, "Assigning line items to subcategories" on page 367, "Assigning line items to investment categories" on page 368, and "Assigning line items to transfers" on page 369.

◆ **Assign categories, classes, and transfers to transactions as usual.**
See "Entering transactions with tax time in mind" on page 373.

◆ **Create a tax schedule report or a capital gains report.**
See how to create these reports on page 374 and page 376.

Assigning line items to main categories

Guidelines for assigning line items to main categories

Be sure to refer to the most recent tax forms available. The TAX.SCD file that came with the tax preparation software contains the most recent forms. Copy the TAX.SCD file into the Quicken 4 folder and make sure it replaces the TAX.SCD file that came with Quicken.

In general, if an amount should appear on more than one line or on more than one tax form, specify the most detailed location.

If you use tax preparation software, check to see where the software requires the amount.

Each category can have only one tax form and line assignment. If you have a category that may vary in its tax treatment, you can either:

- Divide it into separate categories or subcategories for each kind of tax treatment. For example, if you pay estimated tax *and* have tax withheld, use separate subcategories for the estimated and withheld taxes.

  OR

- Use Quicken classes to specify different copies of tax forms. For example, if you file a Schedule C and have personal and business categories in the same Quicken file, you can use the same categories or subcategories for home and for business if you set up and use different classes for home and business transactions. See "Assigning copy numbers to forms and schedules" on page 371.

When you use tax preparation software, the software copies figures from one tax form to another. In the Assign Tax Schedule window, you should choose the form and line where your software requires the amount initially. For example, tax software copies salary information from Form W-2 to Form 1040. So you should assign the line item from tax Form W-2 (not Form 1040) to your Quicken category for salary.

1   **Choose Personal Finance from the Reports menu.**

2   **Double-click Tax Schedule.**

Quicken displays the Create Tax Schedule Report dialog box.

3   **Click Show Options.**

4   In the Assign Tax Forms & Schedules box, click Categories.

If this file is not in your Quicken 4 folder, Quicken asks you to locate the TAX.SCD file. Locate the TAX.SCD file, select it, and click Open.

Use the menu to find the TAX.SCD file. This file should be located in the same place where you installed Quicken on your hard disk.

The TAX.SCD file contains the information Quicken needs to assign line items from tax forms and schedules to your categories.

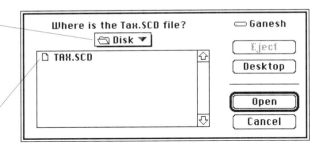

Quicken displays the Assign Tax Schedules dialog box.

5   Select the Quicken category from the list on the left.

6   Select the line item from the tax form or schedule that you want to assign to that category from the list on the right.

The Tax Schedule window lists all your Quicken categories on the left and all the tax forms and schedules including their respective line items you may need to file with the IRS on the right.

The diamonds beside the category appear if you have selected the Tax-related checkbox for that category.

To see all the line items on the tax forms and schedules that you assigned, print the category and transfer list. Press ⌘ L to view the category and transfer list, and then choose Print Categories to print the list.

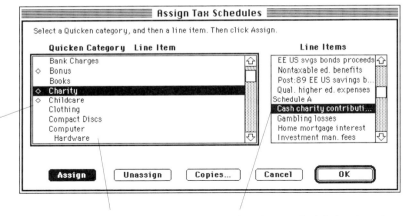

Select the Quicken category from the list here. Scroll up or down to see more categories.

Select the tax schedule line item that you want to assign. Scroll up or down to see more schedule line items.

7   Click Assign.

Quicken displays the line item from the tax forms and schedules across from the category to which it is assigned.

8   Click OK to record the information.

You have now assigned the selected line on the selected tax form or schedule to the category. The tax schedule report will include any transactions having this category.

Assigning line items to subcategories

You assign line items to subcategories the same way you assign line items to main categories.

Guidelines for assigning line items to subcategories

You must assign tax form information separately for each subcategory. A subcategory does *not* use the tax form information for the main category it belongs to. If you do not assign the information separately for a subcategory, the transactions to which subcategories are assigned do not appear on the tax schedule report.

If you have organized some of your tax-related categories as subcategories that belong to main categories, you need to assign line items to the subcategories.

In this example, you would assign line items to the subcategories under the main category "Moving."

Make sure that your tax form and schedule assignments are correct for your situation.

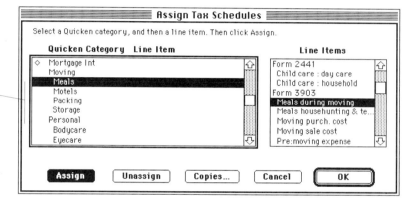

Assigning line items to investment categories

You assign line items to investment categories the same way you assign line items to categories.

Guidelines for assigning line items to investment categories

The investment income report can summarize interest and dividend income by Quicken account or by security name. If you track investments in Quicken mutual fund accounts exclusively *and* all your dividend income is taxable, assign the investment category "•Div Income" to "Schedule B:Dividend income."

Otherwise, do not assign any investment categories to a tax form and line. Instead, gather the tax information for Schedule B as described in "Investment income" on page 301. To gather information for Schedule D, see "Capital gains" on page 299.

Some money funds pay tax-free dividends. If you track these in bank accounts, assign the dividends to a category for which no tax information is specified. You may need to add a special category (for example, "•Div Tax-free") to your category list for this purpose.

The first time you set up a Quicken portfolio or mutual fund account, Quicken automatically adds these investment categories to your category and transfer list.

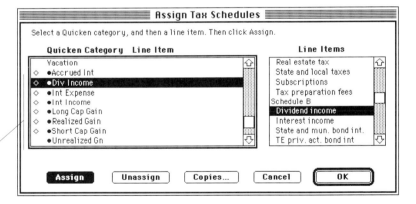

Assigning line items to transfers

When you enter a transfer from one account to another account in an account register, you type the name of the destination account in the Category field. Such a transfer between accounts may be tax-related, so you may need to assign tax information to some accounts as well as to categories.

You assign line items to transfers the same way you assign line items to categories. If you do not use transfers, you do not need to specify tax information for any of your accounts.

In general, you should assign line items only to Quicken accounts that track retirement plans such as IRAs and Keoghs. These are accounts that directly affect your taxes. You should not ordinarily enter tax information for any other types of account. But these are only general guidelines. How you specify tax information depends on how you use your accounts and how you make transfers between them.

For example, if you contribute to your IRA fund, you might record the transaction as a transfer from your checking account to your IRA account. You enter [IRA] in the Category field in your checking account and Quicken automatically enters [Checking] in the Category field of your IRA account.

Guidelines for assigning line items to transfers

Assign tax information for only one of the accounts involved in the transfer.

For example, you assign the IRA account to a tax form and line (specifically, use the line "Form 1040:IRA contribution-self"). Any payments into the IRA account will be included in the tax schedule report. Do not assign tax form information to the checking account.

Assign a line item from the appropriate tax form and line item to your IRA account. Any payments you transfer into the IRA account will be included in the tax schedule report. Do not assign a line item from a tax form to your checking account.

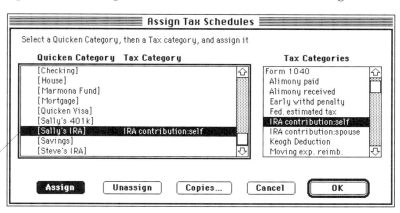

You can specify only one tax form and line number for each account. If you need more tax information for a particular account (for example, if you make a contribution in the same year you receive a distribution), don't assign a tax form and line to the account.

Type of account	How to assign tax information to the account
IRA retirement account	If you contribute to an IRA account, assign the account to the line "Form 1040:IRA contribution-self." (This line is for your gross contribution. Either manually or by using your tax software, you will have to determine how much is deductible.) Note that if you and your spouse each contribute to an IRA, you should track two IRAs with two separate IRA accounts in Quicken. Assign your spouse's account to "Form 1040:IRA contribution-spouse." On the other hand, if you draw money from an IRA account, assign the account to "Form 1099R:IRA total distributions-gross."

If you make IRA contributions for a given tax year during the following year (for example, if you contribute for the year 1993 in March of 1994), a tax schedule report for the tax year will not have the correct IRA information. In this situation, it is better not to assign line items to IRA accounts. Instead, create a transaction report subtotaled by account for the period from January 1 of the tax year to the filing date of the following year. Use all accounts. Filter for selected categories, and select only IRA accounts. The report itemizes all transfers to IRA accounts. Subtract the transfers that are for the wrong tax year. |
| Keogh retirement account | Treat Keogh accounts similarly to IRA accounts. If you contribute to a Keogh, assign the account to "Form 1040:Keogh deduction." If you draw money from a Keogh, assign the account to the line "Form 1099R:Pension total distributions-gross." |
| 401(k) retirement account | The IRS does not require that you report 401(k) deductions from your salary. However, you'll need to specify tax information for your 401(k) account if you use a split transaction to enter your paycheck and show a transfer to your 401(k) account (as in the paycheck example on page 94).

In the split, be sure to enter your gross salary before the 401(k) deduction. Assign your 401(k) account to exactly the same form and line as your salary ("W-2:Salary"). The transfers to your 401(k) account reduce the total for your gross taxable salary.

If you have other pretax deductions from your salary, such as for a health care flexible spending account, assign their categories or accounts also to "W-2:Salary." |

Type of account	How to assign tax information to the account
Checking, savings, cash, credit card, investment accounts (for nonretirement funds)	You do not, in general, need to specify tax information for these types of accounts. Transfers between these accounts are simply monetary transactions that do not affect your taxes.
Mortgage accounts	When you make a mortgage payment from your checking account, only the mortgage interest portion of the payment is tax deductible. Assign a category such as "Mortgage Interest" to the interest part of the transaction. Assign a line item ("Schedule A:Home mortgage interest") to the mortgage interest category. The portion of the mortgage payment that reduces your principal is normally not tax deductible, so you do not need to enter tax information for the transfer.

Assigning copy numbers to forms and schedules

You can file (or receive) multiple copies of some schedules and forms (for example, W-2 and Schedule C).

For example, if you and your spouse each receive a Form W-2, assign classes (such as Sally and Steve) to the salary and withholding categories of your paycheck transactions. Then assign copy numbers to the line items for your salary and withholding subcategories. Assign copy 1 to your class and copy 2 to your spouse's class.

Or if you file multiple copies of Schedule C, assign the class you use for one business to copy 1, the class you use for your second business to copy 2, and so on.

To file (or receive) multiple copies of some schedules and forms, you must set up and use classes for each copy. See "About classes" on page 55 if you need more information about setting up and using classes.

Assign copy numbers if you need	Use classes such as
One tax schedule report that separates your tax information from your spouse's tax information	Sally, Steve
One tax schedule report that separates your personal finances from your business finances	BizCorp, DesignCo
One tax schedule report that separates tax information about each company you worked at in the tax year from the other companies	Apple, Intuit, K&O
One tax schedule report that separates tax information for each rental property you own	Oak Street, Apt 1 Oak Street, Apt 2 45 Weiss Avenue

1   **Choose Personal Finance from the Reports menu.**

2   **Double-click Tax Schedule.**

Quicken displays the Create Tax Schedule Report dialog box.

3   **Click Show Options.**

4   **In the Assign Tax Forms & Schedules box, click Copies.**

Quicken displays the Assign Copies dialog box.

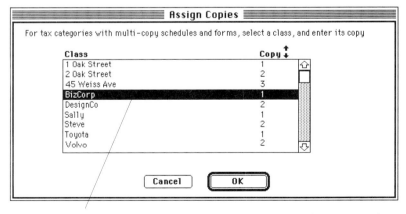

Enter a copy number for each class. Select the class, and then use the arrows to change the numbers.

5 **Assign copy numbers to each class for which you need multiple copies:**

- Select the class.

- Click the Up Arrow to decrease the number by one or click the Down Arrow to increase the number by one.

6 **Click OK.**

Entering transactions with tax time in mind

When you write a check or enter a transaction for a tax-related category in a register, you don't need to do anything extra—just enter a category as usual. But remember that the category you enter may affect the figures for your tax forms.

For example, if you write one check or use your credit card to cover business travel expenses and business meal expenses, be sure to enter the two amounts separately using a split transaction, because the two expenses are assigned to different lines on Schedule C.

Assign the line item "Schedule C: Travel" to your category for travel.

Assign the line item "Schedule C: Meals and Entertainment" for your category for meals and entertainment.

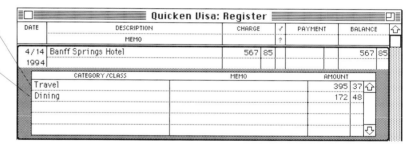

Creating tax reports

You can create tax reports at any time, not just at the end of each year or tax period. See *Chapter 19, Creating reports,* beginning on page 319, for full details about running reports.

Creating tax summary reports

A tax summary report shows the total amount of tax-related income and expenses.

You can create a tax summary report if you have already marked categories as tax-related. See "Marking categories as tax-related" on page 363.

You cannot export tax summary reports to tax preparation software.

1   **Choose Personal Finance from the Reports menu.**

2   **Double-click Tax Summary.**

3   **Enter a report name that states the tax period.**

4   **Enter a date range that covers the tax period.**

5   **Click OK.**

Creating tax schedule reports

A tax schedule report gathers figures from all accounts in the current file and from all categories that have been assigned to a tax form and line. Several categories or accounts can contribute to the same figure in the report. For example, the line "Salary" on Form W-2 can include both regular salary and bonuses.

You can export tax schedule reports from Quicken to tax preparation software.

The tax schedule report lists the exact figures you need in a format suitable for copying or importing into your 1040 tax form and schedules, with these qualifications:

- You must check the figures against any limits defined by the IRS.

  For example, check the maximum deduction allowed for IRA contributions. The Quicken tax schedule report simply gives you your personal totals.

- You need to have already recorded all relevant transactions in Quicken.

  For example, if you assign the investment categories "•Div Income" and "•Int Income" to Schedule B, the tax file subtotals the amount for each category by investment account but not by security.

1   **Choose Personal Finance from the Reports menu.**

2   **Double-click Tax Schedule.**

3   **Enter a report name that states the tax period.**

4   **Enter a date range that covers the tax period.**

5   **(Optional) To restrict the report to certain accounts, click Show Options, choose Accounts from the Restrict By menu, and then click Selected.**

   You may need to do this if, for example, your IRA account is a CD you track as a bank account. (You do not have to report the interest it earns.) If you exclude an account to which you assigned tax form information (for example, your IRA account), the report still lists transfers made into or out of the account if the account at the other end of the transfer is included.

   Quicken prompts you to select the accounts to be included in the report. Select the accounts you want to use and click OK. See "Assigning line items from tax forms and schedules to categories" on page 364.

6   **(Optional) To restrict the report to certain classes, click Show Options, choose Classes from the Restrict By menu, and then click Selected.**

   You may need to do this if, for example, your file contains checking accounts for you and your spouse and you are filing separate tax returns. If you exclude a class for which you defined tax form information (for example, the class for your spouse), the report still lists transfers made into or out of the account if the account at the other end of the transfer is included.

   Quicken prompts you to select the accounts to be included in the report. Select the accounts you want to use and click OK. See "Assigning copy numbers to forms and schedules" on page 371.

7 Click OK.

The resulting report lists your transactions, subtotaled for each tax line on each tax form.

See "Transferring Quicken data to tax preparation software" on page 377 if you are using software to prepare your tax return.

Creating capital gains reports for Schedule D

If you have investment accounts with realized capital gains (following buy and sell transactions), the tax schedule report does not show these realized gains. To obtain figures for your realized gains, run a capital gains report. To get income by security, run an investment income report as described on page 301.

The capital gains report lists your long-term and short-term capital gains transactions in a format suitable for copying or importing into Schedule D.

1 Choose Personal Finance from the Reports menu.

2 Double-click Capital Gains.

3 Enter a report name that states the tax period.

4 Enter a date range that covers the tax period.

5 In the Subtotal By popup menu, select "Short- vs. Long-Term."

6 Click OK.

See "Transferring Quicken data to tax preparation software" on page 377 if you are using software to prepare your tax return.

Transferring Quicken data to tax preparation software

If you use tax preparation software to prepare your Form 1040, you can use data from Quicken's tax schedule or capital gains report in programs that calculate your tax and print completed tax forms.

MacInTax is a *personal* tax preparation program distributed by ChipSoft. TurboTax ProSeries for the Macintosh is a *professional* tax preparation program also distributed by ChipSoft. TurboTax ProSeries is similar to MacInTax, but it has more forms, and is typically used by paid tax preparers.

Exporting Quicken data to tax preparation software

Quicken writes your tax data to a TXF (Tax Exchange Format) file with a standard format compatible with MacInTax and TurboTax ProSeries. Exporting your Quicken tax schedule report or capital gains report to a TXF file eliminates the need to reenter financial data into the tax preparation software.

1   **Create the tax report you want to export and leave it open.**

2   **Choose Export Report from the File menu.**

3   **(Optional) Use the file dialog box to change the location of the file.**

4   **Enter the file name for the tax schedule or capital gains report in the Export To File field.**

If you create both a tax schedule report and a capital gains report, you must create a different file for each report.

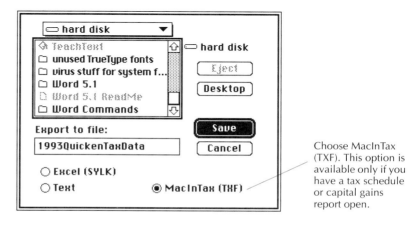

Choose MacInTax (TXF). This option is available only if you have a tax schedule or capital gains report open.

5   **Click MacInTax (TXF).**

Select this option whether you use MacInTax or TurboTax ProSeries.

6   **Click Save.**

Quicken exports the Quicken data to a file that your tax preparation software can import. See the instructions that accompany your tax preparation software to use the file.

Updating your tax form information

Occasionally the IRS changes the information required on IRS tax forms and schedules. When this happens, Intuit provides an updated list of line items, tax forms, and schedules (the TAX.SCD file) to the manufacturers of tax preparation software.

Most changes to IRS tax forms occur in January and very often affect only specialized forms that most people do not need to file. If the IRS makes any changes to the forms you file, however, you will need to obtain a new copy of the TAX.SCD file.

If you use MacInTax or TurboTax ProSeries, your Final Edition of the software includes an updated TAX.SCD file in time for you to file your annual returns. All you need to do is copy this TAX.SCD file to your Quicken 4 Folder. If you install Quicken after you have installed the Final Edition of the tax preparation software, make sure that the latest version of TAX.SCD file is in your Quicken 4 Folder.

Using financial planning calculators

Quicken's five financial planning calculators enable you to try "what-if" scenarios for loan planning, loan refinancing, investment planning, retirement planning, and college planning.

About financial planning calculators

Quicken provides five financial planning calculators that enable you to do "what if" calculations. You can use these calculators to answer questions such as:

If I refinance my mortgage and get a 9% interest rate, how much money will I save each month?

- If I invest $10,000 of my savings and receive an annual yield of 12%, what will the value be in 5 years?

- If I retire in ten years and put $2000 into my IRA account every year until then, how much money will I have available?

- If I set aside $5000 each year until my child is 18, will I have enough to pay for a good, four-year college?

The calculators give you the information you need to make informed decisions on your financial matters. You can play around with the numbers, seeing how different interest rates affect your monthly mortgage payment, for example. In addition, most of the calculators give you a choice of which field you want Quicken to calculate next.

The way you work with each financial planning calculator is the same; only the information and calculations are different.

1   Choose the financial calculator you want to use from the Planning menu.

The selected arrow tells you which field Quicken calculates.

To calculate a different field, click another arrow.

Enter the information in the fields. Quicken recomputes the amount to be calculated when you move the cursor to another field.

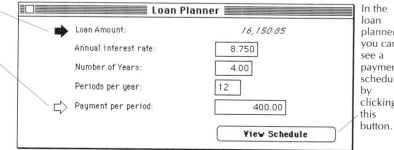

In the loan planner, you can see a payment schedule by clicking this button.

2   Click the amount you want Quicken to calculate.

3   Enter the information into the appropriate fields.

If you need more information about each field, press ⌘ ?.

Be sure to move the cursor out of the last field you fill in so that Quicken can calculate the amount using all of your information.

Calculating loan payments and principal

Choose Loan Planner from the Planning menu. Quicken displays the Loan Planner window.

If you click the Payment Per Period arrow, Quicken calculates what your payments would be for a given loan amount.

For example, if you want to take out a second mortgage on your home, you can learn how much your payments will be if you borrow $20,000 for 30 years at a 9% interest rate.

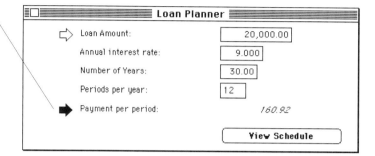

If you click the Loan Amount arrow, Quicken calculates how much you can afford to borrow given a particular payment amount and interest rate.

For example, if you want to buy a new car and you think you can afford to pay $300 a month on a car payment, you can learn how large a loan you can afford if you borrow for 5 years at a 10.125% interest rate.

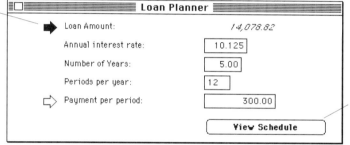

Click this button to see the payment schedule.

Quicken displays this window when you click the View Schedule button in the loan planner.

To print the complete payment schedule, choose Print Payment Schedule from the File menu.

Pmt	Principal	Interest	Balance	Total Interest
		10.125%	14,078.82	
1	181.21	118.79	13,897.61	118.79
2	182.74	117.26	13,714.87	236.05
3	184.28	115.72	13,530.59	351.77
4	185.84	114.16	13,344.75	465.93
5	187.40	112.60	13,157.35	578.53
6	188.98	111.02	12,968.37	689.55
7	190.58	109.42	12,777.79	798.97
8	192.19	107.81	12,585.60	906.78
9	193.81	106.19	12,391.79	1,012.97

Payment Schedule

Use the scroll bar to see more of the schedule, or press Page Up or Page Down to move up or down one screen.

Estimating this year's mortgage interest payments

If you have a fixed-rate loan and have made no prepayments of principal, you can use the loan planner and its payment schedule to estimate what your mortgage interest payments will be for the entire year. This estimate is useful for Form W-4 calculations.

1   Enter the information about your loan from its beginning in the loan planner.

You can calculate either the loan amount or the payment per period. If you know your payment offhand, then click the Loan Amount arrow to calculate the loan amount. (as was done for this example)

Enter the loan's interest rate.

Enter the original loan term.

Enter the number of payments per year.

Enter the payment amount, excluding any changes such as impounds.

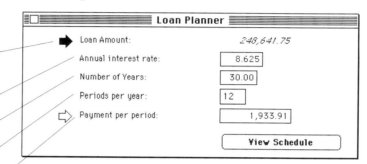

(If you want to calculate the payment per period, click the Payment Per Period arrow. Then enter the original loan balance in the Loan Amount field instead of entering a payment amount.)

2   Click View Schedule.

3   Use the payment schedule as shown here to calculate the estimated interest payments.

Find the payment whose balance most closely matches your loan balance as of the end of last year.

For example, if your loan balance at the end of last year was $248,196, the payment whose balance most closely matches it is payment 3.

Next, find this year's final payment by adding 12 to the payment number you found above.

In this example, payment 15 (= 3 + 12) is this year's final payment.

Then note the total interest amounts for each of these payments.

In this example, the total interest amounts are:

$5,358.16 for payment 3, and $26,692.38 for payment 15.

Pmt	Principal	Interest	Balance	Total Interest
		8.625%	248,641.75	
1	146.80	1,787.11	248,494.95	1,787.11
2	147.85	1,786.06	248,347.10	3,573.17
3	148.92	1,784.99	248,198.18	5,358.16
4	149.99	1,783.92	248,048.19	7,142.08
5	151.06	1,782.85	247,897.13	8,924.93
6	152.15	1,781.76	247,744.98	10,706.69
7	153.24	1,780.67	247,591.74	12,487.36
8	154.34	1,779.57	247,437.40	14,266.93
9	155.45	1,778.46	247,281.95	16,045.39
10	156.57	1,777.34	247,125.38	17,822.73
11	157.70	1,776.21	246,967.68	19,598.94
12	158.83	1,775.08	246,808.85	21,374.02
13	159.97	1,773.94	246,648.88	23,147.96
14	161.12	1,772.79	246,487.76	24,920.75
15	162.28	1,771.63	246,325.48	26,692.38
16	163.45	1,770.46	246,162.03	28,462.84

Finally, calculate the difference in total interest between these two payments. The result is the estimated interest payments for this year.

In this example: 26,692.38 − 5,358.16 = $21,334.22.

Calculating the cost of refinancing a loan

Choose Refinance Planner from the Planning menu. Quicken displays the Refinance Planner window.

Quicken compares your existing mortgage with the proposed mortgage and tells you how long it will take to "break even" — that is, to recoup your refinancing costs.

In this example, the proposed mortgage has biweekly payments, or 26 periods per year. Use the number you enter here to calculate the number of years to break even (see below).

Quicken calculates that it would take 34.47 periods to break even.

To calculate the breakeven point in years, divide the number of periods to break even by the number of periods per year for the proposed mortgage: 34.47 / 26 = 1.33 years.

If you were planning to move before that time, refinancing would not be a good deal.

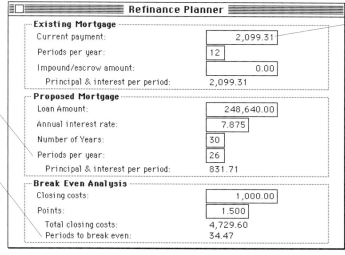

Enter your total payment, including any impound or escrow amount.

Planning your investment savings

Choose Investment & Savings Planner from the Planning menu. Quicken displays the Investment Planner window.

If you click the Present Value arrow, Quicken calculates how much money you need to start with to reach a financial goal.

If you click the Contribution Each Year arrow, Quicken calculates how much you need to invest to reach your goal (the goal is the number that appears in the Future Value field).

If you click the Future Value arrow (as was done for this example), Quicken calculates what your investment will be worth, given a certain period of time, regular contributions, and a constant annual yield.

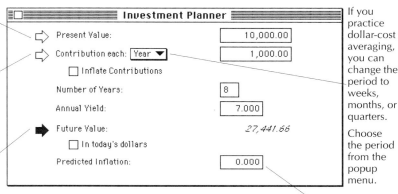

If you practice dollar-cost averaging, you can change the period to weeks, months, or quarters.

Choose the period from the popup menu.

This amount is an annual percentage rate.

In this example, if you presently have $10,000 saved and you contribute $1000 to your account each year (with a 7% yield), your investment grows to $27,441.66 in eight years.

When Quicken calculates your investment's future value, you can see what that amount is worth in today's dollars. by selecting this checkbox. Because of the effects of inflation, ten dollars today buys more than ten dollars will buy eight years from now.

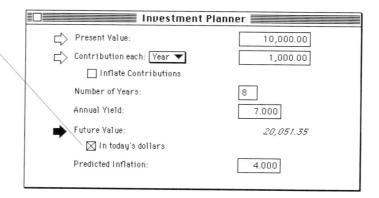

Continuing with the previous example, if you predict that inflation will average 4%, then $27,441.66 buys only $20,051.35 worth of goods today.

The rate of inflation affects what each of your contributions is really worth. For example, if you make annual contributions, then the contribution you make this year is actually worth less than last year's contribution because of inflation. To keep the value of all contributions consistent, you may want to increase the amount of each contribution by the inflation rate.

Click the Inflate Contributions checkbox if you want to see how increasing each contribution affects the value of your investment.

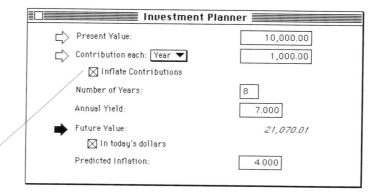

Continuing with the previous example, suppose you increase each annual contribution by 4% over the previous year's contribution. Your investment would be worth $21,070.01 (in today's dollars) at the end of eight years, instead of $20, 051.35 without inflating contributions.

To calculate this year's inflated contribution, multiply last year's contribution by the predicted inflation rate, and then add that amount to last year's contribution.

For example, if last year's contribution was $1,000 and the predicted inflation rate is 4%, then this year's inflated contribution is:

$$(1000 \times .04) + 1000 = 40 + 1000 = \$1040.$$

Saving for retirement

Choose Retirement Planner from the Planning menu. Quicken displays the Retirement Planner window.

The retirement planner lets you look at one retirement account at a time to project how much income that account will provide in your retirement.

If you click the Current Savings arrow, Quicken calculates the amount you need to start with to meet your projected retirement-income goals.

If you click the Contribution Each Year arrow, Quicken calculates how much you need to contribute to your retirement account each year to meet your goals.

If you click the Retirement Income arrow (as was done for this example), Quicken calculates how much a particular investment will be worth given your estimated tax rate and all contributions.

For example, suppose you are 38 years old and plan to retire at age 65. Your IRA account currently has $20,000 in it and you plan to contribute $2000 to it annually until you retire. You've inherited genes for long life, so you plan to withdraw from the account until age 85. As you can see, you have some options about how Quicken shows your retirement income.

You need to provide tax information for Quicken to perform its calculations:

If this retirement account is tax-sheltered (for example, an IRA or Keogh account), select the Tax-Sheltered checkbox. Quicken presets the Retirement Tax Rate appropriately. If it is not tax-sheltered, clear the Tax-Sheltered checkbox. Quicken presets the Retirement Tax Rate and the Current Tax Rate appropriately.

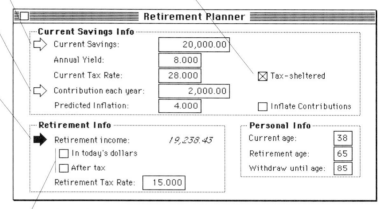

Because these checkboxes aren't selected, Quicken shows your pretax retirement income in future dollars. However, each dollar you receive in the future is worth less (has less buying power) than a dollar you receive today because of the effect of inflation. Consider this when you are planning retirement income. What sounds like a huge sum of money may be reduced to a moderate sum when you account for inflation and taxes.

By selecting the checkboxes to calculate after-tax retirement income in today's dollars, you can see how much your income is reduced from the previous example.

Quicken inflates contributions in the retirement planner the same way it does in the investment planner. See the investment planner example on page 384.

```
┌─────────────────── Retirement Planner ───────────────────┐
│ ┌─Current Savings Info─────────────────────────────────┐ │
│ ⇨ Current Savings:        │  20,000.00 │                │
│   Annual Yield:           │   8.000    │                │
│   Current Tax Rate:       │  28.000    │  ⊠ Tax-sheltered│
│ ⇨ Contribution each year: │   2,000.00 │                │
│   Predicted Inflation:    │   4.000    │  ☐ Inflate Contributions│
│ ┌─Retirement Info──────────────┐ ┌─Personal Info──────┐ │
│ ➡ Retirement income:   6,672.20 │ │ Current age:    38 │ │
│   ⊠ In today's dollars          │ │ Retirement age: 65 │ │
│   ⊠ After tax                   │ │ Withdraw until age:85 │ │
│   Retirement Tax Rate: │ 15.000 │ │                    │ │
└──────────────────────────────────────────────────────────┘
```

Planning for college expenses

Choose College Planner from the Planning menu. Quicken displays the College Planner window.

Quicken's calculations assume that you continue saving until the student graduates.

If you click the Current Annual College Cost arrow, Quicken calculates the annual college costs you can afford given your present savings and the number of years until your child goes to college.

If you click the Current Savings arrow, Quicken calculates what you need to have saved already today given a certain tuition, annual yield on your investment, and the number of years until your child attends.

If you click the Contribution Each Year arrow (as was done for this example), Quicken calculates how much you need to save each year to pay college expenses when your child is ready to attend.

```
▤□▤▤▤▤▤▤▤▤▤  College Planner  ▤▤▤▤▤▤▤▤▤
      ⇨  Current Annual College Cost:        12,000.00
         Years Until Enrollment:          18
         Years enrolled:                   4
      ⇨  Current Savings:                     0.00
         Annual Yield:                     8.000
      ➡  Contribution each year:          2,256.22
         Predicted Inflation:             4.000
              ☐ Inflate Contributions
```

The rate of inflation affects what your investment is really worth. To keep up with the effects of inflation on your investment, you may want to increase your contributions to the investment account by the same rate of inflation. Quicken inflates contributions in the college planner the same way it does in the investment planner. See the investment planner example on page 384.

For example, suppose your child is four years away from attending college. You have $12,000 already saved and figure that in the next four years you can contribute a total of $20,000 more to the college fund. Enter these numbers into the college planner, and Quicken calculates that you can afford an annual tuition of $12,521 in today's dollars.

```
▤□▤▤▤▤▤▤▤▤▤  College Planner  ▤▤▤▤▤▤▤▤▤
      ➡  Current Annual College Cost:        12,521.29
         Years Until Enrollment:           4
         Years enrolled:                   4
      ⇨  Current Savings:                 12,000.00
         Annual Yield:                     8.000
      ⇨  Contribution each year:          5,000.00
         Predicted Inflation:             4.000
              ☐ Inflate Contributions
```

Ordering supplies and other Intuit products

All Intuit products help you complete your financial chores faster and with far greater ease than paying bills by hand.

The Intuit Check Catalog is the best place to learn about these products because it has pictures, more information, and an order form. This appendix answers some common questions about our products. If you have more questions about checks or if you no longer have the catalog, call Intuit. See "Phone numbers" on page 408.

When you're ready to place an order, use the order form in the catalog or choose Order Supplies from the Apple menu to print an order form on your printer.

Intuit checks

The only way to take full advantage of Quicken is to allow the system to print your checks. After all, Quicken already does most of the work to prepare checks. Why duplicate work by writing checks by hand when printing is so easy? You will save hours of valuable time, avoid clerical errors, and prevent unnecessary financial hassle every month.

Intuit offers a complete line of checks and envelopes to meet both personal and business needs. You can order Intuit checks for continuous-feed printers or page-oriented printers such as laser printers and inkjet printers. With Intuit's patented automatic alignment system, you can easily align checks in any continuous-feed printer.

Intuit's Three-Point Guarantee

All Intuit checks are triple guaranteed. We guarantee that:

- Your checks will be accepted by your bank.
- Your checks will work with your Macintosh-compatible printer.
- Your check order will be printed as you submitted it.

If we fail to meet these three conditions, please call right away. We will quickly replace your order or refund your money, whichever you prefer.

Why should I print checks with Quicken?

You should print checks with Quicken for two reasons:

- Using Intuit checks in conjunction with Quicken will save you the maximum amount of time. Once you've entered your data into the program, you can press a button to print checks in just seconds.
- Checks printed with Quicken are legible and attractive, which will help you look more organized and professional.

Is it OK to order checks from Intuit instead of my bank?

ABSOLUTELY. Intuit checks are guaranteed to be accepted EVERY-WHERE your checks are accepted now. They're printed to the exacting standards of the American Banking Association and are pre-approved by all banks, savings and loan institutions, credit unions, and brokers across the U.S. and Canada.

How do I write checks away from home?

For checks you might write away from home, such as at the grocery store, just use the paper checks you already have or handwrite a Quicken check. Then the next time you use Quicken, simply enter the transactions into your Quicken check register. When you order your Intuit checks, indicate the starting number to be considerably greater than your personal check numbers. That way, you avoid any confusion or possible duplication of numbers.

For example, if your personal check numbers are in the 1000 range, begin your Intuit checks at 3001.

Is having two sets of check numbers a problem?

NO. Quicken can easily manage two sets of check numbers in one account. Moreover, the bank has no concerns about which numbers you use on your checks. Check numbers are for your own records.

Should I have check numbers printed on my Intuit checks?

YES. Check numbers are printed with magnetic ink along the bottom of the check where they can be read electronically. When you place a stop payment on a check, the bank's automated equipment reads the check numbers to find and stop payment on the designated check. Some people have requested that check numbers not be printed on checks to avoid problems in case their printer misprints a check. However, with Quicken's patented automatic alignment system for continuous-feed printers, misprints are minimized.

Where do I get Intuit checks?

You can order Intuit checks through Intuit. The enclosed Intuit Check Catalog gives you a complete description of the available check styles and colors. We've also enclosed an order form in the Quicken package for your convenience. If you need more order forms, Quicken will print them for you. Choose Order Supplies from the Apple menu. Order today and Intuit checks will be in your hands in less than three weeks. For faster service, FAX your order anytime to Intuit. See "Phone numbers" on page 408.

What is the Logo Service?

Intuit has a selection of hundreds of standard logos that you can print FREE on your Intuit checks. Just order by number from the catalog. If you want a custom logo, enclose black-and-white, camera-ready artwork with your order. There is a one-time $35 setup fee for custom logos. If touchup, typesetting, or rearrangement is required, additional charges may be incurred. Custom logos cannot be ordered by FAX.

More timesaving Intuit products

These products are also described in the Intuit Check Catalog.

Intuit double-window envelopes

Window envelopes save even more time by eliminating hand addressing of envelopes. Each envelope has two windows. The upper window shows the return address printed on the check and the lower one shows the mailing address that Quicken prints on the check for you. All you do is sign the check and then drop it in the envelope.

Forms leaders

Forms leaders prevent wasted checks. Forms leaders are not recommended for wallet-size checks. See "Phone numbers" on page 408 for the Intuit Customer Service phone number to order Forms Leaders.

Check printer type	Use forms leaders if:
Continuous-feed	Your continuous-feed printer has a tractor head above the print head and you cannot print on the first check.
Page-oriented	Your page-oriented printer does not have an envelope feed and you are using standard three-to-a-page checks and want to print partial pages of checks (one or two checks at a time).

Deposit slips

Intuit deposit slips are preprinted with your account number and name and address. They are available in two books of 100 each. When ordering, be sure to enclose one of your current deposit slips.

Endorsement and return address stamps

To reduce the time it takes to endorse checks and write addresses, use Intuit's endorsement and return address stamps. These pre-inked stamps are good for over 25,000 impressions. They measure 2 3/8-inches x 3/4-inch, with plenty of space for five imprinted lines. To ensure accuracy when ordering an endorsement stamp, enclose a voided sample check from your checking account.

B

Menus and command keys

This appendix describes all the commands on the Quicken menus. Included in the description of most commands is a page number where you can turn for more information about the use of the command.

Some menu commands have Command-key shortcuts. You can use these to enter the command from the keyboard. You can also create your own Command-key shortcuts.

Apple menu

Displays the version number you are using.

Prints an order form that you can use to order Quicken checks and supplies. Fill out the form and send by mail or FAX.

Help (⌘ ?) is displayed here if you have Macintosh system software lower than system 7. Opens Quicken's onscreen Help system.

If you have system 7, choose Help from the Help menu in the upper right corner of your monitor (page 396).

File menu

Opens the Set Up Account window where you can create a new Quicken account in the Quicken data file (page 36).

Displays a menu of all your Quicken accounts. Select an account to open it (page 39).

Closes the active window.

Creates a new Quicken data file and opens it (page 61).

Asks you to select an existing Quicken data file, then opens the file you selected (page 62).

Displays the standard Macintosh page setup dialog box where you can change the size and orientation of paper and other printer settings.

Prints the contents of the active window.
- If a register window is active, the register is printed (page 101).
- If a report window is active, the report is printed (page 326).
- If a graph window is active, the graph is printed (page 350).

Prints all or selected checks you have entered into the Write Checks window or printable transactions you have entered in the register (page 116).

The commands on the File menu create, open, copy, and back up Quicken files; transfer data to and from Quicken; set up your printer; and print checks, reports, and graphs, registers, and budgets.

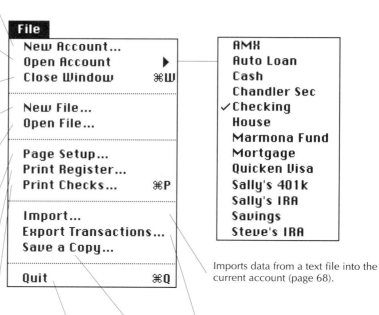

Exits Quicken. Quicken saves your data automatically.

Makes a copy of all accounts in a Quicken file (page 63).

Imports data from a text file into the current account (page 68).

Exports data from an account to a text file.
- transactions (page 68)
- categories (page 53)
- classes (page 53)
- budget amounts (page 356)
- security prices (page 272)
- DOS Quicken data (page 27)
- Quicken for Windows data (page 28)

Edit menu

The commands on this menu help you find transactions; transfer text to and from the clipboard; and make changes to items (such as a category, an account, or an investment security).

Reverses the last change that you made.

Removes the text you selected in a field and places it on the clipboard.

Copies the text you selected and places it on the clipboard.

Copies the text on the clipboard into the field you've selected.

Sets up a new item. The type of item depends on the current window. In a register or the Write Checks window, this command begins a new transaction (page 80). In a list window (such as the Account List window), this command adds a new item to the list (page 36).

Changes a the selected item.

Adds an item to the active window. If the active window is a register, moves to a blank transaction.

Permanently removes an item. You can delete a transaction from a register (page 100), an item from a list, and checks from the Write Checks window.

Voids the transaction you have selected (page 99).

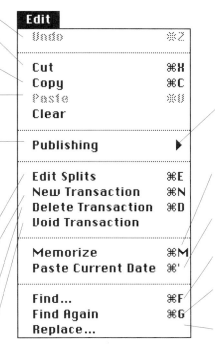

In a register, memorizes the transaction you have selected (page 161). In a report window, memorizes a custom report setup for later use (page 338).

Pastes today's date into the date field of the selected transaction or check.

Finds a transaction based on information you specify (page 97).

Searches for the next occurrence of the transaction you are looking for (page 97).

Finds all transactions that match your criteria and replaces all of them or only those you choose (page 97).

View menu

The commands on this menu display the different lists that Quicken maintains. When you display a list, you can use any of the items that the list shows; you can also add new items to the list and modify old ones. For example, when the account list is on the screen, you can you can display the register for any account simply by double–clicking its name. You can also set up new accounts (thereby adding them to the list), change how an existing account is set up, and delete accounts you no longer use.

Opens the Register window, which shows all the transactions in the current account. You can enter new transactions into the register, or edit ones previously entered (page 80).

Opens the Portfolio window for the portfolio or mutual fund account you've selected (page 240 and page 248).

Lists the categories and account transfers that you can apply to transactions (page 47).

Lists the class names you have set up for the current file (page 57).

Lists the payees that you have set up to receive your electronic payments (page 178).

Opens the list of accounts for the Quicken data file you are using (page 39).

Lists all of the transactions you have memorized (page 161).

Lists the transaction groups you have created for automatic entry of recurring transactions (page 167).

Opens the Setup Loan dialog box if you have never set up a loan before. Opens the loans list if you have set up at least one loan.

Activities menu

The commands on this menu initiate various activities in Quicken, including writing checks, reconciling a Quicken account with your bank statement, and using CheckFree to pay your bills electronically

Opens the Write Checks window where you can enter checks to print (page 104).

Allows you to transfer money from one Quicken account to another without opening either account (page 86).

Opens the register for the destination account involved in a transfer of money and displays the corresponding transaction in that register (page 89).

Allows you to balance your Quicken account register against your bank statement (page 142), credit card statement (page 198), or investment account statement (page 278). Quicken displays the Get IntelliCharge Data command in the place of Reconcile if you have set up the current credit card account to be updated by a by modem or from a disk (page 201).

Allows you to update or adjust the balance of your account registers for Quicken cash (page 223), or asset and liability accounts (page 229).

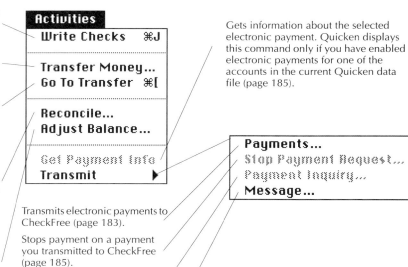

Gets information about the selected electronic payment. Quicken displays this command only if you have enabled electronic payments for one of the accounts in the current Quicken data file (page 185).

Transmits electronic payments to CheckFree (page 183).

Stops payment on a payment you transmitted to CheckFree (page 185).

Sends an inquiry to CheckFree about a previously transmitted payment (page 188).

Displays a window that you can use to send messages to CheckFree (page 189).

Reports menu

The commands on this menu create the different types of reports and graphs available in Quicken. Once you have displayed a report or a graph, you can print a copy of it, use QuickZoom to see a greater level of detail, or memorize your report setup for future use.

Opens a list of personal finance reports from which you choose the type of report you want to create (298).

Opens a list of business reports from which you choose the type of report you want to create (page 311).

Lists the reports you have memorized. To recreate the report, all you have to do is choose it from the list (page 339).

Displays a submenu from which you choose the type of graph you want to create (page 342).

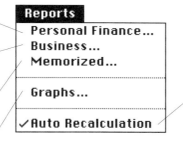

Controls whether Quicken recalculates all totals in an open report whenever you change your data or waits until you change a global report setting. This option is turned on or off depending on whether or not there is a checkmark beside it. If you want Quicken to recalculate all totals in an open report, leave this option selected.

Planning menu

The commands on this menu help you plan for your financial future and save time while planning.

Displays a spreadsheet you can use to set up a budget (page 352).

These commands display Quicken calculators you can use to plan various aspects of your finances (page 379).

Opens the Billminder window to remind you of scheduled transaction groups due, checks to print, or electronic payments to transmit. Choose Billminder to turn Quicken's automatic reminder features on or off (page 169).

Planning
Budget

Loan Planner
Refinance Planner
Investment & Savings Planner
Retirement Planner
College Planner

Billminder

Settings menu

The commands on this menu customize Quicken in various ways.

Displays settings that you can change to affect:

- how account registers look and behave when you enter transactions (page 102).
- customize Quicken checks in various ways (page 102 and page 108).
- change how Quicken memorizes and recalls transactions in account registers (page 102 and page 161).

Turns the display of specific Qcards on or off (page 10).

Changes the number of days before transactions are due before Billminder reminds you of scheduled transaction groups due, checks to print, or electronic payments to transmit.

Changes how categories and classes appear in reports (page 323).

Changes how text appears in reports (page 324).

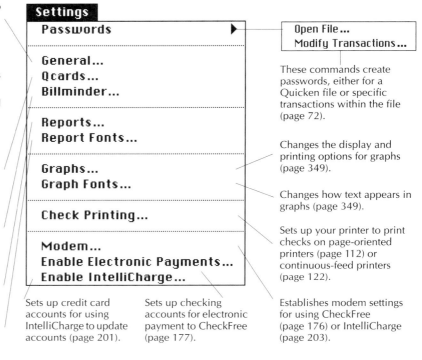

These commands create passwords, either for a Quicken file or specific transactions within the file (page 72).

Changes the display and printing options for graphs (page 349).

Changes how text appears in graphs (page 349).

Sets up your printer to print checks on page-oriented printers (page 112) or continuous-feed printers (page 122).

Establishes modem settings for using CheckFree (page 176) or IntelliCharge (page 203).

Sets up credit card accounts for using IntelliCharge to update accounts (page 201).

Sets up checking accounts for electronic payment to CheckFree (page 177).

Help menu

The commands on this menu give you access to the different forms of onscreen assistance available through Quicken.

Describes how to use Macintosh Balloon Help (for system 7 users).

Turns the display of Quicken Balloon Help on or off (page 11).

Displays a contents listing for Quicken onscreen Help. To display an individual Help topic, click the topic in the list (page 11).

Turns the display of all Qcards on or off (page 10).

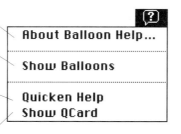

Creating your own Command-key shortcuts

As you become familiar with Quicken, you'll find that you use certain commands more than others. You can make it faster to use your favorite commands by creating *shortcuts* for them. A shortcut lets you execute the command with a simple key sequence: the ⌘ key plus one other key.

You can assign a Command-key shortcut to any menu command, including the account names on the Account menu and memorized report names on the Reports menu.

Assigning a Command-key shortcut to a menu command

1   **Hold down the Command key and click on the menu bar. Don't release the mouse button.**

2   **The mouse pointer changes to a ⌘ symbol.**

3   **Release the Command key and select the menu command to which you want to assign a shortcut.**

4   **With the command selected, release the mouse button.**

Quicken displays a dialog box with the menu name, command name, and existing Command-key shortcut (if any).

5   **Type the key you want to combine with the ⌘ key for a shortcut and click OK.**

6   **For example, if you want the shortcut for an account named Checking to be ⌘-1, type 1 and click OK.**

7   **Quicken creates the Command-key shortcut.**

If another menu command already has the Command-key shortcut you type assigned to it, Quicken asks you to confirm the change. If you confirm the change, Quicken removes the shortcut from the other menu command and assigns it to the command you selected.

Removing a Command-key shortcut from a menu command

1 **Hold down the Command key and click on the menu bar. Don't release the mouse button.**

The mouse pointer changes to a ⌘ symbol.

2 **Release the Command key and select the menu command.**

3 **With the menu command selected, release the mouse button.**

4 **Delete the shortcut from the Command Key field in the Edit Command Key dialog box.**

5 **Click OK.**

Deleting all Command-key shortcuts from the menus

Caution:
This procedure will delete *all* your Quicken settings, including all items in the Settings menu. You will also have to find your data file the next time you start Quicken.

Or press ⌘ Q

1 **Choose Quit from the File menu to exit Quicken.**

2 **Open the System Folder.**

3 **If there's a Preferences folder in the System Folder, open it.**

4 **Select the file called Quicken 4 Preferences.**

5 **Drag the Quicken 4 Preferences file icon to the trash.**

Publishing Quicken report data for use in other applications

With Quicken and System 7, you can publish part or all of the data in a Quicken report for use in other applications.

Publishing Quicken report data

Quicken can publish data from any report to use with another application. To *publish* means to make part or all of a Quicken report available for use with another application. For example, you could publish totals from a Quicken summary report for use in a spreadsheet such as Microsoft Excel. The original Quicken report is called the *publisher*.

When Quicken publishes all or part of a report, it creates a named *edition* to which other programs can subscribe. To use the information contained in a Quicken edition in another application, you launch the other application and then *subscribe* to the edition. The edition remains linked to the data in the original report (the publisher). Quicken can update the information in the publisher whenever you like. (See "Updating editions published by Quicken" on page 401.)

1 **Create the report that contains the data you want Quicken to publish.**

If you need help creating the report, see Chapter 19, *Creating reports,* beginning on page 319.

2 **Select the area of the report that you want Quicken to publish in the edition.**

Just drag across the data to select it. You can include row headings, column headings, amounts, and subtotals in the selection.

3 **Choose Publishing from the Edit menu, and then choose Create Publisher.**

A preview of the data you selected appears in the dialog box.

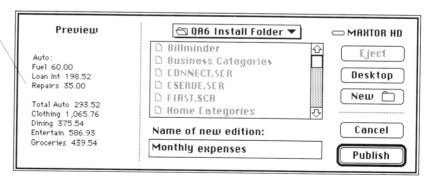

4 **Enter a name for the new edition that Quicken will publish.**

5 **Click Publish.**

Quicken publishes the edition, which is a separate file on your disk that contains the report data you selected in step 2 on page 400.

Updating editions published by Quicken

You can have Quicken update the data in an edition immediately or when you leave Quicken. When Quicken updates the data in an edition, changes to the edition are reflected in all documents that subscribe to the edition.

- To have Quicken update an edition immediately, choose Update Publisher from the Edit menu. Select the edition or editions you want to update and click OK.

- To have Quicken update an edition when you leave Quicken, choose Publisher Options from the Edit menu. Select the edition or editions you want to update and click OK.

Subscribing to a Quicken edition from another application

Many applications running under System 7 can subscribe to Quicken editions. When you subscribe to a Quicken edition from another application, that application places a copy of the edition in the document from which you subscribe. In general, the procedure to subscribe to a Quicken edition from another application is to choose Subscribe To from the Edit menu.

In this example, we publish monthly outflows from a Quicken category report for use in an Excel spreadsheet. Start by setting up a Quicken report that contains the data you want to use in Excel.

1 Set up a Quicken category report with the name "Monthly Cash Flow" and the preset date Current Month. (Choose Current Month from the Date popup menu.)

Or press ⌘ M

2 Memorize the report with a name that's descriptive and easy to recognize.

The name of the report is important because the Quicken report is actually the publisher. When it's time to update an edition, you need to select the publisher from a list of Quicken reports.

3 Select the Outflows part of the report and choose Create Publisher from the Edit menu.

4 Enter "Monthly Outflows" as the name for the edition and click Publish.

Quicken puts the report data you selected in an edition called "Monthly Outflows."

Or press ⌘ Q

5 (Optional) Leave Quicken.

6 Open the Excel spreadsheet.

7 Select the cell or range where you want to place the data.

8 Choose Subscribe To from the Edit menu, select the Quicken edition "Monthly Outflows," and click Subscribe.

In this example, the entire Outflows section was selected and published to an edition called "Monthly Outflows." You can publish any part of a report: row headings, column headings, titles, amounts, subtotal sections, and so on.

In this example, the cell selected in the Excel spreadsheet was A1. If you select any part of the subscriber after the data has been copied into your spreadsheet, you'll see a formula like this:

{=SUBSCRIBER("Your Hard Disk:Folder:Monthly Outflows")}

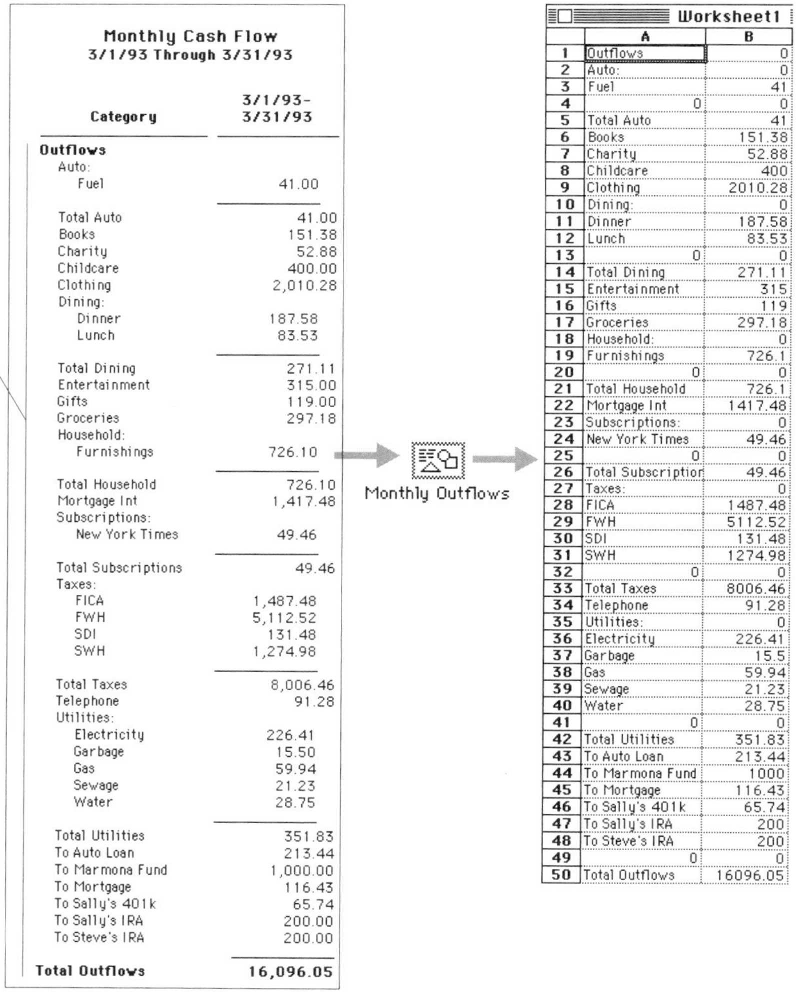

Monthly Cash Flow
3/1/93 Through 3/31/93

Category	3/1/93–3/31/93
Outflows	
Auto:	
Fuel	41.00
Total Auto	41.00
Books	151.38
Charity	52.88
Childcare	400.00
Clothing	2,010.28
Dining:	
Dinner	187.58
Lunch	83.53
Total Dining	271.11
Entertainment	315.00
Gifts	119.00
Groceries	297.18
Household:	
Furnishings	726.10
Total Household	726.10
Mortgage Int	1,417.48
Subscriptions:	
New York Times	49.46
Total Subscriptions	49.46
Taxes:	
FICA	1,487.48
FWH	5,112.52
SDI	131.48
SWH	1,274.98
Total Taxes	8,006.46
Telephone	91.28
Utilities:	
Electricity	226.41
Garbage	15.50
Gas	59.94
Sewage	21.23
Water	28.75
Total Utilities	351.83
To Auto Loan	213.44
To Marmona Fund	1,000.00
To Mortgage	116.43
To Sally's 401k	65.74
To Sally's IRA	200.00
To Steve's IRA	200.00
Total Outflows	**16,096.05**

Monthly Outflows

Worksheet1

	A	B
1	Outflows	0
2	Auto:	0
3	Fuel	41
4	0	0
5	Total Auto	41
6	Books	151.38
7	Charity	52.88
8	Childcare	400
9	Clothing	2010.28
10	Dining:	0
11	Dinner	187.58
12	Lunch	83.53
13	0	0
14	Total Dining	271.11
15	Entertainment	315
16	Gifts	119
17	Groceries	297.18
18	Household:	0
19	Furnishings	726.1
20	0	0
21	Total Household	726.1
22	Mortgage Int	1417.48
23	Subscriptions:	0
24	New York Times	49.46
25	0	0
26	Total Subscription	49.46
27	Taxes:	0
28	FICA	1487.48
29	FWH	5112.52
30	SDI	131.48
31	SWH	1274.98
32	0	0
33	Total Taxes	8006.46
34	Telephone	91.28
35	Utilities:	0
36	Electricity	226.41
37	Garbage	15.5
38	Gas	59.94
39	Sewage	21.23
40	Water	28.75
41	0	0
42	Total Utilities	351.83
43	To Auto Loan	213.44
44	To Marmona Fund	1000
45	To Mortgage	116.43
46	To Sally's 401k	65.74
47	To Sally's IRA	200
48	To Steve's IRA	200
49	0	0
50	Total Outflows	16096.05

Deleting a Quicken publisher and edition

If you no longer need to use an edition published from Quicken, choose Delete Publishers from the Edit menu, select the publisher you want to delete, and click OK.

The edition is a separate file (see illustration above). You can drag it to the Trash like any other file. (You must delete the publisher first in Quicken, or else Quicken will keep publishing the edition.)

Contacting Intuit

As an Intuit customer, you have full access to technical support at no charge for help with any Quicken problems you can't solve yourself. To register for this support, fill out your customer registration card on the first page of this book and mail it to Intuit.

This appendix suggests ways to save yourself time and long distance charges by checking for the easy answers yourself. If you try these suggestions, you may not need to call, or if you do need to call, the support specialist may be able to help you faster because you may have ruled out common problems already.

Saving a phone call

If you have a question about the way Quicken works, the best way to get an accurate, immediate answer is to try looking here:

Help. Press ⌘ ? (or the Help key, if your keyboard has one) to get instant onscreen information while you're working in Quicken. If you want information about a specific task, make sure the window for that task is open and active. You can also look up topics by name in the Help Topics list. See "Using Qcards and Help" on page 10 for more information.

Index. Check this manual's index beginning on page 409 for the topic you need. We've worked hard to make the index useful. Check the index under "troubleshooting" to find tips at relevant places throughout the manual. The index also has entries for common symptoms, such as "missing check numbers."

Specific lists of solutions in the manual. The manual contains lists of solutions to common problems with these specific parts of the program:

If you are trying to	See
Print checks	"Solving check printing problems" on page 135
Print reports	"Printing reports" on page 326
Print graphs	"Printing graphs" on page 350
Balance your checkbook	"Solving balancing problems" on page 150
Send payments to CheckFree	"Solving CheckFree problems" on page 190
Download IntelliCharge statements by modem	"If you have problems downloading your statement" on page 207

Miscellaneous troubleshooting. Here are a few troubleshooting topics that are not covered elsewhere in the manual.

Problem area	Solution
Problems with fonts displayed on the screen	Quicken requires Chicago 12, Geneva 9, and Monaco 9 and 12. (To install fonts if you don't have System 7, you need the Macintosh Font/DA Mover utility.)
Problems with compressed files	Quicken data files and the TAX.SCD file should be marked "Do Not Compress" if you are using AutoDoubler.
Quicken can't open Quicken Help or Supply Order Form	Make sure the Quicken Help file or Supply Order Form is in the same folder as the Quicken 4 application file.

Helping yourself

If you still have a problem using Quicken, the best way to solve it is to try these self-help approaches first:

1 Press ⌘-Option-B in Quicken.

Quicken maintains an index file to improve access to your financial data. When you use this key combination, Quicken reconstructs its index file, which may solve your problem.

Or press ⌘ Q

2 Choose Quit from the File menu to leave Quicken. Then move the Quicken 4 Preferences file from the Preferences folder in the System Folder (or from the System Folder, if your computer is not running System 7) to a floppy disk. Finally, restart Quicken by double-clicking your Quicken data file.

The Quicken 4 Preferences file keeps track of nearly all of your settings except for electronic payment settings (see "Settings menu" on page 396 for descriptions of all settings). If your problem occurs in one of the areas affected by the settings, this step may solve your problem.

After you have moved the Quicken 4 Preferences file to a floppy disk, open the folder where Quicken 4 is installed and double-click the data file (for example, "My accounts") that you were using.

- If this step solves your problem, you need to reset all of your settings (see "Settings menu" on page 396 to locate instructions for changing settings). You no longer need the Quicken 4 Preferences file that you moved to the floppy disk.

- If this step does not solve your problem, quit Quicken, copy the Quicken 4 Preferences file back to the Preferences folder in the System Folder (or to the System Folder, if your computer is not running System 7), and then restart Quicken.

3 Explore the problem a bit before you call.

When you call Intuit with a problem, the support specialist leads you through steps to identify and solve the problem. You can do some of this exploration yourself to eliminate possibilities that don't require technical expertise. The key to troubleshooting is trying the most basic approach first.

- Try the procedure again, starting at the beginning.

Examine the windows and dialog boxes where you entered information. Make sure you are using the appropriate window or dialog box and are choosing the correct options for what you want.

For example, if a report does not include the information you want, check the date range and restrictions in the Create Report window.

- Try a related procedure.

For example, if you have a printing problem, test that the printer is working by trying to print something else. If you have trouble printing checks, try printing a report. If you can't print from Quicken, try printing from a word processor. If nothing prints, you know the problem is related to the printer, not the software. Check the printer connections and the printer selected in the Chooser.

- If something used to work, think about what has changed.

For example, if Billminder doesn't work, did you move the Billminder extension from your Extensions folder? (Or the Billminder INIT from your System Folder, if you are using System 6?)

4   **If you call, be at your computer with Quicken running, and have the following information handy:**

- Exact wording of the error message if you received a message

- Quicken version number (from Quicken, choose About Quicken from the Apple menu to see the version number)

- Macintosh type and model and amount of memory (RAM) installed

- System software version number (choose About this Macintosh from the Finder or About the Finder from the Apple menu to see the version number)

- Extensions (sometimes called INITs) and Control Panels (sometimes called CDEVs) installed in your System Folder

- Monitor type

- Printer manufacturer, type, and model (if relevant to your problem)

- Network configuration, if any

Writing to Technical Support

You can also write to our Technical Support Department. Include the information listed on the preceding page, your day and night phone numbers, the best time to call, and a FAX number if available.

Intuit Technical Support
Attention: Quicken for Macintosh
P.O. Box 3014
Menlo Park, CA 94026

Phone numbers

If you would like	Contact	At this number	During these hours
Assistance using software: **Quicken 4 for Macintosh** **IntelliCharge statement disks or modem use**	Intuit Technical Support	**415-858-6044** **Mailing Address:** Intuit Technical Support P.O. Box 3014 Menlo Park, CA 94026	Monday - Friday 5 am - 5 pm Pacific time
To order: **Software upgrades** **Intuit software products** **CheckFree sign-up forms**	Intuit Customer Assistance	**800-624-8742**	Monday - Friday 7 am - 5 pm Pacific time
Assistance with: **Intuit checks** **Supplies**	Intuit Customer Assistance	**800-433-8810** (in the U.S.) **800-268-5779** (in Canada)	Monday - Friday 6 am - 5 pm Pacific time Monday - Friday 8 am - 8 pm Eastern time
To order: **Intuit checks** **Supplies**	Intuit Supplies	**FAX: 415-852-9146** **Mailing Address:** Intuit Supplies P.O. Box 51470 Palo Alto, CA 94303	Anytime
Assistance using: **CheckFree** **Payment processing**	CheckFree Customer Service	**614-899-7500** **FAX: 614-899-7202**	Monday - Friday 8 am - 8 pm Eastern time Anytime
Assistance using: **MacInTax** **TurboTax ProSeries**	ChipSoft Technical Support	**619-587-3939**	Monday - Friday 8:30 am - 5 pm Pacific time (with extended hours during tax season)
To get an application form for: **Quicken credit card**	Intuit Customer Assistance	**800-756-1855**	Monday - Friday 7 am - 5 pm Pacific time
Assistance with: **Quicken credit card limits** **Billing inquiries, other credit card issues**	Primerica Bank	**800-772-2221**	Monday - Friday 8 am - 9 pm Eastern time
Assistance with: **A lost or stolen credit card**	Primerica Bank	**800-426-2441**	Anytime
Assistance with: **24-hour Quicken credit card balance or last payment amount and date received**	Primerica Bank's Automatic Response Unit	**800-262-9323** Call from touch-tone phone, and enter your Personal Identification Number	Anytime

Index

A

access number, IntelliCharge, 203

account list, 39, 40

accounting periods, closing, *see* transaction passwords

accounts, 35, 42
    adding to a Quicken data file, 36
    assigning to tax forms, 369
    balances in net worth
        graphs, 347
        reports, 305
    category and transfer list and, 47, 82
    Category field and, 82
    combining, 71
    copying transactions from one account to
        another, 69
    deleting, 42
    displaying name or description in
        reports, 323
    editing name, description, or type, 40
    electronic payments and, 177
    Go to Transfer command, 89
    illustration of typical accounts in a file, 7
    income and expense, *see* categories
    maximum number in one Quicken data
        file, 36
    more than one CheckFree account, 177
    multiple windows, 39
    opening, 39
    saving not necessary with
        Quicken, QuickStart-4
    selecting for graphs, 342
    selecting for reports, 332, 335
    setting up, 36
    subtotaling reports by, 330
    transferring funds between, 87
    trouble opening, QuickStart-4

updating from previous versions of
    Quicken, 13
255 in a single file, 36
    see also account list; asset accounts; bank
        accounts; cash accounts; credit card
        accounts; liability accounts; mutual
        fund accounts; portfolio accounts

accounts payable, 227
    accounts payable reports, 311

accounts receivable, 226
    accounts receivable reports, 311

accrued interest for bonds, 256

accrued liabilities, accounts to track, 227

Action field in portfolio or mutual fund
    register, 252

actions, investment, *see* investments, actions

Activities menu, illustrated, 394

actual vs. budgeted categories graphs, 346

actual vs. budgeted net income graphs, 346

actuals
    in budget reports, 298, 358
    in budget variance graphs, 346, 360

adding
    accounts to a Quicken data file, 36
    additional Quicken data files, 61
    shares to a mutual fund account, 247
    shares to a portfolio account, 241
    transactions dated before the opening
        balance transaction, 155
    transactions to the register, 80, 82

address
    check, 105
    stamps, ordering, 390

Adjust Balance command
    asset and liability accounts, 230
    cash accounts, 223

409

B

backing up your work, QuickStart-4, 63

balance adjustments
asset and liability accounts, 230
bank accounts, 98
cash accounts, 223
changing amount of opening balance transaction in check register, 151
credit card accounts, 198, 199
mutual fund accounts, 278
portfolio accounts, 244, 278
when bank account doesn't balance, 151
see also reconciling

Balance Forward section in a report, what it
means, 309

balance sheets, 312
unrealized gains and, 329

balances
account balances in net worth
graphs, 347
reports, 305
bank statement, 144, 145
loan, tracking, 282
opening balance transaction
changing, 41
determining for different account
types, 37
what to enter by account type, 142

balancing your checkbook, 141–156
benefits of, 9
see also reconciling

Balloon Help, System 7, 11

balloon payments for loans, 286

bank
errors caught by reconciling, 145, 153
Intuit checks are accepted by, 388
service charges, entering in register, 80
statements, 9
see also bank accounts; reconciling

bank accounts
opening balance, determining, 33
setting up, 33
setting up for electronic payment, 177
tracking cash in, 218
tracking credit cards in, 195
writing checks in, 103–108

bar graphs, 343

baud rate, how to find which to use, 176

beginning balance on bank statement, 144

Best print quality option, CheckArt and, 135

Billminder, 170
postdated transactions and, 107

bills
accounts payable reports, 311
monthly, grouping, 165
paying credit card bills, 200

bonds
accrued interest for, 256
prices, entering, 242
Series EE, 263
shares, number of, entering, 242
tax-free income and, 265
type of account for, 232
U.S. Savings Bonds, 264
zero-coupon, 265

borrowing, loan planner and, 381

bounced checks, voiding transactions, 99

brokerage accounts
setting up in Quicken, 233
type of account for, 232
see also portfolio accounts

budget amounts, exporting to another file, 356

Budget command, 352

budget reports, 298, 358
global settings for, 323

budget variance graphs, 346, 360

C

checkmarks
    reconciling and, 147
    thin and bold, defined, 148

checks
    adding art to, 132
    changing date to today, 114, 123
    changing in Write Checks, 106
    finding specific number or payee, 97
    for continuous-feed printers, 388
    for page-oriented printers, 388
    logos pre-printed free, 389
    missing or duplicate check numbers, 330
    ordering, 388, 389
    partial first page of checks, 119
    printable, 106, 166
    printed, where to find, 106
    printing, 109–140
        see also printing, checks
    reprinting, 131
    unprinted, reviewing, 106
    voiding, 99
    voucher, printing categories on, 105, 113,
        114, 123
    where to find after printing, 106
    writing, 103–108
    see also check numbers; Write Checks
        window

Checks on First Page icons, 120

"Checks Payable"
    on balance sheets, 312
    on net worth reports, 305

children's investments, setting up types or
    goals to track, 240

"Chk" type for printable checks, 166

Chooser, check printer and, 135

choosing, *see* item you want to choose

choosing an item with the mouse
    defined, QuickStart-4

class list, 57, 90, 91
    printing, 57

classes
    assigning to IntelliCharge
        transactions, 209
    assigning to transactions, 90
    categories and, 55
    copying, *see* classes, exporting
    deleting, 58
    displaying descriptions or names in
        reports, 323
    editing name or description, 49
    entering in register, 91
    exporting to another file, 58
    forward slash (/) and, 90
    job tracking and, 55
    job/project report and, 314
    more than one per transaction, *see* split
        transactions
    rental properties and, 55, 57
    reports, selecting for, 333
    separating personal and business
        finances, 91
    subtotaling reports by, 330
    transfers and, 87
    typing in Category field, 90
    see also class list

cleared (√) column in register, 81

cleared (√) transactions, 148
    defined, 149
    marking during reconcile, 146
    when copying data to new file, 66

clicking the mouse, defined, QuickStart-4

Client Support, CheckFree, how to contact, 408

clients
    setting up classes to track, 314
    see also customers

closing
    accounting period
        see transaction passwords
    assets or liabilities, 229

code, area and zip, entering (CheckFree), 177

Move Shares In investment action, 250

Move Shares Out investment action, 250

moving
    budget amounts to another file, 356
    categories
        in the category and transfer list, 51
        to another file, 53
    classes
        in the class list, 58
        to another file, 58
    data files from one location to another, 68

mutual fund accounts, 235
    adding shares to, 247
    adjusting the share balance of, 278
    asterisk (*) in register, 252, 254
    capital gains distributions, 257
    commissions and fees, 253
    dividends, 257
    entering transactions, 251
        for dates in past, 274
    income distributions, 257
    interest income, 257
    IRA custodial fees for mutual funds, 259
    loads or front-end loads, 256
    market values, 271
    reconciling, 278
    reinvestments, 258
    revising initial transactions, 274
    rounding amounts in, 253
    setting up, 235, 236, 245
    share balance, 271
    transfers in, 259
    see also Portfolio window; securities

mutual funds
    prices, entering, 242
    shares, number of, entering, 242
    type of account for, 232
    see also mutual fund accounts; portfolio
        accounts

names, *see name of specific item*

negative amortization, 287

negative dollar amounts, entering, 264

net savings amount in budget reports, 298

net savings and expense comparison
    graph, 345

net savings category in graphs, 345

net worth
    defined, 226
        excluding sold assets or paid
            liabilities, 229

net worth graphs, 347

net worth reports, 305
    unrealized gains and, 329

New
    Account command, 36
    Category command, 47
    Class command, 57
    File command, 61
    Goal command, 240
    Loan command, 282
    Merchant command, 178
    Security command, 240
    Split Line command, 95
    Transaction command, 80
    Transaction Group command, 165
    Type command, 240

new balance on bank statement, 145

notes
    accounts, 37, 41
    added Note field on check, 102

NSF checks, voiding transactions, 99

Number field
    lightning bolt in, 177
    PRINT in, 106
    SEND in, 180

numbers
    check
        duplicates, 102
        finding in register, 97
        OK to have 2 series of numbers, 389
        why preprinted, 105
    confirmation from CheckFree, 185
    telephone, 408
        help using Quicken, 408
        merchant number for billing questions
            (CheckFree), 178
        modem for CheckFree, 176
        modem for IntelliCharge, 203
        ordering supplies, 408

O

onscreen Help system, 11
Open
    Account command, 39
    File command, 62
opening
    accounts, 39
    files, 62
opening balances
    adjusting, 143
    amount is from the ending balance of your
        latest bank statement, 142
    changing, 41
    determining for bank accounts, 33
    determining for different account types, 37
    entering year-to-date transactions, 34
    on bank statements, 144
options (puts and calls), 266
order, transactions in register, 81
order of transactions
    in register, 81
    in reports, 330

ordering
    address and endorsement stamps, 390
    checks, 387, 388
    deposit slips, 390
    supplies, 389
organization of your Quicken data, 61
"Other"
    in graphs, 343, 346
    in reports, 85, 337
overdraft protection, credit card accounts, 197
overspending
    graphs show patterns, 345
    viewing patterns, 5

P

P & L statements, *see* income statements
page breaks in a report, previewing, 326
Page Preview button, 326, 327
page-oriented printers, 119
    printing checks on, 112–121
        partial first page, 119
paper check, CheckFree uses to pay bills, 183
paper is too short error, 121
parentheses, entering in Quicken, 177
partial page of checks, printing, 390
passwords, 72
    file, 72
    IntelliCharge statements by modem, 202
    transaction, 64, 74
    year-end closing and, 76
patterns in graphs, 343
payables, *see* accounts payable (A/P by
    vendor) reports
paycheck deposit example, 94
Payee field, entering names (CheckFree), 179

R

rate of return graphs, 348

real estate
    investment trusts, type of account for, 232
    types of account for, 233

rearranging categories in the category and
    transfer list, 51

Recalculate button, 322

recalculating totals in split transactions, 95

recalling
    memorized electronic payments, 182
    memorized reports, 339
    transaction groups, 167
    transactions
        automatically, 158
        manually, 162

receipt, for CheckFree payment, 183

receivables, *see* accounts receivable (A/R by
    customer) reports

Receive column, cash account, 222

Reconcile command, 141–156
    credit card accounts and, 198
    see also reconciling

Reconcile window
    difference this statement is not zero, 150
    difference this statement is zero, 149
    difference this statement is zero but there is
        a previous difference, 150

reconciled (✓) transactions, 148

reconciliation reports, 149, 317

reconciling, 141–156
    adding transactions dated before the open-
        ing balance transaction, 155
    adjusting the opening balance, 143
    benefits of, 9
    checkmarks and, 147
    correcting transaction errors, 148
    entering earlier transactions, 155
    first time, 142

how to undo, 148
interest earned, 146, 152
marking transactions that appear on a bank
    statement, 146
missing transactions, 147
mutual fund accounts, 278
portfolio accounts, 278
reconciled transactions, 148
    defined, 149
reconciliation reports, 149, 317
Save a Copy and, 66
service charges, 146, 152

recurring transactions, *see* memorized transactions

refinance planner, 383

refinancing loans, 295, 380

Register window, *see* registers

registers, 79–102
    automatic sorting in, 81
    bank accounts, 81
    cash accounts, 222
    cleared (√) column in, 81
    deleting transactions, 100
    entering transactions dated before the
        opening balance transaction, 155
    finding a transaction, 97
    illustration, 81
    keyboard shortcuts for, 96
    liability accounts, 228, 229
    moving around in, 96
    mutual fund accounts, 251
    portfolio accounts, 251
    printing, 101
    reviewing, 95
    scrolling in, 96
    searching for a transaction, 97
    updated automatically (CheckFree), 172

reinstalling Quicken, QuickStart-2

Reinvest Dividend investment action, 250

Reinvest Interest investment action, 250

Reinvest Long investment action, 250

Reinvest Short investment action, 251

reinvestments, entering in portfolio or mutual fund accounts, 258

REITs, type of account for, 232

removing
    shares from account, 250
    see also deleting

renaming, see editing

rental properties, setting up classes to track, 55, 57, 314

report output window, editing transactions and, 322

Report Settings command, 323

reports
    account descriptions or names in, 323
    categories determine usefulness, 44
    category/class descriptions or names in, 323
    creating, 319–339
    defined, 5
    exporting to a file, 325
    fonts in, 324
    formats, 328
    global settings for, 323
    investigating detail for, 337
    memorizing, 338, 339
    "Other" in, 85, 337
    preset dates for, 320
    previewing printed page breaks, 326
    printing, 326
    publishing for use in other applications, 399
    QuickZoom in, 337
    recalling memorized, 339
    resizing report columns, 321
    restricting, 336
    restricting by dollar amounts, 332
    saving to a file, 325
    selecting items to include, 331, 335
    sorting, 330
    sorting by check numbers, 330
    start printing at the center of the page, 326

    subtotaling different ways, 330
    tax-related, 374
    unrealized gains in, 305
    wildcard characters and, 336
    see also names of specific reports

Reports menu, illustrated, 395

reprinting checks, 131

Request Confirmation (Changing a Transaction) setting, 102

Require Category on Transactions setting, 102

resizing report columns, 321

Restore button, discards changes to transaction, 81

restoring data from a backup, 63

restricting data in
    graphs, 342
    reports, 331
        saving report restrictions
        see memorizing, reports

retirement planning, 385

retirement plans, types of account for, 233

Return key, change action of, 102

return of capital, 264

Return of Capital investment action, 251

return on investments
    average annual total return graphs, 348
    investment performance reports, 302

reverse amortization, 287

reviewing
    check register, 96
    split information, 95

risk, setting up investment goals to track, 240

rotary phone, setting up for, 176

rounding amounts
    in budgets, 355
    in mutual fund accounts, 253
    in portfolio accounts, 253

row headings for reports, changing, 330

S

salary, entering a paycheck deposit, 94

SAM Intercept software, installing Quicken and, QuickStart-1

sample checks, printing, 125

Save a Copy command, 76, 77
  prior uncleared transactions and, 66

Save command, lack of, QuickStart-4

saving
  background, QuickStart-4
  not necessary with Quicken, QuickStart-4
  report instructions, *see* memorizing, reports

savings
  net, 298
  planner, 383

Schedule D (Capital Gains), 376

scheduled payment date, finding to stop a payment, 185

schedules
  loan payment, 290
  tax schedule reports, 374
  tax, assigning to categories, 366

scheduling
  bills to pay, 107
  electronic payments, 181

scrolling register with scroll box, 96

Search menu, 97

searching, *see* Find command; finding

securities
  average annual total return, 302
  buying, 255
  buying on margin, 262
  capital gains reports, 299
  deleting, 270
  entering automatically, 158
  giving shares you own, 261

graphing performance, 348
lots for, 273
market values, 271, 306
receiving additional shares as a gift, 261
selecting for graphs, 342
selecting for reports, 334
selling, 255
selling designated lot, 273
selling short, 265
setting up, 240
subtotaling reports by, 330
symbols for, 240
tracking ones you don't own, 276
types, 240
see also investments; return on investments; security prices; security types

Security field in portfolio account register, 252

security prices
  deleting, 270
  entering, 242
  importing, 234, 272
  price history for one security, 269
  updating, 267
  viewing for one security, 269, 348

security types, 240
  entering automatically, 158
  selecting for reports, 334
  subtotaling reports by, 330

security (safety)
  why CheckFree is secure, 172
  see also passwords

selecting text or an item with the mouse defined, QuickStart-4

self-transfer transactions, 309

Sell investment action, 251

selling securities, 255
  short sales, 265

SEND in the Number field, 180

Series EE bonds, 263

sorting
- automatic in the register, 81
- category and class information in reports, 323
- register printout by check number, 101
- reports, 330
- transactions, 330

source accounts for transfers, 8, 86

speed, modem, how to find which to use, 176

Spend column
- cash account, 222

spending
- graphs show patterns, 5, 345

split transactions, 92, 95
- classes, 92
- defined, 44
- editing, 95
- Go to Transfer command, 89
- printing categories on voucher checks, 114, 123
- recalculating total, 95
- reports, excluding detail from, 330
- reviewing, 95
- transfers, 86, 89

Splits button, 95

spreadsheets
- exporting Quicken data to, 325

standard checks, 114, 123

starter categories, *see* categories, first-time setup

starting Quicken
- double-clicking data file, 18
- first time, 32
- updating from earlier versions, 14

statements
- bank, reconciling, 141–156
- income (profit and loss), 313

Stock Split investment action, 251

stocks
- account type for, 232
- prices, entering, 242
- prices, retrieving via modem, 234
- shares, number of, entering, 242
- stock dividends, 262
- stock index, tracking, 276
- stock splits, 261
- *see also* investments; securities; shares

stopping payment (CheckFree), 185

strike prices, inability to track, 234

subcategories
- example in report, 5
- promoting to category, 52
- rolled up into categories in graphs, 343
- setting up, 48
- tax forms, assigning to, 367
- *see also* categories

subclasses, 58

subscribing to a Quicken edition from another application, 400

subtotaling reports, 330

summary reports, 307

suppliers, *see* accounts payable (A/P by vendor) reports

supplies
- ordering, 387–390
  - CheckArt and, 132
- telephone number for information, 408

supplies order form, 389

SYLK (Excel-compatible) export file format, 325

symbols, where to enter, 240

System Folder, Quicken 4 Preferences file and, 398

System version needed to run Quicken, QuickStart-1

System 7 Balloon Help, 11

copying to a new file, 65

correcting in register, 98

dated before the opening balance transaction, entering, 155

defined, 80

deleting, 100

deleting a transfer, 89

excluding from reports or searches, 336

exporting from one account to another, 70

finding in register, 97

how sorted in register, 81

inserting in register, 80

marking for review (IntelliCharge), 209

multiple categories per transaction, 92

opening balance transaction in register, 33

paycheck, entering, 94

postdated, below line in register, QuickStart-3, 81

protecting with passwords, 72

recurring, grouping, 165

sorting in reports, 330

splitting, 44, 92, 95

　　see also split transactions

transfers, 89

uncleared, 148

unreconciled, 148

voiding, 99

where is transaction? Find command, 97

year-to-date, reconcile, 155

Transfer Money command, 87

Transfer Money investment action, 251

Transfer not present message, 67

transferring

data from DOS Quicken to Macintosh Quicken, 26

data from Windows Quicken to Macintosh Quicken, 26

transfers, 86–89

assigning to tax forms, 369

category and transfer list and, 86

Category field and, 82

credit card accounts, 197

editing or deleting, 49, 89

explained, 8

Go to Transfer command, 89

including in budget, 356

mutual fund accounts, 259

payroll reports and, 315

portfolio accounts, 259

Save a Copy and, 67

selecting for reports, 334

transmitting payments (CheckFree), 183, 184

error during, 184

Treasury bills

redeeming, 264

types of account for, 233

troubleshooting

check printing, 135

CheckFree, 190

general, 405

IntelliCharge, 211

IntelliCharge modem statements, 207

memory

　　see "Memory and Quicken" topic in Help

modem problems, 190

paper is too short, 121

printer driver versions, 111

reconciling Quicken bank accounts with bank statements, 150

report starts printing at the center of the page, 326

transmission problems, 190

tuition, planning for college, 386

TurboTax ProSeries, updating tax assignments, 378

turning on or off

Billminder, 170

electronic bill payment, 177

Qcards, 10

QuickFill, 158

TXF format, 325

types, security, *see* security types

U

"Uncategorized" in graphs, 85

uncleared transactions, copying to new file, 66

Undo command, 98

"Unfavorable" in budget variance graphs, 346

unit trusts
  return of capital, 264
  type of account for, 232

unprinted checks
  accounts payable reports and, 311
  balance sheets and, 312
  net worth reports and, 305

unrealized gains
  including in reports, 329
  investment transaction reports and, 303
  net worth reports and, 305
  portfolio value reports and, 306

unreconciling reconciled transactions, 148

updating
  asset or liability account balance, 229
  cash account balance, 223
  data from previous versions of
    Quicken, 13
  security prices and market values, 267

Use QuickFill setting, 158

U.S. Savings Bonds, redeeming, 264

V

values, *see* market values

variable
  annuities, 232
  rate loans, 291

vendors, accounts payable reports, 311

version
  printer driver, 111
  updating to a new version of Quicken, 13

View By popup menu, 358

View menu, illustrated, 393

Void Transaction command, 99

voiding a transaction, 99

voucher checks, 113, 123

W

wallet checks, 113, 123
  printing single, 119

wash sales in capital gains report, 299

where is transaction?, Find command, 97

wildcard characters (.. and ?), 336

window envelopes, 390

windows
  multiple accounts open at once, 39
  see also names of specific windows, 442

Windows Quicken data, 26

Wrap Around Beginning/End of File on
  Searches setting, 102

Write Checks window
  electronic payments and, 179
  finding a transaction in, 97

writing checks, 103–108

X

x-axis, displays months, accounts, or categories, 343

Y

y-axis, displays dollar amounts, 343

years
  budgeting by, 353
  starting a separate data file for a new year, 61, 76

year-to-date
  estimated interest payments, 294
  transactions, reconciling, 155

Z

zero amounts, memorizing transactions with, 161

zero-coupon bonds, 265

zoom, *see* QuickZoom

Numbers

3-dimensional graphs, turning off, 349

401(k) retirement plans, types of account for, 233

403(b) retirement plans, types of account for, 233

Symbols

( ) parentheses, entering in phone numbers, 177

* (asterisk)
  mutual fund accounts and, 252, 254
  phone system symbol, 190
  portfolio accounts and, 252, 254

.. (two periods) wildcard character, 336

/ (forward slash) separator in Category field, 90

: (colon) separator in Category field, 83

? (marked) field in credit card register, 209

? (question mark) wildcard character, 336

~ (tilde) wildcard character, 336

√ (cleared) column in register, 81

√ (cleared) transactions, 148

√ (thin checkmark) in the √ (cleared) field, 148

✓ (bold checkmark) in the √ (cleared) field, 148
  IntelliCharge register and, 211

✓ (reconciled) transactions, 148

Have product ideas? A change of address?

Use the postage paid Customer Communication Card to send them to us.

QUICKEN CUSTOMER COMMUNICATION CARD

Please use this card to communciate suggestions, or a change in your address.

Name: _____

Address: _____

_____

City: _____ State: _____ Zip: _____

Is this a new address? ☐ Yes ☐ No

Quicken used for: ☐ Personal ☐ Business ☐ Both

Suggestions: _____

_____

_____

_____

_____

_____

*If mailing from outside the U.S., place this card in an envelope and apply proper postage to assure delivery.

Macintosh 4.0　　　　　　　6/93　　　　　　134001

✂ Cut here

Hold onto your Special Offer Coupons Below!

As a Quicken owner, you're eligible for special offers from Intuit. As long as you send in your registration card (in the front of this manual), Intuit will be able to contact you with these special offers.

SPECIAL OFFER COUPON
Quicken 4 for Macintosh

When Intuit announces a special offer, just return the specified coupon. The offer will specify the exact coupon number (1 or 2) required. The original special offer coupon *must* be returned. A copy or facsimile is *not* acceptable.

✂ Cut here

✂ Cut here

SPECIAL OFFER COUPON
Quicken 4 for Macintosh

When Intuit announces a special offer, just return the specified coupon. The offer will specify the exact coupon number (1 or 2) required. The original special offer coupon *must* be returned. A copy or facsimile is *not* acceptable.

Use the postage paid Customer Communication Card to send us your product ideas, or a change of address.

SPECIAL OFFER COUPON #1
Quicken 4 for Macintosh

Mailing Address:

Name, First: _____ Initial: _____ Last: _____

Company (if applicable): _____

Street: _____

City: _____ State: _____ Zip: _____

If outside USA, Country*: _____ Postal Code: _____

Telephone: (_____) _____ ☐1 Day   ☐2 Evening

Check one item for each question:

Quicken used for: ☐1 Personal   ☐2 Business   ☐3 Both
Main reason for use: ☐1 Time Savings   ☐2 Organization/Insight
Own modem: ☐1 Yes   ☐2 No

134001

When you send in a Special Offer Coupon, be sure to fill out the entire coupon.

SPECIAL OFFER COUPON #2
Quicken 4 for Macintosh

Mailing Address:

Name, First: _____ Initial: _____ Last: _____

Company (if applicable): _____

Street: _____

City: _____ State: _____ Zip: _____

If outside USA, Country*: _____ Postal Code: _____

Telephone: (_____) _____ ☐1 Day   ☐2 Evening

Check one item for each question:

Quicken used for: ☐1 Personal   ☐2 Business   ☐3 Both
Main reason for use: ☐1 Time Savings   ☐2 Organization/Insight
Own modem: ☐1 Yes   ☐2 No

134001